Idle Talk, Deadly Talk

NEW WORLD STUDIES

J. Michael Dash, Editor

Frank Moya Pons and
Sandra Pouchet Paquet,
Associate Editors

Idle Talk, Deadly Talk

The Uses of Gossip in Caribbean Literature

Ana Rodríguez Navas

University of Virginia Press
Charlottesville and London

University of Virginia Press
© 2018 by the Rector and Visitors of the University of Virginia
All rights reserved
Printed in the United States of America on acid-free paper

First published 2018

ISBN 978-0-8139-4161-5 (cloth)
ISBN 978-0-8139-4162-2 (paper)
ISBN 978-0-8139-4163-9 (ebook)

9 8 7 6 5 4 3 2 1

Library of Congress Cataloging-in-Publication Data is available for this title.

A Ben, Elena y Beatriz

Contents

Acknowledgments	ix
Introduction: Gossip's Embattlements	1
1. "A Mouthful of Dynamite": Gossip and the Failure of Community	25
2. "Parallel Versions": Gossip, Investigation, and Identity	65
3. "An International Scandal": Gossip, Dissent, and the Public Sphere	110
4. "Páginas en Blanco": The Legacy of the Caribbean Gossip State	159
Conclusion: Radical Gossip	207
Notes	215
Works Cited	251
Index	275

Acknowledgments

THIS WAS a project many years in the making, and its completion owes more than I can say to the colleagues, friends, and family whose generous help made the process both possible and enjoyable, and the finished product far better than it would otherwise have been.

I am deeply grateful to everyone at the University of Virginia Press. My special thanks go to Eric Brandt, J. Michael Dash, and Ellen Satrom for their enthusiastic support and to the anonymous readers for their sharp and thoughtful feedback.

Material support for this project came from a Princeton University Library grant, which in 2016 provided the means for extended access to their collection. Two summer stipends awarded by Loyola University Chicago similarly enabled me to visit various archives and attend key conferences at which I received helpful advice from a number of scholars. Among them I particularly thank Susan Gillman, Lucy Evans, Maria Cristina Fumagalli, and Víctor Figueroa.

Early versions of two portions of this book appeared previously as "Words as Weapons: Gossip in Junot Díaz's *The Brief Wondrous Life of Oscar Wao*" in *MELUS* 42, no. 3 (2017): 55–83, and as "Gossip and Nation in Rosario Ferré's *Maldito amor*," in *Chasqui: Revista de literatura latinoamericana* 45, no. 1 (2016): 65–78. I thank the journals' editors, Gary Totten and David William Foster, for allowing their inclusion herein.

At Loyola University Chicago, Scott Hendrickson's support deserves special mention. Susana Cavallo also provided beneficial guidance at various stages of this project. Clara Burgo, David Posner, and Maria Robertson-Justiniano have been valued and supportive friends and important sounding-boards as I have worked on this book. I am deeply grateful to my mentor, Deni Heyck, whose warmth, endless kindness, and sound advice have been enormously important to me throughout my time in Chicago.

A number of other friends were also generous with their time and energy, and put a tremendous amount of care into reading the evolving manuscript. Michael Wood and Sylvia Molloy were enthusiastic from early on, and their support helped propel this project forward. Maria DiBattista has been a devoted mentor and friend, one to whom I owe much more than she knows. Nuria Sanjuán Pastor was an energetic, sharp, and generous reader; so too was Nathalie Bouzaglo, on whose support and advice I have so often relied. I am especially honored to have benefited from Peter Hulme's friendship and good-humored critical eye. María Gracia Pardo, Natalia Pérez, Víctor García Ramírez, and Eliana Vāgālāu were valuable interlocutors and helped improve various portions of this book. Allyson Doorn's focus and dedication helped rectify oversights and rid the manuscript of typos and inconsistencies.

Other friends and family have accompanied me on this journey and given me much-needed support of various kinds, from advice and encouragement to food and childcare. I thank Vivian Auyeung, Ganesh Gandhi, Valerie Keller, Mada Leanga, Anne Moffitt, Roberto Martínez Bachrich, Nadia Mufarregue, Chente and Chabela Navas, Michele Simeon, and Michael Wachtel. My love and gratitude also go out to my wonderful siblings, Daniel, Vanessa, and Alessandra.

My late father, Ricardo Mario, was the first to teach me to love and to engage with the complexities of the Caribbean. My parents "in love," Jeanette and Eric, and my wonderful mother, Rosa Matilde, believed in me and provided practical support cheerfully and frequently so that I could pour myself into this project. This book would never have been written without them; more importantly, I am lucky they are part of my life.

Finally, my daughters, Elena and Beatriz, have been incredibly tolerant of the countless intrusions that come with a project such as this, and have filled my life with love and joy along the way. And no words can ever come close to conveying my love and gratitude to my husband and partner, Ben, who is always there, full of radiant love and a degree of support that is truly extraordinary. This book is as much their accomplishment as it is mine.

Idle Talk, Deadly Talk

Introduction

Gossip's Embattlements

> Chisme de chisme, todo es chisme.
> —Luis Rafael Sánchez

THE CARIBBEAN is full of gossip. It is in our speech, our songs, and our stories; on our beaches and in our bodegas; in our fictions and our poetry; in our newspapers, our politics, our history, and our memories. Over the centuries this has, perhaps understandably, been a source of considerable consternation: the nineteenth-century Cuban physician Tomás Romay Chacón, for instance, condemns gossips as enemies of society and disturbers of the peace whose sharpened tongues "cause infinite discord and enmity" but admits that to suppress the island's gossips would be impossible. "To our disgrace, their number has grown too many, and we ourselves have joined their ranks," he writes (226).[1] To Édouard Glissant, the Caribbean's "obsession with gossip" was the sign of a people picking at its own spiritual and cultural wounds—"since, in the absence of national production and facing global cultural constraints, a people turns against itself" (335–36). V. S. Naipaul describes the gossip of the Caribbean as claustrophobic and oppressive, and writes of longing "to get away from the easy malice of the small place I grew up in, where all judgments were moralistic and hateful and corrupting, the judgments of gossip" (*A Writer's People* 49). For Derek Walcott, meanwhile, gossip is a feminine practice—though not uniquely so, "since men are sometimes better at bitchery than women"—that underpins the "comic gift" he dryly perceives as characterizing, and perhaps degrading, Caribbean literature. "Allowing that this is possible, we can understand why [. . .][2] our calypsoes generally go no higher than the intimate malice that one woman might share about another. Our so-called asperities, 'picong,' 'mauvaise langue,' 'ole talk,' even 'liming,' are the art of gossip," he writes ("Gift of Comedy" 131). Clearly, there is more to this superficially easygoing speech form than just idle chatter. In this, the first book-length study of gossip in the literature of the Caribbean, I show that, as the foregoing suggests, gossip serves many roles in the region: it circulates information and traverses power structures; it carries weight, causes harm, defines, limits, and constrains; it is often deliberative, sometimes dangerous; it cleaves together and cleaves apart; and, as we will see, it can at times be deadly.

In beginning this task, we should first acknowledge that the suspicion or disparagement of gossip is far from unique to the Caribbean. Plutarch, despite making historical gossip his stock in trade, saw gossips as fools devoured by their own inquisitiveness and talkativeness: "Vipers, they say, burst in giving birth, and secrets, when they escape, destroy and ruin those who cannot keep them," he notes (431). The Talmud considers gossip to be akin to apostasy, and worse than murder, fornication, or idolatry: "Gossipers, receivers of gossip, and those who bear false testimony deserve to be thrown to the dogs," believers are sternly warned (*Pesachim* 118a).[3] For Geoffrey Chaucer, backbiting was "spiritual manslaughter" (561), a figuratively violent act of transgressive speech; for Miguel de Cervantes, it was both vicious and an inescapably human vice. Virtually the first word out of an infant's mouth, insists Berganza in *El coloquio de los perros* (1613), is vicious slander aimed at his nurse or mother— "There is no gossip, if you examine them closely, whose life isn't full of vice and insolence," replies Cipión (32). Michel de Montaigne perceived gossip as mere babble: the idle prattling of chambermaids and fishwives, but by extension also the empty pontificating of the educated classes (Butterworth 6). Later, for Martin Heidegger and Søren Kierkegaard, gossip became the willful elevation of meaningless chatter over the life of the mind, while for Walter Benjamin and Roland Barthes it represented a form of malicious, even murderous, linguistic nihilism. The common thread in such accounts is the perception of gossip as both frivolous and toxic: idle talk, yes, but also talk that renders more edifying discourse impossible, that ruins reputations and poisons relationships, and that frays the fraternal bonds upon which societies depend.

Despite such readings, in recent decades gossip has undergone a redemption of sorts. Building on the work of anthropologists and sociologists who have viewed gossip in utilitarian terms, a small number of literary scholars have sought to rescue the practice, suggesting that it can be far more than just idle chatter or toxic tittle-tattle.[4] Patricia Meyer Spacks, in particular, seeks to redeem gossip by downplaying its risks and emphasizing its role in building intimate communities, asserting that the gossip that seeks to harm others is "probably relatively rare" (4–5).

Spacks allows that some gossip may be vapid or vicious but focuses her attention on the "serious" gossip that she perceives as offering "a resource for the subordinated" and representing "a crucial form of solidarity" for the sidelined and downtrodden (5). Based on such readings, literary scholars such as Jan Gordon, Susan Phillips, and Ned Schantz have explored gossip's role in the construction of intimate communities, of spaces for public discourse, and of means whereby the marginalized can speak back against the powerful.

The value of such work cannot be overstated; still, these scholars have explored gossip largely in British and American texts, predominantly of the nineteenth century, and their readings have quite naturally been colored by their sources. *Idle Talk, Deadly Talk* is founded upon the assumption that gossip plays a different role in the literature of the postcolonial, post-authoritarian, multilingual Caribbean than it does in the genteel drawing rooms and garden parties of Jane Austen or Henry James. As Joyce Carol Oates notes, where *Jane Eyre* assures us that "all things of significance are related to one another in a universe in which God means well," Jean Rhys's creolized rewriting of Brontë's text insists instead that "nothing is predictably related and emotions like terror may spring suddenly from the most innocent of sources" (55). Viewed through the former lens, gossip may easily and correctly be understood as an intimate, empowering, and broadly positive social practice. Seen from Rhys's perspective, however, it may well reveal other aspects: bleaker and more urgent, perhaps, or simply better aligned with the unstable, fraught, and fragmentary realities of the Caribbean. I seek here not to write against Spacks and other scholars who focus their attention on "good" gossip but rather to suggest that the spectrum they envision—good gossip at one end, bad at the other—is broader and potentially richer than their paradigm typically encompasses. In what follows, I show that reading gossip in other places, other texts, and other political or historical contexts can provide new and valuable insights into its deployments and potential significance.

This book examines gossip as represented and mobilized in Caribbean literature since the early sixties, a critical and chaotic watershed for the region coinciding roughly with the triumph of the revolution in Cuba, François Duvalier's consolidation of power in Haiti, the assassination of Rafael Leónidas Trujillo in the Dominican Republic, and the independence of much of the British West Indies. This starting point coincides with the onset, as Silvio Torres-Saillant remarks, of several decades of enthusiastic political engagement and intensely creative intellectual production in the Caribbean—and also, I would add, of a more consistent and politicized use of gossip as a literary theme and narrative strategy. That is not to say, of course, that gossip began in the 1960s, any more than sexual intercourse "began / In nineteen sixty-three"; still, the sexual freedom that Philip Larkin perceives as taking root in the United Kingdom "between the end of the 'Chatterley' ban / And the Beatles' first LP" (167) does in some ways correspond to the outpouring of political and intellectual energy seen in the Caribbean from the early 1960s onward. Torres-Saillant rightly notes that women's voices gained new prominence in the regional production of this period, as did questions of (homo)sexuality; meanwhile, the discourses of marginalized communities won increasing recognition as important sites of resistance and self-articulation.[5] Gossip is not exclusively the province of women, queer communities, or other marginalized groups. Still, this "gender-sensitive way of looking at the past and imagining the future" (*Intellectual History* 153) created fertile ground for writers and facilitated the literary adoption of gossip both as a theme and as a narrative strategy. In the past six decades, I suggest, gossip—hitherto typically regarded by Spacksian scholars as an intimate, mannered, and cozy practice—has frequently appeared in the literature of the Caribbean as a political, contested, and potentially dangerous narrative form.

In exploring gossip's place in the Caribbean, I am not describing literary or cultural phenomena that are exclusive to the region. Many aspects of gossip that I locate in Hispanic Caribbean texts are also found across Latin America: Manuel Puig and Juan Carlos Onetti use gossip to foreground epistemological challenges; Augusto Roa Bastos and Miguel Angel Asturias explore gossip's role in authoritarian regimes; and even the fictions of Jorge Luis Borges, according to Edgardo Cozarinsky, are organized in terms of an ontological revisionism that emulates the process of gossip.[6] Facets of the gossip I describe in the Caribbean can be found in other regions, too: the revisionist gossip of Rosario Ferré or Junot Díaz has parallels in the writing of Salman Rushdie; the paranoid and panoptic aspects of gossip traced by Antonio José Ponte resonate with its depiction in Andrei Voznesensky's Soviet-era poem "Ode to Gossips"; and the exclusionary, rabble-rousing gossip of Luis Rafael Sánchez's "¡Jum!" echoes that of Benjamin Britten's opera *Peter Grimes*.[7] One of the reasons that the Caribbean is a fruitful place in which to study gossip, in fact, is that as a multilingual and multicultural crossroads, marked by slavery, colonization, authoritarianism, and diaspora, it shares connections or historical commonalities with countless other parts of the world, from sub-Saharan Africa to South Asia. It should not surprise us, then, if the gossip of the Caribbean echoes, or is echoed in, the gossip found in a great number of other cultural and linguistic contexts.

These resonances between gossip's role in the Caribbean and its deployments in distant places and disparate traditions can be seen as playing out, in microcosm, within the Caribbean itself: far from monolithic, the Caribbean is a fluid, linguistically and culturally diverse space, a cluster of communities with clear historical commonalities but also with their own cultural identities. Language, of course, is the most obvious dividing line between the literatures and cultures of the region: in the Caribbean, as Torres-Saillant notes, language remains "the ultimate border" between nations and peoples who might otherwise find shared ground in common histories and geographies. "When it comes to mediating the rapport between Caribbean societies, linguistic difference, more than any other obstacle, has the power to encourage and preserve the otherness of neighbors," he warns (*Intellectual History* 26). I aim herein to engage with, if not overcome, this problem. By highlighting some of gossip's roles in the literature of the Caribbean's three dominant linguistic traditions, I show that the practice has a regional significance that seeps through, and frequently transcends, linguistic barriers. Gossip hops between islands, and even where language barriers prevent people from gossiping with one another, they often wind up gossiping in similar ways in response to their common historical, cultural, and political conditions.

This study, then, has two interrelated goals: first, to illustrate the degree to which the literature of the Caribbean has been marked by, and is often organized through, the use of gossip; and, second, to expand the existing scholarship of gossip by elaborating upon certain neglected aspects of the practice's uses and functions in literary texts. My guiding supposition is that gossip is both more malleable and more morally ambiguous than has previously been presumed; it is neither inherently malign nor benign—neither good nor bad—but is, rather, a potent, often political, and above all plural narrative form that serves markedly different uses in different contexts. Gossip is a form of what Michel Foucault calls "subjugated knowledge"—widely seen as deficient, unauthorized, or naive, and as such often overlooked, but in fact ubiquitous and powerful when properly understood (*Society* 7–8). I am particularly interested in uncovering the various ways through which Caribbean literature, in engaging with the region's postcolonial status, entrenched inequalities, and history of political oppression, can help us to more fully understand gossip's role in the creation of public narratives. Gossip, in confronting the fraught, unstable realities of the Caribbean, emerges as not just a tool but a weapon:

a system for self-assertion and resistance, but also at times for oppression and the suppression of dissent. The region's gossip can sometimes be harmless, trivial, or idle, and does still help build communities and broker intimate relationships. But it can also destroy reputations, destabilize accepted facts, heighten fear and paranoia, and in the process reveal itself as urgent, consequential, and violent.

The Study of Gossip

That literary scholars of gossip have largely overlooked the Caribbean is somewhat surprising, for the modern study of gossip has its roots in the region. Spacks's seminal 1985 work *Gossip,* the foundational text for literary scholarship on the practice, is informed by the anthropologist Max Gluckman's 1963 article "Gossip and Scandal," which in turn was written in honor of Melville Herskovits's pioneering anthropological studies of gossip in Haitian and Trinidadian communities. From Herskovits's work, Gluckman gleans the key insight that the gossip is both "a journalist, and [. . .] a Judas," alternately transcribing and traducing the lives of his or her subjects, and goes on to elucidate gossip's role as a means of mapping social boundaries and maintaining the cohesion, as well as the morals and values, of social groups (308). Spacks's chief innovation, in fact, is to bring Gluckman's insights into the realm of literary theory, and to push back against past conceptions of gossip as worthless or toxic by suggesting the possibility of "good gossip," which she takes to be communitarian, truthful, and aimed at fostering kinship and other intimate relationships. In this, Spacks also builds upon Thomas Pavel's 1978 essay "Literary Criticism and Methodology," which suggests that "good" gossip is analogous to what he calls "optimistic" criticism (147), which assumes the possibility of saying something about a text: it is, at its core, an exercise in constructing and exploring hypotheses about a given situation. Following Pavel, Spacks views gossip as a form of emotional or moral investigation: a group of intimates seeking to understand and fully grasp the nature and behavior of others by speculating about their actions. Spacks is aware of the wide spectrum of phenomena encompassed by gossip and acknowledges that gossip "has good aspects and bad ones, that it attests to community but can violate trust, that it both helps and impedes social functioning" (258). Nonetheless, she circumscribes her study to a very specific kind of positive and salutary gossip, grounded in her belief that, on balance, "gossip is good for you" (258).

Spacks's framing of gossip as a fruitful, community-building narrative practice left a mark in the literary study of gossip that cannot be underestimated: most subsequent studies of gossip (including this one) are indebted to Spacks's work. Jan Gordon's *Gossip and Subversion in Nineteenth-Century British Fiction: Echo's Economies* (1996) examines the importance of gossip for the development of the novel, and literature more broadly, in nineteenth-century Britain; Ned Schantz's *Gossip, Letters, Phones: The Scandal of Female Networks in Film and Literature* (2008), with a similar focus on British works, considers gossip's connections to other forms of communication that evaluate the behavior of others. More recently, scholars have looked beyond the strictly literary to explore gossip as a cultural phenomenon.[8] Susan E. Phillips's *Transforming Talk: The Problem with Gossip in Late Medieval England* (2007) posits that gossip, which she describes as "idle talk," merits serious consideration given its centrality in the literature and culture of the period. For Phillips, "Idle talk is not simply women's speech in late medieval England; it is both the obstacle and the tool of priests and pastoral writers" (6). Her work thus avoids an exclusive focus on gossip as marginalized speech in order to better examine gossip as a culturally relevant practice within medieval religious practices and literature. Also written through a cultural lens, Sean Latham's *The Art of Scandal: Modernism, Libel Law, and the Roman à Clef* (2009) examines early twentieth-century British literary circles to present an intriguing view of the degree to which readers' thirst for scandalous gossip informed literary sensibilities and drove the release of prurient revelations in the period's many romans à clef.

As the foregoing suggests, much of the existing scholarship on gossip has followed Spacks in focusing on the practice's role in British and American literature. There are, of course, exceptions: Nathalie Solomon and Anne Chamayou's 2006 collection *Potins, cancans et littérature* offers useful readings of gossip in texts by Franz Kafka and Marcel Proust, among other, mostly French works, while a 2014 special issue of *Forum for Modern Language Studies* entitled "Literature and Gossip" represents a rich and valuable effort to explore the topic through works of multiple, though still predominantly European, traditions. Such forays beyond the ground covered by Spacks raise important and sometime discomfiting questions: in the latter volume's introduction, for instance, Nicholas Martin presents a pessimistic view of gossip and comes to wonder "whether gossip itself can be recovered or rehabilitated through literature" (140). Martin appears troubled by the very association of gossip with literature, which he argues could emerge tainted by the connection. "Gossip has its (literary) uses, but it is widely regarded as, above all, unproductive, idle, sterile waste," he warns (139). Martin here falls back on a kind of pre-Spacksian reading of gossip, and in so doing helps to reveal the extent to which Spacks and her successors' readings of gossip are influenced by their sources. In taking the study of gossip beyond the Anglo-American corpus, the essays Martin collects reveal not only the ample ground still left unexplored but also the limitations—not the invalidity, but rather the insufficiency—of "good gossip" as a framework for exploring the practice's role in other cultural contexts.[9]

The pitfalls inherent in monocultural readings of gossip have long been acknowledged by scholars, especially in fields such as anthropology and sociology. As early as 1963, Gluckman was already arguing for a view of gossip "as a culturally controlled game with important social functions" and concluded that "in different kinds of groups the role and function of gossip will vary with their specific histories and their situations in the larger society" (312). Despite their tacit debt to Gluckman, Herskovits, and other ethnographic researchers, however, literary scholars have tended to shy away from comparative, or even non-Anglocentric, readings of gossip. This has led to missed opportunities, in terms of both the lessons that can be learned from the literary production of other regions, including the Caribbean, and the contributions being made by those regions' scholars. One notable example is that of the Argentine essayist Edgardo Cozarinsky, whose 1973 study "El relato indefendible" anticipated but went unnoticed by the pioneers of Anglo-European gossip scholarship. The upshot of such oversights is that the literary scholarship on gossip has hitherto told an incomplete story, and has yet to systematically account for the practice's strategic value in postcolonial contexts or, more precisely, its function in works concerned with questions of subalternity and power as they crisscross the questions of race, gender, class, and other issues with which gossip often deals.

This is not to say that the role of gossip in the postcolonial Caribbean and other subaltern regions has gone entirely unremarked. Researchers such as Carol Bailey, Juan Pablo Dabove, Bénédicte Boisseron, and Nalini Natarajan have explored gossip's function in specific works from the Caribbean region; similarly, Rukmini Bhaya Nair's work on gossip in the novels of Salman Rushdie offers an intriguing vision of gossip as everyday talk "creatively empowered to reclaim the metaphors of an elite history," a tendency very much in keeping with gossip's deployments in the Caribbean (995). Other scholars have examined gossip as part of broader literary, historical, or interdisciplinary studies; Raphael Dalleo's

Caribbean Literature and the Public Sphere: From the Plantation to the Postcolonial (2011) and Lauren Derby's *The Dictator's Seduction: Politics and the Popular Imagination in the Era of Trujillo* (2009) are notable examples. My contention, however, is that gossip is far more widely present, and more potent, in the literature of the region than these relatively few studies would suggest, and that a more systematic approach can provide important new insights regarding both the literature of the Caribbean and the nature of gossip itself.

The Meaning(s) of Gossip

To begin to address gossip's role in the Caribbean, we must first try to agree on what "gossip" actually is. For such a ubiquitous practice, this is harder than might be expected: if "gossip" means many things to many people, it is in part because it is remarkably difficult to pin down. Appeals to the dictionary only take us so far: the *Oxford English Dictionary* understands gossip as "trifling or groundless rumour," or, more favorably, as "unrestrained talk or writing, esp. about persons or social incidents." A gossip, it is suggested, can also be a person, "mostly a woman, of light and trifling character, esp. one who delights in idle talk; a newsmonger, a tattler." *Merriam-Webster,* meanwhile, speaks of gossip as a "rumor or report of an intimate nature" or "a person who habitually reveals personal or sensational facts about others."

Turning to the Spanish language reveals other nuances: according to the *Real academia*'s *Diccionario de la lengua española,* the word *chisme* signifies "true or false news or commentary that generally seeks to turn one person against another, or which is whispered about someone." The Spanish-speaking Caribbean also uses the word *bochinche,* a slang term that suggests particularly vicious or slanderous gossip or rumor but that can also mean an uproar or hubbub, or a wild and licentious party. Turning again to the *Real academia,* we find *bochinche* defined as "gossip, sometimes calumnious, against a person or family, that grows louder and more slanderous as it passes from one person to the next." The Covarrubias dictionary of 1611, meanwhile, defines *chismoso* as "he who goes to another with news that he should keep quiet [. . .] and tells it with malice to stir up trouble and cause differences; and thus recounts things in the worst possible terms." *Chismosos* are, in this definition, *cizañeros,* or malicious gossips, who "sow discord between brothers" and are "ministers of Satan" (s.v. "chisme"). Clearly, for the Spanish speaker—or at least the Spanish lexicographer—*chisme* connotes a more malicious, adversarial, and potentially abrasive practice than gossip does for their English counterpart.[10]

This is further revealed in the etymology of the words denoting the practice. The English word *gossip* derives from the Old English *godsibb,* or godparent, and thus the ties between intimates—initially of either gender, although over the centuries the word has increasingly been used to denote female relationships. In Spanish, however, the word has almost precisely the opposite connotation. The word *chisme* is thought to derive either from the Latin *cimex,* via *chinche* ("chisme," *Breve diccionario etimológico*), meaning a bug, especially a bedbug, or from the Latin *schisma,* a rift or schism ("chisme," *Diccionario de la lengua española*). Other etymologies suggested by Covarrubias include a Greek term suggestive of lockjaw or an Arabic diacritic used to indicate unvoiced letters; though etymologically implausible, the suggestions stress the hushed, furtive quality of the act. Gossip is barely blown into the ear, the dictionary notes, and hence "those who go with gossip to the judiciary" are known as *soplones*—snitches, or literally blowers of gossip. Other Spanish terms similarly emphasize the negative qualities of gossip: per the *Real Academia, murmuración* is "talk that causes harm to one who is absent," while *malediciencia* derives from *maldecir* in the specific sense of caustic and denigratory speech against an absent other. Tellingly, the Spanish verb *comadrear,* which according to *Diccionario de la lengua española* signifies gossip between women and derives from *comadre,* is a seldom-used colloquialism; *chisme,* with all its pejorative and disruptive connotations, is far more widely used. Gossip, in the Spanish language, then, is etymologically rooted not in intimate and gendered solidarity but rather in the exposure of uncomfortable secrets and the social rifts engendered thereby.

The various French terms for gossip tend to stress the practice's viciousness and uselessness rather than its intimacy. The word *commérages,* though of similar etymological roots to the English *gossip* and the Spanish *comadrear* through the word *commère,* is defined by the *Dictionnaire de l'Académie française* as "idle talk that is indiscreet and of a malicious or malevolent tone"; the *Trésor de la langue française* similarly defines *commérage* as "the act of comporting oneself as a gossip, and of talking idly and indiscreetly, often with maliciousness, about trivial subjects; futile commentary, lacking interest." The *Dictionnaire de l'Académie française* takes a similarly negative view of *cancan* ("idle talk, malevolent or malicious gossip") and *potin* ("idle talk aimed at another and often tainted by bad-mouthing, gossip"). Interestingly, *potin* is also defined by the *Académie française* as "great noise, din," while *faire du potin* is defined by the *Trésor* as "to cause a scandal." *Cancan*, similarly, is defined as "noise or racket, inappropriate scandal" in Émile Littré's 1874 *Dictionnaire de la langue française*. As Brigitte Bercoff discusses, *cancan* is rooted in *quanquam*, a Latin word used to initiate long, scholarly discourses that explicitly correct and rebut the arguments of others. "It is, in reality, an instrument of power," Bercoff argues (18). The more current term *ragot* is defined by the *Trésor de la langue française* as "gossip, idle talk, generally malicious or malevolent" and is derived from the archaic verb *ragoter,* defined in turn as "to tell (something generally malicious or malevolent)" and "to quarrel." Etymologically, the *Trésor* posits that *ragoter* comes from the late Latin verbal form *ragere*, to scream in fury. The French terms for gossip thus bridge the connotations of the Spanish and English terms: rooted in the close relations between women but tainted with indiscretion and negativity and, like *chisme* and *bochinche,* closely connected to the fomentation of uproar, scandal, and social antagonism.

In the Caribbean, of course, we must also contend with a profusion of slang terms for gossip. Darío Espina Pérez's *Diccionario de cubanismos* (1972) records that *buquenque, lengua larga,* and *trapezondero* all signify both a gossip and a troublemaker. Interestingly, in the postrevolutionary Cuban context, *lengua larga* can also suggest a snitch, while *trapezondero* can suggest a wheeler-dealer, or someone who "does business at the margins of the law." María Vaquero and Amparo Morales's *Tesoro lexicográfico del español de Puerto Rico* (2005) similarly stresses the disruptive aspects of gossip, with *bochinche* defined as gossip, scandal, and tumult, and a *bochinchero* defined as one who "foments scandal and disorder" by saying "things that they should not say." Similarly *lengüetero* and *lengüilargo* both suggest a loose-tongued person who is at once a gossip, a troublemaker, and a chatterbox. Orlando Inoa's *Diccionario de dominicanismos,* meanwhile, defines *bajeado,* deriving from a word meaning infected and used to denote opponents of the Trujillo regime, as one who was "gossiped about with the authorities," while *bártulo* means both "propaganda" and "rumors," and terms such as *enreíto* and *fufu* suggest both gossip and a confusing or tangled situation. In a 1971 essay about gossip, Dominican humorist Mario Emilio Pérez lists further terms such as *dar tijeras* (to "give scissors," or colloquially, to "bitch"), *cortar un traje* (literally to cut someone's suit or dress, but figuratively to speak behind someone's back), and *bandear* (to pursue, but also to injure) as synonyms for *chismear.*

Creoles and African linguistic influences further enrich and complicate any attempt to understand the meanings and uses of gossip in the

Caribbean. Lydia Cabrera's *Anagó: vocabulario lucumí*, a study of Afro-Cuban Yoruba vocabulary, offers *chóke chódo, soró pipo, ofofó, afofó eleyo,* and *nforo* as terms for one who gossips, along with *lépe lépe,* meaning "bad-mouthing, gossip, or commentary," *charéreke* meaning "an imbroglio, or to make trouble using gossip and falsehoods," and the flexible word *odi* as a catch-all term for evil things such as "sickness, death, thirst, gossip, curiosity, vice, or infamy." Haitian Creole, meanwhile, offers terms such as *zin* or *zen,* with the rough meaning of gossip that bears news; *tripotay,* which derives from the French *tripotage,* in the sense of intriguing or plotting against someone; *télédiol* (also spelled *télédyol* or *télédjol*), which combines télé- with the Creole word for "mouth" to signify the oral grapevine, or *téléphone arabe;* and *chwichwi,* which refers more specifically to rumors.

The Anglophone Caribbean, similarly, has countless words with subtly differing meanings and nuances. Richard Allsopp's *Dictionary of Caribbean English Usage* lists terms such as *bad-mouth* and *mové-lang,* which focus on the malicious or injurious aspects of gossip; *blag, lick-mouth,* and *ole-talk,* which emphasize titillation and the idle enjoyment of gossip; *susu,* which suggests surreptitious or whispered speech; *koté-si koté-la* and *bring-and-carry,* which focus on the information-bearing quality of gossip; and *mèlé,* which derives from the French *mêlée* and is suggestive of scandal and conflict. Even the word *talk,* Allsopp notes, is understood as meaning gossip or rumor, rather than simply a speech act, in places such as Barbados, Grenada, and Guyana. Fascinatingly, the French word *commérages* also echoes through both the Francophone and Anglophone Caribbean: the phrase *ma commère* has, in various Francophone Creoles, given rise to the word *makoumè,* suggesting an effeminate man and by extension a queer, homosexual, or transgender person. In the Anglophone regions, this has been adopted—using spellings such as *makomè, macmay, macoomeh, macme,* and so on—both as a derogatory term akin to "auntie man" and as a term for a particularly inquisitive or meddlesome gossip. Derivatives such as *mako* and *maco* (which also resonate with the French word *maquereau,* meaning pimp) are also widely used to suggest gossips, busybodies, and people who pry into or spy on the affairs of others.

This linguistic richness is thrilling but presents an obvious challenge; after all, even scholars who confine themselves to the English word *gossip* have found it an elusive target. As Sarah Wert and Peter Salovey note, "Almost as many functions of gossip have been argued as writers who write about gossip" (77). Spacks claims that, much as Barbara Herrnstein Smith writes of poetry, gossip cannot be usefully defined since it "means many things to many people and even, at different times and in different contexts, to a single person" (4).[11] In the three decades since Spacks's assertion, relatively little progress has been made toward a comprehensive working definition of gossip: the books and articles that examine gossip for the most part proceed without clearly defining it. Indeed, as Martin argues, scholars are still debating apparently foundational issues such as "whether or not gossip has an author—or an implied audience or target" (137). Often, he further warns, one scholar's definition will contradict another's, for "while some theorists insist that gossip must name its target, others note that gossip is often couched obliquely and is careful to avoid naming names in order to avoid any possible recrimination" (137). Many scholars forgo the attempt to define gossip in absolute terms, seeking instead to delineate the qualities they take as being quintessential to it. For Martin, for instance, gossip is "characterized by rhetoric about exclusive knowledge, the need for secrecy as well as a series of actual or implied nods and winks" (137). Others focus on gossip as a transactional communicative process: it is, Andrew Counter writes, "a form of communication addressed by no one in particular to no one in particular, in which both sender and receiver participate for the intrinsic pleasure of the act, and are invested in the specific content of the message only to the extent that it appeals to their curiosity" (158).[12] Cozarinsky's more expansive definition runs along similar lines: "Gossip is, above all, a transmitted story," he writes. "One tells something about somebody, and one transmits this story because the somebody or the something is exceptional" (21). Gossip, in this reading, is the sharing of privileged information: we gossip about things that are outside the norm, or not widely known, and that we anticipate will spark the curiosity of our interlocutors.

In this study, I understand gossip as a malleable form that at its most basic constitutes an act of revelation in which a person discloses or comments upon private, privileged, or unauthorized facts or stories about an absent third party, typically without regard for, or in active opposition to, the wishes of their subject. In this conception of gossip I include the information or knowledge conveyed in such an act, as well as its specific form and style; in other words, if gossip is private information made public—a formulation that recurs in gossip scholarship—then it encompasses not just the content it transmits but also the act itself and the manner of its transmission. Gossip, after all, is highly performative: it tends to revel in its own transgressive surreptitiousness and to take theatrical pleasure in the value and nature of the information communicated.[13] Gossip has a compelling style and etiquette all of its own, and by adopting its grammar and vocabulary we agree to abide by its rules, at least for the duration of the exchange: we whisper not only to avoid being heard by others but also because of the pleasure we draw from performing their exclusion, from performing our own membership in the gossiping in-group, and from highlighting our mutual participation in a restricted and unsanctioned act. Indeed, it is through this performative aspect, in large part, that gossip achieves what has been taken by many scholars to be its most important aspect: its ability to presuppose, reinforce, and even create ideological alignment between speaker and listener.

Gossip, then, is a gossipy act, disclosing gossipy information, performed in a gossipy way; that is to say, it is an act of unsanctioned disclosure, relaying information that is private and often scandalous or salacious, and featuring the linguistic and performative markers we typically associate with gossip. These individual factors may be present in differing degrees in any specific instance of gossip; taken together, however, they are unmistakable. If we know gossip when we see it, it is chiefly because we recognize some or all of these structures and processes at work. Not all are necessarily required, and certainly not all three in equal degrees, in order for us to be in the presence of gossip. As the title of this volume suggests, gossip's prototypical medium is the spoken word, and many scholars refer to gossip as "talk." Still, as we have seen, gossip need not exclusively be a spoken medium. As Bruce Stovel writes, gossip's style "is spoken; even when gossip occurs in letters and not in person, the letters reproduce the patterns of spontaneous speech, not those of formal prose. Furthermore, gossip employs a distinctive kind of spoken style: allusive, full of veiled reference and innuendo, of nuance and *double entendre*" (29). Spacks, Cozarinsky, and other scholars also note the degree to which the oral cadences of gossip can be harnessed in literary texts, a process I take as rendering the text gossip-like through its emulation of the performative aspect of spoken gossip. We can see gossip in the prototypically gossipy talk of two close friends—but we can also perceive it, in varying degrees, in a newspaper gossip column, in social-media messages, in marginalia, in political speeches, in literary fiction, or even in history books. In what follows, I will examine various avatars of gossip of these kinds: texts that stage acts of gossip and their effects, writers who disclose gossipy information through their texts, and narrators who adopt or emulate gossipy modes of communication.

This approach also allows us to begin to distinguish between gossip and related forms—including, most notably, rumor. As the dictionary definitions above suggest, gossip and rumor are closely akin to one another, and the terms are sometimes used interchangeably; they are not, however, identical, and while there may be overlap, not every rumor is a form of gossip, and not every act of gossip is an act of rumormongering.[14] Ulises Carrión calls rumor a more general form than gossip: one that springs up in many places, from unidentified or unidentifiable sources, and that is ultimately differentiated from gossip by its status as "a collective creation, whereas gossip is always transmitted from one person to another" (41).[15] Gossip, by contrast, suggests certainty, and depends upon information from a traceable and generally explicitly described source: if not based on firsthand knowledge, it at least has (or is implied to have) a specific provenance. By extension, gossip (rightly or wrongly) presupposes and asserts its own accuracy and truthfulness: where rumor raises the possibility of an alternative version of events, gossip—in its rhetorical structures, its contents, and the relationships it implies—more forcefully asserts and depends upon its own purported accuracy. There is no bright line here; the question is one of degree. Sudhir Kakar argues that rumor is "a more dignified term for gossip" but also a more dangerous variant, focused less on mapping social relations than on stoking anxiety and providing life-and-death information (58). I would take issue with Kakar's claim that gossip is inherently less dangerous than rumor, but certainly rumor's typical content diverges in important ways from that of gossip: we gossip about specific individuals, for instance, while rumors typically deal in more nebulous claims about events. In what follows I will occasionally discuss or draw upon rumors, and in so doing will attempt to illustrate the degree to which such rumors are, and are not, gossip-like.

The framework described above is not so very different from the conception of gossip used by Spacks and others. To the extent that I diverge with past scholarship, it is in my emphasis on gossip as a malleable and plural form, and in my attempt to understand "gossip" not only in the senses typically connoted by the English *gossip* and the French *commérage,* but also in the senses implied by the Spanish *chisme* and *bochinche.* Gossip can, per the French and English usages, be "idle talk" that reveals or discusses fairly trivial things—the chatter that binds intimate communities together—but it can also, as the Spanish terms suggest, be something more boisterous, divisive, and dangerous. At its core, gossip is a fundamentally adversarial act, concerned with questions of power: to gossip with someone is to gossip about (or against) someone else, and to assert complicity and a common position vis-à-vis the gossip's subject. This is evident in the intrusiveness of gossip: insofar as it conveys illicit information or knowledge, gossip is founded upon the act of trespassing into private lives. Even when otherwise benign, the pleasure taken in gossip stems in large part from the enjoyment of power derived from such scrutiny and intrusion; at its most malicious, gossip not only relishes the private shame and misfortune of others but also seeks to take ownership of, expose, and thereby exacerbate that shame and misfortune. In either case, gossip concerns itself not just with information but with judgment. Gossip is necessarily biased and committed to its own ideological reading and presentation of the information it discloses. As such, it is a narrative not just of disclosure but also of revision: it explicitly seeks to offer new versions or readings of previously established narratives. This is a feature, not a bug: it is through its revisionism, its ideological charge, and its avowed lack of neutrality that gossip is able to make such a clear intervention in issues of honor and reputation, and thus exercise power over the lives of its subjects.

Gossip in the Caribbean

One of the lasting effects of Spacks's work is that gossip, as a means for promoting solidarity among intimates, has been increasingly understood in gendered terms, especially with regard to acts of self-assertion by women and, by extension, other marginalized groups. Gossip's position as an instrument of defiance, however, extends beyond simply its historical function as "women's talk." As Spacks notes, the urgency with which those in power seek to clamp down on gossip stands as testament to the form's potency: "History testifies to the persistence and the power of gossip [. . .]. Moralizers have taken gossip seriously even when they declared its lack of seriousness. It supplies a weapon for outsiders—a weapon appropriately directed at the façade of reputation people construct around themselves. And the weapon can be converted to a bond: a means of alliance, a way of feeling united as insiders" (45). If Spacks perceives gossip as a weapon, however, it is one with bated edges. The struggle in which Spacks's gossipers engage is typically a moral or societal jockeying for position, not the high-stakes, genuinely dangerous struggle found in other contexts. Gossip, Spacks writes, is fascinating because it is forbidden, or at least frowned upon. But it is naughty rather than deadly: "We know it's wrong, but it doesn't *kill* anyone," she writes (11). Seen from this angle, gossip's role in forging common narratives appears far less fraught.[16] Naturally, scholars of Anglo-American and European literature, writing in the shadow of Jane Austen's gossip and the old English *godsibbs,* frequently resort to similar readings. In this view, gossip is the act of individuals forging a common identity on their own terms, not of people vying for control of a narrative already claimed and enforced by others.[17]

In the Caribbean, gossip can and does serve as a means of building intimate communities, allowing women and other historically marginalized groups to assert their voices in and beyond the domestic sphere. Indeed, gossip's traditional associations with female speech and domesticity are still vividly present in the region's literature, as seen, for instance, in Olive Senior's use of gossip to map women's communities. But the nascent and brief mentions of gossip in scholarship about the Caribbean have tended to move away from readings of gossip as primarily a feminine practice.[18] Writing in 1973, the anthropologist Peter J. Wilson saw gossip—which he defined as "talk about reputation and respectability"—as fundamental to the establishment of male reputation and a crucial part of both male and female discourse on the Colombian island of Providencia (161). More recently, scholars of Caribbean literature have taken similar approaches: Jason Cortés's *Macho Ethics: Masculinity and Self-Representation in Latino-Caribbean Narrative* (2015), for instance, touches upon gossip's role in masculine, even macho, mythmaking in Luis Rafael Sánchez's *La importancia de llamarse Daniel Santos* (80–81).

As I demonstrate in the chapters that follow, Caribbean literature is full of both men and women who gossip, perhaps because, in the Caribbean, the practice often functions as a pervasive and politicized narrative form intensely bound up in struggles for narrative control. Conventionally gendered gossip is still present, but it is only one facet of a practice that can also present a violent and even destructive aspect more typically associated with hypermasculine identities—though not, in the Caribbean, by any means restricted to men, any more than intimate gossip is solely the province of women. Gossip thus acquires a kind of gender neutrality, albeit one more present in gossip's deployments and practical uses than in its depictions and perceptions. Many (though by no means all) Caribbean cultures still chiefly perceive gossip as being women's talk or as a feminine or effeminate practice that reflects poorly on male participants. It is tempting to read this in linguistic terms: as we have seen, words that imbue gossip with a feminine quality—godsibb, *commère*—are prevalent in the Caribbean, but so too are gender-neutral terms such as *télédiol, bochinche*, or *bad-talk* that frame gossip through its uses and consequences rather than its participants. Gossip is certainly read in the region as something that women do and thus in certain deployments as a feminine practice, but it is *also* read as something done by men—or, perhaps more accurately, simply by people. Though still, at times, the language of the subordinated, gossip is also deployed by more powerful figures, frequently but not exclusively male, as they participate in public life: dictators and dissidents, conservatives and radicals, journalists and Judases. In 1926, the Puerto Rican novelist Rafael Martínez Alvarez wrote: "Here, we have gossip between politicians, gossip between women, merchants, men of letters, journalists; between the brothers and sisters of the same society; between the ministers of the Lord: Catholics, protestants, and rabbis; and, in the social field, calumnies shipped in bulk . . ." (Alva 220).[19] Certainly, this remains true of the more recent Caribbean, where the idea of gossip as a politicized and politically relevant form goes beyond the apparatus of the state and those close to it. Gossip, evidently, is also tied to the functioning of the *polis* more generally—to the public sphere, to the wider body of citizens constituting a community or society, and to the nation.

What unites the various forms of gossip described in the chapters that follow, then, is neither gendered speech nor the creation, through such speech, of intimacy; rather, it is an adversarialism that, while subtly present in a great deal of gossip, is especially potent and prominent in the Caribbean. Just as the communities described by Spacks often derive their intimacy from their policing of group boundaries, so the gossip of the Caribbean frequently defines itself in opposition to its subject, the maligned other. Intimacy and inclusiveness, in gossip of this type, are zero-sum: possible only insofar as they are based upon the exclusion and denigration of a common foe. In the Caribbean, gossip is frequently governed by such adversarial relationships. From the calypso singer's barbed rhymes and the songs of the Haitian combites to the vicious slanders published in Trujillo-era gossip columns, words serve as weapons, elevating and strengthening one person or group—or their preferred narrative—at the expense of another.

It is gossip's pliability and accessibility, its ability to be co-opted by both the powerful and the disenfranchised, that make it so ubiquitous in the region. Gossip, as we shall see, is often deployed in Caribbean literature as a symbol or manifestation of narrative, historiographic, and epistemological discomfort. Stuart Hall argues that the historically polarized nature of Caribbean societies makes it "impossible to approach Caribbean culture without understanding the way it was continually inscribed by questions of power" (28). Dalleo similarly connects gossip with questions of power when he asserts that gossip often serves as "a sort of counterpublic," where those without other means of access to the public sphere can share knowledge (102). But while gossip does function as a counterpublic in Caribbean writing, its uses go well beyond that role, with its narrative embattlements serving to map fractured identities and entrenched antagonisms. In this way, gossip also plays a crucial part in the negotiations through which Caribbean nations forge their societies and their public and political lives. What follows will demonstrate the degree to which Caribbean societies—both geographical and discursive—have used gossip to stage their narrative struggles, and will explore gossip's place in the region's structures and dynamics of power and domination.

The oppositional and revisionary nature of gossip is not unique to the Caribbean but may be more easily visible there. The Caribbean, after all, still bears the marks of dictatorship and state terror, and of conquest and colony; it is still grappling with what Antonio Benítez-Rojo calls the single constant problem of "violence, continuous violence, historic violence" (357). As Martin Munro aptly notes, the Caribbean's cataclysmic history endures in "political systems based on apocalyptic systems of for or against, honor or blood, death or glory" (*Tropical Apocalypse* 11). In such deeply polarized contexts, gossip acquires a palpable urgency. Gossip, in the Caribbean, is not merely the stuff of idle chatter but rather a practical and often deeply political practice: a means of navigating and staging narrative tensions and of waging the narrative battles through which the region's identity, politics, and culture come to be forged.

Idle Talk, Deadly Talk

The four chapters that follow account for some of the chief uses of gossip in the Caribbean and propose that recent Caribbean literature has availed itself of gossip to engage with some of the region's key questions. In what follows I read novels and short stories but also poems, popular music, political essays, pamphlets, personal letters, and memoirs; still, my aim is not to be exhaustive, and in a region so rich in gossip, much ground remains to be covered, not least in terms of the area's pre-1960s literary production.[20] This volume is neither a survey nor a panorama; I do not seek to sort and classify all the instances, or even all the uses, of gossip in recent Caribbean literature, and there are many other Caribbean texts that could fruitfully have been explored here. Neither do I offer a systematic examination of the differing deployments of gossip across the diverging (yet connected) linguistic, cultural, and historical contexts of the region: my goal is not to show how Puerto Rican gossip, for instance, differs from Jamaican or Haitian gossip. Rather, I seek to use the multilingual, multicultural Caribbean as a proving ground: a space, very different from those in which gossip has traditionally been studied, that allows us to more readily apprehend certain aspects of the practice. In so doing, I demonstrate gossip's role in staging the breakdown of communities and of neighborly bonds; its fraught status as a form of knowledge and means of negotiating identities; its utility to political dissidents, especially in shaping international public opinion; and, finally, its role in retroactively representing and challenging the narrative dynamics of authoritarian regimes. It is my hope that in so doing, I go some distance toward helping scholars of the Caribbean to better understand the ways in which gossip exists in and informs the region's literature and, by extension, illuminates the Caribbean's cultural dynamics and public discourses. I seek, too, to expand the horizons of current gossip scholarship and to show that other kinds of gossip, and other ways of gossiping, merit serious examination as we explore this strange, shifting, and endlessly fascinating form of discourse.

The first chapter explores the degree to which gossip in Caribbean literature diverges from the largely benign, prosocial practice described in recent Anglo-American scholarship. The pasquinades that tear apart a town in Gabriel García Márquez's *La mala hora* (1962) show the potentially damaging and corrosive role that gossip can play in communities marked by the legacy of violence and insurgency; rather than using gossip to foster intimacy, García Márquez uses the practice to stage the failure of community. Other texts from the region, including García Márquez's *Crónica de una muerte anunciada* (1981) and works by Roger Mais, Luis Rafael Sánchez, and Jean Rhys, serve to illustrate the degree to which gossip, seen as a conservative force that polices societal norms, can come into conflict with more intimate, neighborly visions of community. In such texts gossip frequently emerges as a totalitarian force, binding communities together by punishing divergence from group norms, but in so doing also revealing itself as alienating, disempowering, and paranoia inducing. In situations such as these, gossip, or the fear of gossip, often forces individuals to sublimate themselves into fearful passivity. In Antonio José Ponte's essayistic novel *La fiesta vigilada* (2007), for instance, gossip is vividly rendered as part of a suffocating system of constant surveillance, transmuting neighborly proximity into an unspoken threat rather than a source of comfort and community.

The second chapter examines gossip as both an epistemological resource and a battleground. Gossip often serves to highlight the discrepancies between accounts circulating in a given community; this is the case, for instance, in Rosario Ferré's *Maldito amor* (1986), a novella in which gossip mediates the textual reality, the events of which are recounted post facto by characters with agendas of their own. Ferré's work has been read primarily as a feminist text, but I suggest that *Maldito amor*'s layers of contradictory gossip serve not to decisively undermine the patriarchal master narrative, but rather to suggest the epistemological indeterminacy of all narratives and the impossibility of arriving at a definitive version of events. A similar process can be found at work in Jean Rhys's *Wide Sargasso Sea* (1966), which uses gossip to trace social divisions, and the epistemic rifts between groups and individuals engendered thereby. Maryse Condé's *Célanire cou-coupé* (2000), meanwhile, uses gossip to introduce fantastical elements and undermine the authority of the narrator, calling into question the truthfulness of the unfolding tale. Still, while gossip can stage the epistemological challenges of the Caribbean, it can also be a valid and powerful tool for interpreting and making sense of reality. In Ana Teresa Torres's *La fascinación de la víctima* (2008), for instance, a psychotherapist turned detective uses gossip to solve a murder. Gossip may not be altogether reliable, but in Torres's text it remains capable of unlocking hidden truths and providing real insights into "the darkness of the soul" (363).

The third chapter discusses gossip's role in the public sphere, especially in literary acts of political dissent. The Cuban writer Reinaldo Arenas, in his autobiography, *Antes que anochezca* (1992), uses gossip about his own sexual adventures to push back against the repressive sexual politics of postrevolutionary Cuba and to reveal the regime's actions to a global audience. Arenas's braggadocio is a calculated stance against what Emilio Bejel terms an "institutionalized machismo" (141–42): in gossiping about seducing soldiers and police officers, Arenas punctures the heteronormative rhetoric of the *hombre nuevo* and asserts his right to define a queer identity on his own terms. A similar drive for self-definition marks the gossip of Arenas's countrymate, the exile writer Guillermo Cabrera Infante, who uses gossip to map the political and artistic structures of the island and to counter official efforts to erase him from the Cuban canon. Cabrera Infante's essays mobilize gossip's adversarial power and seductive narrative energy to bolster his own credibility as an informant, turning a proliferation of gossipy anecdotes into both a defensive and an offensive weapon. Finally, I address the scarcity of dictatorship novels in Haitian literature of the Duvalier period, and explore Graham Greene's 1966 novel *The Comedians* and François Duvalier's subsequent reputational attacks on Greene. In such cases, writers exploit the public's hunger for gossip to facilitate their own entry into the public sphere, using the promise of inside information to assert their individual voices and undermine the public image of those in power.

The final chapter offers an examination of the legacy of the Dominican dictator Rafael Leónidas Trujillo, whose administration incorporated gossip into its own self-sustaining mechanism of power—a practice remarkably common in authoritarian regimes. The Dominican "gossip state" recognized gossip as a threat to its own narrative monopoly, and sought to control it and turn it to its own ends. This left enduring marks in the country's literature, both in explicitly gossipy memoirs by politicians such as Joaquín Balaguer and in fictional works by writers such as Viriato Sención, Marcio Veloz Maggiolo, and Junot Díaz, who seek both to engage with the regime's use of gossip and to reappropriate the personal accounts and plausible versions of gossip in order to grapple with the country's whitewashed history. In this way, these writers sidestep sanitized, monolithic historical accounts and weave unauthorized versions of their nations' histories from alternate materials: rumor, gossip, and hearsay. The chapter closes with a reading of Kettly Mars's *Saisons sauvages* (2010), a novel that uses gossip to craft, retroactively, the kind of dictatorship novel that Haiti has until recently lacked, and to engage with the compromises and complicity of the survivors of the Duvaliers' dynasty. Finally, the conclusion argues that gossip's place in the contemporary Caribbean stems not from any special trait or inherent peculiarity of the Caribbean peoples, but rather from the fraught historical circumstances that have shaped the region and to which its writers must necessarily respond.

Throughout this book, I conceive of the Caribbean not as a collection of islands defined by water-bounded insularity but rather as a crossroads in a much-traversed ocean, marked by exchange and the interplay of language, ideas, and people. The Caribbean is, to borrow Benítez-Rojo's phrase, a "meta-archipelago" comprising the islands and circum-Caribbean coastline but also diasporic outposts in cities such as New York, Miami, and London. These nodes do not exist in isolation: through them, the Caribbean—already hybrid and heteroglot, as James Clifford notes—is in constant communication with global cultural currents. Despite regional insecurities regarding the Caribbean's relationship with distant cultural centers, this is very much an exchange, powered by active and outward-looking (and rebounding) diasporic currents as much as by insular or passive receptivity. As Robert Fatton Jr. correctly asserts, Haiti's oral grapevine, or *télédiol*, is not merely the legacy of the national government's efforts to control and censor more formal discourse: "It is also the fabrication of information to influence reality itself.

Such *teledyol* is practiced in the homeland and exported to the Haitian diaspora in the United States, Canada, and Europe, where it takes new forms through the technologies of the internet. In a boomerang effect, the diaspora is now becoming the digital hub disseminating back home an electronic *teledyol* reflecting its ever-increasing powers" (168). Now more than ever, gossip is a global phenomenon with decidedly local roots. In his poem "juana bochisme," itself a piece of transcribed gossip, the Afro-Nuyorican writer Tato Laviera insists that "what goes on in new york is known instantly in manatí"—and it is gossip, Laviera makes clear, that links the two, running like a root system between the scattered communities of the global diaspora and the towns and villages of the islands (95). The multilateral exchanges between the various nodes that together form the Caribbean—migration and colonization, departure and return, nostalgia and rejection—foster a Caribbean identity that is unusually and perhaps uncomfortably self-reflective. To be Caribbean is to move fluidly from "inside" to "outside" and back again, seeing one's nation and one's people both from within and from without. This is a destabilizing phenomenon: the voices of exiles, emigrants, and outsiders echo through the region, an antagonistic counterweight to the insular nationalism and univocal narratives frequently preferred and promoted by the region's elites.

Antagonism, the mapping of self and other, the disruption of established narratives—all these are precisely the realms in which gossip operates. Scholars in other fields, perhaps indebted to Herskovits and Gluckman, have portrayed gossip as a critical resource for navigating the instability and inequity of Caribbean societies; the anthropologist Glen Perice writes, for instance, that during political strife in Haiti, gossip and rumor became "interpretive stances" that gave rise to an alternative public sphere ("Rumors" 3). Such readings rest not only on the power of gossip but also on the insufficiency of other discourses; in a region forged through slavery, colonialism, revolution, and authoritarianism, the credibility of official and institutional ways of knowing, from history books to the news media, have been eroded by the abuses of those who have controlled them. Ricardo Piglia notes that in Latin America "reality is not the truth" (qtd. in Caistor 7), and I trace a similar anxiety in the Caribbean, where facts are frequently subsidiary to narrative control and official accounts are often, and rightly, viewed as biased and arbitrary. This deficit of credibility creates a kind of narrative disorientation to which gossip, despite and even because of its own unruliness and unreliability, offers a possible solution: a way of scribbling on and defacing official accounts, and of reinscribing plausible hunches and suspicions onto sanitized official versions of events.

It is for these reasons that the writers studied in *Idle Talk, Deadly Talk* so often turn to gossip to thematize discrepancy, unreliability, and doubt. Gossip reminds us that every narrative is necessarily incomplete: that all stories can be told in other ways or can be revised, undermined, or elaborated upon. The gossip of the Caribbean frequently flaunts its power to challenge and revise existing narratives. In a region marked by conflicting viewpoints and incomplete histories, gossip's utility lies in its ability to plumb narrative gaps and to expose papered-over cracks in established narratives, to account for suppressed voices, and to splinter monolithic official accounts into a more representative proliferation of viewpoints.

Gossip is a valuable resource in such circumstances, but it is far from being a panacea: it can help to build counternarratives but can also corrode social ties, disempower individuals, and silence dissenting voices. Gossip serves as a battleground: a contested space where narratives of power and dissent vie for dominance and where no single narrative is ever safe from challenge and disruption. Gossip thrives in the Caribbean, then, because it thematizes both the region's plurality and its essential instability—societal and political, yes, but also narrative, historical, and epistemological. James Scott writes that gossip "is a discourse about social rules that have been violated" (*Domination* 142), and in the Caribbean, where inequality, tyranny, and long histories of domination bring with them the constant violation of social rules, gossip abounds as a resource both to resist and to reinforce power. Gossip's irreverence, its unauthorized and adversarial nature, confer upon it a narrative energy that other forms of storytelling lack—and make it a critical resource for exploring the contested narratives and fraught, insufficient histories that mark the Caribbean region.

1   "A Mouthful of Dynamite"
Gossip and the Failure of Community

> This carry-go-bring-come, my dear, bring misery.
> —Justin Hinds

GOSSIP, AT its most basic, is the spoken word: unauthorized whispers transmitting scandalous secrets from one person to another or the chatter of friends and kinsfolk picking over the actions and transgressions of absent third parties. Gossip's foundation in orality has made it a key weapon in the linguistic battles that are part and parcel of the Caribbean experience. As Edward Kamau Brathwaite writes, "It was in language that the slave was most successfully imprisoned by the master, and it was in his (mis-)use of it that he perhaps most effectively rebelled" (*Development* 237). In the British West Indies and its diaspora, gossip has been an important way of staging the willful misuse of language and of allowing writers to push back against linguistic hegemony and assert the validity of their own voices. Indeed, gossip has been one of the few forms through which West Indian writers have been able to introduce Creole into mass-market media publications; writing in the mid-1980s, Hubert Devonish noted that in the postcolonial British Caribbean, mass-market newspapers were published exclusively in English, with the exception of cartoons, select quotations from Creole speakers, and gossip columns. "In the case of articles of a satirical and gossipy nature, these involve writing which is aimed at imitating informal speech. The writers of such articles, therefore, use written Creole as a stylistic device," he records (32). Many writers from the region and its diaspora have similarly used gossip not only as a means (or consequence) of emulating spoken speech patterns but also as part of a broader project of writing back against British linguistic and cultural encroachment and, in so doing, of asserting their right to build identities and construct communities on their own terms.[1] The Guyanan poet John Agard, now based in Britain, makes the urgency and adversarialism of such efforts clear in his 1985 poem "Listen Mr Oxford Don":

> I only armed wit mih human breath
> but human breath
> is a dangerous weapon (44)

Agard's wry promise to smash up the grammar and syntax of the English language and make it his own belies the seriousness of his engagement with issues of language and of orality: this destructive assimilation is his Gordian solution to the impasse proposed by Derek Walcott when he asked how he could be expected to "choose / Between this Africa and the English tongue I love" ("A Far Cry from Africa," *Green Night* 18). For Agard, the postcolonial writer expresses his love for the "English tongue" by making it his own—by speaking to and for his own experiences, his own community—even if in so doing he must dismantle the very rules and building blocks of the colonizer's language.

Where Agard focuses on using speech patterns to express his claim on the English language, other writers make more explicit reference to gossip as part of this process. The Jamaican poet Louise Bennett has been at the forefront of efforts to make authentic spoken language part of the written record. Her poetry—and most notably her collection *Jamaica Labrish* (1966)—uses gossip to capture the voices and lived experiences of Jamaicans but also to explore the linguistic and political tensions they face. Her poem "Bed-Time Story" (1982) splices together an imported nursery rhyme, recounted in the Queen's English, with a lovingly staged act of gossip:

> Mary had a little lamb
> —Miss Mattie li bwoy Joe
> Go kick May slap pon har doorway—
> His feet was white as snow. (6)

The contrast between pleasurable gossip and the dutifully recited rhyme, extracted from a grudging parent by a restless child, could not be clearer. Bennett also inserts gossip into one of her best-known poems, "Colonisation in Reverse" (1966), in which the Jamaican diaspora is explored through the "joyful news" about émigrés that the speaker shares with "Miss Mattie." The broad-strokes account of diaspora—"By de hundred, by de t'ousan / [. . .] / Dem a-pour out o' Jamaica" (179)—is simmered down to a more personal act of gossip:

> Jane say de dole is not too bad
> Because dey payin' she
> Two pounds a week fe seek a job
> Dat suit her dignity.

Me say Jane will never find work
At the rate how she dah-look,
For all day she stay pon Aunt Fan couch
And read love-story book. (180)

The transcribed fragment of gossip suggests a reading of the broader poem as an act of gossip about England itself and the "devilment" the colonizing power has coming to it. The narrator's mock-sympathetic poring-over of England's problems—"But I'm wonderin' how dem gwine stan' / Colonizin' in reverse" (180)—is very much in keeping with the register of interpersonal gossip. In this sense, Bennett uses gossip to question the authority of the colonial power, in an act of linguistic subversion that itself serves as a reverse colonization of the one-time linguistic oppressor.

Gossip thus allows communities, such as the Jamaicans of Bennett's poem, to engage in a kind of collective adversarialism, both positively asserting their own group identity and needling the people they define as outsiders. This is a process that works in both directions: gossip is an equalizing force, something practiced by both colonizer and colonized, both the marginalized and the powerful. Marlon James's *The Book of Night Women* (2009) offers a barbed reminder that it is not only the downtrodden who gossip: Massa Roget warns that allowing slaves to gossip among themselves is an invitation to revolt, but also acknowledges that there is no substantive difference between the "discourse" of the slave owners and the gossipy speech through which the slaves, if given the chance, will "conspire and plot" (208). Gossip may be especially significant for those who lack other means of gaining a public voice, but it is by no means exclusively deployed by the marginalized; the insular communities formed by colonizers, so deliberately set apart from the communities of the colonized, are perfect breeding grounds for gossip.[2] The tendency to denigrate gossip, or to dismiss the speech of the colonized as mere babble, is itself a part of the power structure against which such attempts at linguistic reformulation should be considered.

While many Caribbean writers have embraced gossip as a means of writing themselves and their authentic voices into public discourses, others have viewed gossip with a degree of ambivalence or sought to problematize the equation of gossip with authentic or noncolonial speech. In Michelle Cliff's 1987 novel *No Telephone to Heaven,* for instance, Harry/Harriet makes a casual reference to Socrates and, when asked where he had read Plato, reminds his friend that they had been forced to read the Greek philosopher in school: "You forget how them drill us in them labrish? De master mek us read about five of dem dialogue. . . . Teaching us to be gentlemen . . . disdaining us all the while," he says (123).[3] The British teacher, he recalls, told the children that ancient Greece had been a golden age—something that strikes Harry/Harriet as strange, given the era's treatment of slaves and women. If Greece, with all its problems, can be considered golden, why should Jamaica be treated with such disdain? "It nuh stand as warning for all a we—no matter how light? how bright? how much of dem labrish we master?" he reflects (123). In labeling Plato's texts as "labrish," or gossip, Harry/Harriet here poses a challenge: Is he denigrating the classics and the imperial schooling—Walcott's "sound colonial education" ("The Schooner Flight" 346)—that elevates them and by extension dismisses the validity of Creole speech and thought? Or are we to read this as a more positive, equalizing gesture, an attempt to suggest that "labrish" is a valid and intellectually useful practice, with the chatter of Jamaicans like Harry/Harriet and the classic texts of empire ultimately deserving of the same degree of respect and consideration? Harry/Harriet offers no clear answer; rather, his choice of words echoes the paradox he discerns in the dialogues themselves, with their "golden age" in some ways so similar to, yet perceived by the colonizer as so superior to, his own Jamaican reality.[4]

Diasporic writers, too, have sought to cast gossip not just as a way for the marginalized to forge communities and assert collective identities but also as a tool of the oppressor.[5] In his poem "The SUN" (1992), the British Jamaican writer Benjamin Zephaniah attacks tabloid newspapers as gossip mills whose "witch-hunting to shame a name" serves the interests of those who are "friendly with The State" at the expense of black immigrants, whom he dismisses, assuming the voice of a tabloid reader, as "Jungle bunnies" who "play tom-toms" (58). He concludes:

> Don't give me truth, just give me gossip
> And skeletons from people's closets
> I wanna be normal
> And millions buy it,
> I am blinded by The SUN. (59)

Tabloid gossip, for Zephaniah, is, on the one hand, the cynical exploitation of readers' ignorance and prejudice and, on the other, the readers' turning away from true knowledge, and willful immersion in group membership, expressed through an uncritical collective blindness. Gossip, then, is not just an aspect of orality or a way of weaving community and shared identity out of authentic or unauthorized speech. It is also a means of forcefully asserting one's membership in a given community; of asserting, equally forcefully, the exclusion of others from that community; and of exploring (and challenging or reasserting) the dynamics and narratives of power that exist at the boundaries of that community, or that mediate one community's relationship with another.

As I will show in the remainder of this chapter, gossip's uses in the Caribbean thus go far beyond simply the spoken word—and in the process, gossip often becomes not only a tool for self-assertion and the maintenance of intimate communities, but also a means of tracing the fault lines inherent in Caribbean societies and of staging the fractures and failures of the communities they contain.[6] I begin by reading Gabriel García Márquez's novels *La mala hora* (1962) and *Crónica de una muerte anunciada* (1981), in which gossip serves to reveal (but not resolve) the tensions and latent violence in small communities, and is exposed as an agent of stasis: the cement that holds a community together, but also a deeply conservative and even paralyzing force. I next explore this theme in the short stories of writers including Roger Mais, Jean Rhys, Luis Rafael Sánchez, Patrick Sylvain, and Luis Negrón, all of whom I take to use gossip as a means of framing the breakdown of conventional neighborliness and the community's intolerance of outsiders. As Olive Senior notes, gossip is often a means of interrogating difference; in the Caribbean, however, the performance of difference frequently serves not to foster and reinforce the ties between small groups of intimates but rather to accentuate the exclusion of the perceived other. In the texts here studied, gossip mediates and fuels adversarialism: outsiders are persecuted, ostracized, and often subjected to violent acts of vengeance. This system of scrutiny and social policing reaches its apotheosis in Antonio José Ponte's *La fiesta vigilada* (2007), which shows Cuba as a surveillance state in which gossip plays a vital and inescapable role. In Ponte's text, I suggest, neighborliness and convivial chatter give way to a panoptic and totalitarian impulse, with gossip co-opted by the state as it seeks to ensure its own survival.

The Fractured Community: *La mala hora*

In early 2005, the town of Iconozo, a sleepy farming community about three hours' drive southwest of Bogotá, became the unexpected focus of global media attention. Local officials, it was reported, had passed a new law making it illegal for the town's twelve thousand residents to gossip about one another. "To possess a tongue and use it to do evil is like having a mouthful of dynamite," the decree warned, continuing that since "unfortunately our tongues repeat what we hear," perpetrators of gossip would henceforth face up to four years in jail and fines equivalent to about $1,600 (*El Tiempo* May 22, 2005).[7] This was no joke, said one functionary: in a country torn apart by drug trafficking and guerrilla warfare, to gossip about one's neighbors was at best risky and at worst tantamount to actual violence. "I'm less afraid of guerrillas or the paramilitary than of gossips' tongues," the official explained (*El Tiempo* May 17, 2005).

To reporters recounting the episode for European and American readers, the tale sounded like something lifted straight from the pages of Gabriel García Márquez—and while the Colombian author and his magic-realist aesthetic have too often been deployed by foreign journalists as a facile proxy for the Latin American other, this time the press gallery was onto something. Gossip is a constant presence in García Márquez's work, from the seething, collectively voiced rumors of *El otoño del patriarca* (1975) and swirling Faulknerian gossip of *La hojarasca* (1955) to the memorable depiction, in *El general en su laberinto* (1989), of Simón Bolívar as powerless to prevent chatter about his "secretos de alcoba," or bedroom secrets (217).[8] Moreover, the gossip of García Márquez is not the comforting, familiar chatter that helps women and other marginalized groups to forge intimate communities. Rather, it is something more dangerous, more alienated and alienating—something, in fact, that can corrode, or explode, the bonds that hold communities together.[9]

This is most vividly apparent in *La mala hora,* in which a town is plunged into chaos by the appearance of highly personal *pasquines,* or pasquinades, that are nailed to the doors of the town's homes and other buildings.[10] The word *pasquines,* typically translated as "lampoons," here denotes not satire but rather, as Michael Wood suggests, "gossip daubed in blue ink" ("Claims"). Though initially a source of amusement for the less well-heeled townsfolk—"better than a serenade," Trinidad says (*La mala hora* 8)—events quickly take a darker turn, with César Montero killing Pastor after a *pasquín* alleges that Pastor has cuckolded him. The murder is only the first of many violent and dramatic episodes prompted by the pasquinades: based on their gossip, Roberto Asís comes to doubt that he is his daughter's biological father, the disgraced Tovar women are forced to leave town, and Pepe Amador is killed by the police. Even those not directly targeted swiftly learn to fear the pasquinades. Mr. Benjamin frets about the gossip sheets, as does the dentist's wife, Angela; the judge's secretary, meanwhile, muses that "what keeps one up at night isn't the pasquinades, but the fear of the pasquinades" (77). The agitation they spark becomes an all-consuming preoccupation: the doctor reports that "for days, the rumors had been coming to his practice. [. . .] In fact he'd heard talk of nothing else all week" (105). There is a fascination to the pasquinades, a certain lowbrow frisson of excitement; the priest comments that "in the houses of the poor there was talk about the pasquinades, but in a different way and even with healthy enjoyment" (106–7). The rich, who fret about their reputations, believe they have more to worry about than the poor; still, the secretary, who is not presented as a wealthy man, is troubled when he recalls the "story of a town that was wiped out in seven days by pasquinades" (33).[11] He, at least, sees clearly that the pasquinades aren't just a guilty pleasure: they are a direct threat to the social fabric, and perhaps the very existence, of the community.

The nature of the gossipy pasquinades that afflict the town has been the subject of considerable critical debate, with many scholars reading the pamphlets as what Wolfgang A. Luchting calls "clandestine opposition propaganda," in contrast to the official pronouncements of the town's leaders (475). "Each time such 'official' literature appears—circulars, instructions, 'levantamientos,' autopsy-findings—it brings or confirms some repression, i.e., it is conservative; whenever non-official 'literature' is mentioned—the lampoons, caricatures, films, 'clandestine leaflets'—it represents an incitement to or confirmation of rebellion, i.e., it is subversive," Luchting explains (477).[12] But the subversion manifested in the pasquinades is darker and less focused than such readings suggest. In fact, the secretary's concerns—about being personally targeted, but also about the pasquinades' impact on the town's social fabric—are shared by the vast majority of the novel's characters.[13] Mr. Benjamin sees the pasquinades as a "symptom of social breakdown" (124), but they are not just a symptom or consequence of societal decay but are in fact the proximal cause of that collapse. Lynn Walford notes that some critics read in the lampoons a sense of solidarity similar to that of Lope de Vega's play *Fuenteovejuna* (1619), in which residents of the eponymous town protect the killer of an oppressive official by saying, even under torture, that "Fuenteovejuna lo hizo"—Fuenteovejuna did it. But as Walford recognizes, such readings miss the mark: the lampoons, "far from uniting the people, serve to deepen the divisions among them" and consist "not of political protest but character assassination; they inspire not defiance but fear" (40). The lampoons' gossip offers not reassuringly Manichean divisions of the community into *us* and *them* but rather a more chaotic proliferation of antagonisms and suspicions. As such, the lampoons neither empower the townsfolk nor allow them to organize into a coherent political opposition; rather, they are a nihilistic force that frays and eventually breaks the ties that, though much strained, have hitherto bound the community together.[14]

From what, though, do the pasquinades derive their destructive power? It is evidently not, or not only, from the information they disclose. The pasquinades do not, after all, reveal the unknown; rather, they make public that which was already privately circulating as gossip. "They didn't reveal any secrets: nothing was said in them that hadn't already been in the public domain for a long time," Arcadio, the judge, reflects (77). This is a theme to which *La mala hora* repeatedly returns: playing down the pasquinades' power—somewhat disingenuously, given the secret affair in which she is embroiled—Nora de Jacob argues that "they can't say any more about me than what everyone already knows" (141).[15] Another character insists: "In this town, you can't keep secrets" (203). The pasquinades' potency, then, stems not from their specific content, which is already the subject of gossip, and widely if not universally known, but rather from the strange social alchemy that occurs when the community's whispers are transmuted into writing and scandalous knowledge moves from the private to the public domain.[16] There is a liminality to the pasquinades: as Juan Pablo Dabove notes, they are literally affixed to the walls, windows, and doors of buildings—often people's homes—as though to perturb the boundaries of the community's public and private spaces. The pasquinades, Dabove continues, "aren't 'political,' in the sense that they don't pertain to the *polis* (the agora as the site of dialogue between citizens), but neither are they private; they do not pertain to the *domus*" (274). They dwell, rather, in a crepuscular border zone made all the more disturbing by the notices' anonymity. What makes the pasquinades fearsome, Dabove asserts, is less their content than "the sinister nature of the existence of an enunciatory principle that lurks in the shadows" (279). Even so, the real horror stems less from the anonymity of the pasquinades' shadowy author or authors than from the transgressive act of exposing private gossip in public spaces: the critical force lies not in the substance of the gossip but in its revelation. What once was whispered is now nailed to the town's doors, transposed from the private to the public domain, rendered in a form that can no longer be dismissed or brushed aside.

The transposition of gossip into the public domain does not provide the "freedom and permanence" that Jürgen Habermas envisioned when he contrasted the reificatory qualities of the Greek agora with the "transitoriness" and "obscurity" of the private sphere (3). The pasquinades of *La mala hora* do not exalt or elevate domestic life by bringing it into the public sphere; neither do they offer the enlightened discussion among citizens that Habermas describes, nor indeed spark much discussion at all. It is notable, in fact, that the characters of *La mala hora* typically discuss the social problem constituted by the pasquinades—their consequences and ramifications, and the responses they engender—far more than they discuss the actual substance of the pasquinades' allegations. Far from validating private realities by drawing them into the public sphere, the pasquinades instead hold them up for mockery and moral opprobrium, as a shameful spectacle rather than a subject for discourse and debate.[17]

In this sense, the pasquinades operate by stripping away the social niceties that allow societies to function. That is to say, the pasquinades turn private gossip into public declarations that can no longer be ignored; they are gossip stripped of any pretense at discretion, its challenge to individuals' reputations made stark and impossible to disregard. The indiscretions exposed by the pasquinades could be disowned or denied before, when their circulation was private; now, made public, they pose a direct and visible threat to individual reputations and, by extension, to the town's social fabric. Honor and shame here become the driving force behind the gossip, allowing it to stir up old rivalries and unleash new forms of violence and social dissolution. Dabove discerns in the pasquinades "a *panoptical* principle" that becomes "a pure eye through which nobody sees. *Nobody, watching everybody*" (279). There is, however, a notable distinction: the paranoid architecture of Jeremy Bentham's panopticon imposed order by leaving inmates uncertain about whether they were being watched, forcing them to self-police in order to avoid punishment. In *La mala hora*, by contrast, the "pure eye" of the anonymous pasquinades sees through, and rips away, the socially necessary falsehoods and self-deceptions that allow the members of the community to coexist despite their enduring differences and unforgiven grievances. Fear of being watched may often serve to cement group norms, but in *La mala hora* the certainty of having been exposed makes continued coexistence all but impossible and ultimately tears the community apart.

The trouble stirred up by the pasquinades is a blow against the status quo and serves to disrupt the power dynamics of the town. It is telling, in this context, that the town's moral and political leaders, the priest and the mayor, initially downplay the notices' potency. While the entire town fixates on them, with amusement or concern, Padre Angel dismisses them, calling them the result of "envy in an exemplary town" (106); only after he is approached in rapid succession by the doctor, the Asís widow, and a delegation of the town's women does he begin to take the pasquinades seriously. The mayor is just as slow to understand the significance of the pasquinades, which he initially dismisses as "papelitos," or little papers (117). The mayor views gossip through a gendered lens—he dismisses a group of men he sees chatting as "faggots" and mentally accuses them of "gossiping like women" (91)—and views the pasquinades as fundamentally degenerate, effeminate, and toothless. He presumes, without evidence, that women are behind the pasquinades—"I don't know why it strikes me that it's a woman," he says (143)—and when he eventually takes action, his agents' first arrest is of an apparently innocent woman. The mayor's dismissal of the pasquinades as merely women's gossip leads him to underestimate their potency and the threat that they present both to the townsfolk and to his authority. Women's talk, to the mayor, belongs to the domestic sphere and is of little relevance to his own official business; his chief failure, in fact, lies in his inability to understand that the pasquinades (regardless of their author's gender) allow gossip to permeate through the boundaries between public and private life and threaten the status quo from which his own power derives. It is only after Padre Angel explicitly describes the pasquinades as "terrorism of a moral order" (132) that the mayor finally begins to take serious action to address the threat.

The priest's and the mayor's initial reluctance to acknowledge the danger posed by the pasquinades and the energy of their subsequent efforts to suppress them, have quite reasonably led to readings of the pasquinades as a direct challenge to the town's leaders' authority. Undeniably, the only clear beneficiaries of the pasquinades are the rebel guerrillas who, toward the end of the novel, emerge once more as a palpable force in the mountains beyond the town's borders. Still, the pasquinades are not simply seditious; their attacks on individual reputations are so numerous and indiscriminate that they come to constitute an act of aggression targeted at the foundations of the community itself. The pasquinades are adversarial and do indeed undermine the mayor's authority, but if the rebels benefit thereby, it is simply because the gossip sheets foster chaos and create a political vacuum in which a new order can seek to assert itself. In this sense, the damage done by the pasquinades, and the mayor's repressive response, can be seen as parts of a spectrum of self-destructive behavior by which the town is gripped.[18] The ubiquity of the gossip, and the purported omniscience of the pasquinades' perpetrators, begin to suggest that the pasquinades are an emergent phenomenon, percolating out of the town's subliminal and self-targeted anxieties.[19] Gossip deals in secrets, and it is implied that virtually everyone in the town has something to hide; in this sense, there is a bleakly democratic impulse to the exposure threatened by the pasquinades. In *La mala hora,* gossip is a discourse that admits no master and has no favorites: the chaos it engenders may help those who wish to plunge the community back into violence, but the pasquinades themselves are attributed to "the whole town and [. . .] no one" (152) and have no agenda beyond the inexhaustible drive to lay bare that which is concealed.

This is not to deny the validity of readings of *La mala hora* as an allegory of *la violencia* and its aftermath.[20] Still, as García Márquez notes, *La mala hora* contains no massacres or unmarked graves: it is a tale not of pitched battles but rather of collective guilt and unacknowledged sins. It is also a novel that, through its pasquinades, wrestles with the narrative challenges posed by *la violencia* and the difficulty of discerning truth and falsehood in an era of impunity. Reading *La mala hora* alongside *La hojarasca,* J. E. Jaramillo Zuluaga suggests that novels of *la violencia* should be read in terms of an "economy of truth" whereby writers challenge the identification of author and narrator in their texts. Writers such as García Márquez, Jaramillo Zuluaga argues, "sought to dissolve this identification, and introduced atypical narrators, multiplied the narrative voices and thereby provoked an amplification of the 'framework of truth' in their stories, a presentation of the different versions that existed of the same events" (17). It is perhaps for this reason that in *La mala hora,* García Márquez appears less interested in gossip's truthfulness than in its consequences. Many of the pasquinades, after all, fall short of the whole truth: they miss, for instance, the fact that Pastor is secretly engaged to Margot Ramírez—"the only secret that was ever kept in this town," says the widow Montiel (38)—and also Nora de Jacob's affair with Mateo Asís. This does not, however, make them less damaging or dangerous: gossip, in *La mala hora,* is less concerned with unearthing the truth than with exposing unvoiced suspicions, unforgotten grudges, and unforgiven transgressions. The official discourses of the mayor and the priest are shown, through the pasquinades, to be insufficient, and gossip, in its adversarialism and irreverence, is shown to be uniquely well suited to staging the multivocality, the plural and dissenting viewpoints, needed to interrogate the social reality of *la violencia*.

Still, there is a brutality and a vindictive nihilism to the pasquinades that goes beyond the widened "framework of truth" described by Jaramillo Zuluaga. Implicit in the gossip that plagues the town is the promise that, beneath a genteel veneer of social convention, the causes of *la violencia* remain, dormant but not dispelled. As José Luis Méndez writes, the struggles of the individual characters of *La mala hora* point to a larger collective problem, with the real protagonist emerging as "the problematic community that [. . .] exhausts its energies in a fratricidal and senseless struggle" (75). It is through gossip—gossip writ large and made undeniable, gossip textualized and dragged forcibly into public view—that García Márquez stages this ongoing fratricidal struggle and, peeling back the comforting hypocrisies of a troubled community, reveals the unresolved tensions that are the enduring legacy of *la violencia*.

Talk and Apathy: *Crónica de una muerte anunciada*

Gossip does not have to instigate violence to have a corrosive effect on community. In *Crónica de una muerte anunciada,* García Márquez uses gossip to reconstruct a community's collective failure to halt a murder that virtually all the town's residents knew, or came to know, was about to take place. The town's resigned inaction becomes the source of retrospective anguish: "The cockcrow at dawn would catch us trying to organize the numerous interconnected coincidences that made the absurd possible, and it was evident that we weren't doing it out of a desire to clear up mysteries, but because none of us could continue living without knowing precisely what was the place and the mission that fate had assigned to each of us" (126). In piecing together the events of the fatal morning, the narrator finds himself also reconstructing the way knowledge of the impending murder spreads through the community, and tracing the gossip that dominates its social life. One by one, Plácida Linero, Victoria Guzmán, Clotilde Armenta, and so forth are introduced through their contact with Nasar, or with the Vicario twins who murdered him, and each time the text maps what they knew. In the first pages, we learn that Victoria Guzmán "categorically denied that either she or her daughter knew that they were waiting to kill Santiago Nasar" (21); Cristo Bedoya tells the narrator that he thinks his sister "already knew they were going to kill him" (29); and we hear that "many of the people at the docks knew that they were going to kill Santiago Nasar" (30). But *Crónica*'s development, as Carlos Alonso writes, "is guided primordially by a performative rather than by a logical or teleological drive" (153); the text shows not just what individual characters know but also how they learn it. It is, in short, by studying the text's meticulous staging of the circulation of information about the murder—which is to say, the flow of gossip through the town—that we can come to more fully understand the fatalism and apathy that grips the community.

It is gossip, after all, that serves as the primary mode of transmission for news about the impending murder. Clotilde Armenta wakes up her husband "to tell him what was happening in the store" (74); Colonel Lázaro Aponte had just shaved "when the agent Leandro Pornoy revealed to him the intentions of the Vicario brothers" (75); moments later, "his wife told him excitedly that Bayardo San Román had sent back Angela Vicario" to her family (75). The revelations are connected: the colonel "put together the two pieces of news and immediately discovered that they fitted exactly like two pieces of a puzzle" (76). The town is abuzz with chatter about the killing—as the colonel leaves his house, "three people stopped him to tell him secretly that the Vicario brothers were awaiting Santiago Nasar in order to kill him" (76)—and in each new telling, we recognize the cadences of gossip, with its urgency, its excitement, and its confidential tone. The gossip continues to spread: "The Vicario brothers had told their plans to more than a dozen people who went to buy milk, and they in turn had spread the news everywhere before six in the morning" (78). But it soon becomes clear that the town is more invested in talking about the "inevitable" killing than in trying to prevent it. "I only know that by six in the morning, everybody knew," says Flora Miguel (145–46).

Gossip serves as the means for the transmission of the news, yet also emerges as a part of the inexorable force that robs the townsfolk of agency and locks them into their roles as passive spectators. In tracking the transmission of the twins' plans and the many failures or refusals to try to stop them, or even to warn Nasar, the text establishes the town's collective guilt. The townsfolk fall back on fatalism to alleviate their guilt or mitigate their responsibility; still, the narrator's staging of the events demonstrates the degree to which Nasar's death is attributable not to destiny but simply to the town's apathy and inaction. This stasis or stupefaction is cleverly concealed, perhaps even from the townspeople themselves, by the narrative energy resulting from their exuberant circulation of gossip. In this way, *Crónica* represents a failed community: one so immersed in gossip that it sees the twins' disclosure of their plan less as a warning than as a piece of news, a gossipy morsel to be relished rather than acted upon. As the Vicario twins close in on their victim, "the news had spread so widely that Hortensa Baute opened the door just as they passed in front of her house, and was the first to weep for Santiago Nasar" (83). The performative revelation demands a performative response but no actual action: the townsfolk fail to realize that the information they are sharing is real and consequential, and that a man's life hangs in the balance.

Hearing of the killing before it happens, the townspeople absorb it as news of an event that has already occurred; like Hortensa Baute, they begin mourning even before the murder is carried out. Part of the problem, in fact, is that the townsfolk take gossip as offering a definitive, and thus nonnegotiable, account of the events unfolding before them.[21] It is perceived as a history told in real time: a story already written, and thus not one in which they can conceive of attempting to intervene. The very few inconsistencies in the versions circulating in the town serve to highlight the countless areas where people's perspectives do agree: "nobody failed to notice" (42), "nobody would have thought, and nobody said" (52), "it was never known" (57), "many people knew" (60), and so on. Here, as in *La mala hora,* gossip is presented as all-seeing; indeed, Ángel Esteban suggests that "the novel is constructed like a Panopticon" (330), with a "panoptic narrator" occupying a privileged central viewpoint. Still, it is gossip itself that is presented as omniscient, with the narrator simply recording and arranging the versions of events already circulating in the community. Gossip may not actually be all-seeing and infallible, but the town believes it to be so and relies upon it unquestioningly.

Many passages demonstrate the townsfolk's confidence in knowledge received through gossip or highlight gossip's preternatural speed and reliability. Even before San Román begins courting her, Angela Vicario has learned, through casual gossip, of his intention to marry her. The narrator, similarly, writes that between sips of coffee his mother would tell him "what had happened in the world while we slept" and continues: "She seemed to have secret lines of communication with the other people in town, above all those of her own age, and sometimes she would surprise us with anticipated news that she could only have come to know through the arts of divination" (31). These divinations are an expression of gossip's potency—in terms both of the sheer speed with which news travels through the grapevine and, more importantly, of the deference accorded by the townsfolk to news received through gossip. This is not simply speculative chatter: it is "anticipated news" made real and irrevocable in the telling, just as the "death foretold" of the book's title is inevitable from the moment that it is first announced.

Like the pasquinades of *La mala hora,* the gossip of *Crónica* takes on a charge that goes beyond the specific words that pass from one person to another, and that reflects the public scrutiny and attendant questions of honor and shame that gossip brings. The honor killing at the heart of the novel, after all, is set in motion by gossip: the brothers' actions are driven not by righteous anger but rather by a weary obsession with preserving the family's reputation. This dutifulness is based more on fear of the town's judgmental gossip than on any real belief in the moral urgency of killing Nasar. Indeed, the twins' public display of murderous intent is both an attempt to satisfy the town's moral arbiters by performing their willingness to kill, and an attempt to create opportunities for the act itself to be interrupted. It is gossip, and the fear of gossip, about their sister that precipitates the twins' murderous plan, and it is gossip that drives them inexorably forward, even while—as Clotilde Armenta remarks—they hope to encounter "someone who will do them the favor of stopping them" and free them from the "horrible obligation that has befallen them" (77). But gossip's moral conservatism not only drives the twins forward but also prevents anyone from interrupting their performance. Arnold Penuel writes: "Fear of 'el qué dirán' is a potent force in the town, ensuring that the townspeople adhere to their traditional values. This fear colors nearly all the Vicarios' acts. [. . .] Of course the brothers' observance of the code of honor initially is due obeisance to appearances. In view of their obvious reluctance to carry out the murder and the hypocrisy in the townspeople's values, honor becomes little more than an institutionalization of the fear of 'el qué dirán'" (762). Gossip here serves to police group norms and to identify the actions that must be taken to shield the Vicario family from moral condemnation. It is, however, a force to which all are subject: while gossip ostensibly represents the community's collective moral code, no individual member can shape or redirect the flow of that gossip, or even intervene in the horrifying actions set in motion thereby.

In this sense, the twins' performance is paradoxically both an attempt to halt the killing to which they have committed themselves and a confirmation that the killing will in fact take place. The second time the twins visit the market to sharpen their knives, they "screamed again so that it would be heard that they were going to rip the guts out of Santiago Nasar" (79). Knowing full well that news of their intentions will quickly spread through the town, they announce their plans to anyone who will listen. In the process, the text tells us, the brothers forgo opportunities to kill Nasar "immediately and without public spectacle" and instead go "to unimaginable lengths to find someone to keep them from killing him" (67–68). The townsfolk, moreover, were well aware of the twins' purpose in broadcasting their intentions: "No death was ever better foretold [. . .] twenty-one people declared having heard what the twins said, and all of them had the impression that they'd said it with the sole purpose of being heard" (69). The twins' gambit works on one level: word of their intentions spreads so far and so quickly that to Clotilde Armenta "it seemed impossible that it wasn't already known in the house across the street."

The text continues: "There were very few of us who didn't know that the Vicario twins were waiting for Santiago Nasar in order to kill him, and their motive was also known in full detail" (78–79). But knowledge does not lead to action, in part, ironically, because the news has spread so widely that it seems inconceivable that it has not yet reached Nasar. "Nobody asked themselves if Santiago Nasar had been forewarned, because it seemed impossible to everyone that he wouldn't have been," the narrator asserts (30). It is the town's absolute faith in gossip's reach and reliability, in short, that keeps individual residents from accepting their responsibility for preventing the killing.

More than this, however, the town's paralysis reflects an effacement, in the residents' interpretation of their own gossip, of the distinction between signified and signifier: the circulating gossip about the twins' intentions grows indistinguishable from actual facts about completed actions. The gossip and the act itself become all but interchangeable—"noticia anticipada," or anticipated news—for many of the townsfolk. Luisa "hadn't finished hearing the news before putting on her heels and the church shawl" that she only used for visits of condolence (33). Indeed, the town's lived reality appears shaped by gossip: the townsfolk's near-universal conviction that Nasar is innocent is based largely on the assumption that were he guilty, there would be gossip to show it. "Nobody believed that it had, in fact, been Santiago Nasar. [. . .] Nobody had ever seen them together, much less alone," the narrator states. "The town had never known him to have any relationship, other than the conventional one that he maintained with Flora Miguel, and the tempestuous one with María Alejandrina Cervantes that drove him mad for fourteen months" (117–18). Without gossip to substantiate it, Nasar's guilt seems inconceivable: the narrator's sister complains that "nobody could explain to me how it was that poor Santiago Nasar wound up embroiled in such a mess" (32). The town's shared reality depends, it seems, on public knowledge established through gossip: events passed over in silence might as well never have happened.

This is all the more remarkable because *Crónica*'s narrator goes to great lengths to establish the unreliability and incompleteness of the town's gossip. One striking example comes when the narrator reveals his own clandestine liaison with María Alejandrina Cervantes—a secret hitherto concealed even from his three most intimate friends. Hidden from the town's gossip networks, the affair "opens the door to all kinds of informational uncertainties," Angel Rama writes, even raising the possibility that it was the narrator himself who dishonored Angela Vicario (15). Rama is correct about the affair's destabilizing impact, but it is not the only such moment; the narrator is diligent in recording the discrepancies between the various accounts he hears. Not only are there secrets that never become part of the town's gossip—and so, it might be said, simply never exist for the bulk of the townsfolk—but there are also numerous moments in which gossip, as a depository of public knowledge, is shown to be internally inconsistent or simply incorrect. Most people believe the Miguels sleep "until twelve by order of Nahir Miguel," but the truth, the narrator informs us, "is that they left the house closed until very late [. . .] but they were early risers" (144–45). The narrator likewise stresses the town's inability to reach a consensus about whether the morning of the murder was sunny or rainy. Indeed, the narrative of *Crónica* seems almost designed to ring hollow, and to be built around promises that it cannot keep. "The investigative framework of the novel forever seems to imply the imminent uncovering of some hitherto unknown datum that will bestow coherence upon the fateful events of that distant February morning," Alonso writes. "And yet, the novel constantly thwarts all expectations of revelation through what seems a perpetual game of deferrals, extremely detailed but inconsequential information and contradictory affirmations" (152). The hollowness of the narrator's implicit promises echoes the hollowness—the *performativeness*—of the twins' dutiful outrage, and also of the townsfolk's outpourings of grief. When San Román's female relatives arrive, they carefully remove their shoes before walking barefoot in the dust, "tearing out clumps of hair and crying with piercing howls that seemed to be of joy. [. . .] I remember thinking that such grief could only be feigned in order to hide other, larger shames" (112). In grief, as in anger or shame, awareness of the observing community takes primacy over authentic emotion: pain and humiliation are reified through rituals of display, as though only when reflected in the townsfolk's gossip can such responses be truly validated and made real.

On one level, the town's gossip speaks to a strong sense of community and collective identity. The text frequently uses plural constructions—"us," "nobody," "everybody"—to show the extent to which events are understood through collective interpretations and shared moral judgments: "For the vast majority there was only one victim: Bayardo San Román," the narrator declares. "People assumed that the other protagonists of the tragedy had fulfilled, with dignity and even a certain greatness, the parts life had chosen for them. Santiago Nasar had expiated the injury, the brothers Vicario had proven their manhood, and the scorned sister was once again in possession of her honor" (109). Death and murder, it seems, are of less consequence than the town's collective understanding of honor and shame. But there is a neuroticism to this shared understanding: "For years we could talk of nothing else," the narrator records. "Our daily conduct, dominated until then by so many linear habits, had suddenly started to revolve around the same common anxiety" (126). If the novel's protagonist is the town as a collective entity, then the narrative itself, and the gossip it is founded upon, can be read as a critique of collective morality. The hollowness of the narrative—its resolution striven for but never reached—stands as an indictment of individuals willing to subsume their own agency in the collective and surrender themselves to passivity and gossip.

The tragedy at the heart of *Crónica,* in this reading, is the townsfolk's tendency to mistake talk for action. The narrator's mother, hearing of the twins' plan, rushes out not to halt them but rather to tell Nasar's mother what she knows: "It isn't fair that everyone knows they're going to kill her son, and that she's the only one who doesn't know it" (34). Similarly, Clotilde Armenta "shouted at Cristo Bedoya to hurry up, because in this town of faggots only a man like him could prevent the tragedy" (142). Armenta recognizes the need for action but shrugs off her own responsibility, choosing instead only to tell yet another person about the unfolding drama. Even after Nasar's murder, the community responds only with more talk: people mob an investigating judge with unsolicited statements, while Angela Vicario recounts her misfortune "to anyone who would listen" (117). To the narrator, this inaction is the consequence of fate, or fatalism; the inexorable pull of predestination both explains and excuses the town's inaction. But as Penuel notes, the narrator's insistence on the role of fate serves "an ironic intention" that highlights not the unavoidability of the tragedy but rather the townsfolk's failure to respond to clear warning signs (763). "Though chance does play a part in their lives, what they consider fate or destiny is principally a projection of their own passivity," Penuel writes (763). Drawn through morally charged gossip into a stunted and corrupted form of the public sphere, the townsfolk become trapped in pointless discourse: endless chatter that precludes the possibility of action, and collective moral judgment that absolves them of individual moral responsibility. In the end, the town is left paralyzed, with the townsfolk mired in gossip and reduced to passively bearing witness to their own still-unfolding story.

Crónica's gossip-mediated performance of shame and redemptive violence has parallels elsewhere in the Caribbean. Consider, for instance, the popularity of Los Cantantes' "El Venao," a merengue that in the mid-1990s was one of the most-played tunes at Puerto Rican, Dominican, and Venezuelan parties. The word *venao* derives from *venado,* or stag, and suggests someone who wears antlers—that is, a cuckold. The singer addresses his unfaithful lover:

> Ay, woman, the people are saying round here
> That I am a *venao,* I am a *venao*
> [. . . .]
> That when I went to New York you had many lovers
> Pay no attention to this trick, they're rumors, they're rumors
> And don't let them call me *el venao, el venao*
> Because it torments me, *el venao, el venao.*

The singer fears betrayal, but it is not the pain of infidelity but rather the shame of being gossiped about that is uppermost on his mind. In E. Antonio de Moya's telling, the song quickly acquired a life of its own, becoming a "collective innuendo" targeted at men whose partners were unfaithful:

> The untoward song was anonymously whistled to those men by the telephone, or loudly and reiteratively played on the jukeboxes of street-corner *colmados* (grocery stores) every time they passed nearby. To the despair of the victims, mocking customers joyfully danced and sang to the chorus [. . .]. When the fashion of this biting jest faded away in the country several years later, no less than a dozen women had been killed [. . .]. Dozens of women had been badly battered and injured by jealous husbands, and some men had committed homicide or suicide as a consequence of the "killing" *merengue.* (69)

In Puerto Rico, too, police officers blamed a rash of domestic killings on the song: "Every time somebody kills their lover or spouse, they blame it on 'El Venao,'" said Puerto Rican homicide detective Héctor Urdaneta, while the Reverend Milton Picón, the leader of a local morality group, claimed that *venao* had become a "fighting word" that was "shredding the social fabric of the island" (qtd. in Ross 121). But singling out cuckolded men also serves a community-building purpose. In the aftermath of "El Venao," de Moya reports, at least one small Dominican town institutionalized the social policing of masculinity, creating a "Fiesta de Cuernos" in which a single man is named "Community Cuckold of the Year":

> Any unwitting married man could be the year's chosen antihero, the winner of this catastrophic, discrediting and disqualifying surprise. Even worse, as a disclaimer, he would be pressed to prove to others that the accusation is false; if true, he must guarantee that the infidelity was not culturally "justified" by

his presumable lack of masculinity. He must show that he is "still" a man by taking "due" revenge on his wife and her lover. Otherwise he will have to submissively accept the defiling stigma of a cuckold, a synonym for abjection, of being an outcast or a contemptible individual. (69)

The selection of the "Cuckold of the Year" appears to depend on consultations with "key informants," including eyewitnesses, taxi drivers who took the adulterous couple to motels, friends and acquaintances, and even the paramour who cuckolded the prize recipient. Once the winner is chosen, a crowd gathers and dances to his home, where it announces his selection and demands a performative response. "His reaction, of course, should be one of shock, denial and anger, but the crowd will prompt and encourage him to action," de Moya writes. "As a result, the 'celebration' has invariably ended in violent fights, and one or more deaths have occurred every year in the community for this reason" (70). De Moya perceives in such phenomena the confluence of masculinity and issues of power and social control, and the emergence of masculinity as a totalitarian political discourse.[22] We can see here two apparently contradictory but ultimately connected accounts of gossip's role in Caribbean communities: first, that, as in *La mala hora*, it can serve as a corrosive force that undermines solidarity and unity and, second, that, as in *Crónica*, it also emerges as a force—quasi-totalitarian, and certainly indifferent to the suffering of individuals—that binds communities together through the destructive performance of common values. The pasquinades of *La mala hora* are anonymous, indiscriminate, and unfettered from any performance of community; the gossip of *Crónica*, by contrast, is entirely an expression of communal values, to the exclusion of individual agency or responsibility. The death of Nasar, in this sense, becomes a blood sacrifice in the name of the community: through gossip, the town performs its values, its collective guilt, and its complicity—and, in its shared performance, finds a way to bind itself together.[23]

Neighbors and Outsiders: *Listen, the Wind* and *Sleep It Off, Lady*

The bleak vision proposed by García Márquez stands in marked contrast to the views of many past scholars who, insofar as they have explored the more oppressive aspects of gossip, have tended to focus on the ways in which the practice defines in-groups and out-groups, and helps police (or encourage the self-policing) of group norms. We can see this function of gossip at play in many Caribbean texts, but in such texts we also frequently see a heightened awareness of the individual costs that come with communal surveillance. In his posthumous short story collection *Listen, the Wind* (1986), for instance, the Jamaican writer Roger Mais repeatedly showcases the claustrophobia and individual anguish generated as communities constitute themselves through gossip.[24] The eponymous short story "Listen, the Wind . . ." describes a woman who wants her infatuation with her lover, Joel, to remain an intimate secret: lying next to him at night, she delights in the fact that she is "an enigma to the neighbors, because in spite of all their unkind gossip and forebodings of evil, she still kept her secret, and it defeated them, thwarted them, so that their tongues were robbed of that spell of evil that drips with slander and gossiping—like a scorpion that has been deprived of its sting" (68). She goes on to contemplate the womenfolk doing their laundry:

> Above the noise of the paddles with which they beat the clothes, with the soap in them, against smooth, round boulders to get the deep dirt out of them, would be heard the tongues of the women . . . the cruel tongues that tore secrets from the innermost recesses of homes and spread them out before the world like washing was spread upon the river bank . . . the idle tongues, never for a moment quiet, that slavered over another's wounds with gloating and laughter.
>
> But her secret would be locked tight within her breast, and she would smile deep down inside herself. (68)

The protagonist's hatred of the gossiping women is vividly depicted, and the parallels between their wagging tongues and the violent motions of the laundry, with its shaking loose of "deep dirt," are sharply drawn.[25] Despite her disdain, however, the following day the protagonist hears gossip about her lover that proves largely accurate and portends her own disillusionment. The women insist that Joel "needs a strong woman to make a man out of him" and predict that Joel will tire of the protagonist and leave her heartbroken (70). The protagonist rejects the oppressive, threatening warning—"They were vultures all of them . . . great flapping black vultures circling above the still living flesh upon which they hoped to feast," she thinks (70)—but soon learns that in fact the women's words are well founded, and begins to succumb to the suspicions they have foretold. The washerwomen's use of gossip to scold the protagonist and mockingly predict the failure of her love affair is a way of bringing her back in line, and of warning her that her intimate "enigma" is both all too transparent and founded upon a naive misreading of her situation.

She may believe that, in the throes of young love, she exists outside the norms of her community, but in fact the community is still there, watching her and judging her and drawing her back in—as inescapable as the wind that clatters at her shutters, "telling her wild and terrible things" as she lies awake at night (72).

Mais explores similar territory in "Gravel in Your Shoe," in which the unnamed protagonist reflects on her uncomfortable relationship with Miss Matty, a gossiping neighbor. The neighbors' yards are connected by an overhanging ackee tree that, besides serving as a symbol of Miss Matty's encroachment into the protagonist's domestic life, makes encounters inevitable and form "the solid basis of their neighbourliness" (75). Still, the protagonist "hated the old woman's everlasting gossip" and thinks that "if she only had the courage she would have got a man to chop down the ackee tree, and so put an end once and for all to their neighbourliness" (75). In this way, the tree also becomes a symbol of longed-for isolation: chopping down the tree would bring escape from Miss Matty's prying eyes. The dream, however, remains unrealized, for the protagonist herself is caught up in, and constrained by, the web of gossip that she disdains. Were she to cut down the tree, she realizes, "she would never be allowed to hear the last of it. All the people in the lane would talk about it for months" (75). Fear of gossip thus leads the protagonist to restrain herself and refrain from challenging the bonds of community. Even so, the protagonist's fear of gossip proves well founded: in a burst of "neighbourliness," Miss Matty tells the protagonist of "things she thought she ought to know about where her man went evenings after he left home, and what sort of company he was keeping, and how he was spending his money, and upon what kind of women" (75). The insidious gossip destroys the protagonist's peace of mind: once the doubts have been raised, she cannot forget or banish them, and her trust in her husband is broken beyond repair.

This is, evidently, a particularly barbed vision of neighborly relations: not only Miss Matty but the entire local community is portrayed as constantly "bickering at each other, or gossiping, over their back fences" (74). Only the protagonist is portrayed as rising above the intrusive chatter, smiling or singing to herself as she strives to stay beyond their reach. Miss Matty's gossip thus becomes an aggressive act of repossession and a reassertion of the community's claim upon the protagonist: neighborliness, clearly, is about belonging, both in the sense of claiming membership in a group and in the sense of being laid claim to by that group. There is, then, a latent threat to neighborliness, which in Mais's text we are meant to read as essential to and inextricable from the realities of community life. Kenneth Ramchand writes that "Gravel in Your Shoe" recounts the protagonist's struggle against "forces that deny her personhood and her privacy as an individual" (xxi), and her attempts to negotiate the tension between the needs of the community and those of the individual. "One belongs to the group or community, but there is an ultimate aloneness and privacy, a private space necessary to the unique individual," he writes (xxii). But Mais's story addresses not the reconciliation of these opposing impulses but their fundamental incompatibility. As in "Listen, the Wind . . ." the protagonist of "Gravel in Your Shoe" expresses her aspirations to exist beyond the reach of gossip in naive, idealistic terms: "She wanted to live among them like neighbours, with love. A woman had her troubles, her bread to eat in secret that no one might share. No one. Her life to live" (79). Mais's texts suggest, however, that membership in a community makes such privacy unsustainable on the individual level and intolerable on the collective level. The protagonist's closing cry—"But oh Lord Jesus, sweet Jesus, if only they would let her alone" (79)—is a despairing acknowledgment that to sustain itself, the community must lay claim to the intimate lives of its members. The community exists, in large measure, through its gossip; to set oneself apart from this gossip, to refuse to participate therein, is just as divisive and destructive an act as it would be for the protagonist to chop down the ackee tree she shares with her neighbor.

This is the reality that the protagonist knowingly inhabits; her daydreams of a community founded upon love, respect, and privacy are undercut by her realization that to insist upon privacy, or to symbolically spurn the community by cutting down the ackee tree, would only reimmerse her in the gossip she wishes to escape. "They would build up around her such a legend of wickedness as she would never be able to live down. Never be able to hold up her head again among her neighbours. No one would speak to her," she acknowledges. "Their children would never be allowed to play with her children. They would be considered outcasts as long as they lived there" (75). The risk of ostracism and scandal is the sheathed blade carried by every gossip: an unspoken threat that serves as an effective means of policing community norms and suppressing dissent. "If she had courage sufficient unto herself to withstand their hate, their jibes, their speech deliberately and pointedly withheld, their sneers behind their hands, their talk among themselves, their innuendoes, their spite, their backbiting, all—she would get a man in tomorrow and cut down the ackee tree," the protagonist reflects. "But she knew herself in this wanting" (76).[26]

Read in this light, "Gravel in Your Shoe" is the story of its protagonist's succumbing to the inexorable gossip upon which her community is built. The failure is all the more wrenching because the woman not only fears gossip but condemns it in moral and religious terms; she has, she claims, "built her life not upon barren gossip, and mistrust, and all things misbegotten" but rather upon a more kindly and dignified personal code (75–76). The trouble with gossip, though, is precisely that it is *not* barren: rather, it is endlessly, noxiously fruitful. By weaving a "legend of wickedness" about those who transgress group norms, the practice reaffirms its own dominance over the group and its members. But gossip not only threatens those who seek to express their individuality; it also insinuates itself into the lives of those who accept their allotted roles as members of the community. Even the protagonist, for all her qualms, begins to give in to its seductive logic and to entertain gossip about her husband. To reject the community would mean being ostracized and condemned through gossip. But to remain a part of the community, the protagonist must accept and participate in gossip, and reinforce the very system of scrutiny and social policing that she herself so acutely resents.[27]

A similar tension, born of the individual's desire for privacy and the community's intolerance of attempts to step outside its prescribed bounds, runs through many of the stories gathered in Jean Rhys's *Sleep It Off, Lady* (1976). As Elaine Savory remarks, the outsider is a key theme in Rhys's fiction, and Mr. Ramage, the Englishman featured in "Pioneers, Oh, Pioneers," is just such an outsider: he moves to Antigua in search of "peace" and acquires a remote estate. The town's initial appraisal of Ramage, guided by the gossiping Miss Lambton, is positive; still, his reserve soon makes him seem "very unsociable" to his neighbors, and he sparks further chatter by rebuffing "all invitations to dances, tennis parties and moonlight picnics" (13). Ironically, Ramage's reclusiveness fuels the gossip about him: his marriage to a black woman, condemned by the townsfolk through coded references to her "cheap scent" and "aggressive voice," inspires all the more gossip because, as Miss Lambton reports to Mrs. Cox, "he told me that he didn't want it talked about" (15). Here, as with the protagonist of "Gravel in Your Shoe," Ramage's aloofness, and his disdain for the town's chattering voices and prying eyes, becomes intolerable to the townsfolk, who root out and seek to punish his idiosyncrasies. When Ramage is spotted sunning himself naked, the townsfolk fan the indiscretion into a major scandal, with some claiming to have seen him striding about the countryside wearing nothing but a cutlass at his hip. Later, when Ramage's wife takes an unannounced trip to Guadeloupe, her absence sparks a flurry of gossip, anonymous police reports, and even a newspaper article condemning Ramage for "beastly murder" (19).[28] Finally, the gossip spurs a rioting mob to pelt Ramage with stones; in the aftermath, Ramage is found dead after suffering what the townsfolk agree to call "an accident" (21). Even at Ramage's funeral, the town turns to gossip to emphasize Ramage's outsider status and shape the community's narrative of his death. While many come to the funeral because "they felt guilty," their contrition doesn't last long: "Already public opinion was turning against Ramage. 'His death was really a blessing in disguise,' said one lady. 'He was evidently mad, poor man—sitting in the sun with no clothes on—much worse might have happened'" (21). The graveside gossip foreshadows the children's chatter, two years later, that frames Rhys's tale. The children's talk also pointedly echoes the newspaper article that slandered Ramage: "You like crazy people. [. . .] You liked Ramage, nasty beastly horrible Ramage" (11). Even the doctor, who at the time defended Ramage's reputation, comes to modulate his recollection of Ramage, whom he now sees as "certifiable" and "probably a lunatic" (12). By the time the story begins, the town has fully laid claim to the tale of the vilified outsider: their gossip has cohered into consensus and been accepted as fact.

Gossip thus serves both to articulate the figure of the outsider and as the trigger that sets Rhys's story in motion. While the text notes many cases of gossip, it also makes clear that "it was Mr Eliot, the owner of Twickenham, who started the trouble" (16) and who "told this story to everyone who'd listen" until "the Ramages became the chief topic of conversation" (17). Rhys's story features plenty of women and other marginalized individuals who gossip, but it is a wealthy male landowner who starts the specific gossip that leads to Ramage's downfall. Gossip is shown as a swirling presence that penetrates both male and female discourse, infiltrates public institutions such as the press and the police force, and transcends race and social class: it is an all-encompassing force that cannot be safely ignored but also cannot be stopped. The doctor, whose interactions with Ramage convince him that the town's gossip is baseless, fails to prevent people from "talking venomously" (19); later, he writes to Ramage urging him "to put a stop to the talk at once and to take legal action if necessary" (20), advice rendered all the more preposterously insufficient by the fact that, unbeknownst to the doctor, Ramage is already dead. Finally, the doctor subjugates his own experiences to the judgments rendered through gossip, accepting that his views had been "all wrong" (12). This is the "price" that the doctor warns Ramage he will pay for distancing himself from the town: once gossip labels Ramage an outsider, the community swiftly moves to affirm and amplify that judgment, and to punish him not just through ostracism but through physical violence.

Gossip, in Rhys's work, is a heartless and impersonal force: it sustains itself through the communities that it governs but has little regard for the individuals caught up in its machinations. This is evident in "Sleep It Off, Lady," a story in which an elderly woman wrestles with her neighbors' condemnation of her alcoholism. Her well-founded paranoia about her public image—"she knew that the bottles in her dustbin were counted and discussed in the village" (164)—maps onto her struggles with a huge rat, dismissed by Tom, her handyman, as an alcohol-induced hallucination.[29] Later, she emerges from a blackout to find herself copying out the words "Evil Communications corrupt good manners" into a notebook (163). It is the fear of surveillance, of gossip, that stops the old woman from turning to her neighbors, or even her cleaning lady, for help: "Mrs Randolph would be as sceptical as Tom had been. A nice woman but a gossip, she wouldn't be able to resist telling her cronies about the giant, almost certainly imaginary, rat terrorizing her employer" (165). When the old woman finally slumps by the dustbin—a half-drunk bottle of whiskey still open on her sideboard—and is unable to get up, her neighbors pass her by without hearing her pleas for help. A child who finally stops to talk invokes the community's judgment as a reason to leave her lying in the road: "Everybody knows that you shut yourself up to get drunk. People can hear you falling about. [. . .] Sleep it off, lady" (171). Realizing, finally, that to protest the community's judgment is "useless," and perceiving the depth of her own isolation, the old woman succumbs to a "numb weak feeling" that leaves her unable even to call out to passersby (171). Rejected by her community, and literally cast aside with the garbage, she perishes.

Gossip's callousness is on similarly stark display in "Heat," in which the eruption of Mont Pelée and the deaths of forty thousand St. Pierre residents become an excuse for gossip. "It was after this that the gossip started," Rhys writes, with people quickly blaming the eruption on St. Pierre having been "a very wicked city" (40–41). In "Heat," as in "Pioneers, Oh, Pioneers," Rhys suggests that the gossip of Caribbean communities is fundamentally at odds with the discourse of English outsiders: just as Ramage cannot comprehend the risks inherent in his self-exclusion from Antiguan society, so the narrator of "Heat" puzzles over English news reports, based on the testimony of a single survivor, that appear to contradict the popular, gossip-derived understanding of the disaster. Similarly, in "Fishy Waters," a judge hearing a case involving child abuse expresses frustration at the breakdown of law and order in a community so defined by prejudice and gossip: "I cannot accept either hearsay evidence or innuendoes supported by no evidence: but I have not been in my post for twenty years without learning that it is extremely difficult to obtain direct evidence here" (59). The judge has learned through bitter experience that gossip's judgments are hard to escape, and the true facts of the matter are easily buried thereby. The defense lawyer makes a similar point, contending that the accused man, having already been tried and condemned in the court of public opinion, can hardly be given a fair trial. "Are you not very ready to believe the worst of him? Has there not been a great deal of gossip about him?" he demands (52).

After the case concludes, Matt Penrice, both the defendant's accuser and the child's true assailant, comes to fear that prying eyes will uncover the truth of the matter, and sends the child to live on another island "away from all the gossip and questioning" (60). The gambit fails: in attempting to avoid gossip, Penrice only sparks more chatter about the child's departure. Penrice laments that there is no way to stop the gossip once it has begun, speaking of the chattering islanders in prejudiced, bestial terms: "Do you think these damnable hogs care whether it's possible or not, or how or where or when? They've just got to get hold of something to grunt about, that's all" (61). Finally, he says he wishes only to leave the Caribbean and return to England, where he won't have to worry about "what they say here." Penrice's wife, who loves the Caribbean, reminds him that he will find "envy, malice, hatred everywhere" and that he "can't escape"; Penrice admits as much, saying: "Perhaps, but I'm sick of this particular brand" (62). Rhys insightfully suggests that gossip operates differently—more pervasively, more brutally—in the fraught communities of the Caribbean, but also that the gossiping communities' hypocrisy and bleak indifference are equally present, if differently expressed, in British society.

Performing Difference: Sánchez, Sylvain, and Senior

Like Rhys's "Pioneers, Oh, Pioneers," Luis Rafael Sánchez's "¡Jum!" (1966), one of the first Puerto Rican short stories to openly explore homosexuality, shows a community deploying gossip to police divergence from social norms.[30] The tale's main character, "Trinidad's son," who is presumed to be gay, is described as a "queer bird" and persecuted and ostracized by the townsfolk, who are presented as a faceless collective, a seething "whispering" of indistinguishably plural voices (131).[31] Sánchez, always attuned to spoken language, uses the anaphoric *que,* or *that,* to reflect the rhythmic syntax of gossip from the text's opening paragraph: "That Trinidad's son was tightening his cheeks until he suffocated his asshole. That he was a queer bird taking a vacation on land and sea. That he would don his Sunday best even when it was Monday or Tuesday. And that his vest was festooned with genuine-lace clovers" (131). The story records the transformation of these remarks, first into judgments, then into insults. The title itself signals a similar process: as Juan Gelpí notes, it is an interjection that "denotes threat as much as strangeness. Threatened by strangeness, by the *different,* the community charges, using anaphora" (119). Trinidad's son sequesters himself, remaining in his home "like a cloistered nun" (133), but like Ramage, his efforts to avoid gossip only heighten the inescapable urgency of the community's whispers. Trinidad's son is progressively abandoned by his cook, his washerwoman, his barber, and finally his neighbor, who installs a fence that literally redraws the boundaries between their houses. Insults, insistent and incantatory, ring throughout Sánchez's text; finally, Trinidad's son, irrevocably marginalized, tries to leave the town, only to find as he steps into the street that the townsfolk have coalesced into a mob. He is pushed and shoved to the edge of the town, then driven into the river that serves as the community's boundary; finally, as the whispers crescendo into a full-blown riot, he drowns, succumbing almost gratefully to the water—"warm water, warmer, warmer" (135)—that also drowns out the jeering of the crowd.

Agnes Lugo-Ortiz perceptively notes that Sánchez's text is remarkable because its protagonist's "presumed 'otherness' is not a preexistent condition" but is instead reified and amplified by the crowd's pervasive chatter. "It only comes into being through the utterance of the community," Lugo-Ortiz continues. "What the story thematizes is the presence of difference within and the process through which it is made into an outside: violent verbal marginalization and deadly suppression" (129). It is through the speech act, through orality, that "a community that aspires to a totalizing self-definition exercises its law and its violence" (130–31). Still, what Lugo-Ortiz refers to as "the utterance of the community" is not mere speech, but speech in a social context—speech, in fact, that demands to be considered as gossip. It is through gossip that the town's increasing outrage is portrayed: the soft whispers of the opening sentence, "the whispering traveled from mouth to mouth" (131), intensify to become "the whispering flew from mouth to mouth" (132), then proliferate into "an abundant crop of gossip" (133). Finally, the gossip takes a violent turn, becoming a murmuring "like a dart or a sword" (134) that the townsfolk use "to attack him with words" (131). The pain inflicted on Trinidad's son through gossip is deliberate—"in every corner, the men would fling knives from their mouths" (132), the text states—and encompasses both a social judgment and the implicit threat of actual violence that leads Trinidad's son to leave town.

As Lawrence Martin La Fountain-Stokes writes, this collective brutality is a fundamentally social endeavor that frames the "malicious use of gossip as a way to discipline unruly subjects and create a general negative social reaction: gossip as a form of ostracism and persecution" (3–4). As in Rhys's "Pioneers," once put into circulation the gossip cannot be contained: in both texts, the significance and fragility of individual reputations in small communities is clearly displayed. Reputation, after all, is simply a proxy for that which is said about a person in a given community: gossip, then, becomes self-justifying, with the very fact that a person is being spoken ill of serving to validate the claims made about them. What begins as an acknowledgment of perceived difference gains affective charge and spirals into collective outrage, as speculative gossip coheres into readily accepted fact: accusations, by tarnishing the reputation of their target, serve to cement his position as an outsider, and thus his status as a threat to the community's integrity.

This can be readily seen in "¡Jum!," as the details of Trinidad's son's divergences from group norms—in appearance, in behavior—are captured and shared through gossip, and distilled into derogatory terms or hateful phrases that are repeated by the faceless residents of the town. The accusations multiply, reverberating and seething formlessly like the procession that drives Trinidad's son to the river. As in both *Crónica* and "Pioneers, Oh, Pioneers," the crowd becomes an unthinking unit, its individual members absorbed into the collective performance of judgment and exclusion. Whispers swell into yells; finally, the mob's shouted insults blend in with the barking of the dogs they have set upon Trinidad's son. Stripped of individuality, and thus of individual responsibility or restraint, the pursuing crowd becomes "the town, [. . .] then the mutts and finally, always and again, the town" (134).

A similar episode of gossip-mediated mob violence occurs in Patrick Sylvain's 2011 short story "Odette," set in the aftermath of the Port-au-Prince earthquake, in which the elderly, shocked, and perhaps senile titular protagonist, after witnessing the death of her granddaughter, takes up residence in a tent city. A kindly neighbor gives Odette a red head wrap, and she falls asleep nervously fiddling with and tapping her walking stick. Soon, however, neighborliness gives way to embittered scrutiny: "Despite the constant chatter of her fellow evacuees, the tapping made a persistent noise in the humid hot air that seemed intrusive to some and meditative to others. Eventually, she began to inspire gossip" (24). Singling out Odette is both a means of entertainment and a form of catharsis for the bored residents of the camp. "The gossip was a way to both pass the time and deflect resentment, which, without an identified target, would have reattached itself to its originator. Odette thus became an unwitting target over the next several weeks, as words traveled from mouths to ears to other mouths," Sylvain writes (24). In the minds of the gossips, Odette's senility becomes "a secret code" and her red head wrap "proof of what many had heard for years: that she was such a lougawou, a wretched person, that even her own child had abandoned her" (24). People begin to gossip about her supernatural powers, claiming that she had predicted evil happenings ranging from a car accident to a coup d'état, and insinuating that she caused the death of her own daughter. Odette is excluded from the improvised community of the tent city and unable to defend herself: "People would have been happy to ask her about all of this, except Odette had not uttered an intelligible word since that horrible afternoon in January," the text notes. Still, she perceives and fears the gossip: "During the long sleepless nights of tent city life, gossip spread at a distorted speed, occasionally ricocheting past Odette's ears. [. . .] She started crossing herself multiple times before falling asleep" (24).

The gossip of Sylvain's story shows, among other things, the decay of neighborly bonds in the wake of the city's destruction. A kind gesture inadvertently precipitates gossip that makes Odette the target of her tent-city neighbors; later, as the gossip crescendoes, a former neighbor who has been providing Odette with food merely stands passively—she "just watched and sobbed" (25)—as the tone grows denunciatory and the crowd coalesces into a mob. Odette perceives "the voices discussing her outside" and the "talk [. . .] about her flying around in the dark, her being a witch" as an intrusion. "She had been living alone for so many years now that all this sudden company was agonizing," Sylvain's text reads (25). Significantly, the fierce gossip of the crowd is perceived as "company," in a distortion of the ordinary sense of cordial visits and pleasant conversation. In fact, the swelling gossip is the sound of the crowd whipping itself into a near riot; soon, the neighbors' chatter grows into a rendering of judgment, and then the battle cry of a burgeoning mob:

The entire tent city seemed to be alive with commotion. The news that Odette, the lady lougawou, was about to be dealt with brought ecstasy to many.

A small group of stick-wielding women were already inside her makeshift tent. She felt an arm around her neck, which was followed by the tearing sound of the front of her dress and then a slap at the side of her head. All she remembered saying was: 'Ki sa m te fè?' What did I do?

As the torrent of slaps continued, she wrapped both her arms around her head. Had it not been for a police pickup that was parked nearby, her body would surely have been hacked. Even in the presence of the officers, some managed to land a kick or a slap. (26)

Gossip, in the aftermath of unthinkable destruction, runs unchecked by the usual social norms; even the presence of police officers does little to prevent the crowd from taking arbitrary, cathartic vengeance against Odette. The tent-city residents' anger at their own loss is turned outward, fueling a violent upsurge of collective rage that—much as with the chatter of the townsfolk in *Crónica*—serves to reaffirm the participants' membership in a community, albeit at the expense of the helpless old woman they select as their sacrificial victim.

Gossip plays a similarly aggressive, if more subtle, role in another story by Sánchez, "Etc.," in which the male narrator's account is interrupted by women's gossip about a man who loiters on the street corner and sexually assaults women he finds attractive. The women turn out to be talking about the narrator, disclosing not just his predatory behavior but also the fact that his wife is unfaithful to him. Through their gossip the narrator is exposed, and his threat diminished along with his narrative authority, as the women hijack the tale and turn the narrator into an object of mockery. Gossip becomes an act of aggression, as Gelpí insightfully notes: "The etcetera of the title alludes [. . .] to what is missing in the text. That which is missing in the story, and which interrupts the characters' routine, is the feminine verbal aggression, the gossip through which one of the Franklin store's clerks unmasks the character" (118). As Gelpí discerns, Sánchez's text plays on the homophony in Spanish between two forms of aggression: *dar chino* and *chismear,* or to commit sexual assault and to gossip. The clerks' gossip about the story's protagonist corrects the narrator's own account and adds a crucial piece of information: that he himself has been cuckolded. Gossip here becomes a weapon of attack. The airing of dirty laundry—"sacar los trapos al sol" in Spanish—constitutes a ritual of retribution by the community against one of its members, with gossip becoming a means of punishing and emasculating the transgressor. The community once more asserts itself through gossip at the expense of a perceived outsider.

In *The Harder They Come* (1980), Michael Thelwell similarly tells the tale—itself recounted through a pages-long, carefully transcribed act of gossip—of a "syndicate" of young, poor Jamaican men who gossip both to reinforce their own bonds and to take revenge upon an attractive woman who spurns their advances. The men use gossip to map the woman's rejection of them and her dalliances with more affluent men, and toy with simply reporting her affair with her wealthy employer to the man's wife; in the end, however, they are more creative, pooling their resources—a gold watch, a pair of fancy shoes—to make one of their number appear far better off than he is. Next, they plant gossip about their friend to make him seem an eligible bachelor: "It was arranged for her to learn via the grapevine that he was a clerk in a downtown store, who was studying accounting in night school and was assured of a big job when he finished his studies" (228). Finally, when their friend succeeds in bedding the woman, the men gather outside his room, and one takes the friend's place in the midst of the couple's lovemaking; the ruse is discovered only when it emerges that the substitute is far better endowed. Both the well-endowed man and the woman become the subject of gossip, but the man is given an affectionate nickname—"Longah"—while the woman is hounded out of her job, in a move presented as just punishment for her rejection of men of her own social class. "So everybody say. You can ask anybody in Trench Town. Ah true man," insists Bogart, who narrates the gossip (228). The episode recalls anthropologist Peter Wilson's description of gossip as a reputational contest between men and women, with men gossiping about their sexual conquests to bolster their own standing at the expense of the reputations of the women they describe, and women countering by gossiping about the "foolish" or "ignorant" behavior of the men. Still, Wilson notes, this gendered contest is not fought on level ground. While men gossip about women chiefly in order to elevate their own social standing, the woman's first priority is defensive: she must protect "that vulnerable part of her social personality, her pretense to respectability" (162). Moreover, Wilson argues, since respectability is relative, women tend to seek to tarnish the reputation of their rivals, with even gossip about male misbehavior often intended to denigrate other women by association.

The tendency to boost one's own status through gossip about others can be seen in Luis Negrón's 2010 short story "Muchos o de cómo a veces la lengua es bruja," in which two "very concerned neighbors" (73) chatter about a long line of people—a child, a brother-in-law, the sons of three acquaintances, a school librarian, and others—who they claim are *patos,* or homosexuals. The two women egg one another on, in false sympathy for the families of the various people they believe to be gay, but by defining the men they discuss almost exclusively in terms of female relationships—"Alta's boy," "Margot's son" (73, 78)—they effectively use them as reputational props, serving to diminish the women in question. The gossip session is underpinned by the ostentatious performance of anxiety—"Look, my hairs are standing on end," one woman tells the other (78)—with the pair reassuring one another that they aren't prejudiced even as they approvingly describe episodes of persecution and physical violence against people suspected of being gay. Negrón's work is indebted to Sánchez's, and, as in "¡Jum!," gossip gives rise to direct action against its targets. Still, in this instance Negrón suggests that the women are fighting a rising tide. The proliferation of *patos* in the women's world is described as a "rich threat" (79)—a wry nod to the vicious pleasure the women take in condemning and judging their neighbors, but also to the shifting sexual reality, the Caribbean queering, depicted in Negrón's stories. The threat is real, and there really are "muchos" homosexuals surrounding the women, the story concludes: "Por lo que se ve, no es para menos" (79)—"from what we can tell, it's no small matter" (68).[32] Society is changing, and while the women resort to gossip to shore up their way of life, for once social condemnation will not be enough to undo the changes, any more than the prayed-straight therapy sessions that the women discuss are enough to render their targets heterosexual.

Still, it is through gossip that the women of Negrón's story articulate and process the changes taking place—and the *others* they see gaining sway—in Puerto Rican society. This resonates with the more placid use of gossip in the stories of the Jamaican writer Olive Senior. As Lucy Evans perceptively remarks, Senior's stories present gossip as "a means through which community is articulated and reinforced" (56)—but while at some times "the gossiping community serves as a support network" for its members, at others it functions as a mechanism whereby "close-knit rural communities can exclude those who do not conform and integrate" (64). These are flip sides of the same coin: often, gossip obtains and maintains its status as a support system for some of a community's members precisely by excluding, criticizing, or ostracizing those who are deemed to have trespassed beyond the community's moral boundaries. The female characters of "Ballad," Evans notes, "are brought together in mutual critique" of Miss Rilla, with whose makeup, jewelry, and general comportment they eagerly find fault. "Their rejection of Miss Rilla brings them together, reinforcing the dominant ideology to which they all subscribe," Evans writes (64). As Evans notes, Senior's stories show women playing a wide variety of roles, often defined by their varying degrees of compliance with or resistance to "a European ideal of respectability" (65). The apparently petty social grievances revealed and policed through gossip thus reflect broader tensions inherent in the communities and societies of which Senior writes; the differences in which gossip deals, in other words, are more complex and more significant than they seem. In stories such as "Real Old Time T'ing," "Lily, Lily," and "The Lizardy Man and His Lady," as Carol Bailey writes, gossip serves to challenge the conception of "'difference' as a primary basis of social organization in colonial/modern Jamaica." The protagonists of these stories, Bailey asserts, "use gossip as a means of foregrounding the self, and in so doing call into question their own investment in the systems they interrogate" (124). Bailey is aware that gossip can serve as a means of social control, but also sees in gossip's interrogation of "difference" a means of exposing a society's defining anxieties about race, class, and morality. "Beyond maintaining control and exposing social codes, gossip [. . .] reveals a subject's own insecurities and investment in the system she critiques," she writes. "Senior uncovers the social investment that gossip both reveals and embodies" (124).

This is apparent not only in the stories explored by Bailey but also in many of Senior's other works. *Dancing Lessons* (2014) features a well-connected "sambo girl" named Millie who defies expectations and refuses to settle down with a single man, sparking gossip that she is "a loose woman" (50)—a claim the narrator questions. "I don't think she was; though she had a reputation as a 'walk-bout,' Millie didn't care," the narrator reports. "Unlike her younger sister Vie, who had to stay home to mind the three children she already had at age twenty, Millie was 'free, single, and disengaged,' as she liked to describe herself to any who dared criticize her" (50). Millie does not simply ignore the community's gossip about her: she dives into it, uses it, and makes it a part of her own process of self-assertion:

> Millie on her days off was free to walk. And talk. She walked to the shop, she walked to the post office, she walked to visit her friends and relatives when her mind took her, in the process harnessing all news and gossip and trailing behind her the ugly chit-chat that followed women who did not stay at their yard and—even worse—had no children of their own. Yet, because Millie had

such a pleasant, smiling face, with dimples, and a temper to match, everyone liked her, even the women, so the remarks passed behind her back were nowhere as stinging as they would have been were she less well liked, or less well connected in the marketplace of gossip. (50)

As the narrator makes clear, not everyone is able to evade the slings and arrows of neighborhood gossip with quite as much dexterity as Millie; it is her ability to do so that makes her remarkable. Still, Senior's text suggests, gossip is a marketplace from which a savvy trader can come away having made a profit, and in which difference can, for some participants, become a thing to be asserted rather than feared. As Bailey writes, gossip may appear to be about other people, but Senior—writing about "postcolonial societies that are still haunted by the preoccupation with difference that created them" (131)—sees clearly that the differences about which people gossip are actually a commentary upon their own self-image. The things people gossip about reveal their hopes, prejudices, and fears, and speak eloquently about the uncomfortable truths and frailties upon which their communities are founded.

Community and Society: *La fiesta vigilada*

The scholarship on gossip and community can be loosely divided into what might be called traditional and revisionist schools. The former asserts that gossip is fundamentally corrosive to community, and that through its assaults on reputation and dignity it breaks down the fraternal neighborliness and mutual trust upon which the community depends to sustain itself. The latter, which might also be termed the Spacksian reading, suggests the existence of "good" gossip, which strengthens such ties by brokering and bolstering intimate relationships, and by allowing marginalized groups to assert their views.[33] In the texts examined in this chapter, however, a third possibility reveals itself: that gossip can serve to trouble the distinction between *Gemeinschaft* ("community") and *Gesellschaft* ("society") proposed by Ferdinand Tönnies, and elaborated upon by Jean-Luc Nancy and others.[34] In the Spacksian view, gossip—or at least "good" gossip—is a prototypical discourse of *Gemeinschaft*: it allows the ties of kinship and friendship to proliferate and strengthen themselves, and authentic, intimate relationships to spring up amid the institutional affiliations and obligations that mediate the drab modernity of *Gesellschaft*. As we have seen, however, Caribbean writers tend to view gossip's role in mediating community with suspicion. Community itself, in fact, is a particularly fraught concept in the region—a consequence, Celia Britton convincingly argues, of the region's uniquely troubled past. Caribbean societies are the "pure product of colonization," Britton writes, and consequently "there could be no 'natural' sense of community evolving peacefully over the years; rather, the *problem* of community, conceived both in terms of collective practices and institutions and on the subjective level of collective identity, generates a deep-seated anxiety" (*Sense of Community* 1). In such a context, gossip appears not as a means of generating utopian, pseudofamilial microcommunities but rather as a decidedly dystopian force: the intimate communitarian structures of *Gemeinschaft* placed in the service of the *Gesellschaft,* and used not to reinforce neighborly bonds but rather to oversee and enforce the bleaker reality of a society seeking to sustain itself. Gossip, in other words, evolves into a totalitarian force seeking to stifle individual self-expression and to punish those who challenge the status quo or wander beyond the community's carefully policed boundaries.[35]

This can be seen, to varying degrees, in the texts examined in this chapter. Even Senior's portrayal of gossip, which of the texts discussed leans closest to a Spacksian approach, is marked by an acute awareness of the societal tensions and postcolonial anxieties manifested in the intimate interactions she describes. If *La mala hora* hews closer to the traditionalist view, showing a society torn apart by gossip, meanwhile, *Crónica* shows a society held forcibly together by gossip, but at the expense of individual agency. Rhys and Sánchez show gossip being used to brutally punish, or label and exclude, transgressors, with deadly results. Mais, pointedly, describes a woman who longs for *Gemeinschaft*—to "live [. . .] like neighbours, with love"—but who is frustrated by gossip's impersonal policing of community behavior and by the apparent impossibility of self-actualized existence in such a society. And if Negrón's ironic portrayal of gossip's social policing hints at the waning power of the moral arbiters in question, it also acknowledges the immense power such gossips have long exercised, and still seek to assert, over the sexual and romantic lives of queer Puerto Ricans. Gossip is shown as not simply a means for small, neighborly groups to constitute themselves but also as a tool that binds communities together without regard for intimacy, authenticity, or individuality. It becomes, in short, a means for the *Gesellschaft* to assert and sustain itself more forcibly, by co-opting the prototypical discourse of the *Gemeinschaft.*

The texts hitherto examined explore gossip's totalitarian aspect chiefly via its deployment in informal social and power structures. In some

Caribbean works, however, the connections between totalitarian gossip and authoritarian politics are made more explicit. This is the case in Antonio José Ponte's *La fiesta vigilada,* a novel-essay—told in the first person, as opposed to the ensemble visions of many of the preceding texts—that shows the irreparable damage done to a community, and to its individual members, when gossip is co-opted by the state.[36] The state's suffocating presence is, as many have noted, the central concern of Ponte's work. María Guadalupe Silva writes that Ponte's texts are marked by the "constant presence, in each space of public and private life, of the Cuban state and its regimes of authority" (70), which are depicted as "an expansive and totalitarian system" (72). Less often remarked, however, is the degree to which this system is dependent upon networks of friends and neighbors who become "espías," or spies, prying into one another's private lives and reporting each other's intimate secrets to the government. The spies to which Ponte refers are actually just gossips, like the prying neighbors of "Gravel in Your Shoe": private citizens who engage in conventional chatter about which of their neighbors have more money than they should, receive strange visitors, or behave "suspiciously." But where Mais's neighbors gossip among themselves, Ponte's transmute their chatter into espionage by reporting it to the government. The text's insistence on calling such people spies is both an ironic gesture, mocking the informers by inflating their status, and a serious one that acknowledges the effects of their intrusion. Similarly, Ponte speaks of "the surveillance of the neighborhood committees" and "that of the uniformed forces" in the same breath, both puncturing the self-importance of the gossips and signaling their assimilation into the state's surveillance apparatus (236).[37]

Above all, however, Ponte stresses that his lived reality is one in which every friend, neighbor, or even bystander is potentially a spy.[38] Everything is observed, and everything must be observable: "Better that no tree should stand between the buildings; frankness should reign between comrades," he wryly notes (184). Here, once more, the tropes of community life are perverted to serve the needs of the impersonal and uncaring but powerfully self-sustaining surveillance state. Gossip becomes a dispersed form of surveillance, in contrast to the central and unitary surveilling eye conceived of by Bentham and described by Foucault. Still, the assumption by Cubans of responsibility for their own surveillance is very much in keeping with Foucault's conception of the panopticon as an instrument for creating a self-policing community; it should, he argues, "be a machine for creating and sustaining a power relationship independently of the person who exercises it; in short, the detainees should be caught up in a situation of power of which they themselves are the bearers" (*Surveiller* 203).[39] The gossip-mediated social surveillance practiced in Cuba is notable for combining peer-to-peer social scrutiny with a centralized government structure: in Ponte's text, gossip obtains its power not simply through the subject's awareness of being watched and judged, but through the acutely felt threat that what is seen by one's peers will be repeated to state security agents and will filter back into official networks of oversight and control. This is a plausible concern: Lillian Guerra's *Visions of Power in Cuba* details the Castro government's use of "eavesdropping, snooping, gossip gathering, and shouting matches on the street" as a form of social control, with particular reference to the role of the *Comités de Defensa de la Revolución* (209). Guerra argues convincingly that the CDRs mediated "a unique system of power best described as a grassroots dictatorship," with *cederistas* given the right to assess the revolutionary credentials of their neighbors and to forge new identities for themselves as self-appointed agents of the state—both tasks in which gossip became a vital and widely used resource (200).

Ponte sets his own experiences among a constellation of other spy stories, primarily English, pulled from history and literature. Pondering Graham Greene's 1958 novel *Our Man in Havana*, Ponte discerns a similarity between the novelist's fascination with the lives of others and the prying eyes of the gossip-spy. He also reflects on the journalist Timothy Garton Ash's discovery of his Stasi file in the former East Germany, noting that the file is composed of three kinds of documents: photocopied letters, transcribed phone conversations, and "reports from neighbors and acquaintances of the surveilled" through which Garton Ash "was able to reconstruct a day from more than thirty years ago" (214). Ponte is especially fascinated by this last set of documents, which Ash uses to recompose "successions of Bloomsdays" through reports describing the way he "would come in and carry his bicycle to the landing of the staircase that led to his floor" (214–15) and so on and so forth, in tedious detail. This trivia is the stuff of mundane gossip, not spy novels, but it is precisely through the accumulation of such quotidian information, Ponte suggests, that the surveillance state obtains such sweeping control over its citizenry. Ash's discoveries feed Ponte's exhausted sense of being constantly watched, a well-founded paranoia that seeps into his own daily experiences. When the economy changes and money starts flowing in to Havana, Ponte immediately recognizes that "the suspicion of someone who lived above their means would become a motive for frequent snitching" (127). During a Celia Cruz performance, meanwhile, he can't help but assume that among the orchestra members there is "some colleague (or several) ready to snitch" (133). The state thus achieves oppression through perceived omniscience: Ponte's paranoia, and his sense of living in a panoptical surveillance state, penetrates all aspects of his life.

Despite this suffocating paranoia, the guarded tone of *La fiesta vigilada* appears motivated by the pursuit of a kind of restrained intimacy that suggests a frustrated yearning for kinship and for connections between the narrator's experiences and those of others. For Adriana Kanzepolsky, *La fiesta vigilada* raises important questions: "How to appropriate [. . .] the memory of the city, and above all one's own memory, when the discourse of the State threatens with its presence to seep into all the cracks? That is, how to narrate a discourse in the first person when [. . .] the 'I' insists, page after page, that the public has taken the place of the private?" (64). Ponte's watchful first-person narrator grapples with these questions, offering himself as a voice for the destroyed community, a "we" that finds its sense of self precisely in the shared experience of persistent isolation and mistrust. "We were all the police," Ponte writes, fusing the first person and the destroyed community in the dual experiences of watching and being watched (236). Ponte thus also reflects upon the alienation of the individual in a surveillance state in which "one was always under suspicion" and in which even introspection becomes a sterile, carefully regulated activity, with communal acts of self-criticism serving as "a bad mix of the agora and the confessional box" (123). Despite this, Ponte's paranoia is not limited to his own stifling sense of being watched but encompasses the suffering of others, too, such as the orchestra members in the example above, or the construction workers who, as Ponte observes, are "always at risk of losing their job due to someone's denunciation" (201). Paranoia, Ponte suggests, is a simple fact of life for those living under surveillance.

Perhaps because he himself understands the impulse to scrutinize—as he reminds his reader, the novelist is a kind of spy—Ponte senses the alienation not just of the watched but also of the watcher. "The Muscovites needed to spy incessantly due to a profound incapacity for understanding," he writes. "Given that they did not understand the contemporary world, nor the history that since 1917 had been carrying them towards the most absolute darkness and the peak of horror, they spied. Because of emptiness, because of idleness" (150–51). Not just the victims of the gossip-spies but the entire community—the entire city—is corroded by the pervasive prying that paradoxically also serves to hold it together. Anke Birkenmaier notes that in Ponte's text, "the city is conceived of as an entity threatened by 'others': visiting foreigners, spies, surveilling neighbors" (250). It is telling, then, that Ponte makes explicit the connection between the figure of the gossip-spy and the motif of ruination that runs through *La fiesta*. "All spying aspires to the simultaneity of the interior and the exterior that is an attribute of ruins," Ponte writes (203). The spy—like the gossip, one could argue—is concerned with revealing that which lies within and rendering public, through a process of destructive exposition, that which others wish to keep hidden from view. In such an environment, in the *ciudad vigilada*, the society sustains itself, but there is no real sense of community: there is *Gesellschaft* without *Gemeinschaft*. "The city belonged, in the long run, to nobody," Ponte writes.[40] "Life in each neighborhood became a collective shipwreck, with surveillance between neighbors as the clutching of a drowning man that drags another to the depths" (202–3). There is no sense of belonging or of fraternal bonds, no real kinship: only a shared sense of loss, of paranoia, of hopeless resignation. Gossip, in such a setting, is a far cry from the Spacksian chatter that allows the forging of bonds between small groups. In these Caribbean texts, gossip is at best vestigial, a reminder of lost intimacy. More typically, gossip becomes a powerful but impersonal, even totalitarian force: a means of binding the social group together, but one that shows little concern for the freedoms lost or the individual lives sacrificed along the way.

2 "Parallel Versions"
Gossip, Investigation, and Identity

> We know people by their stories.
> —Edwidge Danticat

IN HER 1992 poem "Crick Crack," the Grenadian poet Merle Collins compares the founding myths of the Afro-Caribbean to the stories of her childhood. The "nanci-stories" were clearly labeled as fictions, she recalls, and listeners knew that "somebody was going to take a high fall on a slippery lie." By contrast, Collins warns, the stories of the discovery of the Americas, of the emancipation of slaves, and of the end of apartheid, bear no such labels:

> When we were children the signals were clear
> somebody say crick we say crack
> [......................]
> But some stories come
> with no crick with no crack
> [..................]
> so what is the mirage and
> what reality?
> do we know what is truth
> and what is truly fiction? (193–95)

The Caribbean, Collins suggests, is fundamentally marked by this narrative tension, the only solution to which, she argues, is for its peoples to tell new stories and forge new histories that properly reflect their lived experiences and shared past. Still, to do so is no easy task, and the poem concludes with a hissing note of defiance that is also resigned to the continuing force and power of the region's official narratives:

> tales of hunting will always
> glorify the hunter
> until the lioness

  is her own
  hiss-
  -torian (196)

The mistrust of the official narrative, the authorized histories of "tall, tall, tall" white men, is urgently felt (196). But Collins also juxtaposes her defiant closing declaration with its own source material, an Ewe proverb, which she places immediately before her closing stanza: "Until lions have their own historians, / they say, / tales of hunting will always / glorify the hunter." Collins's repetition is a feminist riff on a rather masculine proverb, injecting a female lioness into the talk of lions and hunters. By turning the "his" of "history" into an ungendered, animalistic hiss, the poem insists that even if lions learn to tell their own stories and write against imposed truths, the tale will remain incomplete unless women (or lionesses) also seize the right to tell their stories on their own terms.

  This is in keeping with Collins's adoption of the oral patterns and images of stories traditionally told by adults to children. Still, her evocation—at once plaintive and mocking—of the easy certainties of childhood seeks to highlight the contingency of truth and fiction, mirage and reality, in the contemporary Caribbean. Despite her closing exhortation, Collins ultimately suggests that for the people of the Caribbean, the most pressing need is not to write new histories but rather to understand that much of what is presented as truth is in fact fiction, and that not all lies come clearly labeled.[1]

  Collins's suspicion of official narratives is, of course, widely shared in the Caribbean, a region triply marked by the sanitized histories of conquest and colonialism, the imposed discourses of authoritarianism, and the constant encroachment of cultural materials from dominant literary and artistic centers in Europe, the United States, and Latin America. Such suspicion creates fertile ground for gossip. But resorting to gossip in the face of untrustworthy or inauthentic accounts, and the epistemic instability that they bring, in turn raises questions about the epistemic quality of gossip. If official accounts cannot be trusted, why should we think any differently of information gleaned through gossip? Can gossip be a stable building block in a positivist, epistemically valid account of the world—or is it just another mirage, another fraught fiction, in a region rife with untrustworthy tales?

  The epistemic validity of gossip is a puzzle that has been previously addressed, if not fully solved. Tommaso Bertolotti and Lorenzo Magnani describe gossip as mediating a bilateral exchange between individual and collective depositories of knowledge, and emphasize the practice's role as a form of collaborative knowledge making. Karen Adkins, meanwhile, situates gossip within a broader tradition of feminist epistemological investigation, attempting a "historical resuscitation" intended to demonstrate the epistemic worth of gossip in narratives of both men and women (215). Both genders use gossip to construct knowledge, Adkins notes, as do scientists, historians, and many other epistemically respectable investigators. It thus follows, she claims, that the divide between authoritative knowledge and knowledge obtained through gossip is an illusion; gossip is revealed not as "women's knowledge" but rather as an ungendered means of sharing and weighing information. "The material and means of gathering knowledge feminists have brought to light always already occur with all of us," Adkins asserts (230).

Such investigations are valuable and, I will argue in this chapter, have significance for gossip's deployments in recent Caribbean literature. The contradictory gossip of Rosario Ferré's *Maldito amor* (1986) serves a refractive role, rendering firm or final truths unreachable, in a gesture entirely in keeping with the instabilities that Ferré perceives in the Puerto Rican nation. Jean Rhys's *Wide Sargasso Sea* (1966), to which Ferré's text is indebted, similarly uses gossip's fraught epistemic status to trace fault lines in Caribbean society. Maryse Condé's 2000 novel *Célanire cou-coupé*, meanwhile, presents an apparently omniscient narrator who defers to gossip and public opinion and is thereby seduced into presenting fantastic tales as plausible or truthful. Finally, Ana Teresa Torres offers a counterpoint to these murky epistemic spaces: in *La fascinación de la víctima* (2008), a psychotherapist plays detective, using gossip to arrive at meaningful new truths about an unsolved crime. In telling stories of and for a region full of tales that begin "with no crick with no crack," and in exploring the truths and fictions of a region characterized both by distrust of official narratives and by ubiquitous gossip, Caribbean writers thus often come to reflect on the fascinating and treacherous epistemic status of the gossip and rumors through which they construct their narratives. In so doing, they—like Collins—address not just the truthfulness of Caribbean narratives, but the broader and thornier question of how to forge authentic collective and individual identities in a region where truth and falsehood remain sharply contested.

Family and Nation: *Maldito amor*

Adkins's reading of gossip as an ungendered form of knowledge production is pertinent to Rosario Ferré's novella *Maldito amor*, a work that engages with questions of both truth and identity and that has been widely interpreted as a feminist text. Lidia Santos argues that Ferré's project is to rewrite the Latin American canon from a female point of view, while Cynthia Sloan remarks on Ferré's efforts to disrupt the "dominant cultural constructions that have silenced women's voices" (35). It is easy to see why Ferré's text has inspired such readings: though dominated by the florid account of Don Hermenegildo, a lawyer and historian who tells the "official" version of the De la Valle family's saga, *Maldito amor* ends with a radical act of subversion. Gloria, the family's long-suffering mulatto nurse, recounts a divergent version of events as she sets fire to the family's home, in the process perhaps killing Hermenegildo. Gloria's narrative revisionism and final act of arson have been read as a double blow against patriarchal master texts, and by extension against broader gender-, class-, and race-based hierarchies. Marisel Moreno describes Gloria's burning of the home as "the final debunking" of Puerto Rico's foundational myth, an attempt to "rebel against the hegemonic order and patriarchal structures that the De la Valle family [. . .] comes to symbolize" (97). Gloria's and Hermenegildo's sparring accounts are thus conceived of in terms of an essential duality: one account triumphs over and replaces the other in a narrative clash that reveals the tensions and power struggles of Puerto Rican society.

Such readings, though valuable, overlook the refractive nature of *Maldito amor*, which advances not solely through the accounts of Hermenegildo and Gloria but also through a plurality of other contradictory yet complementary tales told by various family members and associates. The text's narrative complexity can be understood by reading these diverging accounts as gossip, particularly in their aim to revise other narratives or to reveal secrets that shed fresh light on them. The characters of *Maldito amor* disclose, through Hermenegildo's transcription of their gossipy speech, what they claim to be private truths about others; in so doing, they actively contradict the other characters' versions of events. One account does not simply replace another; rather, through gossip, it establishes its place in a narrative lattice in which every character's account undermines—and crucially, is undermined by—each of the others. The driving force at work here is not a simple dismantling of master narratives but rather an exploration of the essential precariousness of *all* narratives, carried out incrementally but insistently by all the text's characters, female and male alike, through the gossip that they share.

As this suggests, the gossip of *Maldito amor* is forcefully adversarial: the De la Valle family members are engaged in a narrative struggle with gossip as their chief weapon. There is real power, both symbolic and practical, to the characters' words. By revealing what they know (or claim to know) about others, the characters of *Maldito amor* gain tangible advantages over one another, and not always in proportion to the agency and authority they might otherwise possess: the account of Titina, the family housekeeper, for instance, is given equal weight to that of Arístides, the family's only surviving son. Gossip in *Maldito amor* thus becomes a vital form of self-expression and a means of giving voice to one's own viewpoint even, or especially, in the face of more securely established narratives. In this, the novella portrays gossip as a potent leveling force and tool for dissent, and as a discourse and social practice uniquely equipped to allow the subordinated to challenge the narratives of the powerful.

This aspect of *Maldito amor* clearly resonates with feminist approaches to the text, and it is reasonable to read Ferré's deployment of gossip, a form so often seen as gendered, as a means of troubling master narratives, patriarchal or otherwise.[2] Still, *Maldito amor* goes further, using gossip as a means not just of questioning hegemonic narratives but also of rendering a more fundamental epistemological uncertainty. In Ferré's novella, gossip promises new truths and the disruption of prior understandings, yet it is also presented as partisan, inescapably (and often deliberately) colored and distorted by the perspectives and agendas it advances, and by the moral judgments it hands down. While each character's gossip insists upon its own truthfulness and demands credulousness of its interlocutor, it ultimately fails to deliver the promised "real" or "true" insights. In this way, the text reminds its reader that both master narratives and the alternative tellings that strive to replace them are equally precarious. Neither can deliver a final or definitive truth but only another version or perspective; both, therefore, are equally vulnerable to being displaced by new, more seductive accounts.

Ferré's warning is particularly urgent in Puerto Rico, a nation perpetually groping for a definitive account of its political standing and yet unable to crystallize different voices and viewpoints into a single coherent vision of its national status and identity. Similarly, there is no larger truth or even consensus to be found in *Maldito amor,* and no common narrative for the characters, in their fragmented perspectives and worldviews, to share. In using the De la Valles as a metonym for the Puerto Rican *gran familia,* Ferré's text elaborates a failed epistemology of national significance. It stages, in other words, the failure—perhaps the *inevitable* failure—of Puerto Ricans to arrive at and agree upon a single common truth, and vividly renders an existential uncertainty that is both cause and symptom of the nation's inability to satisfactorily resolve its own status.

Ferré conceived of *Maldito amor* as a tropical version of Akira Kurosawa's *Rashomon* (1950), a "fabulous film," she told Walescka Pino-Ojeda, in which three accounts of a murder "tell the same story, but from completely different points of view, and in the end one doesn't know who is right" (82). Like *Rashomon*'s witnesses, Ferré's characters tell and retell the same basic events but with each version revising or casting doubt upon those that came before. Hermenegildo's account of the life of the De la Valle family patriarch, Ubaldino, is derailed by the entrance of the housekeeper, Titina, who lets slip that the family killed Nicolás, Ubaldino's son, to keep him from giving away the family fortune. Next, Arístides tells Hermenegildo that Nicolás had been a homosexual forced into an unhappy marriage with Gloria, that he had been cuckolded both by Ubaldino and by Arístides himself, and that his death had been either a suicide or an act of revenge by workmen subjected to his sexual advances. Arístides's account is followed by that of Laura, Ubaldino's wife, who claims her supposedly chivalrous and aristocratic husband had actually been a syphilitic philanderer descended from a local black man, and alleges that Nicolás's marriage had been a sham intended to shield Gloria from Arístides's lascivious advances. Finally, Gloria, one eye already on the gas can, asserts that she and Nicolás had in fact been passionately in love, that Ubaldino's political career had been tainted by corruption, and that Nicolás's death was the result of either filicide or fratricide. Each character, in short, gossips about the others, yielding a succession of contradictory accounts that, as Ferré suggests, "produce what we might call a domino effect, in which the first version knocks down the second, which knocks down the third, until in the end it's impossible to determine what the truth was because it all ends in questions" (Pino-Ojeda 82). As in *Rashomon,* there is no overarching narrative authority to provide the reader with a definitive version of events; besides a few basic facts, there is little upon which the characters agree.[3]

As these tales unfold, the text strays from the formal, hagiographic account intended by Hermenegildo and enters a brash, scandalous realm more akin to a Latin American *telenovela* than to the idylls of a *novela de la tierra*. Still, the action, with the exception of Gloria's final act of arson, takes place offstage and is enacted through second- or third-hand retellings, rendered through multiple layers of prurient and obsessively detailed gossip about the lives of others. The tellers of these tales, moreover, are not content simply to describe a series of events; rather, they construct their stories according to the rhythms and cadences of gossip. Describing his brother, Arístides tells Hermenegildo: "Under his savior's pose, beneath his airs of deliverer and liberator, he was really a closet queen, a poor degenerate fool who skewered and twisted and danced before their horrified eyes at the first opportunity he had of being alone with them; who doled and measured out the land and the houses he had promised on the basis of who would and who wouldn't, who could be man enough to trade in his dignity for a piece of bread or a brick" (SDD 45).[4] Arístides doesn't just set out the facts: he relishes their telling, and revels in his ability to titillate his listener with specific and sordid details. Lingering over Nicolás's sexual transgressions, Arístides acts as a stereotypical gossip, thoroughly enjoying the performative disclosure of another's secrets. Of course, Arístides's juicy tidbits seek not only to entertain and engage his listeners but also to seduce them into accepting the truthfulness of his version of events. To the extent that Arístides succeeds, through gossip, in converting his listener into an accomplice or ally, he wins a narrative victory: in accepting Arístides's version of events, one must necessarily reject other, contradictory accounts.[5]

The same is true of the other stories presented by the various characters given a voice in *Maldito amor*. Rather than simply providing their own individual perspectives, each character actively seeks to elevate his or her version above the others and to have his or her telling accepted as the only true account. This highlights a key aspect of gossip that separates it from other forms of storytelling: the hidden truths it purports to reveal about its subjects frequently come at the expense of other accounts and explicitly seek to revise or overwrite another person's version of events. What is more, as Arístides instinctively realizes, the gossip that triumphs in this narrative clash is not necessarily the most truthful but rather the best told, most memorable, or most sensational.

In this sense, *Maldito amor* exploits and foregrounds gossip's inherent adversarialism. The characters are well aware of the rival threads of gossip that swirl around them, "roaming the town like stray dogs," and seek to tame, dominate, or control them, often through gossipy ad hominem attacks on those who spread the tales (MA 129). Talking about Gloria, Titina states that "in Guamaní to be single and walk the streets means you're risking your reputation, and now Arístides and his sisters are spreading the rumor that Gloria is loose with men, may God save her soul" (SDD 21).[6] Hermenegildo, meanwhile, laments that rumors narrated "by strange and untrustworthy people" have tainted the family's reputation (MA 132).[7] Arístides, too, insists that Gloria is merely a "scheming, ambitious hussy" and that he "won't let her let loose her pack of lies upon the town, trying her best to ruin us" (SDD 35).[8]

Such exchanges underscore the fact that the primary source of gossip's power is its ability to wreck reputations. The characters of *Maldito amor* are acutely aware of the image they present to the world, and invest their energy in keeping their private transgressions out of the public eye. When the family's good name is tarnished, Arístides says he wishes to move to the capital, "where no news of our dishonor or of our shame has as yet arrived" (*SDD* 36). Laura, similarly, complains of Ubaldino's aunts' "ugly habit" of gossiping about "which families of Guamaní had a strain of black blood in them, and which had managed to remain white" (*SDD* 70). She counters with gossip of her own, telling Hermenegildo about how she learned, through gossip, "the secret, the unmentionable mystery" the aunts had tried to hide: that Ubaldino's mother had married a black man (*SDD* 74). Like Laura, the text's other characters seek to eradicate one another's gossip and negate threats to their reputation with new tales of their own. It is indicative of gossip's place in the power dynamics of *Maldito amor*, too, that the characters have, in many cases, held on to the information they share for years or even decades. The versions they now divulge have long been part of their worldview but were hitherto kept private—in order to protect "our good names," Arístides claims (*MA* 142)—and are brought to light only when the imminent death of Doña Laura threatens the characters' individual interests.

The narrative clashes of the De la Valles do not, then, take place in a vacuum: rather, they have specific and significant consequences. Arístides's account of his brother's sexual escapades is more than just backbiting; it is a calculated attempt to counter the suggestion that Nicolás was killed by his own family, and to convince his listener that in fact Nicolás's insatiable sexual appetite led his abused employees to sabotage his airplane. This pattern is repeated throughout *Maldito amor,* with gossip that initially seems merely trivial often proving to have far-reaching consequences. Titina's gossip, for instance, triggers Hermenegildo's hunt for a will that promises to determine the mill's future ownership and sets off the chain of events that culminates with Gloria's act of arson. Gossip, the text repeatedly insists, has real power and real consequences, and the characters harness it to their benefit.

The power struggles thus enacted through gossip in *Maldito amor* frequently play out according to the gender dynamics noted in feminist readings of Ferré's work. It is through gossip, after all, that the text's female characters—most notably Gloria, but also Laura and arguably Titina—succeed in asserting their voices, viewpoints, and versions of the narrative.[9] The women's stories, moreover, are somewhat less easily discredited than those of Arístides or Ubaldino: the male characters' values align them with and lead them to defend the white, male-dominated, land-owning class of Puerto Rico, while the women, as underdogs in a patriarchal society, demand the reader's sympathy. This supports past readings of *Maldito amor,* and Ferré's broader corpus, as mounting a strong feminist critique that, as Moreno asserts, "challenges and parodies the paternalistic canon" and seeks to tear down patriarchal constructions of the Puerto Rican nation and its history (83).

Ferré's use of gossip can be read, then, as an aspect of the feminist thought that undoubtedly marks the text, but such readings do not tell the whole story. It is not just the female characters of *Maldito amor* who use gossip to assert their voices: all the characters gossip, men and women alike. The chatter of the housekeeper, Titina, is gossip in its most stereotypical, feminine form; so, too, are the informal oral accounts of Gloria and Laura. But Arístides's sexual boasts and sniping at his brother's supposed debauchery, and the moralizing *machismo* and homophobia implicit in his comments, are equally recognizable as gossip. The same can be said of Hermenegildo's overwrought, faux-historical account, which is littered with asides about his subjects' private lives, up to and including accounts of their toilet habits and marital relations. The gossip of *Maldito amor* is not, then, uniquely feminine, any more than it is uniquely oral or informal; the registers and rhetoric vary, but all the novella's characters take pleasure in revealing secrets and personal details that others would prefer to keep private. Gossip emerges in the text as a democratic narrative form: men and women, rich and poor, white and black are all equally avid gossips, and all use gossip to gain narrative power over one another.

Ferré's conception of gossip as a narrative leveling process contrasts with the previously discussed traditional view of the practice as women's talk. Ferré's text hints at the cultural stereotypes and gendered history of gossip; her depiction of Titina, especially, reflects the popular image of the female gossip who is intimately acquainted with the private lives of those for whom she works. But by allowing spiteful gossip to filter into (or, more tellingly, *emerge from*) the formal and masculine registers of Hermenegildo's literary and historical account, and the forcefully macho speech of Arístides and Don Julio, the text challenges the notion that gossip is inevitably gendered. Instead, gossip is framed as something both petty and dangerous—to be kept at arm's length, but also a tool used, by men and women alike, to reveal, denounce, or overpower.

Read in this way, the conflict between the male and female characters in *Maldito amor* is less sharply delineated than many scholars have assumed.

Certainly, the female characters' narrative interventions do often puncture and deflate the hegemonic, patriarchal account crafted by Hermenegildo. But the women are neither alone in doing so—Arístides similarly seeks to correct the record about his brother's habits—nor exclusively focused on challenging Hermenegildo. Time and again, the female characters' narratives struggle against and seek to undermine one another, too, suggesting that their interventions should not be read solely in terms of gender. Neither are such interventions solely enacted by marginalized characters. Don Julio silences his wife, Doña Elvira, with physical blows but also with the humiliating reminder that "her saintly De la Valles, like the rest of Guamaní's hacienda owners of yore, had also been slave drivers," a slur that becomes gossip when recounted by Hermenegildo (*SDD* 14). What ultimately emerges, then, is not simply a gendered dichotomy but rather a more plural and atomized framework in which the characters speak against each other. The unifying factor, it seems, is less gender than the characters' use of gossip to assert their stories and undermine those of their rivals.

This implies a significant break with what one might term the conventional reading of *Maldito amor*, which suggests that Gloria's incendiary final chapter, in supplanting Don Hermenegildo's narrative, offers a factually accurate account of the De la Valle family. Such a reading is both plausible and seductive: Gloria is in many ways the fulcrum upon which the family's saga turns, and by the time the novella concludes with her account, she has been alternately celebrated or maligned by most of the other characters. Having been used and abused throughout the text, in the last chapter Gloria is at last no longer *acted upon* but rather is granted the right to act and speak for herself, and to tell her story without Hermenegildo's mediation. It is almost with relief that the reader comes to accord to Gloria's testimony the weight of truth and to accept it as the key to the puzzling contradictions that have preceded it.

Ferré's text seems actively to encourage such a reading. Consider, for instance, its treatment of Hermenegildo's account, with its conception of Puerto Rico as, in Ferré's words, "a lost paradise, a feudal and agrarian world, in which, supposedly, injustice and hunger did not exist" ("Memorias" 112). Hermenegildo, at once a lawyer, a historian, a biographer, and a journalist, represents four different facets of the official narrative of Puerto Rico's past. But just as Ferré questions his account, so too her text repeatedly reveals gaps and obfuscations in Hermenegildo's version of events. He fails to mention, for example, that Don Julio Font, whom he consistently portrays in a negative light, is a black man, an omission that the reader can plausibly infer is intended to mask his own racism. Similarly, Hermenegildo passes over Ubaldino's corruption and philandering in silence in a bid to "protect his good name" (*SDD* 24). As the tale unfolds, however, the characters directly challenge Hermenegildo's authority, with Laura, for instance, warning that a man could never understand her family's story. Finally, it falls to Gloria to offer a direct rebuttal of Hermenegildo's utopian vision: "Guamaní had never been a paradise, as Don Hermenegildo says in his romantic novel." Instead, she continues, "for centuries it had been an epidemic-infested hole, where most of the Guamaneños remained illiterate and before turning thirty-five would die by the hundreds from tuberculosis, uncinariasis, and hunger" (84). Gloria's words are grittier and more realistic in tone than Hermenegildo's romanticized telling, and appear the more truthful for it. The act of arson that accompanies her words, too, might lead the reader to assume their truthfulness. Why would she take such radical action, after all, unless she is nursing an honest grievance?

The apparent privilege accorded to Gloria's account has led many critics to conclude that Gloria serves as a kind of authorial proxy who voices Ferré's own views. Given Ferré's avowed feminism, it is reasonable to assume that it is with Gloria that her personal sympathies lie, and the same can be presumed of many of her readers. As Oralia Preble-Niemi notes, "Each reader of the novel must make an individual decision about what the truth is in the various matters brought up by the dramatized narrators," and amid the "polyphonic and heteroglossal" noise of *Maldito amor,* the reader will tend to trust the account of the character whose "class or ideological system more nearly conforms to his or her own" (21). But if such factors lend Gloria's account their weight and plausibility, they also serve to highlight its contingency. Gloria's account, for all its merits, derives its claim to truth status not from any objective set of facts but rather from a series of subjective judgments, and the potential congruence between her views and our own, or Ferré's, does not render her version necessarily more complete or truthful. No matter what the reader may think of her, Gloria has not nullified the other characters' accounts; she has simply communicated, like the other characters, her own unique and partial perspective, albeit in a particularly dramatic way.

The reader should not be too quick to decide, then, that *Maldito amor*'s female voices offer the real or true version of the family's saga, or to read Gloria's words as somehow privileged or final. For one thing, as Paul Allatson writes, the story of the De la Valle family does not in fact end with *Maldito amor*—some family members reappear in other stories published alongside Ferré's novella, suggesting that the family narrative has survived Gloria's act of arson. Even the destruction of the sugar mill is neither as dramatic an upheaval nor as definitive a transfer of agency as it might seem: Arístides has already decided to end the family's association with the property by selling it to the Americans. And while Ferré gives Gloria the last chance to shape the text's narrative, her final words are in fact adapted from the nineteenth-century Puerto Rican *danza* "Maldito amor," the same song crooned, in Hermenegildo's telling, by Ubaldino's mother two generations earlier. These borrowed words hint at Gloria's continuing entanglement in the family's tale and suggest the impossibility of the clean break to which her narrative aspires.[10]

This is another reason to deprivilege Gloria's account and to view it as a commentary on, rather than a rupture with, the epistemological instability that has gone before. Gloria sees, more clearly than any other character, the fractures and contradictions that the De la Valles have hitherto concealed in order to uphold a sanitized version of the family narrative. By burning down the family home, she seeks to silence all those who, in speaking, have sought to establish the primacy of their own versions of events; in so doing, she also hopes to establish her own version as the single and definitive account.[11] But Gloria's violent actions are simply an amplification, an impassioned staging, of the same process found in every other character's account: the drive to silence others and to assert the truth of the speaker's viewpoint. Gloria's act of destruction, which affects not just the family's home but also the potential for Hermenegildo, its chronicler, to continue recording the family members' stories, is an attempt to impose a state of amnesia, to obliterate even the memory of the text's diverging accounts. Were Gloria's attempt to succeed it would mean, as George Handley notes, that Gloria's own narrative "would become History, a new master narrative" ("Testimony and Truth" 76). This is the final victory that Gloria seeks; she fails to realize, however, that even if it were possible for her "river of blue benzine" (*SDD* 82) to wash away the other characters and erase their accounts, other alternative accounts, other gossip, would soon emerge to take their place. Simply asserting one narrative more forcefully, or silencing conflicting voices more brutally, cannot confer the definitive epistemological closure that Gloria craves.

Read in this way, Gloria's actions can be seen as bringing to a head an epistemological anxiety that pervades the novella as a whole. Like all gossips, the characters of *Maldito amor* promise to reveal the truth and are explicitly concerned with asserting and elevating their own narratives as the "true" version of events; it is this impulse that leads Laura to declare that she "only wanted to scream, to proclaim the truth" (*MA* 176). But in its very urgency, such an imperative betrays the fragility of its own promise. The frantic pursuit of narrative primacy is, paradoxically, an indication precisely of the multiplicity of "truths" that circulate and also of the degree to which any given account's popular acceptance is a sign less of its objective truth status than of its teller's victory in an ongoing battle for narrative control. Each individual act of gossip promises the definitive inside scoop, but taken in aggregate the conflicting tales of *Maldito amor* in fact call into question the very possibility of definitive versions. The result of the cascading contradictions is, as Julio Ortega writes, a text that progressively "erases itself [. . .] in an act of radical negativity" (91). As in Kurosawa's *Rashomon*, the text provides neither a framework against which to evaluate the characters' statements nor direct access to the facts at hand; the reader is given no easy way to determine what really happened. It is this double movement, promising truth while foregrounding its ultimate inaccessibility, that defines *Maldito amor*'s use of gossip.

Ferré's exploration of the epistemic implications of gossip resonates with Edgardo Cozarinsky's conception of the practice. Cozarinsky writes that gossip "subverts before the narrator the realist illusion, uncovers for them countless aspects of a reality that habit or apathy had dilapidated" (31). Cozarinsky's premise is that gossip, even when ostensibly focused on trivial, everyday situations, serves to reveal new aspects of reality. By refracting a narrative into multiple parts and perspectives, gossip allows texts to discover the plural realities masked, or rendered dilapidated, by our tiresome habit of perceiving reality as "one, precise, tangible" (31).[12] Indeed, it is this very habit that the characters of *Maldito amor* seek to leverage in telling their tales: they count on their listener's desire for a single coherent narrative, for it is this tendency that allows their own tales to supplant those of others rather than simply being taken as one viewpoint among many.

There are echoes here of the impetus that Cozarinsky traces in Proust's work, for whom gossip proceeds "like the positive sciences in their battle to dominate 'data' and possess a 'truth'" (24). Gossip, Cozarinsky suggests, provides data points that Proust organizes into a coherent narrative. But there are other ways of conceiving of gossip. Henry James, Cozarinsky notes, does not see knowledge acquired through gossip as necessarily cumulative; rather, James's passion for gossip shapes and is shaped by his notion of the many-windowed house of fiction, where the reader's view of the surrounding landscape depends upon which window they look out through, which is to say, which character's viewpoint they follow. James's works, Cozarinsky writes, are marked by an "absent center" (28), in that events cannot be directly accessed but can only be seen obliquely through the idiosyncratic and fragmentary perspectives of the various characters. Where Proust uses gossip to deduce the truth, James uses gossip to emphasize the incompleteness and partiality of the narratives he weaves.

The characters of *Maldito amor* are, like James's, built around an absent center. The text refuses to intervene in their bickering or to rule on the truth status of their conflicting accounts. But Ferré goes further than James. Those standing at the windows of James's "house of fiction" are presumed to make a good-faith attempt to describe what they see outside; the discrepancies between their accounts primarily reflect the different frames through which they view the world. Ferré's characters are similarly constrained by their varying viewpoints, failures of recollection, or naive responses to what they see—but their accounts are also overtly adversarial, constructed in full awareness of the tales that came before, and underpinned by self-serving calculations about how they will be perceived and used by others. James proposes truths that are inaccessible or difficult to grasp; Ferré seems to agree but goes further, offering characters who do not even try to communicate the truth and instead lie or confabulate to suit their own prejudices and private goals. In *Maldito amor*, Ferré writes, "Literature, language itself, is at the center of the characters' struggle for power. Everything they say is gossip, lies, unfettered calumny, and nonetheless it is all true" ("Memorias" 112). James's fragmented viewpoints are here recast as a narrative power struggle: every glimpse is not only incomplete but also filtered and distorted according to the speaker's own agenda.

Still, Ferré insists, despite the lies and distortions, "it is all true." With that she seems to suggest that *Maldito amor* is not a puzzle that can be solved, or at least not one that has a single answer. Rather, every speaker's version is a puzzle of its own: a story containing a private truth, which can be discerned despite, or even through, the speaker's calculated obfuscations and manipulations. This irreducible plurality underpins Ferré's claims that her characters challenge Hermenegildo's sweeping historical account by offering "the story of the port of Guamaní, where everything changes and there is no stable reality" ("Memorias" 112). Hermenegildo's account may be the "official version," but *none* of the versions offered present the reader with a "stable reality." The female characters, in their marginalization, are perhaps more aware than Hermenegildo of this instability, but while they are able to use their gossip to reveal the inadequacy of Hermenegildo's narrative, they are no more able than he to present a fixed and final version of the family's tale or to fully erase the countless versions that have gone before.

The contradictions and narrative clashes of *Maldito amor* demand to be understood as speaking to a national condition, with the De la Valles' claim to be descended from Puerto Rico's first governor, the conquistador Juan Ponce de León, standing as an invitation to read the family's struggles as an allegory of the island's own troubled history. This is particularly significant given that Puerto Ricans have, for much of their history, used the metaphor of the *gran familia* to portray their nation as a single happy family. Hermenegildo, early in *Maldito amor,* uses the words "great family" to describe Guamaní residents of "good stock," suggesting, perhaps, that Ferré intends for her reader to view the concept of the *gran familia* with the same skepticism she invites them to accord to Hermenegildo's other romantic but elitist and exclusionary notions about his country's culture and identity. As Ricardo Gutiérrez Mouat and other scholars argue, Ferré's project is to show the connection between neocolonial Puerto Rico and the political, erotic, and familial conflicts of the De la Valle clan, and by extension of all Puerto Rican families. Gutiérrez Mouat writes that Ferré "envisions each Puerto Rican family as a scale model of a nation in perpetual civil war, divided between the proponents of assimilation with the United States and those in favor of independence" (285). What ties both the nation and its families together is a shared past constituted through their shared stories, but the gossip of *Maldito amor,* by constantly opposing and calling into question the accounts of others, foregrounds the fundamental contradictions that fracture what should be common narratives and highlights the precarious balance in which the *gran familia* hangs.[13]

Ferré's problematization of the narrative foundations of the Puerto Rican *gran familia,* in casting its stories as willfully adversarial rather than stable or consensually realized, recalls Ernest Renan's notion that forgetting is "an essential factor in the creation of a nation" (7). Renan sees nationhood as springing from disparate groups' willingness to forget their differences and forge a common identity. Homi Bhabha argues that Renan's act of forgetting is thus a collective assertion, a performance, of unity and will to nationhood: "To be obliged to forget [. . .] is the construction of a discourse on society that *performs* the problem of totalizing the people and unifying the national will," Bhabha explains (230). In this sense, the act of forgetting is a daily referendum, a constant reaffirmation of nationhood. In *Maldito amor,* however, gossip functions as a narrative of revision and rediscovery, bringing to light grievances and transgressions that were hidden or at risk of being forgotten. The text thus presents Puerto Rico as a nation that has not yet achieved the kind of unity Bhabha invokes; just as the De la Valles cannot agree about the details of their own family history, so Puerto Rico cannot arrive at a coherent and consensual view of itself. It cannot, in other words, agree on what to remember and what to forget.

What is more, *Maldito amor* further suggests that in the Puerto Rican context, forgetting becomes a divisive rather than a unifying act: not an outgrowth of or path to national unity but rather an amnesia unilaterally imposed by factions seeking to shape the nation's narrative to serve their own ends. Ubaldino's career as a nationalist politician leads him, Ferré writes, to "practice a series of forgetting exercises, to weaken his memory as much as possible" (*SDD* 83), allowing him to sidestep uncomfortable aspects of Puerto Rican reality. This might seem a Renan-esque exercise in nation building, but Gloria, in gossiping about Ubaldino's forgetfulness, suggests instead that it is the self-serving construction, by a corrupt politician, of a one-sided history from which the underprivileged are conveniently excluded. Hermenegildo himself says nearly as much, arguing that while every family has skeletons in its closet, "it's better to forget these unhappy events, erasing them with the edifying accounts of his heroic exploits. Every country that aspires to become a nation needs its heroes [...] and if it doesn't have them, it's our duty to invent them" (*SDD* 24).

If forgetting can be a path to national unity, then, it is also a fraught and contested process. *Maldito amor* thus uses gossip to assert a larger point: that every historical fact, and much of what passes for knowledge, is the site of an epistemological battleground. If it is not seen as such, it is only because the battle has already been fought, and a given set of facts and interpretations has triumphed. But if gossip is a means of challenging narratives, it also stands, in its ubiquity, as a metaphor for the relentlessness of doubt itself. For Cozarinsky, "the 'truth,' which confers so much dignity on history, is merely the absence of contradiction among received versions of a fact" (16). Ferré would agree: for every nugget of historical information, be it personal or national, there are countless possible revisions and alternative versions, spoken or unspoken. If one cannot be sure about the story of a single family, then how can one possibly hope to establish the truth of long-ago events or of so-called historical facts?

Through gossip, *Maldito amor* reveals the epistemological frailty of historical narrative, but offers neither a real alternative, nor much hope that an alternative is even possible. Gossip allows disenfranchised Puerto Ricans to challenge unsatisfactory historical accounts and to shatter hegemonic views of the country's past into shifting and contradictory versions. But gossip does not provide a tool with which to distinguish or judge between these versions. The story that replaces or corrects a master narrative is not necessarily more complete or "true" simply for having challenged it, nor by virtue of its being told second. This is another reason to doubt Gloria: her radical solution might bring some satisfaction on an individual level, the text implies, but one cannot resolve an entire nation's historical and epistemological anxieties with a can of gasoline. This is an intractable problem: the notion of a complete and lasting solution, like Gloria's attempt to unilaterally end the family's story, is ultimately little more than a fantasy.

What emerges from the text is a peculiarly despondent and atomized vision of Puerto Rican nationhood, in which consensus and unity are unreachable chimeras.[14] Such a view resonates with other readings of the island's troubled history. In his classic essay "El país de cuatro pisos," José Luis González claims that Puerto Ricans are rightly concerned about "the persistent lack of consensus that our people shows in what concerns the future and definitive political organization of the country, that is, the so-called 'problem of status.' In that sense, one easily recognizes the reality of a 'divided people'" (25). Similarly, *Maldito amor* can be read as a meditation on the island's failed struggle to definitively resolve either its own identity or its relationship with the United States as a colonizing power. Ferré describes Puerto Rico as a "schizophrenic country with a Hamlet complex" ("Memorias" 111), profoundly marked by its own ambivalence—its lack, in other words, of a "stable reality." The Hamlet complex of which Ferré speaks resonates with Mallarmé's description of Shakespeare's prince as "ce seigneur latent qui ne peut devenir," a latent lord who cannot become (300). Puerto Rico's status as a site of colonial and postcolonial epistemological struggles, Ferré suggests, forces an awareness of the limitations even of self-knowledge, and the island, in its uncertainty, is left inescapably torn between independence and statehood, stasis and reinvention, and the question of whether to define itself through or against its colonial status. Like Hamlet, the island is seen as ripe with its own potentiality but hesitating, trapped between the many versions of its past, present, and future.[15]

"The Other Side": *Wide Sargasso Sea*

Ferré's novella can be read as an overt homage to Jean Rhys's 1966 novel *Wide Sargasso Sea*, which similarly retells a master narrative and reflects on questions of identity from the perspective of marginalized female characters.[16] Antoinette's experiences can, as Gayatri Spivak points out, be read as "an allegory of the general epistemic violence of imperialism" (251), while in Benita Parry's compelling counterreading, the Martiniquan servant Christophine can be viewed as an "articulate antagonist of patriarchal, settler, and imperialist law" (38). By borrowing details from Charlotte Brontë's original narrative Rhys seeks to interweave the two texts and, as David Leon Higdon notes, "give the illusion that this is [. . .] the other truth" (106). Yet throughout her text, Rhys shows characters struggling to deal with truths portrayed as fragmentary and insufficient and confronting the epistemic challenges of the Caribbean. *Wide Sargasso Sea* is marked by what Saikat Majumdar terms "a deliberate lack of signifiers, gaps between signifiers and signifieds, a Beckettian abundance of all 'nameless things' and 'thingless names'" (110). The text, Majumdar continues, "destroys all possibilities of epistemological certitude. No authoritative, omniscient voice resolves conflicts created by fragmented, multiple viewpoints. Antoinette is 'undecided, uncertain about facts—any facts.' The letters of Daniel Cosway, the Obeah voice of Christophine, the unsettling effect of the ambience on Rochester, the recurring motifs of madness, all give but a hallucinatory glimpse of the 'truth'" (110).

The epistemological significance of Obeah in Rhys's novel has been remarked by Maria Cristina Fumagalli, who considers it a form of discredited or subjugated knowledge, in much the same way that Carolyn Cooper describes folk superstitions as being part of a "body of subterranean knowledge" typically associated with "the silenced language of women and the 'primitiveness' of orally transmitted knowledge" (65). Indeed, as Parry notes, Rhys explicitly contrasts Christophine's informal, Obeah-based wisdom with the lettered knowledge and official histories of the colonizer: "Read and write I don't know. Other things I know," Christophine insists (133). But such knowledge is not a direct substitute for conventional epistemology; rather, it is a fragmentation or destabilization thereof. Carine M. Mardorossian proposes that Obeah gives way "not to a sense of anchored historicity but to a proliferation of narratives" (73). The same, of course, could be said of many forms of gossip—and, indeed, it is remarkable that Christophine's status as an Obeah woman is itself introduced into the text through an act of gossip. After a passage in which Antoinette reflects on the spiteful gossip she has heard about her mother—"I had heard what all these smooth smiling people said about her when she was not listening and they did not guess I was"—she recalls "that woman" also saying: "It's evidently useful to keep a Martinique Obeah woman on the premises." Antoinette reflects: "She meant Christophine. She said it mockingly, not meaning it, but soon other people were saying it—and meaning it" (17–18). The gossip spreads, as gossip tends to do, gaining seriousness and credibility along the way; soon, Antoinette herself is passing on gossip, breathlessly reporting her own daydreams about Christophine's purported Obeah practices. The point is not so much that the gossip is entirely wrong: Christophine does present herself as an Obeah practitioner and concocts a potion (or poison) in response to Antoinette's plea for help.[17] Rather, the issue is that the Obeah gossip continues, unsubstantiated and unchecked, even as it taints both Antoinette's perception of Coulibri and her relationship with Christophine. Just as Antoinette's childish conviction that she intuitively understands Obeah without ever having been taught about it is allowed to go unchallenged, so too is the chatter about Christophine's supernatural activities left to swirl through much of the novel without being directly contradicted or affirmed.

This slipperiness, and this spitefulness, plays a key role in Rhys's presentation of gossip, which she frames as a potent source of information, but also of instability and doubt, for the characters of *Wide Sargasso Sea*. The racial tensions implicit in the gossips' commentary on Obeah come to the fore in Antoinette's strained relations with Tia, the black child whom Christophine recruits to be her friend after other black children start bullying her. When the pair squabble over a few pennies—and after Antoinette calls her a "cheating nigger"—Tia retaliates by unleashing a stream of gossip questioning Antoinette's purported wealth: "That's not what she hear, she said. She hear all we poor like beggar. We ate salt fish—no money for fresh fish. That old house so leaky, you run with calabash to catch water when it rain. Plenty white people in Jamaica. Real white people, they got gold money. They didn't look at us, nobody see them come near us. Old time white people nothing but white nigger now, and black nigger better than white nigger" (14). Tia reaches for the nearest weapon at hand—malicious gossip that she has overheard—just as she later reaches for a jagged stone to symbolically shatter the bond between the two of them as Coulibri burns. Peter Hulme's comments about the stone-throwing incident apply to Tia's earlier outburst, too: the episode, he writes, draws together "the grotesque injustices of colonial violence with the story of an innocent childhood dream of friendship shattered by the realities of a racially-divided society" ("Locked Heart" 83–84). Both the thrown stone and the tossed-off gossip are childish acts that speak to deeper wounds, larger injustices. Indeed, it is by repeating the gossip of adults that Tia comes to assimilate—and to educate Antoinette about—the racial divisions that define their world, just as it is through a symbolic, mutually painful act of violence that she finally underscores the inaccessibility of her world to Antoinette.

The social scrutiny indistinctly perceived—but acutely felt—by the young Antoinette is far clearer to her mother, Annette, who quarrels again and again with her husband, Mr. Mason, over the islanders' hatred of her:

> "The people here hate us. They certainly hate me." Straight out she said that one day and it was then he laughed so heartily.
>
> "Annette, be reasonable. You were the widow of a slave-owner, the daughter of a slave-owner, and you had been living here alone, with two children, for nearly five years when we met. Things were at their worst then. But you were never molested, never harmed."
>
> "How do you know that I was not harmed?" she said. "We were so poor then," she told him, "we were something to laugh at. But we are not poor now," she said. "You are not a poor man. Do you suppose that they don't know all about your estate in Trinidad? And the Antigua property? They talk about us without stopping. They invent stories about you, and lies about me. They try to find out what we eat every day."
>
> "They are curious. It's natural enough. You have lived alone far too long, Annette. You imagine enmity which doesn't exist. Always one extreme or the other." (19)

The marital row encapsulates a key theme in Rhys's treatment of gossip: not only that it is dangerous but also that it is dangerous in ways beyond the comprehension of English visitors and more easily grasped by those who identify with the Caribbean rather than the colonizing power. Mason, like Rochester, represents what Hulme calls the "white English 'norm,'" while Annette is both Creole and Martiniquan and is "therefore alien to the 'English' creole of Jamaica" (80). Her outsider status (from the perspective of Mason, himself an outsider in the Caribbean, but also from that of the Jamaicans) makes her the target of gossip but also gives her a more acute understanding of the risks inherent in being ostracized. Indeed, islanders of all races and classes really are chattering maliciously about the Mason household, from the "idiot" son to the "six-foot snake" on their privy seat, with special venom reserved for Annette, "a widow without a penny to her name" (17). The couple's argument continues, with Mr. Mason resorting to casually racist clichés to justify his position:

"They're too damn lazy to be dangerous," said Mr Mason. "I know that."

"They are more alive than you are, lazy or not, and they can be dangerous and cruel for reasons you wouldn't understand."

"No, I don't understand," Mr Mason always said. "I don't understand at all." (19)

Mason's facile profession of incomprehension—transmuted by the word "always" into something weightier than a mere attempt to extricate himself from a marital tiff—underscores his own status as an outsider and his basic indifference to the reality of the colony where he temporarily resides. If he is reluctant to leave Jamaica, it is because, in a sense, he never really arrived: where his wife understands and fears gossip, Mason has simply established a quiet outpost of his own English reality, in which he dwells with neither understanding of nor interest in the islanders' malicious chatter.

Such episodes prefigure the alienation and incomprehension that give rise to Antoinette's later betrayal by Rochester.[18] Daniel Cosway's letter, itself a remarkable piece of epistolary gossip, tells Rochester that *"the truth is better than a lie"* and that he has been *"shamefully deceived"* (56). Cosway rattles off a litany of bits of gossip and family lore, all explicitly framed as a true account set in opposition to the prevailing narrative to which Rochester has hitherto been privy. *"They tell you perhaps that your wife's name is Cosway [. . .] but they don't tell you what sort of people were these Cosways,"* Cosway writes, continuing:

> There is madness in that family. Old Cosway die raving like his father before him.
>
> [. . .] Her father and mine was a shameless man [. . .].
>
> [. . .] Ask the older people sir about his disgusting goings on, some will remember.
>
> When Madam his wife die the reprobate marry again quick, to a young girl from Martinique—it's too much for him. Dead drunk from morning till night and he die raving and cursing. (56–57)

Cosway repeatedly claims reluctance or unwillingness to speak—he writes only *"after long thought and meditation"* (56)—before going on to disclose juicy details, in a rhetorical gesture that echoes the performative patterns of spoken gossip. He writes of Annette's marriage to Mr. Mason, for instance, that *"there is much I could say about that but you won't believe so I shut my mouth"* before immediately going on to reveal, *"They say he love her so much that if he have the world on a plate he give it to her—but no use. The madness gets worse and she has to be shut away for she try to kill her husband—madness not being all either"* (57–58). Like most gossips, Cosway claims inside knowledge of his subject matter, thanks to his supposed status as Antoinette's half brother; still, his parentage remains an open question, and he later admits to having had limited contact with his purported family.[19] It is clear that much of what he writes is actually sourced from gossip; he repeatedly refers to what *"they say,"* and indeed some of his claims directly echo the gossip that Tia once relayed about Antoinette's family. *"Nobody would work for the young woman and her two children and that place Coulibri goes quickly to bush,"* he writes. *"She have no money and she have no friends"* (57). Cosway reports, too, that he wrote his letter in response to island-hopping gossip about Rochester's marriage: *"News travel even to this wild place and next thing I hear from Jamaica is that old Mason is dead and that family plan to marry the girl to a young Englishman who know nothing of her"* (58). And it is to gossip that Cosway repeatedly turns to validate his account: "Still you don't believe me? *Then ask that devil of a man Richard Mason three questions and make him answer you. [. . .] If he keep his mouth shut ask others for many think it shameful how that family treat you and your relatives"* (59). Later, his first letter having been ignored, Cosway repeats: *"You don't believe me? Then ask someone else—everybody in Spanish Town know"* (71). The secrets he discloses are in fact common knowledge, inaccessible only to Rochester, the English outsider with whom nobody gossips.

Cosway himself misreads Rochester; his second letter strikes a more threatening tone—*"You want me to come to your house and bawl out your business before everybody?"* (71)—and when the pair finally meet, Rochester rebuffs Cosway's clumsy attempt at blackmail. Still, Cosway's allegations unsettle Rochester. As Veronica Gregg remarks, Cosway's letter has been largely ignored by critics, and viewed as little more than a device for stoking Rochester's suspicions about his wife. Certainly, the letter has that effect; still, its gossip also serves a broader function: not just fueling Rochester's doubts but serving to stage his alienation and—much like Mr. Mason—his fundamental incomprehension of the "dangerous and cruel," and epistemologically unstable, reality he now inhabits. He reaches out to Antoinette after speaking with Cosway, asking whether there is "another side" to the story, and she gives him the only honest answer possible: "There is always the other side, always" (77). For Handley, Antoinette's awareness of and tolerance for uncertainty is "a cognition that the novel ultimately values as more truthful" than Rochester's conviction that the truth is something "knowable and something to be subjugated" (*Postslavery* 158). But Antoinette's understanding of the truth as relative and plural is of little consolation to Rochester, raised on the easy certainties of empire. As Gregg notes, Cosway's story "as told to the Englishman cannot be disproved. It can only be denied or disbelieved" (114). The truth of the matter, in other words, emerges as a social construct; it is accessible only by weighing partial, agenda-driven, and self-motivated accounts. This renders it inaccessible to Rochester's drier, more positivist approach; perhaps inevitably, his doubts, irresolvable and festering, lead him to distance himself from his wife. Christophine tries to explain to Antoinette the effect that local gossip is having on her husband. "Plenty people fasten bad words on you and on your mother. I know it. I know who is talking and what they say," Christophine says. "The man not bad man [. . .] but he hear so many stories he don't know what to believe. That is why he keep away. I put no trust in none of those people round you. Not here, not in Jamaica" (68). Terrified of being deceived, Rochester falls prey to deceit; his belief in the power of secrets—which is also a belief in the existence of a hidden truth, fixed and irrevocable—makes him vulnerable to and unable to parse the multitude of lies and half-truths to which he now finds himself exposed.

Rochester's descent into suspicion and uncertainty is underpinned by and fuels his increasing "othering" of both Antoinette and of the Caribbean itself. Majumdar suggests that Rochester's initial fetishization of the exotic slips into something more troubling: "Rochester falls prey to the desire for a world which, with its 'otherness,' lies beyond his grasp and thwarts the authority of imperialism as the standard of absolute value" (112). As discussed in the previous chapter, gossip here marks the fissure lines in a failing community and reveals the unbridgeable gaps—and the power dynamics at play—between Creole and English-born, between colonizer and colonized, between races.[20] But it also marks the epistemological rifts inherent in, and perhaps responsible for, the atomized community that it portrays. Rochester's European positivism is of little assistance as he picks his way through the threatening, overgrown and ant-infested forests of Dominica: "How can one discover truth I thought and that thought led me nowhere. No one would tell me the truth," he complains (62). Increasingly, he becomes convinced that Antoinette, or the Caribbean itself, has access to more exotic epistemologies, inaccessible to the British visitor. "I was certain that everything I had imagined to be truth was false. False," he confesses. "Only the magic and the dream are true—all the rest's a lie. Let it go. Here is the secret. Here. *(But it is lost, that secret, and those who know it cannot tell it.)*" (100–101). It is the desire to cling to this fleeting, secret truth—this realization that, as Helen Lock writes, there are "competing epistemologies" at play (101)—that leads him to resent and ultimately lock up Antoinette. Rochester, Lock continues, has been literally "changed 'out of all knowledge'; his epistemology has failed him, yet he is unable to comprehend an alternative" (103). The real breakdown, Lock argues, is Rochester's, for it is Rochester who comes to equate a hidden secret with both his wife and the Caribbean they call home.

There is an irony to this: Rochester, so uncomprehending of gossip, both fears scandal and relies on gossip to validate his suspicions about his wife. As the narrative arcs back to England, Rochester seeks to prevent chatter about his own family secret; still, as Rhys makes clear, gossip is not something that occurs only in the Caribbean. At Thornfield Hall, Mrs. Eff tries in vain to clamp down on the gossip of the household servants, even threatening to dismiss those who continue to gossip: *"Next day Mrs Eff wanted to see me and she complained about gossip,"* recounts Grace Poole. *"I don't allow gossip. I told you that when you came. Servants will talk and you can't stop them, I said"* (105). Indeed, the impossibility of stamping out or prohibiting gossip is apparent to everyone. *"Then all the servants were sent away and she engaged a cook, one maid and you, Leah. They were sent away but how could she stop them talking?"* Poole asks. *"If you ask me the whole county knows. The rumours I've heard—very far from the truth. But I don't contradict, I know better than to say a word"* (105). Poole refers, almost in the same breath, to the potency of gossip, to its frequent inaccuracy, and to the hopelessness of seeking to correct or contain the spread of rumors. Even the ruling classes, for all the power they wield over their servants cannot "stop them talking" once the talking has begun.

As in the Caribbean, gossip here serves to stage the mutual resentment and lack of trust between social classes. But if Rhys presents gossip as a form of counterdiscourse, a space in which the marginalized can obtain a degree of narrative agency, she does not shy away from the challenges such narrative clashes present for the parsing of truth and falsehood. Like Ferré, she presents her narrative through multivocal, sometimes contradictory accounts that are peppered with gossip. "As if piecing together bits of gossip, the reader must puzzle alone for the information behind these statements and attitudes," Colette Lindroth writes. "The reader, like Antoinette herself, must decipher hints, overheard whispers, snatches of distant conversation, gossip, and speculation to determine the direction of the narrative" (88). Rhys stops short of denying the reality or accessibility of truth: the puzzles she leaves for her reader are not as fundamental or all-encompassing as the uncertainties embedded in Ferré's refractive, contingent text. Still, she allows Antoinette to grasp the truth and understand something of its limits—"It is always too late for truth," she thinks (69)—and also to intuit that ultimately suspicion and belief, not truth, will determine her fate. Like Ferré, Rhys challenges her reader to look beyond the text's apparent truths and epistemological signposts, as though to signal not just the insufficiency of the master narrative against which she writes but also the difficulties inherent in seeking a single, definitive version of what is true and what is false—what is mirage and what is reality—in the colonial and postcolonial Caribbean.

Seductive Stories: *Célanire cou-coupé*

Much like Ferré and Rhys, the Guadeloupean writer Maryse Condé is attuned to the epistemological challenges and possibilities of gossip.[21] Her novel *Célanire cou-coupé* (2000) is told by an ostensibly omniscient narrator who frequently provides the reader with startling insights—presented in a remarkably matter-of-fact way—into the thoughts and indiscretions of the novel's various characters. King Koffi Ndizi is unfazed by Hakim's sexual preferences, the reader is casually informed, because he once shared them: "He was not ignorant of his inclinations, but viewed them indulgently, having groped a number of boys in his youth. Along with incest, sodomy is a king's privilege" (22). In the same breath, the narrator informs us of Ndizi's long-running plot to overthrow Thomas de Brabant, the governor's deputy. "Koffi Ndizi and Hakim had tried to hide a mamba in one of his desk drawers and also to bribe his cook to poison his meals," we learn. "One time, they had buried a doll that looked like him in the guts of a black cat. Nothing!" (22). The relaying of the details of acts kept utterly secret by their perpetrators suggests the narrator to be all-knowing—but in the first pages of the novel, the limits of the narrator's knowledge are also quickly brought into focus: "At the moment when this story begins," the narrator states, then interjects: "(but is it the beginning? Where is the beginning? Who can say!)" (14–15). The narrator explicitly questions his or her own monopoly on narrative authority and often does so, moreover, by deferring to another form of authority: common knowledge, gossip, and speculation. The narrator clearly has privileged insights, but for the full picture such insights are worth no more, and perhaps much less, than opinions circulating through the grapevine. This is a pattern that repeats, in various ways, throughout Condé's novel:

despite appearing to have unfettered access to the deeds, memories, and motivations of the novel's characters, the narrator frequently delves into murkier spaces, recounting, re-creating, and even coming to rely upon the hunches and intuitions that circulate, in the form of rumor and gossip, among an extensive supporting cast of villagers and townsfolk.

Acts of gossip are seldom shown in detail in *Célanire;* rather, they are stipulated or taken for granted. We see individuals gossiping but rarely learn the content of their chatter: when Thomas de Brabant dines with senior officials and clergy, for instance, we simply learn that they "drank too much, and gossiped ferociously" (59); similarly, when Hakim and Betti Bouah meet, they swap "the latest gossip" (52). This opacity also extends to the gossip of unnamed figures: in the public parks, mothers spend their time "whispering secrets and the latest gossip to one another" (170–71); in the Peruvian bar where Amparo and Yang Ting meet "the chatter was non-stop" (223), and in the ship aboard which Célanire and Thomas head home, the female passengers "badmouthed each other" (235). Inasmuch as we learn the content of gossip and rumor, it is typically presented in the aggregate, without attribution to specific speakers. Tales of the governor's failings, from his lackluster public-work projects to his struggles with his weight, are "whispered everywhere" (194), but we never learn by whom. Consider, too, the moment in which Célanire first returns to Guadeloupe:

> Throughout the land the same whisper went up. Incredible but true! Célanire, Célanire was back! What could have brought her back? Did she not know her countrymen? Did she not know that they would not be able to resist exhuming the corpse of a rape that had caused such a stir at the time, and of gorging themselves again and again on its filth? No matter that she had become the wife of the governor: she and her husband would find themselves sullied. Unless she was back to add a few final touches to all the evil she had previously done? In any case, this return did not bode well. (139–40)

We hear the words spoken, but without attribution or context; the effect is of a collective voice, perpetually murmuring in the background, as though gossip percolates up through, or serves to mediate, the collective consciousness and common knowledge of the community.[22]

In this sense, the gossip of *Célanire* serves as an oral grapevine, reinforcing and defining communal ties through the transmission of news and information. This notion of gossip as a form of news service is widespread in the Caribbean: consider the *radio-bois-patate* and *télédiol* of the Francophone Caribbean, which Jarrod Hayes aptly terms "an alternative mode of truth production" and a fundamental narrative building block in the region's literature (322); Cuba's "Radio Bemba," which evolved from guerrilla radio broadcasts into a rich network of both political information and celebrity gossip; or the Trinidadian word of mouth described by Elizabeth Nunez in *Bruised Hibiscus* (2000). Nunez's novel begins by tracing the spread of news about a body's discovery: "There was an intricate network of people who could be counted on—men's women, women's men, husbands, wives, mothers, fathers, daughters, sons, brothers, sisters, aunts, uncles, friends—who passed the word from mouth to mouth as they thought they should; news too sensational, too shocking to keep to themselves, news it was their duty to share" (4–5). News acquired through the grapevine supplements and in some cases replaces news from official sources: Cedric turns to gossip to confirm his hunch that a murdered woman was white, despite newspaper reports to the contrary. Nunez shows gossip from the viewpoint of its recipient, as an interpretive process informed by one's presuppositions and prejudices, rather than as a source of objective or necessarily reliable information. Rosa, Cedric's wife, chooses to believe contradictory rumors blaming the killing on Boysie Singh, a real-life gangster; her friend Zuela, meanwhile, dismisses the gossip about Singh and concludes that the killing was actually a crime of passion.[23]

In *Célanire,* characters similarly rely on information gleaned through quick-traveling gossip—not necessarily accurate, but always compelling—to navigate their community and their relations with others, and frequently turn to gossip in their efforts to find out more about the various enigmas in which Célanire herself is embroiled. Some of the news thus transmitted is relatively banal: the details of Tonine's funeral are "spread by word of mouth like wildfire," prompting all who hear to attend (203). Elsewhere, the grapevine transmits the kinds of scandals and bedroom secrets in which gossip often deals: "some good souls" inform Amarante that Célanire "was now carrying on publicly with Élissa de Kerdoré" (176). In other instances, gossip is shown as a repository of past knowledge: upon hearing of Célanire's affair with Élissa, Amarante recalls "the old gossip: they whispered that, in her childhood, Célanire had caused the death of Ofusan, just as she had caused the downfall of Dr. Pinceau. And who knows what else?" (177). Similarly, Yang Ting's murder is kept in people's memory through their gossip: "In Lima, people still talk about the story" and "if you go for a drink at Juanito's in Barranca, or at Brisas del Titicaca near the Plaza Bolognesi, they will tell you the story and add many unverifiable details" (222–23). Even the location and brutality of

Yang Ting's murder are thus memorialized, through rumors that the room where the crime took place is haunted: "Soon the rumor spread everywhere, and nobody wanted to live there" (224).[24] As the transmission of details surrounding Yang Ting's death reveals, the novel's gossip and rumors may be a source of news or background knowledge, but are no slaves to the truth; they promise useful information, certainly, but also deal in distortions, "unverifiable details," and even ghost stories.

Gossip of this sort is news, then, but news with a splash of something more intoxicating and seductive. Besides being a potent informational resource, the free-flowing gossip of *Célanire* is also highly performative, with embellishment and bias portrayed not as defects but rather as intrinsic parts of the narratives being woven. Though grounded in a private act of speech, gossip aggregates into something public: it can become a spectacle, even a spectator sport. To gossip can be a private act, entered into with the expectation of confidentiality—but, as we will see in the next chapter, it can also be to participate in a chain of communication, with the implicit expectation that what one says will be repeated, amplified, and even broadcast throughout the community. This, again, is a feature rather than a bug: some kinds of gossip, at least, can be furtive without being secretive and can be shared with an eye to a broader audience. For gossip of this sort, which makes up much of the gossip of *Célanire*, the more spectacular the revelation, the better; truth, or at least plausibility, still matters, but it matters markedly less than the startling or salacious quality of the tale being told. Indeed, this seductive aspect is perhaps a part of the reason that *Célanire*'s narrator is repeatedly drawn back to gossip. The facts matter, and the narrator strives to return to them, but the circulating stories are simply too juicy not to recount—and once the narrator begins to share them, they become almost impossible to set aside, even at the risk of losing track of what is true and what is false.

In this way, the pursuit of the spectacular can lead gossip to become a speculative form, dealing not just in what is actually known but in what is merely supposed or suspected. We are delving, here, into the territory described by C. A. J. Coady as a "pathology of testimony." Rumors and myths may be false, Coady argues, but gossip—nonpathological gossip, at least—"is standardly sincere, and may be true and known to be true" (253); indeed, to knowingly spread falsehoods through gossip, he argues, is to engage in an act that has transcended (or sunk beneath the level of) what may properly be termed gossip. "To my ear, the phrase 'lying gossip' does not ring true; the more accurate description of the activity is just 'spreading lies,'" he asserts (263). What Coady sees as a pathology, however, I view as fundamental to gossip, which depends for its validation not on hard facts, but rather on its plausibility: not on factual truth but rather on an affective alignment with the emotional needs and preexisting prejudices of its participants. Olive Senior—a writer who freely declares herself a gossip—notes that gossip "presupposes a loop that connects teller to listener, binding both to the subject of the story" with the "ultimate judgement [. . .] based not on veracity but believability" ("Writer as Gossip" 49–50). Speculative gossip is, in *Célanire,* a way of giving voice to the hunches, suspicions, and slanderous suppositions that bubble beneath the surface of the community; it is at once a negotiation and an affirmation of the group's collective judgment of a situation. Crucially, however, gossip seldom if ever acknowledges that it has drifted away from the pursuit of pure factuality; even as it gives way to speculation and prejudice, gossip typically continues to insist upon its own truthfulness and remains a space in which common knowledge is delineated and transmitted. It is, in short, a space in which speculation can give rise to claims that are communally accepted as truths—and that, once accepted, are seldom reexamined. As Condé's novel shows, gossip, for all its bias and embellishments, can thus cohere and weave itself into a community's stock of common knowledge: in its partisanship, it offers a morally and ideologically clear map of the community, even if in so doing it undermines or displaces more accurate accounts of the events it describes.

A part of the process whereby the factual schemas proposed through gossip come to dominate the public discourse and cement themselves as "common knowledge" is by seeking to exclude those who refuse to participate in gossip. As previously discussed, to exist outside the realm of gossip is to be fundamentally othered: not simply a member of the in-group or the out-group but a member of no group at all. When Melody testifies against Papa Doc, it is the lack of gossip about her that proves most unsettling and serves to undermine her claims.[25] "Where did this Melody come from, whose testimony had condemned me?" Papa Doc wonders. "Nobody had seen her, nobody knew her. Before working for me, she had not been in the service of any good family. Neither in Grande-Terre nor Basse-Terre had anyone ever seen her before" (123). But Célanire herself also exists in this liminal space, distancing herself from the community's gossip and effectively othering herself as a form of self-assertion: "She had never shared their simple enthusiasms, their excitements, or their fears. When they confided secrets to each other, she covered her ears" (16). Here, Célanire is shown as actively distancing herself from the intimacy and complicity that are crucial for communal bonds. In a corresponding gesture, meanwhile, she actively cultivates or seeks to provoke gossip about her scar, knowingly stoking speculation by concealing it from view:

> Of course, there was always that rotten handkerchief knotted tightly around her neck. What did it hide? The most fantastic explanations took root and circulated. At sixteen, Célanire had been disfigured by a crazed lover that she had spurned. He splashed acid at her eyes, but in his rage his hand trembled and he caught her throat. That occurred in an African country several years before she married Thomas. Thomas, who was then governor, had used his position to have the guy transported to a penal colony. Doubtless, he was there still. Or they insisted that in her childhood her head had been all but ripped off with a skipping rope, and sewn back on by a surgeon in Guadeloupe who had then raped her. And so on and so forth . . . One can see that the common thread in all this gossip, where pieces of truth had been crassly stitched to bits of fable, was that Célanire was a woman who should be handled with caution. (237–38)

The public narrative, like Célanire herself, is a patched-together creation, a Frankenstein's monster, and by making herself the subject of gossip Célanire ultimately gains a measure of respect. Indeed, Betti Bouah is reduced to childlike fear by Célanire's scarf, which he suspects conceals "the mark showing that she was the 'horse' of dangerous aawabo" (48). The mark Bouah believes Célanire to carry is an intimate secret—examples of other such marks include warts and fused toes—of the kind typically interrogated through gossip, but by covering her throat Célanire assumes an active role in inciting and steering the circulating gossip. "The dread she provokes stems mainly from this scar's invisibility, from an unconfirmed suspicion that Célanire is hiding a 'secret terrible,'" notes Nicole Simek. "Her 'monstrosity' lies in this interpretive instability, as well as in her control over those who would 'read' meaning into her scar" (105). Célanire manipulates the gossip about her, or at least the information available to the gossips, as a means of asserting her own agency, and her independence from and indifference to the community's moral judgments.

But while Célanire can control, to an extent, the facts that she discloses, she can do little to stanch the slow drip of pure speculation that, throughout *Célanire,* emerges with little or no factual basis, is repeated as gossip, and gradually becomes accepted as "fact" by the community as a whole. Condé's *roman fantastique* is rife with examples of lurid speculation—often concerning Célanire's purported monstrosity—being disseminated through gossip and becoming accepted as factual accounts of the events in question.[26] After a cleaner gossips about Célanire's homosexual liaisons, for instance, sinister tales begin to spread:

A hunter who had gone deep into the woods to catch thrushes and ortolans claimed that before dawn he had run into Célanire, who seemed to be waiting, sitting under a wild cherry tree, her lips smeared with blood. [. . .] She chased him, so he climbed to the top of an ebony tree. She apparently did not know how to climb trees, and in a rage had paced up and down at the base of the tree. This show had lasted until sun-up, when she had bolted off back to Ravine-Vilaine.

Given such gossip, the good that Célanire was doing passed unnoticed. (206)

In this remarkable passage, the narrator reflects on how gossip's seductive quality overpowers other narratives that, though potentially more accurate, are less flashy and less fascinating to the listener. The narrator attempts to retain some distance—it is only what a hunter "claimed," and what "apparently" happened—but nonetheless passes along and helps to perpetuate the gossip. Célanire's supposed bestial transformation recalls an earlier episode in which a nurse claims to have seen Célanire shedding her body just as a snake sheds its skin: "One night while the rain and wind were rattling the shutters, she had gone unexpectedly into her room and seen, before the wide-open window, a small pile of soft, shapeless flesh and skin. Hidden behind a closet, she witnessed the return of the young woman during the small hours of the morning. Her mouth smeared with blood, she had squeezed herself back into her fleshy trappings and calmly returned to bed" (84–85). The narrator insists that we should dismiss this gossip as mere superstition: "Can one really believe such nonsense and badmouthing?" (85). But the narrator immediately undercuts this dismissal of the gossip: "One thing that wasn't a lie was that in the June session, the Home put forward six candidates, of whom four were girls, for the native certificate of elementary studies. They all passed, even the girls[. . . .] In everyone's eyes, the quick transformation of the Home reeked of pure witchcraft." (85). The superstitious "nonsense and badmouthing" is followed by facts, presented as indisputable, which rhetorically one would expect to serve as a counterpoint to the gossip. In fact, however, the new details support the common view that Célanire is in fact embroiled in some kind of witchcraft and that her success can only be explained through black magic. Gossip here appears to overcome the narrator's own better judgment and begins to infiltrate their supposedly factual account.[27]

There are other notable occasions when *Célanire*'s narrator suggests that it is possible to discern the truth or falsehood of the gossip on display but then explicitly fails, or refuses, to do so. In describing Célanire's recuperation, for instance, the narrator disavows any privileged insights into the specifics of her treatment, falling back on a more probabilistic approach to the facts of the matter: "We don't know whether Madame Eusebio gave Célanire the medication recommended by Doctor Iago Lamella," the narrator admits. "Cod-liver oil? Shots of camphorated oil? Hardly likely! She did whatever entered her head!" (236). Crucially, the narrator then goes on to describe in far more detail, and with far more certainty, the nature of the meals prepared for Célanire by Madame Eusebio: "Because we do know with certainty, down to the last detail, the diet that she made her follow. Twice a day she would go down into the heat of the kitchens, tie an apron around herself, and prepare her patient's tray. The most outlandish stories circulated about her behavior, spread by the cooks and the kitchen boys. For them, without a doubt, Madame Eusebio was a bruja, like those of the southern coast of Peru. Rather than milk, she needed blood, more blood, always blood" (236). The passage effaces the boundary between knowledge and speculation, between fact and gossip. We are told that we can "know with certainty" what Célanire ate, but having promised facts, the narrator steps back to describe her diet through the "outlandish stories" and insinuations of witchcraft that circulate among the kitchen staff. The slippage is significant: the narrator, the storyteller from whom the reader's own knowledge derives, appears to have been lulled by the rhythms of gossip into forgoing "certainty" and choosing dramatic hearsay over dry facts.

This concept of choice is significant and serves as a reminder that the knowledge built up through gossip is less monolithic than its ubiquity might suggest. Gossip is not a means of imposing a fixed narrative onto a community but rather a means for communities to negotiate, or try to negotiate, consensual ways of knowing.[28] In *Célanire* we typically see the effects of this process, rather than the process itself at work; still, there are hints at the negotiations continually being effected through gossip. In some moments, the narrator makes clear that the opinions being shared have not yet reached the level of a consensus. As *Célanire* concludes, for instance, the people of the island are troubled to see lychee trees bearing fruit before their proper season, and arrive at wildly divergent conclusions: "What did such an abundance presage? Surely, a series of catastrophes. Given that March was not hurricane season, some peered over at La Soufrière. It is true that, after several weeks, it was once again letting out fumes, foul-smelling like farts. Others remembered that it was the tenth anniversary of an earthquake that had reduced La Pointe to rubble. Discordant voices insisted that on the contrary, the lychees heralded good fortune" (241). There is little sign of the speculation settling into a consensus; we are simply presented with contradictory interpretations of the event's significance. Similarly, the consensuses arrived at through rumor and gossip are at times shown as being restricted to subgroups of the community: one event "deeply shocked the Africans," while another "stunned both Blacks and Whites," with the narrator's insistence on racial group identity serving as a reminder that even convergent opinions do not always efface the perceived boundaries between groups (92–93).[29] These divisions and fault lines highlight gossip's status as a means of delineating group beliefs, but also of cohering and defining subgroups through the differences in opinion arrived at and articulated through gossip.

Celia Britton traces a similar strategy in Édouard Glissant's *Malemort* (1975), in which the narrative is conveyed through reported speech, generating a refractive effect that dilutes the authority of any individual version. For Britton, "The plurality of discourses is crucial to Glissant's promotion of diversity against the domination of a single universalizing truth" (*Glissant* 168). Similarly, Valérie Loichot writes that for Glissant, "the intermingled voices are those of the community. They mix, dissolve, and clash in the person of a 'nous,' allowing the reconstruction of a clearly Caribbean voice" (73). But where Glissant's narrator defers to the voices of others in order to cultivate polyphony, Condé's narrator appears torn between the urge to deliver firsthand, ostensibly objective knowledge of the type a reader expects from an omniscient narrator and the desire to tap into the circulating narrative, grounded in gossip and commingled with superstition, that represents the social consensus about the events and people in question. What we read in *Célanire*, then, is not the "reconstruction of a clearly Caribbean voice" but rather the convulsions of a people struggling to maintain a collective voice, a collective identity, in the face of individuals and actions that do not fit neatly into existing moral or factual schemas.

The gossip that bubbles through *Célanire*, then, is not merely informational, and does not serve solely to assert community or group membership, but is also an interpretive challenge. This is an aspect of the text, if not of its gossip, that has been remarked before: Simek highlights the "dizzying mélange of parodic techniques" at work in *Célanire*, which she asserts function to make Célanire's identity "*incomprehensible,* in the etymological sense of something that cannot be contained within the normative parameters of categorization or representation" (258). As Simek rightly notes, the fracturing of the narrator's authority in the novel's first pages serves as a signpost that warns the reader of the interpretive difficulties that lie ahead. Similarly, Dawn Fulton writes convincingly of the ways in which conflicting accounts of characters' deaths generate a "heightened interpretive tension" as divergent tellings are "forced to occupy the same discursive space" (106–7). Célanire herself is the focal point of a similar tension, Fulton continues, with her cultivated opacity rendering those around her unsure of her true nature and ultimately leading them to view her as monstrous. "Versions and explanations conflict, firsthand accounts of her behavior meld into rumor and exaggeration, and interpretation vacillates with shifts in audience," Fulton writes (104). Indeed, she argues, the text itself becomes a "monstrous" narrative, with disparate versions from various sources patched together into a discomfiting and piecemeal narrative. "The narrative is thus 'monstrous' in the sense that it does not represent a coherent whole through the lens of any particular interpretive context," Fulton writes (105). Fulton's reading is accurate, but one can add that gossip is the common thread running through many of these fragments of information and interpretation. The epistemological challenge that Fulton traces in Condé's work manifests not just in the diverging episodes that Fulton analyzes but also runs deeper, as the text's narrator alternates between presenting an omniscient perspective on the events described and sharing the other versions that have crystallized in the town's gossip.

The seepage of gossip into a purportedly objective and omniscient narratorial account reflects the difficulties inherent in telling stories about a community so immersed in the stories it tells about itself. Is it more accurate, more truthful, to focus on objective facts and ignore the lived reality, or realities, reflected in a community's gossip? Or is it better to report the speculations, exaggerations, and embellishments taken as true by a community's members, even at the cost of twisting or overshadowing the more mundane "true" version of events? To what extent, furthermore, can a narrator make a fair judgment between these two approaches, given the seductive power of gossip and the temptation to tell listeners not just true stories but captivating ones? And ultimately, in such a setting, what does it mean to have knowledge? Condé herself offers no solution to these epistemological challenges; indeed, she shrugs off the question and asserts that *Célanire* "is really a book that has nothing to teach people, that one can understand as one chooses. It has whatever meaning one wants it to have" ("A Conversation" 12). This is in keeping with her broader project; as J. Michael Dash notes with reference to *La traversée de la mangrove* (1989), Condé's work is driven by an "inexorable skepticism" that makes her "one of the quintessential practitioners of postmodern narrative in the

Caribbean." The titular mangrove—itself read by Hayes as a metaphor for the narrative's gossipy structure—is impossible to ford or navigate. "Consequently," Dash writes, "no totalizing system or master narrative is possible in such a world" (*Other America* 120).

Gossip, in this reading, once more recalls Coady's notion of a "pathology of testimony," in that it not only fails to provide access to objective truths but in fact impedes access to such truths. The narrator is faced with the unresolved challenge of both presenting facts and adequately representing the stories that circulate in the community. In this sense, Condé presents speculative gossip as a way not of approaching epistemic truths but rather of interrogating the psychological truths of individuals, and the shared truths by which the community defines itself and inscribes its own understanding of the truth. Gossip may not itself always present the truth, Condé's novel asserts, but no story can be complete, or fully truthful, without acknowledging the myriad speculative and revealing narratives that circulate through gossip.

Gossip and Investigation: *La fascinación de la víctima*

The texts examined thus far in this chapter deploy gossip as a means of highlighting the epistemological challenges of the contemporary Caribbean and view the region through a postmodernist lens: gossip, in its plurality and its multiple perspectives, is seen as speaking to the refractive and contingent nature of truth itself. Still, some writers do seek to show gossip as a possible solution to, rather than simply an expression or allegorization of, such challenges. In the preface to *Falsas crónicas del sur* (1991) Ana Lydia Vega claims to have woven her short stories from the oral traditions of the coastal towns of the Puerto Rican south. Indeed, several of Vega's introductory notes acknowledge the stories' roots in "Radio Bemba" (162) and "oral tradition in its street form of town gossip" (174). Vega remarks: "In this geography configured by sugarcane and the sea, beneath plants that hang like garlands from electric cables, the public and the intimate, for better or worse, are confusingly intertwined" (162). The confusion is inescapable, Vega argues, but the "protean multiplicity of events" (1) traced by gossip maps the connections that define communities, and can still reveal something meaningful about the nature (and knowledge) of the community in question.

Abilio Estévez's *Inventario secreto de La Habana* (2004) similarly reports several stories purportedly sourced from gossip, claiming that "to speak of Havana one must speak of its *malas lenguas*," or evil tongues

(111).[30] Unlike Vega, who tends to highlight gossip's playfulness and its informational value, Estévez repeatedly stresses gossip's maliciousness, claiming that "in Havana, all tongues are viperine" (113). But while Estévez foregrounds both his disdain for and apparent distrust of gossip, his inclusion of gossip as a source mirrors Vega's and similarly affirms gossip's value as a means of reconstructing stories that might otherwise be forgotten. Here again, gossip's questionable veracity does not necessarily render it less useful or diminish its ability to communicate significant truths about the society in which it circulates. Both Vega and Estévez take a rather impressionistic approach that allows them to sidestep some of gossip's thornier epistemological challenges. The truth or falsehood of a specific bit of gossip matters less, they propose, than the simple fact that regardless of its epistemic reliability, gossip offers valuable insights into stories circulating in a given time and place.

Still, some writers go further, suggesting that gossip can nonetheless serve as a reliable means of uncovering and ascertaining specific facts. This, certainly, is the case in *La fascinación de la víctima,* a 2008 novel by the Venezuelan writer Ana Teresa Torres, in which the protagonist, a psychoanalyst turned sleuth named Elvira Madigan, uses gossip as a potent investigative tool while she navigates a corrupt and toothless judicial system and ultimately successfully solves a murder. Madigan's inquiries begin when a patient, Adriana Budenbrook, seeks help coping with her sister's murder. Adriana is convinced that her grief can be assuaged only by learning the truth about the murder—it is, Madigan quickly perceives, "more a case of who did it and why, than the need for personal help" (11)—and to fulfill her duties as a therapist, Madigan increasingly assumes the role of private investigator. In fusing these roles, Torres's novel reflects on the epistemological and narrative connections between the psychoanalytic process and the detective story—a kinship Freud understood and one that has been well explored in the scholarship of Peter Brooks and others. In *La fascinación,* however, psychoanalysis and detection bear fruit only when brought into conjunction with gossip, which is presented as an equally valid and potent investigative method. The most significant clues that Madigan uncovers are arrived at and interpreted through gossip: she reconstructs the killing through secrets disclosed by others, and the novel's narrative is propelled forward by the incremental discovery, through intimate, dyadic conversations, of new perspectives on a decades-long, still-unfolding story.

In this way, *La fascinación* presents gossip as a relatively benign social practice, transmitting valuable and largely reliable knowledge about a community's members, rather than as the narrative power struggle presented in *Maldito amor* and *Wide Sargasso Sea,* or the barbed and speculative communal judgments shown in *Célanire.* That is not to say that the gossip of *La fascinación* is not adversarial, or that it has bated edges: the gossip Madigan hears is still an act of violation, insofar as it is the revelation of facts that its subject wished to keep secret. Still, Madigan's interlocutors are not chiefly concerned with twisting the facts to their advantage; rather, they seek to obtain a measure of fleeting and perhaps largely symbolic power through the act of violation itself, by claiming the right to reveal the private stories of others. This is clear, for instance, when Adriana's father, Adrian, is accused of killing Adriana's half sister. His business partner, Leo Altman, declares that "he killed her. [. . .] Adrian could not accept a daughter who would sully his life" (275) and tells Madigan she has given him "the chance I have waited for my entire life. [. . .] The chance to say out loud that Adrian Budenbrook was a murderer" (276). In soliciting information, Madigan gives something to her interlocutors: there is a power in the sharing of gossip, a power in the act of denunciation—and, as the passage shows, a power that is realized when latent, unspoken knowledge is reified in the act of disclosure. If the gossip of *Maldito amor* is specific, self-serving, and urgent and the gossip of *Célanire* is diffuse, always simmering in the background, then the gossip of *La fascinación* lies somewhere between the two: it is less explicitly self-interested than the gossip of Ferré's novel and less obliquely presented than that of Condé's text but exists as a tangible presence, foregrounded and shown directly as a constant of social interactions that offer real utility to both listener and speaker.

It is these social interactions that drive the novel forward: Madigan does not so much interrogate her witnesses as simply chat with them, with traditional evidence replaced by personal insights obtained through acts of gossip. One of Madigan's chief sources, Aída Machado, is a society journalist—a professional gossip, as it were—who, once befriended, shares "her opinions, her jokes, and her gossip" and in the process reveals crucial clues (236). Lisbet, a minor character whom Madigan meets at a party, spends most of her time regaling Madigan with "very old gossip," including the story of how, during the dictatorship of the 1950s, "the gossip about Luis Emilio Orozco's conspiring" led to his being jailed (324). It is from this disclosure, in fact, that Madigan finally deduces the motive for the killing. Even the killer himself, Tomás Orozco, gossips with Madigan, casually revealing intimate details that help bring about his downfall. Orozco recognizes the risks in gossip—he laments that "to wind up on Aída Machado's lips was dangerous" (159)—but cannot resist participating. Torres's Caracas is filled with "constant babbling" (73), but gossip can also be a kind of currency, with Madigan's interlocutors taking pride in the secrets that they alone can pass on to her. Adrian's daughter, Adriana, speaks frankly of her father's fabrication of "the family's official version" of its past but goes on to brag that she is the only person to whom he told "the true story" (234). Machado herself, meanwhile, boasts of knowing "everything that happens in this city" and that "nothing escapes me" (237). Gossip, here, is not just a way of knowing but a way of asserting exclusive knowledge—even if, ironically, such exclusivity can be fully asserted only by imparting that knowledge to others.

As this suggests, the novel portrays Venezuelan society as deeply invested in gossip. As a Canadian expatriate, Madigan soon realizes that if she is to arrive at the truth about the crime, she must integrate herself into the social milieu of her new home and persuade the people with whom she interacts to grant her access to their secrets: to obtain gossip, in other words, she must herself become a gossip. This is a process complicated by Madigan's status as an outsider; still, despite spending much of the novel running up against dead ends, Madigan remains doggedly, even naively convinced that the truth is real and accessible, even if it is dispersed among the many friends, acquaintances, and other characters upon whose gossip she depends. In gathering together the threads of the truth she seeks, Madigan encounters multiple versions of the same events, much as we see in the works of Ferré and Condé; Madigan, however, is convinced that these contradictory accounts can be reconciled or reassembled to arrive at a true account of the events in question. At one point, Madigan marvels at how well informed one of the murder victims had been: "How on earth did Pablo Narval find out all that?" She answers herself: "The same way that everything in this country winds up being known" (343)—that is, through gossip and hearsay. Gossip, in this instance, becomes a valuable resource, a storage house for fragments of information through which, with the right tools, valuable knowledge can be discerned.

This is not an easy task. Not all of Madigan's interlocutors are uniformly truthful, and at times she feels overwhelmed, "lost in a web of assumptions and misunderstandings, blinded by an intolerable family novel" (204–5). Still, she remains convinced that even if the truth is being kept from her, it remains potentially accessible: "Someone must want to know the truth, someone must yearn for that truth to be realized," she insists (231). To approach the truth, Madigan ruminates at length upon what she has heard and frequently herself gossips about the gossip to which she has been made party, telling not only Adriana, her patient, but also her friend and fellow therapist Ingrid Horowitz and the police detective Boris Salcedo. These acts of gossip recall the analyst's session, or the detective's conversations with his sidekick: an active process of narrative composition through which information is unraveled, weighed, and organized. This is not to suggest, of course, that every piece of information received through gossip is true or that Torres's novel presents the pursuit of truth, or truth itself, as uncomplicated. Madigan acknowledges that the insights she gathers from gossip are not in themselves reliable or final, and that they are in fact "parallel versions that could contain truths, half-truths, lies, or half-lies" (161), but she approaches this epistemologically treacherous ground with a detective's rigor and a therapist's sensitivity. By weighing and editing the diverging accounts she collates through gossip, she engages in a painstaking process of narrative reconstruction that ultimately allows her to uncover the truth about the crime she is investigating.

It is useful here to return to Cozarinsky's view of gossip as refracting narratives into multiple complex and heterogeneous parts. Torres's novel similarly shows gossip troubling the surfaces of realities that had seemed unitary, but goes a step further: where Cozarinsky sees gossip as irrevocably shattering unitary narratives—or, rather, as revealing such narratives to be illusory and insufficient—*La fascinación* insists upon the possibility of teasing out, from disparate and contradictory fragments, what Madigan repeatedly describes in positivistic terms as "truth" and "order."[31] *La fascinación* is not naive about the possible distortions present in gossip, but neither does it despair of finding truth. The epistemological pessimism that pervades *Maldito amor, Wide Sargasso Sea,* and *Célanire* are here replaced with the Proustian conviction that gossip has the potential, even if it often goes unrealized, to provide access to hidden truths—and that, in fact, gossip can be a more effective means of arriving at such truths than many other mechanisms of inquiry. Where Ferré and Condé's texts mobilize gossip to illustrate and explore the difficulties in arriving at coherent versions of reality, *La fascinación* sees gossip instead as providing, if not a complete solution, at least an effective medium through which to advance toward a solution. The definitive answers arrived at by the novel's resolution clearly break with the view of gossip as a means of destabilizing narratives and problematizing the notion of objective truth. Gossip is presented, like police work or psychoanalysis, as a powerful and substantive way of knowing.

The congruencies between criminal investigations and psychoanalytic inquiry—and, to a lesser extent, gossip—have not gone unnoticed by scholars. In *Body Work,* Brooks asserts that analysts and detectives use similar methods because of their similar aims: "Like the detective story, the analysis is an inquest, moving back from present symptoms, clues presented to the analyst, to the signs left by earlier events, and eventually back to the beginning in order to construct the chain of events leading up to the scene of suffering. The narrative chain, with each event connected to the next by reasoned casual links, marks the victory of reason over chaos, of society and sanity over crime and neurosis, and restitutes a world in which etiological histories offer the best solution to the apparently unexplainable" (233). But if detectives, as Geoffrey Hartman writes, seek "graphic details" that feed their "lust for evidence" (165), then gossips, in their love of lurid specificities, do much the same. Just as importantly, the gossip, the psychoanalyst, and the detective not only seek new details; they also weigh them, consider them, and pore over them obsessively in an attempt to distill them into coherent and internally consistent narratives. In a discussion of Agatha Christie's Miss Marple tales, Spacks briefly notes the points of contact between the three fields: "As a mode of interpretation, gossip, like psychoanalysis, helps people make sense of the past in the light of the present, and of the present in relation to the past. A simple literary example is the detective story, in which the detective uses hearsay and gossip to construct retrospective explanation" (230). Though she does not trace the epistemic connections between the three forms of inquiry, Spacks notes that in Christie's work, the role of the gossip "metaphorizes that of the writer" by shaping new truths: "Gossip constitutes information; it becomes *truth,*" she writes (230).[32] In *The Seductions of Psychoanalysis,* similarly, John Forrester explores the connections between gossip and analysis, writing that "gossip is remarkably akin to analysis, both in its powers of revelation of the truth and in its revelation of the power of the truth" (250).[33]

Still, few writers or scholars have connected psychoanalysis, detective work, and gossip as directly and fruitfully as Torres does in *La fascinación.* In Madigan, the three modes of inquiry are channeled through a single character who uses them, interchangeably and often simultaneously, to arrive at truths that address the text's central mystery, and to forge a revelatory narrative that sheds light on the hidden motives, actions, and interior lives of others. While in some ways psychoanalysis and criminal investigation might appear to be prioritized—Madigan *is* a therapist, the text *is* a detective novel—Torres's text makes clear that gossip is just as potent a means of inquiry. Analysis and detective work alone bear scant fruit in Torres's novel; it is only by supplementing them with gossip that Madigan gains the insights she needs to solve the crime and provide her patient with closure. In scrutinizing people's words and exploring their actions through both their own accounts and those of others, Madigan is finally able to reveal not only the true facts surrounding the killing but also the true nature of some of the people with whom she speaks. Through gossip and deduction Madigan discovers that her patient has concealed certain key facts, including the scandalous detail that the murder victim was not Adriana's sister but her daughter, the result of incest with her father.

Indeed, once Madigan lays out the whole story, Adriana confesses that "it's curious, I began this because I couldn't live without knowing who did it and now that seems to me the least important part of all. What I discovered was [. . .] the darkness of the soul, of my father's soul, of my daughter's, of my own" (363). The words recall Adriana's earlier intuition that knowing the truth about the murder would restore her mental health. But Madigan has done more than simply reveal the murderer's identity or uncover a few *secrets d'alcôve*. Gossip has made possible Adriana's journey into "the darkness of the soul"; from a psychoanalytic standpoint, it has generated the narrative epiphany through which Adriana can begin to heal her psychic wounds. Torres, in portraying Madigan in the combined roles of therapist, detective, and gossip, and in showing gossip as providing the crucial impetus that allows Madigan to succeed both as analyst and as investigator, thus seeks to elevate gossip and establish it as a vital member of a narrative and investigative trifecta. Gossip, in *La fascinación*, is presented as a practice that can supplement other modes of inquiry and provide a means of unearthing the truth.

This is especially important in the Venezuelan context, where official institutions are viewed with suspicion, and where even Salcedo, the police detective, shrugs off his duties with the words "You can't try to solve everything" (13). Salcedo's words recall Carlos Monsiváis's assertion that in Latin America "there is no crime fiction because there is no trust in justice" (11). Of course, we can quibble over how literally to read Monsiváis's claim; in recent years, numerous writers from both Latin America and the Caribbean have turned to crime fiction to reflect upon the failure of their societies' civil institutions and their governments' inability to provide justice.[34] We can see this clearly in Torres's novel: Salcedo knows the man imprisoned for the crime was merely a scapegoat but does not care to investigate the conspiracy underlying the case, admitting to Madigan that "in this specific case they pay me not to discover it. [. . .] I received orders to leave things as they were" (13). But Salcedo also presents his shortcomings as something more fundamental: an epistemological deficiency rooted in the very methodology of police work. In a scene that again recalls Kurosawa's *Rashomon*—and thus also the narrative fragmentation of *Maldito amor*—Salcedo tells Madigan: "Listen to ten informants, and you'll get ten versions" (85–86). What is needed, what Salcedo lacks, is a way to look beyond the informants' words and uncover their unspoken secrets. It is precisely this interior glimpse that Madigan derives from gossip, allowing her to tease out, from the parallel versions she hears, a narrative that fills the vacuum.

Madigan's dogged belief in the existence of a coherent, true version of events stands in sharp contrast to Salcedo's jaded worldview. This can at times make her (and perhaps the novel, too) seem naive, and it is worth remembering that Madigan is explicitly cast as an outsider who does not fully understand how Venezuelan society works.[35] Still, it is striking that Torres allows her psychoanalyst turned detective to succeed in reaching the kind of recomposition, or epiphanic narrative revelation, that is the ultimate goal of psychoanalysis, of crime fiction, and perhaps also of gossip. *La fascinación* shares Monsiváis's cynicism about the failures of the region's justice systems and about the inapplicability of conventional detective fiction in such a context. But Torres also posits a solution. Madigan uses gossip as both an investigative and a therapeutic tool: not to problematize or challenge official discourses but rather to confront, process, and ultimately overcome Venezuela's failed civil and judicial institutions. Through gossip, Madigan seeks truth, but she also seeks a means of coming to terms with the suspicion, mistrust, and cynicism that lies at the heart of Venezuelan society. When the state fails, Madigan suggests, it can still be possible to find solutions through self-reliance and appeals to the knowledge and insights of others.

In this sense, Torres's text should be read as a twist on the tradition of crime fiction marked by suspicion of the state, of justice, and of the possibility of definitive truths. In keeping with this tradition, Torres's novel portrays Venezuela's criminal justice system as broken: the guilty go free, and police detectives, faced with the impossible task of restoring order in a society full of violence, approach cases with mere apathy. But Torres also uses crime fiction to explore gossip's role as a potent way of building and sharing knowledge in societies where people know better than to rely on the state and its institutions for trustworthy answers—or indeed for *any* answers. Where Ferré presents official narratives as untrustworthy, self-serving, and biased, Torres's even bleaker text offers nothing but silence, a system whose failures are so deep that answers are no longer demanded or expected. Still, Madigan, harnessing the power of gossip, is able to develop an informal but effective rebuttal to official indifference. In so doing, moreover, she develops a more complete picture, uncovering not just hidden facets of the lives of the people she encounters but also the solution to the crime. What begins as a simple whodunit becomes, through gossip, a more ambiguous and psychologically complex journey that engages with slippery questions regarding the status of knowledge, truth, and narrative.

Knowledge and Intimacy

We have now seen gossip used to challenge master narratives and show the contingency of all narratives; to condense speculation into consensus and common knowledge; and to sidestep corrupted official discourses and systems of investigation, and attempt a more direct and personal engagement with the interior lives of others. All these deployments are anchored not in the philosophical interrogation of what can or cannot be truly known but rather in the understanding of knowledge as a deeply personal phenomenon, in which each person's reality can be markedly different, and in which to gain knowledge oftentimes means to gain insights into the individual experiences and perspectives of others. There is, in short, an intimacy to knowledge that gossip, through its occupation of the liminal space between the public and the private, and through its intrusion into the intimate secrets of others, is uniquely well situated to explore. Forrester suggests that like the intuitive insights of psychoanalysis, gossip "leads us to an epistemological impasse" (244), for it provides truths that cannot be verified through appeals to positivist inquiry but that nonetheless have a profundity and power that demands their admittance into our schemes of knowledge. "Knowledge had by gossip only barely maintains its claim on that word, sketching out the no-man's-land of fiction which equally constitutes the social knowledge by which we live," Forrester writes (244).[36] The texts examined here share this notion of gossip, not necessarily as a tool for arriving at the stark epistemic truths dreamed of by philosophers, but rather as a means of negotiating the hazier and perhaps higher truths by which societies define themselves and by which individuals navigate their societies.

A similarly intimate epistemological view is taken by Brooks in *Body Work,* which casts the desire for knowledge as an erotic process: scopophilia and epistemophilia, he suggests, are sides of the same coin. "The desire to know is constructed from sexual desire and curiosity," he writes

(5). The Freudian impulse to uncover the intimate secrets of another, in other words, is for Brooks largely the same impulse that drives us to seek knowledge, to question, and to probe our condition, our very reality, for deeper and more absolute truths. To venture into the unknown is not only an exploration; it is also an intrusion, even a violation of spaces hitherto sacrosanct.[37] "The private is an object of never-ending curiosity—of a basic 'epistemophilic' drive—precisely because, whatever its violations, it remains the space to which we assign final secrets," Brooks writes. "Intimacy is of the body, and the body is private" (51).

Brooks sees parallels between the erotic gaze and the lust for knowledge, but we can just as easily trace parallels with the prying eyes and wagging tongue of the gossip. As Brooks notes, this erotic and epistemic duality bubbles forth in literary narratives; as the body becomes a focal point of literary attention, so too emerges "a literature driven by the anxiety and fascination of the hidden, masked, unidentified individual. The invention of the detective story in the nineteenth century testifies to this concern to detect, track down, and identify those occult bodies that have purposely sought to avoid social scrutiny" (*Body Work* 26). Gossip, clearly, offers a similar means of social scrutiny and is explicitly concerned with the hidden bodies, and, by extension, the hidden interior worlds, of its subjects. It is perhaps a more subtle drive than the lust for knowledge described by Brooks—as we have seen, gossip can be used not just to probe for truth but also to manipulate and misdirect the investigations of others—but it is, nonetheless, always preoccupied with knowledge, and with understanding and grasping the knowledge of others.

Just as Brooks locates epistemological awareness in the voyeuristic intrusions of high modernists such as James and Flaubert, so too in the gossip of the Caribbean can we trace an urgent drive to rethink, restate, or recalibrate existing discourses and ways of knowing. Like Brooks's gaze, gossip is by its nature intrusive: a liminal and transgressive practice that not only probes the boundaries of the public and the private, but also seeks to bring into plain sight that which its subject wished to keep hidden, and to take possession of things held privately by another. As Brooks rightly perceives, the act of taking possession is epistemologically potent: the nosy servants of *Madame Bovary,* looking in at Emma through a broken windowpane, are not only breaching the boundary between private and public but are reformulating their own understanding of the world and violently but efficaciously finding new ways of knowing and understanding. The prying eye of the gossip, in this sense, can be read as providing another tool for those who, as Brooks suggests, wish "to work through epistemological complications to revelatory moments of looking, to moments of smashed windowpanes that call for revaluations" (*Body Work* 118). Gossip, like voyeurism, is a potentially destructive and implicitly violent act; yet for all that, much as Brooks suggests of the corporal gaze, it can be a powerful means of knowledge production, and a way of knowing especially well suited to the fraught uncertainties and boundless suspicions of the Caribbean.

3 "An International Scandal"
Gossip, Dissent, and the Public Sphere

> La historia no es más que la ilación de dos o tres chismes decisivos.
> —Guillermo Cabrera Infante

IF GOSSIP is, as Niko Besnier argues, "a quintessential tool for political action in private realms" (*Production of Politics* 12), then it has become so chiefly through its ability to blur the boundaries between the public and the private.[1] The act of gossiping, after all, is in large part the act of making public that which was once an intimate secret: while gossip, in its classic form, is private speech, it can also be understood as engagement with a network of speakers—a public, or perhaps a counterpublic— that goes well beyond the immediate participants. Gossip, then, is among other things a way for private speakers to address and even insert themselves into the public life of their community. Lisa Lowe argues that gossip plagiarizes public discourses even as it remains "parasitic on the details of 'private' life," thereby transgressing and eroding the boundaries between public and private spheres (116). This makes gossip—alongside kindred forms such as rumor—a powerful resource for those excluded from more formal public discourse. Domesticity, after all, is only one kind of marginalization; as scholars such as Ranajit Guha have ably illustrated, in colonial and postcolonial contexts, gossip and rumor can become a locus of resistance against authority. Indeed, by facilitating communication and organization, and allowing entry to or replicating some of the functions of the public sphere, gossip and rumor come to serve, in Guha's words, "as the most 'natural' and indeed indispensable vehicle of insurgency" (256).[2] This has certainly been the case in the Caribbean: as Raphael Dalleo notes, gossip "appears frequently in Caribbean literature of the modern colonial period as a sort of counterpublic where those excluded from the dominant public sphere pass along knowledge" and serves "as a more democratic, oral alternative" to the literary public sphere. "This trope of gossip as a counterpublic created by the restrictiveness of the official public sphere [. . .] suggests an anticolonial interest in exploring how groups excluded from official discourse still express themselves," Dalleo writes (102–3).

As described in the preceding chapters, gossip certainly does play the role Dalleo describes in Caribbean literature, and not only in that of the modern colonial period: through gossip, we frequently see groups and individuals reshaping their understandings of community, negotiating the tropes and truths they take as valid or meaningful, and constituting, maintaining, or disrupting the publics and counterpublics they inhabit and slip between. Such readings focus in large part, however, on the construction of predominantly local public spheres grounded in the family, the village, the neighborhood, and the city. This does not make them less valid, but it suggests they may not tell the whole story. In focusing on the recent Caribbean, I read the region as a globalized archipelago: forged by the traumatic influx of conquistadors, colonizers, and slaves but now defined by bidirectional networks of cultural influence, diaspora, exile, and tourism. To speak of gossip's role in the public sphere of the contemporary Caribbean, it is necessary to consider not just the public and private discourses of individual island nations but also the Caribbean's place—and the Caribbean writer's place—in a global network of literary, political, and historical discourses. This is especially true since the Caribbean has, in this period, been marked both by authoritarian regimes that have sought sweeping and even totalitarian controls over the public sphere, and by a corresponding outpouring of literary and political exiles who have sought to write back against perceived oppressors and to radically reshape their home countries' perception and place in the global public sphere.

Reading Caribbean writers in terms of a global or transnational public sphere is inherently somewhat problematic: as Nancy Fraser notes, the public sphere, as conventionally conceived, is a discursive space in which a given nation's citizenry negotiates and asserts a democratic consensus in order to hold its leaders accountable. Public sphere theory, Fraser states, insists for these purposes upon "a Westphalian political imaginary" in which the public sphere is bounded by and accounts for a single coherent and strictly defined nation-state (8). Such a framing is difficult, if not impossible, to reconcile with a geographically dispersed and politically heterogeneous "transnational public sphere"—and yet, Fraser insists, such a reconciliation must take place if public sphere theory is to remain relevant in the modern, globalized and post-Westphalian world. "A critical conception can no longer restrict its attention to the direction of communicative flows in established polities," she writes. "It must consider the need to construct new addressees for public opinion, in the sense of new, transnational public powers that possess the administrative capacity to solve transnational problems" (23).

Fraser's argument rests upon the conviction that the nation-state is no longer a sufficient space in which to negotiate questions of power and that transnational discussion, and the appeal to transnational institutions, must be part of public sphere theory's evolution if it is to "keep faith with its original promise to contribute to struggles for emancipation" (24). This is doubly true of the Caribbean: already, as I have previously argued, a space that demands to be understood as a meta-archipelago of interconnected islands and diasporic outposts in fluid and constant communication but also, lamentably, the site of entrenched power struggles and politics of domination that have too often curtailed opportunities for participation in conventionally conceived, nationally bounded public spheres.[3]

Fraser envisions the evolution of a global public sphere in which "new transnational public powers [. . .] can be made accountable to new democratic transnational circuits of public opinion" (24). For the writers discussed in this chapter, however, appeals to the nascent transnational public sphere of which Fraser writes would have been largely fruitless—not least because such a participatory space has yet to clearly emerge in any meaningful way. Instead, their efforts to address a global public sphere resonate more closely with Pia Wiegmink's notion of activist performers who "make use of symbolic political acts in order to make their agendas visible to a wider public" and "create a space for public discourse by means of performance" (2). The writers detailed in this chapter conceive of themselves not simply as intellectuals but as provocateurs, seeking to make a splash and thereby insert themselves, and the scandals of Caribbean authoritarianism, into the global consciousness. Like Wiegmink, they "perceive the public sphere as a battleground of competing publics that struggle for public attention" and understand that "before certain political issues become subject of political discussion and debate, these matters must be uttered and made visible in public" (2).

In this sense, the public sphere of which I write is not entirely Habermasian, for it is a space in which rational debate is subsidiary to or, at best, exists alongside an ongoing narrative battle. Instead, I hew closer to the Belgian philosopher Chantal Mouffe, who writes of an "agonistic model" of democratic engagement and artistic activism, and conceives of public space as "the battleground where different hegemonic projects are confronted, without any possibility of final reconciliation" (3). The Caribbean writers here studied have little faith in the free, democratic process of consensus building proposed by Habermas: they align far more with Mouffe's notion that "the impediments to the Habermasian ideal speech situation are not empirical but ontological and the rational consensus that he presents as a regulative idea is in fact a conceptual impossibility" (3–4). What remains, for such writers, is the possibility of disruption and adversarialism: the refusal to be silenced and—in the absence of a viable local public sphere—the ability to cause a ruckus on the global stage and disrupt the reputations and public images of their island's authoritarian leaders.

In what follows, I explore gossip as a strategy, at once literary and political, that can be used not just in local acts of subversion but also as a means of gaining entry to, and reformulating, the international public sphere. Reading Reinaldo Arenas's 1992 autobiography, *Antes que anochezca*, as an act of self-gossip, I show how his hypersexualized braggadocio serves to undermine the Cuban government's prudishly macho conception of the revolutionary *nuevo hombre,* but also and especially to capture the prurient imaginations of foreign readers. Another Cuban exile, Guillermo Cabrera Infante, uses gossip about others—including despised political figures but also persecuted artists toward whom he is largely sympathetic—to cement his own position as a knowledgeable broker of information about the island. A similar impetus can be seen in Jamaica Kincaid's *A Small Place* (1988), an essay written for a foreign audience, which uses gossip to criticize both Antigua's corrupt government and the oblivious tourists who flock to the island. Finally, I turn to the regime of François Duvalier, which—having effectively silenced Haitian writers—understood Graham Greene's 1966 novel *The Comedians* as a reputational attack and responded by publishing a gossipy pamphlet, intended for international consumption, containing a litany of insinuations and ad hominem attacks on the British writer. All these figures sought to reshape the public perception of Caribbean nations in real time, using gossip with the explicit goal of reconfiguring and redirecting contemporaneous international public discourse. In the next chapter, I will explore similar issues from the perspective of writers who have used gossip as a means of exploring the legacy of authoritarianism, with a focus on more inward-looking questions of memory and national identity. Here, however, I focus on the immediate, the contemporary, and the global.

Sex and Dissidence: *Antes que anochezca*

Few writers gossip with quite the same riotous disregard for propriety as the Cuban novelist Reinaldo Arenas, whose autobiography, *Antes que anochezca*—described by Manuel Pereira as "a monotonous collection of minor gossip with an emphasis on the obscene" (56)—is packed with ribald anecdotes about the sexual indiscretions of a long list of Cubans. Arenas gleefully recounts the tale of a police officer who would detain a good-looking young man, then drag him into the bushes to "suck his member" (264).[4] He writes of how Hiram Prado was expelled from the Soviet Union "after he was caught sucking the cock of a young Russian during a Bolshoi Theater performance"—and subsequently arrested when, back in Cuba, he fellated a man behind a theater curtain only for the curtain to go up, leaving him exposed on center stage (98). He dwells, too, on a "happening" at the home of a poet named Carilda (likely Carilda Oliver Labra, although only the first name is given) who strips to her panties, quarrels with her husband (whose prostate problems are also described in detail), and winds up being chased naked through the streets by her sword-wielding spouse, while begging him "not to cause such a scandal in my hometown" (268). Many of these stories are told with a certain affection: Virgilio Piñera, whom Arenas loves and respects, is shown not just as a brilliant writer but also as a sexual adventurer, with Arenas lingering over the tale of a well-endowed cook who continues to stir his soup as he penetrates Piñera. Other tales are more spiteful: Hiram, the friend turned informer who helps the authorities locate Arenas, is described as having his "most fulfilling" sexual dalliances with his own eighty-year-old grandfather until he "could only have a real orgasm" when being penetrated by the old man (234). Similarly, the critic José Rodríguez Feo, who abandoned Piñera after his fall from grace, is described as a pimp who runs a male brothel "where strong men worked as bartenders and, on the side, engaged in such other activities as clients might request" (82). Whether vicious or affectionate, however, the stories are gossip in the classic sense, offering up juicy revelations about the scandalous indiscretions of their subjects in a manner clearly intended to titillate and captivate the reader.

Arenas's text is notable for the extent to which it recounts not just the deeds of absent third parties—the usual targets of gossip—but also Arenas's own adventures. "Autobiography is a form in which one gets to gossip about oneself," asserts Joseph Epstein (18), and Arenas takes full advantage of the fact, filling the text with tales of his comic sexcapades.[5] Arenas also shows himself gossiping about other people and in fact recounts how he used gossip to play tricks on various acquaintances, often with hilarious results. In one passage, Arenas details what he terms "the War of the Anonymous Letters"—a rapidly escalating exchange of pasquinades between members of his literary circle. The "war" begins with the circulation of anonymous bulletins accusing Arenas of murdering a child; he responds by covering Havana's public restrooms with graffiti against Pepe Malas, the presumed author, "stating that he was the most faggoty faggot of them all, and that he was an informer for State Security. [. . .] Whenever he went to a rest room in search of adventure, he would see those messages and run away" (264). Finally, Arenas and a friend pen an anonymous communiqué urging right-thinking Havanans to condemn orgies supposedly being held at the church where their acquaintance Samuel Toca lives. "The communiqué was really not too far from the truth because Samuel would bring anyone he met into the church, including a cop who happened to be a closet queen," Arenas confides (264). The authors lists the participants in the supposed orgies, including their own names "as a cover-up," then quietly inform Toca that Malas is responsible for the stunt (265). Toca is threatened with eviction from his cell at the church, and Malas has several teeth broken in the beating Toca subsequently gives him; still, "no one took the letter seriously," Arenas claims (266). Elsewhere, Arenas notes a similar episode in which he sent a "Termination of Friendship Notice" to friends who had failed to stand by him "at a time when friendship really mattered" (238). Hiram made more than a hundred copies of the letter and sent them to all Arenas's friends, causing "dreadful confusion"; Arenas responded by sending Hiram a notice of his own, then penning a series of tongue twisters making fun of him. "This was another of the weapons I used against those who had harmed me," he declares. By 1977, he claims, his tongue twisters had "become famous throughout Havana," targeting more than thirty "well-known people in the city's theater and literary worlds" (238–39). Arenas's social network, it seems, was mapped through reputational pranks, pasquinades, and acts of spitefully adversarial gossip.

As these episodes show, the tone of Arenas's autobiography is frequently comedic: numerous scenes, from the "incessant farting" of his fellow convicts to the episode in which a former lover attempts to break into Arenas's apartment (Arenas reaches through a hatch, unseen, bops the man on the head with a stick, and disappears; the process repeats until the man, bruised and confused, stumbles away), would not be out of place in a Mel Brooks movie. A similar cartoonishness marks the incessant sexual shenanigans he describes: busloads of men grope and fellate one another;

husbands duck into changing rooms for hurried homosexual encounters and then rush back out to take family photos; and Arenas, swimming underwater, fellates men as they stand chatting with unwitting third parties. "I would suck his penis powerfully until he ejaculated, and would then swim away with the help of my flippers. The person he was talking to at a little distance would notice no more perhaps than a deep sigh at the moment of ejaculation," Arenas claims (101). Such scenes demand to be read as fantasy or hyperbole, but Arenas makes it hard to be entirely sure.[6] They are also clearly intended to sharpen the contrast between the comic text and the tragic reality: despite the jokes, after all, the farting prisoners are in fact the inmates of a concentration camp. A similar pathos underlies Arenas's sexual adventures, which are grounds for persecution and subject to undignified scrutiny by the Cuban government. Late in the text, Arenas is forced to explain the exact nature of his sexual preferences, and to parade himself back and forth in front of psychologists "to see if I was queer" (281). Taken in isolation, the episode would be a violation; presented after hundreds of pages of bawdy and joyful sexual encounters, however, it is stripped of much of its power. It reads, in fact, like a punch line: Arenas has suffered, but by turning daily life in the Castro regime into a tropical sex farce, he also manages to have the last laugh.

Arenas's frenetic tone also serves to blur the line between gossip and slander: throughout *Antes que anochezca,* he offers a cocktail of truthful and presumably exaggerated or fabricated tales, with little effort to differentiate between them. Are we really to believe that Hiram fornicated so avariciously with his grandfather that he drove the old man to a premature death? Or that so many Cuban officials—from a lesbian State Security officer to a policeman who fantasizes about Arenas throwing nude parties—are truly closeted homosexuals? It's hard to say, in part because Arenas, in sharing countless other gossipy, titillating tales, has already drawn us to a place of nodding complicity: in a country in which men appear to be making love behind every bush and in every public restroom, it is all too easy to accept the stories that Arenas tells about his enemies.

Such episodes demonstrate Arenas's mobilization of gossip as a means of revenge. Abilio Estévez describes *Antes que anochezca* as "an act of vengeance" and, in a phrase borrowed from José Rodríguez Feo, "a masterpiece of slander" ("Between Nightfall" 861). Arenas's text is marked, Estévez writes, by its commitment to "defamation and vengeance as method" (865). But *Antes que anochezca* is not just a settling of old scores: it is also a fervently political document that demands to be read as a dissident writer's decisive intervention in the international public sphere.

Nerea Riley describes Arenas's work—"so angry, subjective, bitchy, paranoic in the face of injustice" (493)—as a form of literary vendetta, and correctly notes that his energy derives from an acute sense of persecution. In this sense, Arenas's listing of his enemies' scandalous indiscretions is an act of defamatory vengeance against the people named, but also against the Cuban revolution in general and against Fidel Castro in particular. This is not the nostalgia of the lifelong exile but rather the urgent and defiant work of a writer who still feels ensnared by, or has only just managed to escape, a regime that personally targeted him.

Arenas thus uses gossip to retaliate, and to write himself and his works back into the Cuban narrative. He is acutely aware that Havana has sought to destroy his literary reputation: when accused of corrupting a minor, he claims the charges were brought to avoid turning him into a political symbol.[7] "By convicting me of a common crime, they would avoid an international scandal," he writes (206). Arenas's writing is a process of rescandalization: a refusal to accept the regime's condemnation, a celebration of his own apparently endless appetites, and a gleeful flaunting of the homosexuality that the regime saw as a counterrevolutionary embarrassment. The delirious and denunciatory mode that Arenas adopts allows him to assert his own identity and to present a page-turning exposé of the persecution he faced for the two things that he most prized: his writing and his sexuality.

It is sex, of course, that emerges most vividly from Arenas's text, with virtually every page of his autobiography containing another erotic adventure. This cataloging of sexual antics is quintessentially gossipy, but it is also an act of defiance: Arenas displays and foregrounds the homosexual acts for which he was persecuted, casting them as both joyful and rebellious. Sandro Barros emphasizes the political significance of Arenas's professed erotomania, describing it as "without a question personal and political, since the very presentation of desire is framed within the subversive homosexual act of reclaiming the body as private property." Arenas's text turns pleasure into a symbol for individual freedom, Barros argues, but also symbolically comes "to represent the rejection of the State's effective control over one's body" (6). Rafael Ocasio similarly suggests that Arenas turns his own "hypersexualized" body into "his main weapon in the opposition to Castro's revolutionary practices" (197). But *Antes que anochezca* does more than just chronicle Arenas's own erotic encounters: it also presents, through gossip, a panorama of homosexual practices under Castro. Arenas argues that the systematic repression of homosexuality brought about precisely the opposite of what it intended:

an unleashing of sexual activity that extended to the most ideologically committed sectors of Cuban society. Arenas writes: "I think that the sexual revolution in Cuba actually came about as a result of the existing sexual repression. Perhaps as a protest against the regime, homosexuality began to flourish with ever-increasing defiance. [. . .] I honestly believe that the concentration camps for homosexuals, and the police officers disguised as willing young men to entrap and arrest homosexuals, actually resulted in the promotion of homosexual activities" (107). Here, Arenas turns the table on the Castro government: having been convicted as a corruptor of minors, Arenas makes the case that it was the government itself that, by politicizing the sexual act, drove young people to begin fornicating as a form of defiance. Arenas's own lovemaking, in fact, is presented as the homoerotic conquest of the *hombre nuevo* and of the Castro regime's cult of machismo: "I think that in Cuba there was never more fucking going on than in those years, the decade of the sixties [. . .] when the sexual act became taboo while the 'new man' was being proclaimed and masculinity exalted. Many of the young men who marched in Revolutionary Square applauding Fidel Castro, and many of the soldiers who marched, rifle in hand and with martial expressions, came to our rooms after the parades to cuddle up naked, and show their real selves" (105). This is a gossipy subversion of the aggressively macho image put forth by the Cuban government: the real *hombre nuevo*, Arenas suggests, is engaging in military drills and revolutionary parades one moment and locked in a homosexual embrace the next. Arenas thus both queers the macho—all those young, lusty soldiers are sexually available to him—and incorporates macho ethics into his own queer identity: the braggadocio and boundless sexual appetite manifested in his text constitute a macho gesture of defiance and a refusal to allow Castro's government to define his sexuality as somehow shameful or effete.[8]

Arenas's politicization of his sexuality is entirely in keeping with the views of both heteronormativity and homosexuality espoused by Cuba's revolutionary leaders. Emilio Bejel describes how, from the early 1960s, the Cuban government added "an aggressive homophobia" to the ideological apparatus of the revolution (96) in an effort both to create a culture "free of the impurities of the bourgeois past" and to forge an *hombre nuevo* whose machismo and heterosexual virility was matched only by his readiness to "sacrifice for his country" and "renounce utilitarian values" in the name of socialism (99). The *hombre nuevo* was envisioned as fiercely heterosexual and energetically devoted to the regime but also as paradoxically meek, at least in the sense of being unquestioningly obedient and politically compliant. As Lillian Guerra notes, the revolution preached radical nonconformity with the capitalist traditions of the past and the exterior, but simultaneously insisted on absolute conformity with the Marxist values and cultural logic of the *nouveau regime*. To be homosexual—especially, as in Arenas's case, to be openly and exuberantly homosexual—was to be fundamentally at odds with this project. Guerra remarks: "Those who distorted or diverged from a mandatory heterosexist gender order were 'ideological diversionists' who jeopardized the collective prosperity of society[. . . .] Real and imagined homosexuals were considered particularly virulent carriers of ideological diversionism" (228–29). Through gossip, then, Arenas turns the Cuban government's institutionalized homophobia against it: in celebrating and hyperbolizing his own homosexual liaisons, he both stakes out a position as a dangerous rebel and underscores the fact that countless other young Cubans, including many apparently devoted to the regime, are also engaged in politically subversive sexual acts.

Arenas jubilantly documents the "erotic rebelliousness" of the postrevolutionary period, repeating countless ribald tales about young people, especially soldiers, engaged in homosexual affairs. A trip to the beach is "like entering paradise because all the young people wanted to make love, and there were always dozens of them ready to go into the bushes" (92). The eroticization of the *hombre nuevo* continues on a train ride: "The train was full of recruits; everybody was sexually aroused and having sex in the bathrooms, under the seats, anyplace. Hiram used his foot to masturbate a recruit who seemed to be sleeping on the floor. I was lucky enough to be able to use both hands" (92). Later, Arenas and Hiram visit a military camp where sex-starved recruits crowd around them, wrapped in blankets or completely naked, then throw an orgy in an abandoned tank (93). The sex is endless: one friend claims to have "made a small fortune during his stay for the Revolutionary parade" by having sex with more than twenty people a night, "at ten bucks each" (52), while Arenas and Hiram calculate that by 1968 they had bedded some five thousand men apiece. Arenas adds that he and Hiram "were not the only ones carried away by this kind of erotic rage; everybody was: the recruits who spent long months of abstinence, and the whole population" (93).

As Barros proposes, Arenas's "rhetorical homosexualization of the revolutionary *macho*" is, among other things, a denunciation of the perceived hypocrisy at the heart of the revolutionary establishment (1). Arenas contrasts his own sexual energy with the repression of the revolutionary government. "All dictatorships are sexually repressive and anti-life. All affirmations of life are diametrically opposed to dogmatic regimes," he writes. "It was logical for Fidel Castro to persecute us, not to let us fuck, and to try to suppress any public display of the life force" (93).⁹ But he also shows his persecutors as caught up in the sexual fervor of the moment, even as they seek to suppress it. An official at the Ministry of the Interior is portrayed as showing off his erection on a bus, then taking offense and beating up someone who makes a pass at him. Later, the official threatens Arenas while strutting around his home in a towel, flaunting an erection and surreptitiously masturbating. "The man, who was persecuting us for being gay, probably wanted nothing more than for us to grab his penis, rub it, and suck it right then. Perhaps this kind of aberration exists in all repressive systems," Arenas writes (95). Fidel Castro's personal friends, such as Armando Rodríguez and Alberto Guevara, are shown living a "scandalous homosexual life" without repercussions, thanks to their political connections (77). Even Arenas's teachers, so dedicated to turning young boys into "cadres of the Revolution," engage in torrid homosexual affairs with their charges, with one supposedly having relations with almost a hundred boys (50). "Sometimes the young men lined up by his room to fuck him; I actually saw this," Arenas insists. "In addition, a classmate of mine, reputed to have one of the largest penises in school, told me that he was a favorite of that professor of Marxism" (51). Both the students—future revolutionary leaders denying their homosexuality while jumping the fence each night to have sex with local men—and the teachers are shown as hypocrites, just like the many fornicating policemen and politicians who help sustain the regime's repression of homosexuals. But the hypocrisy is portrayed as endemic—something that "exists in all repressive systems." In this sense, the gossip that Arenas presents about specific figures is often also gossip about Castro's regime, with the cowardice and hypocrisy of individuals becoming a synecdoche for the failings of the revolution itself.

The sexual freedom that Arenas relishes is not itself free from corruption: Arenas presents his time in prison as the antithesis of the good-natured lustiness he describes elsewhere. The "queers" and "fairies" who inhabit the prison are not the untroubled lovers of Havana but rather embittered rapists who drive newly arrived adolescents—"fresh meat"—to suicide, or engage in bloody razor fights aimed at disfiguring rather than killing their rivals. "I had no sexual relations while in prison, not only as a precaution but because it made no sense; love has to be free and prison is a monstrosity where love turns into bestiality," Arenas writes (187). When he arrives in prison, moreover, Arenas is defined through gossip as a "hard-core criminal who had raped an old woman, murdered God knows how many people, and was a CIA agent"—a claim, presumably encouraged by his captors, that serves to strip away the joyful sexual identity that Arenas has forged for himself (187). It is by penning letters to prisoners' girlfriends, and thus becoming the "literary boyfriend or husband for all the prisoners" (188), that Arenas is able to reclaim and reassert his identity: not as a homosexual but as a writer. This cuts to the core of Arenas's project: though it is easy to view him chiefly as a sexual dissident, this is only the case because he expresses his sexual dissidence so forcefully through the written word. Arenas's autobiographical sex caper, in other words, is a document dedicated not just to revealing sexual rebellion but also to exploring the role that writers play in pushing back against the public narratives of authoritarianism.

Castro's "Palabras a los intelectuales" looms large in Arenas's imagination as he seeks to chronicle the erosion of intellectual freedom in postrevolutionary Cuba. The country's writers were sometimes fearful or diminished, and sometimes defiant in the face of intellectual repression; either way, Arenas records, to write freely was to be fundamentally at odds with the regime, and punishment and retaliation were never far off. Few writers, including Arenas himself, were able to navigate these perils without compromise, and Arenas's autobiography is full of intellectuals who betray themselves or others. The persecution of homosexual intellectuals initiated by the Padilla affair is portrayed in terms that strikingly recall the operations of gossip: private denunciations flare into public scandals aimed at policing the *parametraje*, or parametrization, of social norms. The Castro regime uses performance, both of shame and of judgment, to enforce its persecution of gay writers, Arenas asserts: "Public humiliation has always been one of Castro's favorite weapons: the degrading of people in front of a public always eager to make fun of any weakness in another, or of any person who had lost favor. It was not enough to be accused; you had to say you were sorry and beat your chest before an audience that would applaud and laugh" (139).

Amid the humiliations and betrayals and compromises, however, literature continues: Arenas and others write furtively and share their work among small groups of intimates. Notoriety even helps promote the work of some targeted writers: "As the persecutions intensified, the people were more and more eager to get to know the works of censored writers. Lezama became very popular, and some people knew Padilla's banned verses by heart" (136).[10] Arenas gossips about peers who, fearful for their safety, report details of the gatherings where writers share their work: "Undoubtedly those meetings had already been infiltrated by agents of State Security, writers turned informers, such as (we later found out) Miguel Barnet, Pablo Armando Fernández and César López. Whatever was read in one of those places was reported to State Security by the next day" (136). By cataloging these literary turncoats, Arenas uses gossip to map his social network and sort his acquaintances into in-groups and out-groups, much as he did with his Termination of Friendship Notices. "This was one of the most vicious acts perpetrated by Castroism: to break the bonds of friendship. To make us mistrust our best friends because the system was turning them into informers, into undercover agents," Arenas writes (154).[11] But if Arenas uses gossip to name and shame those he perceives as having betrayed him, he also makes a larger point by documenting the progressive corrosion of the Cuban public sphere: an insidious process through which intellectuals were either parametrized away from public life, or co-opted through fear and self-interest into the Castro regime's intelligence networks.

By gossiping about his fellow writers, Arenas personalizes the damage done by the Castro government and seeks to memorialize and make sense of the regime's actions. Following Piñera's death, he uses gossip to question the official, sanitized account of his demise and to suggest that Castro himself, offended by Piñera's work, had ordered his murder. "Fidel Castro has always hated writers, including those favoring the government, such as Guillén and Retamar. But in the case of Virgilio, this hate was even fiercer, perhaps because he was a homosexual," Arenas writes (274). This is expository, denunciatory gossip, but it is also an attempt to lay the blame for Piñera's killing directly at Castro's feet. Throughout *Antes que anochezca,* indeed, Arenas emphasizes Castro's personal responsibility for the government's actions, frequently invoking the Cuban leader by name when describing the regime's excesses. In this way, Arenas leverages the personal adversarialism upon which gossip is predicated: his own writing becomes less a counterrevolutionary gesture than an act of direct antagonism, and the regime itself is cast not as a vast and faceless bureaucracy but rather as an expression of the flaws and prejudices of a single man.

The reduction of the regime to its leader might suggest a symbolic reclamation of power: to gossip about Castro is arguably to domesticate and belittle both the leader and, by proxy, the Cuban government as a whole. Certainly, Arenas takes pleasure in describing the anger and frustration with which he imagines Castro receiving news of his evasion of his security forces. While he was on the run, Arenas writes, Castro "had given the order to find me immediately; in a country with such a perfect surveillance system, it was inconceivable that I had escaped from the police two months before and was still on the loose, writing documents and sending them abroad" (174). But if Arenas shows himself thumbing his nose at Castro, he also shows Castro as enjoying sweeping control over the island: despite his defiance, Arenas is eventually captured, and a confession is quickly wrung out of him. "This only proves my cowardice, my weakness, the certainty that I am not the stuff of which heroes are made," he writes (204).

Arenas's performative insistence that he is not a hero is likely not intended to be taken entirely seriously; despite his admitted failures, Arenas consistently presents himself in terms of his dogged commitment to opposing Castro's government, and especially to doing so through his writing. Indeed, the adversarialism of Arenas's text is such that Castro's efforts to suppress Arenas's work become, in Brad Epps's words, "the condition of possibility of Arenas's writing itself," with Castro emerging as "the phantasmic coauthor of Arenas's writing, the authority who by striving to disauthorize Arenas ultimately only authorizes him all the more" (246). If Arenas's forced confession and reduction to a jailhouse ghostwriter serve to underscore Castro's near total control over the Cuban public sphere, they also provide a reminder that his power is not absolute, and that other publics exist beyond Cuba's shores. Even as he gives in to Castro's power, Arenas declares himself "comforted" by the thought that while still at large, he had preemptively disavowed his confession: in a series of letters to international organizations including the United Nations and the International Red Cross, he had insisted that his attacks on the Castro regime "were absolutely true to fact, even if at some point I denied them" (204). Likewise, while in prison Arenas is consoled by the thought that "although my keepers continued to threaten me, they also feared foreign public opinion" (204). Even at his darkest moments, Arenas remains convinced that through writing he can sway foreign audiences and do real harm to Castro and his government. Indeed, this is the fight in which Arenas declares himself to be engaged throughout his autobiography: to write, despite everything, and to be published, despite Castro's efforts to the contrary.

Arenas gains a more nuanced understanding of the global public sphere after leaving Cuba, coming to realize the complicity and cowardice (in his view) of foreign intellectuals who supported the Castro regime, and the extent of the Cuban government's "tremendous propaganda machine and numerous international connections," which include "cultural centers, bookstores, publishing houses, and public-relations agencies spread worldwide" (300–301). Against such opposition, Arenas faces a tough fight—"I realized that the war had started all over again, now in a much more underhanded manner," he writes (288)—but demonstrates his enduring faith in the power of public opinion by penning an open letter, cowritten with Jorge Camacho and signed by many prominent intellectuals, calling on the Cuban government to allow a plebiscite like that which helped end Pinochet's rule in Chile. "The newspapers published the letter, and it turned out to be a terrible blow for Castro; it proved that his dictatorship was worse that Pinochet's, and that he would never allow free elections in Cuba," he writes (xiv).

Not all of Arenas's postexile efforts to shift public opinion are made through gossip: no longer living in Cuba, he is free to use other methods, from delivering speeches to writing letters to newspapers, and even reading excerpts from *Granma* and sections from Cuban statutes verbatim to incredulous academic audiences. Still, facing blowback for his political views, Arenas returns to gossip to recriminate those who slight him or obstruct his efforts.[12] Publishers who refuse to pay Arenas are listed by name; Severo Sarduy, meanwhile, comes in for special criticism for refusing to return manuscripts previously smuggled out of Cuba, paying a pittance for the rights to the French editions of Arenas's work, and spitefully telling Arenas's credulous aunt that her nephew was now a wealthy man. Gossip similarly plays a role in the feud between Arenas and Angel Rama, detailed by Ocasio, with Arenas alleging that Rama had "signed 'documentos subversivos' [. . .] that favored Castro-financed guerrilla groups throughout Latin America," a widely reported claim that likely contributed to Rama being denied a US visa (192).[13] Even in exile, especially in exile, Arenas continues to use gossip to catalog his few faithful friends and the actions of his many "sordid and money-hungry" enemies (288). More than anything, though, Arenas uses gossip to sway public opinion against Castro. Arenas is clear eyed about the shortcomings of both communism and capitalism: "Although both give you a kick in the ass, in the communist system you have to applaud, while in the capitalist system you can scream. And I came here to scream," he writes (288). But after so many furtive liaisons, so many whispered tales and suppressed scraps of writing, the ability to scream, to publish and be damned, is all that Arenas seeks. "I scream, therefore I exist," he declares (301).[14]

Of all Arenas's screams from exile, his last rang loudest: *Antes que anochezca,* his final work, was his most decisive intervention in the public sphere, not least because it also serves as an extended suicide note. In a final act of self-gossip, *Antes que anochezca* concludes by reproducing

Arenas's actual suicide note, dubbed a *carta de despedida,* or farewell letter. Arenas certainly intended his note to be read far and wide, arranging for it to be distributed not just to his friends but also to a larger public. The note is a political gesture, one final attack: though brief, it is dense with political declarations, personal attacks on Castro—"There is only one person I hold accountable: Fidel Castro," he declares—and the unspoken conviction that public speech, public writing, is a weapon that can bring down tyrants (317). Arenas's suicide note is an attempt to reframe his death as a political gesture: not simply another life ended by AIDS but rather, as Benigno Sánchez-Eppler suggests, "a politically marked Cuban suicide, with undisputed access to a Cuban grandeur worthy of monumentalization" (180). By making his suicide note a political and literary gesture, Arenas seeks to insert himself—all his life, with all its excesses and deprivations—into the public sphere, as a parting blow against the Castro regime. As Sánchez-Eppler notes, "The life so masterfully ended is explicitly handed over fully self-inscribed into the *res publica*" (177). Arenas closes his note with a defiant rallying cry—"Cuba will be free. I already am"—but, almost as an afterthought, offers the postscript "TO BE PUBLISHED" (317). It is both a practical instruction and a fitting epitaph for a writer who strove all his life for publication and for entry into the public sphere—just as avidly as he sought out sex, and with far more seriousness.

The Gossip Broker: *Mea Cuba* and *Vidas para leerlas*

Arenas's text has been widely read as a work of *testimonio:* a searing, personal account of hardships endured and persecution witnessed.[15] This can, however, be rather discomfiting for its reader. *Antes que anochezca* stands as "one of the most wrenching testimonials of oppression and rebellion written in our tongue," notes Mario Vargas Llosa, but is undervalued because it "has the perverse faculty of leaving its readers bruised and uncomfortable, as though waking from an infernal nightmare" ("Pájaro tropical"). The rawness of Arenas's text, and the bitterness behind the braggadocio, makes it a difficult pill to swallow. John Beverley proposes that "the complicity a testimonio establishes with its readers involves their identification—by engaging their sense of ethics and justice—with a popular cause normally distant, not to say alien, from their immediate experience" (37). Arenas's autobiography depends upon just this process: ironically, in a text so full of seduction and consummation, Arenas makes little effort to seduce his readers but simply assumes that they will be outraged by the abuses he describes. Arenas's undeniable charisma and his depiction of Castro's Cuba as a nonstop sex romp keeps us turning the pages, but his gossip seeks to denounce rather than to convince. The reader is left simply to accept or reject Arenas's viewpoint; there is little middle ground and little attempt to win over those who may waiver between the two ideological poles that Arenas presents.

Like Arenas, the exiled Cuban writer Guillermo Cabrera Infante also relies on gossip to weave himself into the international public sphere. Where Arenas uses gossip as a means of vengeance and self-assertion, however, Cabrera Infante uses gossip as a more subtle tool, intended both to lure his readers into ideological complicity and to tell the story of Cuban exiles, including but not limited to Cabrera Infante himself, in a way that directly rebuts and is designed to outlast the Castro regime's own international propaganda efforts. This is not to say that Cabrera Infante gossips less than Arenas; in fact, Cabrera Infante gossips with remarkable avidity. Still, where Arenas builds his entire autobiography out of gossipy anecdotes, Cabrera Infante's gossip is as much a question of style and tone as of the specific information he relays. There is, of course, plenty of explicit gossip in Cabrera Infante's writing, especially in the political essays, written between the 1960s and the early 1990s and collected in 1992 in *Mea Cuba* and *Vidas para leerlas,* on which I here focus. Still, he gossips not only through carefully staged scenes and anecdotes but also through a near constant stream of tossed-off asides and insinuations, backhanded details, and self-indulgently vicious digressions. Gossip, in fact, is as much a part of Cabrera Infante's literary style as the wordplay and puns for which he is better known.

Cabrera Infante does more than simply emulate the style and formal structure of gossip, however: he also puts juicy meat on its bones. We see vividly, in his ad hominem attacks, the "degeneration of argument into insult and accusation" that Jean Franco perceives in Cuban discourse more generally in the wake of the Padilla affair (96). We learn in passing, for instance, that Che Guevara had a speech impediment and that Fidel Castro habitually filched cigars. But we also learn the intimate secrets and personal quirks of countless Cuban literary and artistic figures, including many whom Cabrera Infante considered his friends and allies. In *Vidas,* for instance, he gleefully reveals that Piñera was known as much for his romantic trysts as for his literary works, and that Enrique Labrador Ruiz once drank Pablo Neruda under the table.[16] Cabrera Infante makes no attempt to conceal the fact that his essays are woven from gossip. *Vidas* borrows its title from Plutarch, "but it isn't comparable to the

Plutarchian model—except in that Plutarch gave considerable importance to salon gossip and court rumors," he remarks, adding parenthetically that Plutarch's master, Herodotus, "was called in Greece not the father of history, but the king of gossip" (*MCAD* 807). The effect, in *Vidas* and elsewhere, is of a panorama of Cuban art and politics, with Cabrera Infante dispensing, through barbed and breezy gossip, his own superior knowledge of the significant figures of the postrevolutionary period.

This aspect of gossip—the promise of the inside scoop—is one that marks Cabrera Infante's essays, not least because Cabrera Infante really did have a privileged view of the Cuban revolution and the early years of the postrevolutionary regime. As editor in chief of *Lunes de revolución,* Havana's most celebrated cultural magazine, Cabrera Infante had a ringside seat for many of the defining moments of Cuba's postrevolutionary cultural life: his brother codirected *PM,* the short film that sparked Castro's clampdown on intellectual and artistic freedoms; he was present for Castro's "Palabras a los intelectuales" speech; his work played a part in the Padilla affair; and so on. As Raymond D. Souza notes, Cabrera Infante's firsthand knowledge of the period's key literary and political figures "is enough to make a Cubanist weep" (82).[17]

Even from exile, Cabrera Infante remained in close contact with vast numbers of other Cubans writers and intellectuals, and worked hard to maintain his image as a "king of gossip" and source of inside information about happenings on the island. Those who visited his London apartment frequently came away having been pumped for information and pumped full of fresh gossip in return. In a letter to Cabrera Infante from 1967, Julio Cortázar acknowledges Cabrera Infante's role as a gossip broker and marvels at the speed with which news travels to him from Havana: "I've heard plenty of talk of the 'Arab telephone,' but the Cuban beats it for (or by) a long chalk. One can speak of a script in Havana, and the name of its author will arrive in London before the speaker has returned to Paris, proving once more the truth of the profound adage that my aunts used to say: it's a small world." Gossip may turn a large world into a small one, but not all of Cabrera Infante's friends were as appreciative of the writer's tendency to gossip. In a letter from 1980, Manuel Puig chides Cabrera Infante for his excessive gossip and begs him to be more discreet: "I beg you not to disclose things about me that you've learned as a friend. [. . .] I know that these things stem from an anxious drive for general amusement, for continuous humor, but sometimes things get complicated." In another letter, Yale professor Emir Rodríguez Monegal tells Cabrera Infante that he has urged Rita Guibert, the author of *Seven Voices,* to refrain from publishing gossip about Castro that Cabrera Infante had shared with her: "I talked with Rita Guibert about removing from your interview the phrase about certain of Fidel's intimacies," Rodríguez Monegal writes. "Your interview was too good to go into such details. Rita promised me she'd remove the blessed phrase." Cabrera Infante's implacable drive to gossip was not just well known to his friends and peers; it was a critical part of Cabrera Infante's identity and hard-won public image, even if, as Puig and others recognized, it could also be intrusive, reckless, or even dangerous.

While Cabrera Infante's gossip is grounded in the promise of the inside scoop, it also carries the implicit threat that those who ignore it will be made to look foolish or be deceived by pro-Castro propaganda. In one gossipy aside, Cabrera Infante suggests that revolutionary heroine Haydée Santamaría, the founder of Casa de las Américas, may not have been the brightest bulb in the box. "One time Haydée told me, and not in confidence: 'What an ignorant, stupid peasant I am! I always thought that Marx and Engels were just one philosopher. Like Ortega y Gasset, you know,'" he reports (*MCAD* 538). But his point is not simply that Santamaría is dim-witted; it is that she is uncritical. He continues:

> Of more relevance were Haydée's revelations after returning from her first trip to Russia. She then trustingly confided in me: "In Moscow, I met Ekaterina Furtseva. You know, the minister of Culture. [. . .] She explained to me, woman to woman (or better, comrade to comrade), what happened to the writers and artists who died in the Stalin era. They didn't kill them because they were hermetic poets, bourgeois novelists, and abstract painters. No. In truth, they had them shot because they were Nazi spies and not artists. How about that? All agents of Hitler! There was no solution but to exterminate them. Do you understand?" Yes, I understood. Ah, what an innocent and dangerous revolutionary she was! (*MCAD* 538)

The reader is invited to join Cabrera Infante in rolling their eyes at Santamaría's credulity. But Cabrera Infante's invitation contains a delicately veiled threat: you and I, gentle reader, know better than that, he implies—and thereby also insinuates that if readers reject his opinions or scorns his gossip, then they risk proving themselves as credulous and dim-witted as Santamaría.

This is, for Cabrera Infante, a two-way, adversarial process: just as he seeks to condemn and sideline those who allow themselves to be taken in by the Cuban state, so too he believes himself to be besieged by people who question his authority. An exchange of letters in the *London Review of Books* following the publication of "Infante's Inferno" in 1982 makes this clear. The Cuban poet Pedro Perez Sarduy writes rejecting Cabrera Infante's characterizations of Cuba under Castro and questioning Cabrera Infante's ability to accurately depict the island from exile: "I had recently arrived in England from Havana and was amazed that someone who for over fifteen years had been out of his native country, Cuba—my country—should attempt the remembrance of things for him long passed. I was especially amazed since Guillermito, as he was known in his early satiric days, was one of those writers who never did know what happened." Perez Sarduy goes on to quote Padilla's denunciation of Cabrera Infante as "a social misfit *par excellence,* a man of the humblest extraction" and to mock Padilla and Cabrera Infante for gossiping in exile. "Now, in a different time and space, they whisper secrets to each other over the phone," he writes. Finally, he bemoans the ease with which Cabrera Infante wins attention by gossiping about the Castro government. "Guillermo Cabrera Infante is not only a much-embittered and out-of-touch man now: he never did know what happened in Cuba," he insists. Cabrera Infante, unwilling to let such challenges to his credibility go unanswered, fired back a letter labeling Perez Sarduy a nobody, with no inside knowledge or personal connections upon which to draw. "Who is Pedro Pérez, and why is he saying these ludicrous things about me? He claims he knew me as Cain but I swear I don't know him from Adam," he writes in his response in 1983. He then seeks to turn the attack into a sign of the degree to which his own gossip has gotten under Castro's skin—thus affirming his own authority—and to cast Perez as a proxy for the regime. "His letter I do recognise, though. It's the typical production of the apparatchik: a massive missive made in Moscow[. . . .] I enjoy detecting the hidden Goebbels in every party political broadcast."

This conceit—that Cabrera Infante's gossip is so urgent and important that it represents a festering thorn in Fidel Castro's side, and that any criticism is therefore part of a pushback orchestrated by the regime—is one to which Cabrera Infante returns time and again throughout his political writing. Sometimes he suggests that he is at risk not just of getting hauled over the coals in literary journals but of more sinister and dangerous attacks. When Cabrera Infante's London apartment is mysteriously broken into—and nothing taken, despite valuables having been left openly on display—he decides that Castro is behind the episode, and compares himself to Georgy Markov, the Bulgarian exile killed by the KGB with a ricin-tipped umbrella. There is obviously some distance between a break-in, however mysterious, and a political assassination. Still, by framing Markov as a fellow gossip, killed after disclosing "a series of intimate revelations about the life and miseries of the unnamable Bulgarian tyrant," Cabrera Infante seeks to share in the "aura of James Bond" that marked the media's portrayal of the Markov case (*MCAD* 470–71). The risk of retaliation is real, Cabrera Infante insists: "To presume that Castro governs only within Cuba is to refuse to admit that a political exile is a fleeing enemy to whom is extended not a silver bridge, but a long arm that can reach him anywhere," he warns darkly (*MCAD* 468–69). Nonetheless, he flaunts his unwillingness to be silenced. "I'm only worried about the fate of my family, stranded in Cuba [. . .]. But I had to speak, and to begin to tell these things," he insists (*MCAD* 480).

Despite Cabrera Infante's ostentatious performance of courage in the face of danger, however, he is chiefly threatened by reputational attacks, not ricin-tipped umbrellas. He repeatedly claims that Castro has worked, directly or indirectly, to slander him and obscure his contributions to Cuban letters. After Cabrera Infante's break with the regime in 1968, the official periodical of the Cuban military, *Verde olivo,* published a litany of personal attacks, suggesting that Cabrera Infante had relied on nepotism to have his work published, accusing him of collaborating with the CIA, and noting primly that only a debauched mind could have dreamed up the drunks, junkies, and prostitutes that populate the Havana of *Tres tristes tigres* (Avila 22). It would be easy enough for Cabrera Infante to brush off such partisan attacks were it not for what they signified: not just one critic's disapproval but the regime's determination to make his works disappear. Over the years that followed, the arbiters of Cuban culture did their best to airbrush Cabrera Infante from the country's literary history, and he was pointedly excised from the *Diccionario de la literatura cubana* (Venegas 109). Such attacks, for Cabrera Infante, carried a real sting: "Nothing kills a writer like being forgotten," he laments (*MCAD* 913).

The state's totalitarian impulse for narrative control, Cabrera Infante suggests, can be enacted through force in Cuba but must be achieved through more subtle means in the international public sphere. "Nothing works in Cuba besides two things: the police and propaganda. The police for the interior, propaganda for the exterior," he writes (*MCAD* 779). Writers on the island and the manuscripts left behind by exiles are entirely within Castro's power, Cabrera Infante asserts, declaring himself "truly worried" about the unpublished works of writers such as Piñera and Arenas, which he claims will be left to rot in a basement of the State Security building known to insiders as "Siberia" (*MCAD* 553). Even writers who have fled the island are still within reach of Castro's propaganda machine—a machine, Cabrera Infante makes clear, that is itself fueled by gossip. Cabrera Infante details Castro lashing out, two decades after Carlos Franqui's 1968 break with Cuba, with "mere gossip" about Franqui having abandoned his mother (*MCAD* 634). The reputational attack is intended, Cabrera Infante claims, as a warning shot, a means of silencing Franqui: "But why slander Franqui now and not then? The answer is simple. Franqui has just finished a portrait of Fidel Castro with all his warts. Franqui knows his model very well, and knows many private stories and can tell them. There is no other reason for the current mendacity" (*MCAD* 634). The Castro regime deploys gossip and defamation, Cabrera Infante argues, as means of keeping exiles tangled in its web. But despite being erased from official photographs and subjected to personal attacks, Franqui—like Cabrera Infante, the reader is surely meant to realize—bravely responds with gossip of his own. His *Retrato de familia con Fidel* (1981) contained "scoops and news, some of them sensational," Cabrera Infante writes, including an account of Castro, piqued at being sidelined during the Cuban missile crisis, muscling his way to a control panel and personally launching missiles at an American spy plane (*MCAD* 642–43). The widely reported anecdote tarnished Castro's carefully cultivated image, and Cabrera Infante retells it with the theatrical enjoyment of a street-corner gossip passing on a juicy bit of hearsay.

This brings to the fore a paradoxical aspect of Cabrera Infante's use of gossip: while he does share plenty of firsthand information, he also stakes his credibility on his ability to recirculate stories told to him by others. The official account is mere propaganda, he insists, so only through personal reports—whispered accounts smuggled out of Cuba by, or to, exiles such as Cabrera Infante—can international observers learn the true nature of Castro's revolution. Cabrera Infante also stresses the regime's efforts to repress gossip in Cuba, thus increasing his own value as a gossip broker. In passing on information about the shooting of Trotskyites and Catholics, for instance, Cabrera Infante credits the writer Calvert Casey, emphasizing that Casey heard it "on good authority" through "clandestine connections" (*MCAD* 850) and was punished for what he disclosed. In a similar episode that Cabrera Infante relays in a 1981 *London Review of Books* article, Casey suffers for spilling the beans about Castro's persecution of homosexuals:

> Even poor, peaceful Calvert Casey got into trouble when he dared tell a Mexican writer of the Left, just one more political tourist, that there were camps for homosexuals all over Cuba, and they were not exactly summer camps. This was a carefully guarded secret which Calvert knew about through the

gay grapevine. Next morning, as in a guilty hangover, the Mexican tipped off Haydée Santamaria that she had counter-revolutionaries in her house, who told tales, very dangerous lies for Casa de las Americas. He whispered a gringo name, Casey. Calvert was severely reprimanded and demoted. (BC)

Cabrera Infante shows Casey relying on gossip to both discover and disclose the regime's secrets—and ultimately paying the price for doing so, thanks to the whispers of an informant. The only gossip that is permitted, Cabrera Infante claims, is that of neighbors who reveal one another's secrets to the government. "Castro has forced the Cuban people to become snitches," he writes. "He has created a Cuban version of the Nazi Blockwarts in the *Comités de Defensa de la Revolución,* in which each Cuban is forced to spy on their neighbor, the children on their parents, and each one on the other" (*MCAD* 753). Cabrera Infante here closely tracks Ponte's description of the spying that takes place between neighbors in Castro's Cuba, as discussed in chapter 1. Still, where Ponte wryly compares prying neighbors to official security forces, Cabrera Infante draws a comparison with Nazi Germany, in a gesture designed to paint the revolution in the starkest possible terms before his global audience. There are no shades of gray here: to memorialize, for Cabrera Infante, is also to sensationalize, and thereby inject his own thoroughly partisan understanding of the revolution into the public sphere.

The counterhistory that Cabrera Infante assembles through gossipy, one-sided, and often rather histrionic anecdotes has not always been well received. In a July 1981 letter to the *London Review of Books,* where one of *Mea Cuba*'s lengthiest essays originally appeared, Nissa Torrents and Christopher Abel complain: "His article is littered with unsupported assertions and is heavily reliant upon gossip and hearsay that would be inadmissible as evidence in the analysis of any political system. [. . .] He tends to confuse fiction with a personal attack on the regime that sinks even to the banalities of describing his opponents as 'paunchy' and 'bald.' [. . .] Indeed, the author of the article undermines his own case by trivialising points that he clearly considers important." Cabrera Infante's article, the letter concludes, is "merely a catalogue of undisguised prejudices by an idiosyncratic author whose private likes and dislikes are presented as political journalism." Torrents and Abel correctly identify Cabrera Infante's method but misinterpret his goal: he seeks not to offer a balanced analysis of the Cuban situation but rather to gossip about, and against, Castro's regime. Read as gossip, Cabrera Infante's diatribe makes much more sense; in this light, we come to understand not just his offhandedly partisan attitude but also the political calculations behind his approach.

Cabrera Infante's discussion of the Castro regime's persecution of homosexuals, for instance, is mapped through insinuations and insults; he describes the policies as stemming from an "infamous collective illness" marked by "an obsession with queers, queens and kinks" that originates with Fidel Castro himself. "Why this 'pathological' aberration? Fidel Castro is, as gays in the United States like to say with terrible grammar, *mucho macho*," Cabrera Infante writes. "On the other hand, Che Guevara considered homosexuals to be sick people who must give way to the politically healthy 'new man' made by Communist Cuba" (BC). The implication, echoing Arenas, is that the ostentatious performance of *machismo* by Castro and Guevara, and the revolution's persecution of gays, speaks to an unvoiced insecurity: in short, the revolution is queerer than it looks. Like Arenas, too, Cabrera Infante pivots from insinuation to undiluted gossip: "There are multiple levels of irony here. The other Guevara, Alfredo, was a notorious fag, protected by Fidel's own brother, Raul Castro," he writes. Gossip becomes an argument as well as an attack: by gossiping about the regime's tolerance of well-connected homosexuals, Cabrera Infante makes the case that its anti-gay policies stem not from ideological imperatives, but merely from the whims and prejudices of hypocritical officials.

This is a critical aspect of Cabrera Infante's gossip: it is not mere logorrhea but rather a serious political gesture (or, as Wiegmink might argue, a performance) intended to gain attention, generate controversy, and establish Cabrera Infante's own status in both the exile community and the international public sphere. The backlash against his gossip thus became a confirmation of his significance; indeed, the criticism leveled by Torrents and Abel was precisely the kind of literary ruckus that Cabrera Infante had been hoping to stir up. In a 1981 letter to Rodríguez Monegal, he brags about plans to republish "Bites from the Bearded Crocodile" in Germany, Japan, Mexico, and Spain, and notes the resistance to his article: "I'm sending you, too, a photocopy of one of the letters (typical *castrista* professor, like those you've suffered) and my answer," he wrote. "These people never seem to learn that if you mess with us [. . .] you'd better be careful." Cabrera Infante's jeering, gossipy prose, it seems, was meant to stick in the craws of his *castrista* critics and to provoke violent reactions that would get Cabrera Infante's message noticed on the global stage. During the 1960s, in fact, Cabrera Infante used precisely this strategy to secure a wider audience. In 1968, he wrote to *Life en español* editor Alberto Cellario pitching a polemical article on Cuban cultural affairs. "I've accumulated so many facts, so much material, and have a knowledge not only first-hand but from being the originator of many of these incidents and revelations," he assured Cellario, continuing: "If you want I can send the *Primera Plana* articles, the attacks, my answers, etc., etc." Once again, Cabrera Infante promises the inside scoop: the envisioned article, he writes, "would deal specifically with a sensitive angle that has never been touched on by anyone who studies the Revolution." Cabrera Infante here makes clear that his own inside knowledge and the controversies that his writing generates go hand in hand. He is also frank about his ambitions: *Life en español* would be attractive "for the reach it would give and the penetration it would grant to my documents and allegations," he explains.

Cabrera Infante's insistence on his credibility, and on the accuracy of his depictions of the Castro regime, repeatedly leads him to clash with writers who view Castro's Cuba through a more forgiving lens. One such case is the British writer Graham Greene, whom Cabrera Infante depicts in his writing as a dupe suckered into becoming a "faithful servant" of Castro's propaganda machine (*MCAD* 989). Elsewhere, he is more explicit: "Greene chose to be inimical to Batista and amicable with Castro for religious reasons. He sees himself as Castro's paraclete, whereas he is only the devil's advocate," he writes (II). Greene, he suggests, allowed himself to be seduced by Castro's romantic image and to imagine himself an insider—but he was, in Cabrera Infante's telling, only ever a useful idiot, an outsider put to work to polish the global public image of the Castro regime.

To establish the inadequacy of Greene's knowledge of Cuba, Cabrera Infante follows his usual methods, first claiming personal insight into Greene's time in Cuba: "I know, because it was I who arranged Greene's first meeting with Castro," he brags (*MCAD* 694).[18] In contrast, Cabrera Infante suggests, Greene is a mere interloper, with only the crudest understanding of the Cuban situation. Cabrera Infante mocks Greene for his insistence on calling key Cuban figures by their first name—Fidel, Haydée—as a means of suggesting familiarity with the island. Greene suggests Cubans refer to their leaders by their first names as a sign of affection; in fact, Cabrera Infante asserts, Cubans are simply terrified of being seen as opposing Castro. "One of the most hideous tyrants in America ever, the Mexican Porfirio Díaz, was always called respectfully by Mexicans Don Porfirio: only enemies called him Porfirio," Cabrera Infante notes (II). Such nuances, however, are lost on outsiders. Greene sees but does not understand, Cabrera Infante suggests—the corollary to his attack being that to truly grasp the reality of the Cuban nation, we need the guidance of an insider such as Cabrera Infante himself.

Cabrera Infante seeks to further diminish Greene by firing off a flurry of barbed digs and fragments of gossip. Cabrera Infante mocks Greene's friendship with the Soviet defector Kim Philby and writes scathingly of how Greene regaled Castro during one of their meetings with tales of how he used to play Russian roulette as a young man. The tale reflects poorly on Greene, who toyed with suicide at an age when most young men "play more vital games," Cabrera Infante writes (*MCAD* 655). Cabrera Infante also repeatedly mocks Greene's depiction of Batista's Cuba as a pleasure island packed with casinos and brothels. Greene himself spent plenty of time and money in Batista's Cuba, Cabrera Infante claims, and now writes "like a Victorian moralist (one of those who would hide their perverse sex beneath the Macferlan of their good manners)" (*MCAD* 695). In the English version of *Mea Cuba,* Cabrera Infante adds that Greene divined Cuba's moral shortcomings using "Aaron's rod"—a mocking biblical reference, but also a phallic, Lawrencian euphemism intended to suggest Greene's alleged hypocrisy and past debauchery (*MC* 295).

Here, once more, Cabrera Infante blurs the line between revelatory gossip and ad hominem attacks. The adversarialism continues in the letters that followed the publication of Cabrera Infante's article, with Greene himself scolding Cabrera Infante for various errors: "When one attacks one should get one's facts correct. This Mr Cabrera has failed to do," he writes tersely ("Letters: "Cain's Cuba"). Characteristically, Cabrera Infante's response is more verbose: "Cuba is more than somebody else's facts. She is my constant concern. But Greene, like many modern writers, confuses facts with truth. He of all people should know that the Gospels are revealed truth—but are they fact? Moreover, he seems to believe that dates are facts. Is the year Jesus was born faith or fact? For a doubting Catholic, Greene reveals himself to be as factual as a materialist" ("Letters: Cain's Cuba"). Elsewhere, Cabrera Infante claims that his original article "provoked a tantrum by Graham Greene, who tried to defend the indefensible: Fidel Castro's obscene political presence" (*MCAD* 695). As before, Cabrera Infante sees Greene's anger, and his own response, as a vindication of his methods. Writing about the episode in the English translation of *Mea Cuba,* where he reproduced his response to Greene, he claims that Greene was "totally rebuked" by his reply (*MC* 308). He concludes with another first-person anecdote, about a time the pair crossed paths at a bookstore owned by Greene's brother, where Greene was attending a party. "There, front and center, tall, looking more than ever like a fish-faced phony, was Greene with a glass of wine in his hand," Cabrera Infante writes.[19] "Before turning around and going back to the street, I saw his bloodless face redden. Did he fear a real slap rather than a literary one? Or was it the wine?" (*MCAD* 695). The episode is told through gossip, but the aim is clear: to depict Greene as cowed—and perhaps more important, speechless—in the face of Cabrera Infante's truth telling. Through a personal attack, Cabrera Infante aims to establish himself as the only credible source of information about the reality of Cuban life under Castro, and to ensure that it will be his account that endures to shape Cuba's perception in the public sphere.

Cabrera Infante may not have demolished Greene's vision of Cuba quite as effectively as he claims. In a broader sense, however, he was largely successful in giving reach and traction to his account of the Cuban revolution: a great many of Cabrera Infante's tales have now become widely accepted and repeated parts of the revolution's folklore. In disseminating his own versions of events, however, Cabrera Infante also seeks to force his readers to address the Cuban revolution on moral rather than ideological terms. As he writes, "My position is an extreme moral, not political, opposition" (*MCAD* 759). Gossip is well suited to this project: to gossip, after all, is a collaborative act that not only renders judgment but also presumes moral alignment between its participants. Cabrera Infante's texts, by drawing the reader in with gossipy anecdotes and the promise of privileged insights, seek to foster a complicity that will ultimately give way to shared outrage and incite what Rafael Rojas calls "a moral reaction to political barbarism" (*Tumbas* 35). This may involve a turning away from philosophical debate about the merits of communism, but it is far from apolitical. Cabrera Infante accuses the Castro government of engaging in "politics through other means: hooliganism" (*MCAD* 790), and in fact Cabrera Infante uses gossip as a key tool of his own politically charged *gamberrada,* or hooliganism: a way to scrawl dissenting messages in opposition to the Castro government and to hoot and jeer back at the foreign intellectuals whom he sees as helping to shore up the regime's global image. Cabrera Infante is dismissive of the foreign intellectuals who oppose him, writing that "to stir up such *bochinche* isn't to take a stand against me or what I write, but rather to be against liberty in a free country" (*MCAD* 790). But *bochinche*—here used in the sense of a ruckus, though still one incited by gossip—is actually something Cabrera Infante directly seeks to inspire. Just as Mouffe suggests that the artist obtains political significance "by subverting the dominant hegemony and by contributing to the construction of new subjectivities" (5), so Cabrera Infante sees his ability to spark angry debate as a direct blow against the narrative hegemony of the Castro regime and as generating precisely the kind of messy narrative pluralism that, in Cuba, he sees as effectively suppressed by the Castro government.

This, in fact, is the foremost role of gossip in Cabrera Infante's political writing: a means of stirring up trouble and of undermining too-generous or too-credulous readings of the Cuban revolution by those outside the island. In an essay from *Mea Cuba,* Cabrera Infante ponders the absence of dissident writers in the communist countries of Eastern Europe and argues that Cuba, similarly stricken by silence, "has become a Latin American Albania." He continues: "But few foreigners know this. Political hell is paved with the ignorance of strangers. The Holocaust was fully known only after the war. The gulags were publicised only after the death of Stalin. The atrocities of Castro, not all of them literary, will be known in full only after his demise, whenever that may be" (BC). Cabrera Infante once more compares Castro's excesses to those of the Nazis in the hope of eliciting a visceral reaction from his foreign readers. Such acts of radical hyperbole may sometimes have backfired, making Cabrera Infante easier to dismiss as a crank, but it is indicative of the urgency underpinning his project. Through gossip, he aims to supply insights that would otherwise come to light only after the fall of the communist government. Cabrera Infante describes Castro as "a crude actor" playing his version of *Macbeth* "to the largest captive audience in the Americas" (BC). But the audience, he suggests, extends beyond the island and encompasses the credulous onlookers in foreign parts who applaud while the Cuban tragedy unfolds. Through the moral charge and scrappy adversarialism of gossip, Cabrera Infante seeks to disrupt the performance: to hiss and holler and to force others to join him or shout him down. His goal in gossiping is to problematize, to provoke, and ultimately to substitute outrage and angry debate for credulous acquiescence.

The Historical and the Everyday: *A Small Place*

Arenas and Cabrera Infante are not the only Caribbean intellectuals to appeal to gossip in order to mobilize public sympathy and intervene in the public sphere. Eric Williams, the first prime minister of Trinidad, was renowned for his mastery of informal, almost casual oratory, and his ability to keep a crowd enthralled as he wove gossip, history, and politics together into a single compelling countercolonial narrative. Thanks to his grasp on populist oratory, writes Spencer Mawby, "no other anti-colonial politician was better qualified to question the truthfulness of the uplifting imperial stories which the British liked to tell to themselves and to the colonized" (31). The Barbadian novelist George Lamming offers a widely quoted summary of Williams's populist appeal: "He turned history, the history of the Caribbean, into gossip so that the story of a people's predicament seemed no longer the infinite barren track of documents, dates and texts. Everything became news: slavery, colonization, the forgivable deception of metropolitan rule, the sad and inevitable unawareness of native production. His lectures retained always the character of whisper which everyone was allowed to hear, a rumor which experience had established as truth" (731).[20] Cabrera Infante and Williams were very different figures, operating in different political contexts and with different goals; still, there are similarities in their approaches. In his best-known speech, the "Massa Day Done" address given in Woodford Square in 1961, Williams seeks to personalize Trinidad's social and economic history, offering a detailed account of the "Massa" who extracted personal wealth from Trinidadian society and offered little in return. Williams weaves in gossipy details—the "Massa" who gave his name to a beach and then returned to England to worship in the same church as his ancestors, the "Massa" who fiercely protested limits on floggings, and so forth—in order to grab his audience's attention and lead them through his argument for Trinidadian nationalism. Williams's collage of historical anecdotes, filtered through gossipy oratory, is remarkably similar to Cabrera Infante's own approach in the historical vignettes of *Vista del amanecer en el trópico* (1981). Williams's approach, with its composite subject, is arguably more a rhetorical or oratorical flourish, a stratagem, than true gossip; still, as we have seen, Cabrera Infante's use of gossip is also very much a stratagem, and one deployed to similar if not identical effect.

Where Arenas and Cabrera Infante used gossip to insert themselves into an international public sphere, however, Williams uses gossip to shape the local, Trinidadian public sphere and to carry his audience along with him as he pushes back against the imposed logic and power structures of empire. Jamaica Kincaid's *A Small Place* (1988) has something of both approaches, using gossip to stage both an angry outward-facing critique of the neocolonial forces she sees at work in the Antiguan tourism trade, and a finger-pointing attack on Antigua's troubled domestic politics. Its first two sections present a disdainful reflection on the impact of rich, white tourists on the tiny island of Antigua; its third, read by some scholars as a reward for white readers who persevere through the first two essays, is an equally embittered reflection on the failings of the island's black political elites. All three sections of the book, as Nalini Natarajan remarks, use gossip—chiefly, in Natarajan's reading, to forge a fragmentary and deliberately inconsistent account of Antigua's political reality. The island nation, Natarajan suggests, is "imagined through an epistemology of doubt" that is "especially noteworthy in the pages that describe the horrors of neo-colonial politics, not as a fact, but as a tourist attraction related in town gossip" (130). She continues: "Gossip is the medium of the text's relentless tirades (against the enemies of Antigua, domestic and colonial); fragmented information (about the doctors, the politicians, the businessmen), repetition (the Library, corruption, colonial atrocities), rumours (the horror stories of domestic violence). [. . .] The fragmented telling, the petty prejudices, the mistakes and inconsistencies, the trivial details, the lack of proof in many of the judgments made make this all a very non-authoritarian, non-positivist imagining of nation" (130–31). Where Natarajan sees gossip as fundamentally "unliterary" and opposed to the radical certainties of the printed word, I prefer to read Kincaid's project as one of scandalization. Natarajan is correct to perceive some of the oral markers of gossip in Kincaid's text, but it is in the content of Kincaid's "relentless tirades" and rumors that gossip's presence can most clearly be seen: not the accessible, populist patter of Williams's speeches, but rather an accumulation of accusations and shocking details intended to serve as spurs to a complacent readership.

Kincaid's short but discomfiting piece is simultaneously accusatory and ashamed, and determined to bring into the light all the untold secrets and failings of Antiguan society and politics. Kincaid suggests that the white tourist, with whom her reader is expected to identify, is the unwitting subject of gossip, mocked by local Antiguans for their accent and appearance, their way of eating, even their intimate habits. "They collapse helpless from laughter, mimicking the way they imagine you must look as you carry out some everyday bodily function. They do not like you," she writes (*A Small Place* 17). Structurally, gossip depends upon having a specific, identified subject; here, Kincaid makes the reader that subject, in a narrative twist that both generates an affective charge and demands that the reader consider his or her own relationship to, or complicity in, the scandals being described. Kincaid also uses gossip, or something very like it, to skewer and deflate the various prominent white figures of Antigua's colonial past. As J. Brooks Bouson notes, the English heroes who gave their names to the streets are revealed by Kincaid to be "maritime criminals," while Princess Margaret is described as "putty-faced" and the Barclay brothers are cast as former slave traders (99). But it is in the third section of *A Small Place,* when Kincaid turns her cannons inward and fires broadside after broadside against the island's black political leaders, that gossip truly comes to the fore. This, she makes clear, is a public accounting of the island's open secrets and the scandals already on the lips of native Antiguans. "As Kincaid's speaker assumes the role of the insider-informant and talebearer, the reader becomes a kind of eavesdropper on island gossip about governmental corruption," Bouson writes (104). In staging the things that Antiguans say about their government officials, Kincaid's text also serves as a condemnation of the fact that their words, their gossip, fails to ignite into political action. Kincaid reflects at some length on why, exactly, Antiguans' gossip about government corruption does not spark a political awakening. Part of the reason, she suggests, is that in Antigua, the scandalization of the everyday makes the scandalization of larger events less compelling. "In a small place, people cultivate small events," she writes. "The small event is isolated, blown up, turned over and over, and then absorbed into the everyday, so that at any moment it can and will roll off the inhabitants of the small place's tongues. For the people in a small place, every event is a domestic event" (*A Small Place* 52). Gossip amplifies the everyday, but historical events are also discussed in the same register and with the same narrow, personal focus. Slavers' flotillas are remembered as if they landed only yesterday; the abuses suffered under slavery, the broken families and beatings and deaths, are equally present and personal. "Then they speak of emancipation itself as if it happened just the other day, not over one hundred and fifty years ago," Kincaid writes. "The word 'emancipation' is used so frequently, it is as if it, emancipation, were a contemporary occurrence, something everybody is familiar with" (55). But where Williams used gossip to make historical events more acutely felt, Kincaid perceives in Antiguans' gossipy relationship with history a kind of flattening: an amplification of the mundane and trivial, and a failure to manifest the proper outrage about the historical situations and government excesses of which she writes. "In Antigua, not only is the event turned into everyday but the everyday is turned into an event," Kincaid asserts (56). This bilateral transformation leads to Antiguans "not knowing why they are the way they are and why they do the things they do" and makes it impossible to "put in their proper place everyday and event, so that exceptional amounts of energy aren't expended on the trivial, while the substantial and the important are assembled (artfully) into a picture story ('He did this and then he did that')" (57). Gossip, in Kincaid's reading, serves to exaggerate the trivial and to collapse the truly momentous into something mundane: worth chattering about, but not worth acting upon.

The gossip of the Antiguan street corner, Kincaid argues, thus comes to seem childlike, or even like a form of insanity. It stands apart from the political life of the island, unmoored, as though—like the townsfolk of *Crónica de una muerte anunciada*—Antiguans have mistaken gossip for action. The gossip of the islanders, which Kincaid so carefully relays, is if not the cause then at least a sign of the paralysis and hapless disempowerment that Kincaid perceives in Antiguans' response to the tourism industry and the corrupt government that it sustains. "They say these things, pausing to take breath before this monument to rottenness, that monument to rottenness, as if they were tour guides; as if, having observed the event of tourism, they have absorbed it so completely that they have made the degradation and humiliation of their daily lives into their own tourist attraction," she writes (68–69). The irony, of course, is that Kincaid herself is both gossip and tour guide. Indeed, the two facets of Kincaid's authorial persona are here directly related. It is through gossip that Kincaid reveals her island's shameful secrets, in an indictment both of Antigua's corrupt leaders and of the tourists who blithely sun themselves without realizing that anything is amiss. But Kincaid, unlike the islanders of whom she writes, is not simply chattering to other Antiguans: she is writing *outward*, addressing her text directly to the "white people in the suburbs" (Cudjoe 401) who visit Antigua's resorts—and who read the *New Yorker*, the publication for which Kincaid originally wrote *A Small Place*. Kincaid frames her account as a revelation of family secrets, intimacies to which foreign visitors are not usually privy; her disclosures are thus very much in the register of gossip, and were perceived as such by her fellow islanders. Perhaps unsurprisingly, Kincaid's text initially met with a strongly negative reception in Antigua. "One thing Antiguans said about *A Small Place:* 'It's true, but did she have to say it?'" Kincaid later said. "No one says that it's a lie; the disagreement is did I have to say it" ("Interview" 499). Like Arenas and Cabrera Infante, Kincaid also experienced pushback from the government; her book was suppressed in Antigua, and Kincaid herself was "informally banned" from the island (Bernard 129). Still, Kincaid writes not primarily for her compatriots but for a global audience. By publishing the gossip of her native island, she challenges foreigners—Americans especially, but also the English—to consider their own complicity in Antigua's postcolonial plight, and seeks thereby to raise awareness of the island's political corruption on the global stage.

Speaking in Signs: Haitian Exile Writers

The efforts of Antigua's government to punish Kincaid for her outspoken criticism were muted by comparison with the ad hominem assault launched against Graham Greene by Haiti's government after the publication of *The Comedians* in 1966. Like Kincaid, Greene wrote his novel, along with numerous newspaper columns and letters, in a bid to increase international awareness of the wrongs he perceived. In so doing, however, he sparked a reputational conflict, mediated through vituperative gossip, into which François Duvalier himself entered with gusto. I will return to this point, but first it seems important to ask: Why was it necessary (or why did it seem so to Greene) for a foreign writer to address Haiti's struggles? If gossip offers a potent and accessible tool with which writers can shape international narratives and insert themselves into the global public sphere, why was it Greene, rather than a Haitian writer, who sought to draw back the curtain on the Duvalier regime? In Cuba and, as detailed in the next chapter, in the Dominican Republic, the authoritarian impulse to exert a narrative monopoly made gossip a vital resource for exiled and dissident writers. Haiti endured back-to-back dictatorships and shares many of the social and postcolonial tensions that mark the Hispanic Caribbean. Where, then, are the gossiping dissidents of Haitian literature?

To begin to answer this question, it is first important to acknowledge that Haitian writers have been far less forceful than their counterparts from other Caribbean nations in writing back against authoritarianism. As Dash notes, Haiti and its diaspora "never managed to produce outstanding treatments of political dictatorship" to rival the "far more accomplished novels in Spanish" ("Exile and Recent Literature" 458). Even within the circumscribed efforts at dictatorship novels and other dissident fiction that have marked the Haitian and exilic fiction of the Duvalier eras, however, gossip plays a smaller role than it does in Cuban or Dominican literature. This may be in part simply because Duvalier cracked down harder and earlier on writers than did Castro or Rafael Leónidas Trujillo, leading the vast majority to flee the nation. For Cabrera Infante and Arenas, Cuba remained a fundamentally vibrant island filled with people trying to hustle and gossip their way through the perils of the Castro regime; for many Haitian exiles, in contrast, the nation was seen as a husk, with little bilateral communication and little love lost between exiled intellectuals and the handful of writers who remained behind. The result, Dash writes, was "an unbridgeable gap of mutual suspicion and distrust [. . .] between those who write in exile and those who are *du dedans*" (*Literature and Ideology* 207). If transatlantic gossip allowed Cabrera Infante, exiled in London, to keep his finger on the pulse of Havana's literary and political happenings, the same was hardly the case for most Haitian exiles in Paris or Montreal.

Indeed, the literary vacuum left by the flight of writers and intellectuals gave rise to an exile community that viewed the nation they had fled in bleak terms. René Depestre's long exile "led him to despair for Haiti," Dash writes, and to come to view it as "a world of vermin and dust where only the living dead survive" ("Engagement, Exile and Errance" 750). For writers such as Depestre, direct engagement with this perceived wasteland was simply too painful to contemplate; in *Le Mât de cocagne* (1979), for instance, Depestre uses allegory not to obliquely recover the country lost in exile but rather to create still more distance. "It is as if the brutal excesses of Duvalier's Haiti are too painful to present without the comforting yet distorting lens of allegory," Martin Munro writes (*Exile* 103). Anthony Phelps, in his 1968 poem "Mon pays que voici," makes a similar point when he writes: "*Ô mon Pays si triste est la saison / qu'il est venu le temps de se parler par signes*" ("O, my country, so sad is the season / that the time has come to speak in signs"). The need for distance, the urge to speak in signs, is antithetical to the stark, intimate specificities in which gossip deals; one cannot gossip without speaking directly.

Georges Anglade, who was imprisoned in the 1970s and subsequently spent many years in exile, alludes to Phelps's poem in his 2006 *lodyan* "Les couverts de trop," which charts Haiti's descent into a silence that Anglade suggests began early in the Duvalier era. Tens of thousands of people, he claims, now quietly set a place at their table for those who have disappeared, an "act of duty to their memory" that "had spread all the more rapidly since it was the last way of speaking of them. By signs" (209).[21] He continues, in a powerful passage worth quoting at length:

> People were falling like flies. First the peddlers of political gossip, public chatterers in perpetual motion who had experienced their moment of glory during a long and hectic presidential campaign. Their flood of information, mostly false, delighted the galleries and *tonnelles*. In every camp they batted with bits of gossip, especially ones that hit below the belt. Those among them who did not realize quickly enough afterward, once the new government was installed, that gossiping so openly was becoming a highly risky occupation, paid for it with their disappearance. One day, just like that, vanished into thin air. And the trade itself disappeared, since there was no one left to carry it on. Then the

gossip-mongers, who had been mere amateurs, gave way to the professional tattletales, trained infiltrators who prompted the revelation of rumors and secrets everywhere. The government lay in ambush, having organized a great word-hunt. Fear swooped down upon the square-shaped city. People had to be wary of what they said, even in other people's dreams, and that is not merely a way of speaking. The tale was told, in great detail, that a careless man mentioned that he had dreamed of hatching a plot with a few of his acquaintances. The whole group vanished. It's true!

Commonplace phrases went back into service. The walls have ears, Discretion is the better part of valor, When the candles are out, all cats are gray, There's no cowardice in taking precautions . . . were no longer figures of speech. People thought they saw ears growing on walls. Only whispering survived. The tattletales, who had replaced the rumor-mongers, gave way to hard-line informers. Spies. Calumny triumphed over even the slightest, most discreet lip movements. Arbitrary accusations of coups d'état and conspiracies were made up out of whole cloth, by the dozens. Even the dogs stopped barking at night. It's almost true!

During those cursed times, since every word was suspect and all speech monitored, as was usual, each of us took refuge in puns and word play in order to exorcise our fear of the executioners: *a sign of the times, this time of signs,* we would chant when the heat was on, from the moment when an inspired poet had been fortunate enough to create a triptych on how sad is the season / when the time has come / to speak to each other with signs. The only thing that remained was the gesture around the table, with teeth clenched. (209–10)

But the silence, and the gestural allegorization of suffering, is not something that ended with the fall of the Duvalier dynasty. In fact, Anglade argues, silence has become a defining characteristic of Haitians, with speech itself understood through its risks as presaging "the rapid arrival of a long silence" inflicted by the powerful on the merely glib. "For there are a good two dozen ways of cleverly characterizing speech (to be silenced) in a country where taciturnity passes for profundity and gloom for strategy," he writes (395). Anglade makes a similar point in "La galerie des huit portraits à grands traits," in which he describes the differences between native-born Haitians and those born in diaspora: "I finally understood that the answer lay not in what they were saying. Their difference lay in the fact that they were speaking," he writes. "For just as speaking in order to say what one truly thinks, to differentiate oneself, to propose, to explore . . . is promoted in their culture, so our culture puts a premium on keeping silent at all times and in all places" (369). The point is a telling one: for Anglade and many other Haitian exiles, silence was too ingrained, too hard-learned a lesson, to simply shrug off after leaving the country.[22]

The relative scarcity of gossip in Haitian texts of the period may also be in part due to linguistic and cultural specificities. Haiti has been studied as a Francophone nation, and most of its literature is in French, but the business of daily life, for the vast majority of Haitians, is conducted in Creole. Literature and gossip are thus separated by a linguistic rift (itself also a social rift) that, though by no means insurmountable, may have made gossip a less obvious and readily available resource for the country's predominantly Francophone writers. To the extent that Creole has been embraced by younger Haitian writers, meanwhile, it typically comes at the expense of their entry into the international public sphere.[23] Even those writers who use Creole, however, typically make fairly limited use of gossip as a narrative strategy and fall back on similar strategies of defensive distancing to those used by their counterparts who write in French. Frankétienne's *Dézafi* (1975), the first novel written in Creole, allegorizes the Duvalier regime by describing its protagonist's zombification by a Vodou sorcerer and his subsequent awakening and instigation of a zombi rebellion. In both *Dézafi* and Frankétienne's French rewriting, *Les Affres d'un défi* (1979), Haitians are allegorized as subsumed in a silenced, zombified collective, reduced to guttural grunts instead of meaningful speech. The zombification described by Frankétienne, one of the few Haitian writers of the period who remained active without going into exile, has become a prominent way for Haitian writers to thematize the impact of the Duvaliers' regimes. The focus in such works, however, is on passivity and silence, not the active and adversarial narrative battles in which gossip proves such a potent weapon.[24] Victimization expressed through oblique, allegorical messages, not resistance or dissidence, has been the primary motif in Haitian approaches to the pain and suffering of the Duvalier era.

Horror and Hearsay: *The Comedians*

It was this state of affairs that made it possible, in 1966, for a peripatetic Englishman to write what has become, as Munro notes, the "best-known novel of the Duvalier dictatorship" (*Tropical Apocalypse* 63). Greene's *The Comedians* is not as densely interwoven with gossip as *Mea Cuba* or *Antes que anochezca,* but it makes a similar promise: to lift the lid on the Duvalier regime and break the silence imposed by the Tontons Macoutes.

The Comedians is not explicitly presented as a roman à clef, and indeed is prefaced by an introductory letter in which Greene denies that any of the novel's characters are drawn from life.[25] But its depiction of the country itself and of the suffering of Haitians under the Duvalier regime, Greene insists, is anything but a fiction. "Poor Haiti itself and the character of Doctor Duvalier's rule are not invented, the latter not even blackened for dramatic effect. Impossible to deepen that night," he writes, continuing: "The Tontons Macoute are full of men more evil than Concasseur; the interrupted funeral is drawn from fact; many a Joseph limps the streets of Port-au-Prince after his spell of torture, and, though I have never met the young Philipot, I have met guerrillas as courageous and as ill-trained in that former lunatic asylum near Santo Domingo." Where Haitian writers struggle in the face of intolerable pain, Greene writes with a certain paternalistic detachment of "poor Haiti"; his text is an expression of sympathy (and, by extension, indignation on another's behalf) rather than of personal suffering. Still, *The Comedians* is intended to be read as an exposé: a fictionalization of real events and real pain, often framed through its characters' reliance on gossip in the absence of credible public institutions. In this way, much like the Cuban works examined in this chapter, Greene's novel stands as an explicitly and theatrically adversarial gesture. If it lacks the deep knowledge of local affairs that Cabrera Infante and Arenas bring to their examinations of Castro's Cuba or that Kincaid brings to bear on Antigua, it nonetheless draws on Greene's own carefully cultivated public persona as a worldly and world-famous writer to render credible claims intended to shock, to startle, and thereby to alter international perceptions of the Duvalier regime.

Three years before the publication of *The Comedians,* Graham Greene used an essay in the *Sunday Telegraph* and the *New Republic* to map some of the key themes—Vodou rites, violent repression, chaos, farce—that would run through his fictional representation of Duvalier's Haiti. Under the headline "Nightmare Republic," Greene wrote:

> While you wait for the lights to go on, you sit around oil-lamps exchanging rumors—the rebels are only 24 hours from Port-au-Prince, one optimist declares; the army has suffered a hundred casualties (it is always a hundred when an optimist speaks); a military plane has been shot down. Someone has heard on the Voice of America. . . . On the way to the hotel one night when I was stopped at a road-block, the man who searched me for arms, patting the hips, the thighs, laying a hand under the testicles, asked my companion in Creole, "Is there any news?"

> But there is no such thing as news any more. (The stories which appear in the *New York Times* or the *New York Herald Tribune* as a rule have a San Domingo dateline and reflect the hopes of the exiles.) The President's daughter is said to be on a hunger-strike to induce her father to leave; the President's wife has abandoned him and is in America.... The Spanish Ambassador came home the other night to find a black dog in the Embassy, but none of his staff would touch it because it might house the spirit of Clement Barbot, the President's deadly enemy, shot down a few weeks back on the edge of Port-au-Prince by the Ton Ton Macoute, the evil militia founded by himself. The Ambassador (the story grows and grows) had to put the dog in his car himself and drive it away. He tried to turn it out in the great square by the Presidential Palace, but it refused to move—the dog was too close to Dr. Duvalier. Only when he reached the cathedral did he consent to budge, trotting off into the dark to seek another sanctuary. Of course there was no truth in the story, but it seemed probable enough in this city without news and between certain hours, without light. (18)

Greene segues between rumor (anonymous, hesitant, about things rather than people) and gossip (specific, sure of itself, about named third parties) as he traces the whispered speculation—all of it in fact inaccurate—that echoes through the darkened streets of Port-au-Prince. Typically of gossip, the truth of the claims matters less than their plausibility—and in Duvalier's Haiti, Greene asserts, even the most lurid claims are perfectly plausible. "Anything may happen, any time, anywhere," he writes (19). Having thus justified his methods, Greene proceeds to mine rumor and gossip to expose the reality—for Greene implicitly promises to reveal the Haitian reality, the hidden truth of the matter—of life under Duvalier's regime. He catalogs the hardships of specific (but unnamed) laborers and beggars, the extravagances of government officials, the actions of rebels and of the Tontons Macoutes, and the religious practices of Duvalier himself, presenting a vivid snapshot of a country spiraling into authoritarian chaos.

Greene returned to these themes, and perhaps these methods, as he wrote *The Comedians,* presenting Haiti as a country in which the decay of official institutions—from the dismantling of the independent news media to the collapse of the telephone system—has left gossip and rumor as the main ways for people to figure out what is going on. Gossip is described as swirling through the marketplace and as a resource that expatriates and foreign officials also rely on, albeit chiefly through intermediaries such as servants tasked with keeping their ears to the ground. The ambassador depends on relayed gossip to learn the "news in town," from the inflow of refugees to neighboring embassies to the theft of Doctor Philipot's body. The captain of the *Medea,* too, uses rumors and hearsay to plan his journey, and Brown, the protagonist, passes on gossip about the Tontons Macoutes machine-gunning the home of a former "prize sharp-shooter of the republic" (15).[26] Brown also depends on gossip to learn what is happening in Port-au-Prince; explaining the discovery of Doctor Philipot's body, Brown reconstructs the gossip and rumors through which the news is transmitted:

> It was said that Doctor Philipot had killed himself, but of course no one knew how the authorities would describe his death—as a political assassination, perhaps, engineered from the Dominican Republic? It was believed the President was in a state of fury. He had badly wanted to get his hands on Doctor Philipot, who one night recently under the influence of rum was said to have laughed at Papa Doc's medical qualifications. I sent Joseph to the market to gather all the information he could. [. . .] Joseph came to my office after breakfast [. . .] to tell me the whole story of the discovery of Doctor Philipot's body as it was now known to the stallholders in the market, if not yet to the police. [. . .] One of the militiamen on the road-block below the hotel had taken a fancy to a peasant-woman who was on her way up to the big market at Kenscoff early that morning. He wouldn't let her pass, for he claimed she was carrying something concealed underneath her layers of petticoat. She offered to show him what she had there, and they went off together down the side-road and into the astrologer's deserted garden. She was in a hurry to complete the long road to Kenscoff, so she went quickly down upon her knees, flung up her petticoats, rested her head on the ground, and found herself staring into the wide glazed eyes of the ex-Minister for Social Welfare. (120–21)

The marketplace gossip about the episode, fueled by a detailed account of the sexual encounter that precipitates the cadaver's discovery, outpaces the official account and comes complete with highly speculative accounts of Papa Doc's own reaction, the reasons behind it, and the cause of the doctor's fall from grace. Such accounts may not be the whole story, but they have a greater claim to accuracy than the official account, which, when it comes, is presented effectively as yet another act of gossip:

> "Poor Philipot," the Minister said, and I wondered whether at last we were to receive the official version of his end.
> "What happened to him?" Mr Smith asked with admirable directness.
> "We will probably never know. He was a strange moody man, and I must confess to you, Professor, his accounts were not in good order. There was the matter of a water-pump in Desaix Street."

"Are you suggesting he killed himself?" [. . .]

"Perhaps, or perhaps he has been the victim of the people's vengeance. We Haitians have a tradition of removing a tyrant in our own way, Professor."

"Was Doctor Philipot a tyrant?"

"The people in Desaix Street were sadly deceived about their water." (163–64)

The insinuation and slander perpetrated by the minister is passed on in much the same way as the marketplace gossip, but is less reliable because its agenda is more transparent. The gossip of the marketplace may be speculative, but it at least strives toward the truth; the gossip perpetrated by officials—and the news and rumors that circulate through official media—is corrupt, unreliable, and intended not to inform but to whitewash and deceive.

This is evident in Brown's reading of the gossip column penned by Petit Pierre, an eccentric character modeled upon real-life gossip columnist Aubelin Jolicoeur. Petit Pierre's gossip column isn't entirely accurate—among other exaggerations, Brown reads about how Smith "had been narrowly defeated in the American Presidential elections" (103)—but the florid prose is basically truthful and a more or less reliable record of the comings and goings of Port-au-Prince visitors and residents. The news pages of the same newspaper are far less dependable: Brown mocks a reported plan to eliminate illiteracy, suggesting that the education minister is counting on a hurricane to kill off unlettered peasants, and roundly dismisses claims that rebels had been captured bearing American weapons. "If the President had not quarrelled with the American Mission, the arms would probably have been described as Czech or Cuban," he thinks (103). Gossip may not be infallible, but it is all there is; in fact, for those without access to gossip, it is essentially impossible to keep track of what is going on in Port-au-Prince. Toward the end of *The Comedians*, the manager of a Dominican bauxite mine asks Brown: "What's the Tontons Macoute?" The question is absurd, unthinkable, a sign of how little of Haiti's troubled reality filters into the outside world. "We were less than three hundred kilometres from Port-au-Prince; it seemed strange he could ask me that, but I suppose there hadn't been a story for a long time in any newspaper he read," Brown reflects (292–93). But Brown's own grasp of the Haitian situation—like Greene's, we may suppose—is entirely contingent upon his being able to access the native gossip network through intermediaries such as Petit Pierre and Joseph. Nobody gossips with Brown directly; rather, he receives reports, the authenticity of which he seldom questions, and from which he derives insights that he takes to be accurate but for which the reader has no native witnesses to vouch. Brown struggles when denied access to the intermediaries who pass on gossip to him: "Petit Pierre hasn't been up for days. Joseph has disappeared. I'm cut off from news," he complains when Martha tells him of Papa Doc's "impressive" plan for a televised execution, staged in a floodlit cemetery before an audience of schoolchildren (202). When excluded from the local gossip and rumor networks, Brown is left adrift, isolated even from the manufactured spectacle and propaganda of the regime.

The news that circulates through gossip is not held by Haitians to be completely reliable but only basically truthful in its intent. Necessarily, then, upon hearing gossip, characters ponder its accuracy and significance. The ambassador dismisses "rumours" of the interrupted funeral, saying he "didn't believe them," only to revise his assessment after hearing firsthand evidence from Brown (137). Later, Brown and Martha weigh a rumor, reported by Petit Pierre, that Papa Doc is planning to expel Martha's husband, the ambassador, from the country. "I told her of Petit Pierre's rumour. 'Oh, no,' she said, 'no. It can't be true,' and then she added, 'Luis has been worried about something the last few days.' 'But if it should be true . . .'" (256–57). This is not simply idle chatter: the pair are concerned for their own happiness and especially for Major Jones. "Darling, we'll manage somehow, but Jones—it's life or death for him," Martha tells Brown (257). In Duvalier's Haiti, gossip tracks the rise and fall of individuals and is therefore a serious business—a resource for navigating the treacherous waters of Port-au-Prince, and sometimes a weapon, too. Brown thinks as much after learning from the ambassador that Martha is the child of a German hanged during the US occupation of Berlin. "But why, I wondered, tell me this fact about Martha? Sooner or later one always feels the need of a weapon against a mistress: he had slipped a knife up my sleeve to use against his wife when the moment of anger came" (137). Gossip provides information, a vital resource; but information can also be used against people, to potentially calamitous effect.

In such an environment, gossiping acquires a dual quality: it can be both an act of bearing witness and an act of betrayal. Gossip is dangerous, and Brown is acutely aware of being watched—he notices the gardener eyeing him through the window, and later warns Jones to stay off the road, saying: "The peasants will [. . .] report any white man they see" (287). Hamit, from whom Brown rents the room where he and Martha conduct their trysts, is clearly aware of the power his knowledge gives him: "Hamit watched me, ironic and comprehending," Brown states. "I remembered the stains we had left on his sheets, and I wondered whether he had changed them himself. He knew as many intimate things as a prostitute's dog" (141). The pejorative description of Hamit signals Brown's discomfiture at the very real power Hamit—standing next to the man Brown has cuckolded—now holds over him. But while knowledge brings power, it also confers a kind of responsibility, for it is through gossip that the excesses of the Duvalier regime are publicized and circulated. Brown and his friends realize as much after watching Doctor Philipot's body being taken away by the Tontons Macoutes—an act about which Brown later gossips—with Brown saying: "We were witnesses, but there was no court which would ever hear our testimony" (130). It is through gossip, too, that the "true story" of Doctor Magiot's death becomes known. As Martha says, "The official version is he was killed resisting arrest. [. . .] The true story is that they sent a peasant to his door asking him to come and help a sick child. He came out on to the path and the Tontons Macoute shot him down from a car. There were witnesses" (306). But to be a witness is neither easy nor safe: the couple who find Doctor Philipot's body reveal their discovery only because the shocked peasant woman is unable to stifle a scream. Similarly, when Brown remarks that the servants surely realize that he was involved in moving Philipot's body, Doctor Magiot reminds him that they would be afraid to talk. "A witness here can suffer just as much as the accused," he says (100).

This is especially evident in the remarkable, conflicted character of Petit Pierre, who knows everyone and virtually everything, and who presents himself as an information broker for the Port-au-Prince elite. Petit Pierre is disdainful of newspapers, especially foreign ones—"You don't believe what the American papers say, do you?" he sneers (42)—and equally distrusting of the unsourced rumors that swirl around the city. Gossip, however, is both his stock-in-trade and a form of currency: as Brown acknowledges, Petit Pierre "paid for his drinks only with his pen" (66). Certainly, Petit Pierre's status as a gossip broker provides him with a degree of power: he can get suitcases waved through customs, and his column is read by government ministers, with Brown attributing the "celerity and politeness" with which officials treat Smith to a flattering line in Petit Pierre's column (163). Later, in exchange for information, Petit Pierre gossips about the detention of Captain Concasseur in Miami, helps Brown to understand the repercussions of the incident, and uses gossip about Concasseur's character to help Brown hatch a plan. Petit Pierre begins the exchange with the words "If you would be frank with me [. . .] I might perhaps be of a little help" (104), effectively proposing an informational quid pro quo that illustrates both the power he derives from gossip and the hustling, transactional nature of his existence.

Through such deals, Petit Pierre shields himself from the outrages visited upon other Haitians, but also makes himself the subject of gossip. "He was believed by some to have connections with the Tonton, for how otherwise had he escaped a beating up or worse?" Brown asks (41). Petit Pierre's power seems threatening at times, with Brown remarking that his first visit "was like an interrogation by the secret police" (67). Still, Brown also recognizes Petit Pierre's "odd satirical courage" in occasionally inserting dangerously outspoken gossip into his newspaper column; in this sense, Petit Pierre becomes a figure rather like a court jester, granted limited and temporary license to transgress—to a minor degree, and not without considerable risk—the norms imposed upon other Haitians. Walking this improbable tightrope, Petit Pierre maintains a comic demeanor—"I had always thought that, when the time came, and surely it must one day come in his precarious defiant livelihood, he would laugh at his executioner," Brown reflects (41)—yet not one that belies the tragedy of the Haitian situation. "It was as though he had tossed a coin to decide between the only two possible attitudes in Port-au-Prince, the rational and the irrational, misery or gaiety; Papa Doc's head had fallen earthwards and he had plumped for the gaiety of despair," Brown states (102–3). In a book full of comedians, of people playing roles, Petit Pierre is the most openly comical character and yet also one with a serious and dangerous part to play.

The real risk, for Petit Pierre and all the characters of *The Comedians*, is that Papa Doc will take offense at something they say or write. Duvalier is the subject of a great deal of gossip: Brown reports hearsay that suggests "the Baron" is dead or that he has been missing for months, and also records claims that Duvalier likes "to watch personally the slow death of a Tonton victim" (113). To say such things is dangerous; Doctor Philipot's only crime, after all, was to have "spoken ill of the president" (124). Gossip is, however, the only way to puncture the imposed silence and the bogus reports that emanate from the presidential palace. When the ambassador suggests that "even Papa Doc is a comedian," Philipot responds: "He is real. Horror is always real" (140–41). It is through gossip, chiefly, that the true horrors of the regime are recorded, reified, and rescued from the unreality that pervades the regime's official discourse. In Greene's telling, it is gossip that allows Haitians to peek behind the curtain, behind the costumes and the Vodou posturing, and grasp the real horror of the Duvalier regime.

Horror, in the Kurtzian sense, is a key facet of Greene's work and, as Dash explains, of the traces it has left in the public (or at least American) perception of Haiti. "Just as Joseph Conrad had earlier supplied the dominant images of Africa in the European imagination, in the 1960s

Graham Greene performed the same dubious service for Haiti in the Western imagination," Dash writes (*Haiti and the United States* 101). Greene's "essentially anti-modernist narrative" achieves this in part, Dash writes, by emulating "the travelogue, the eye-witness account, the diary" (115)—all forms that, in their intimacy and promise of inside knowledge, bear comparison to gossip. Greene's text is not as filled with gossipy anecdotes as Cabrera Infante or Arenas's works; still, Dash notes that it is "lurid and melodramatic" (108), "seductive," and above all "familiar and disturbingly memorable" (110)—which is to say that it deals, directly or indirectly, in the same scandalous, exoticized and othering details that are the stuff of gossip. Greene writes for a foreign audience that expects Vodou and tropical chaos, and he meets their expectations, offering up colorful Haitian episodes just as carefully and deliberately as Arenas catalogs his nocturnal (and diurnal and crepuscular) liaisons.[27]

Inescapably, in so doing, Greene's writing is marked by his status as a neocolonial, or at least expatriate, outsider; reading *The Comedians,* one senses a writer enthused by his novel subject but at the same time removed from it. Rather like Brown, whose concern about the potential loss of his hotel pales into insignificance compared to the suffering of the Haitians, Greene is insulated from the events he describes. There is, in fact, a perverse enjoyment—even a kind of schadenfreude—to Greene's treatment of Haiti's woes: while, like Brown, he relies on local informers to explain the Haitian situation to him, his writing is calibrated to appeal to the sensibilities of a predominantly British and American readership already primed to view Haitians as ignoble savages. But while *The Comedians* is written by an outsider and lacks the deep commitment and understanding that a local writer might bring, Greene is not merely pandering to his readers' prejudices: the text is also marked by a didactic impulse and a desire to expose Duvalier's excesses before a global audience. Greene's work, in Dash's reading, gave rise to a new genre of our-man-in-Haiti accounts, in which foreign writers "set out to prove to a scandalized audience the extent to which Haiti had slipped away from the values of the civilized world" (111). Writing in 1969, Bernard Diederich and Al Burt channel Greene when they offer up "scandalous hearsay" and use "details that are either deflating or comical, such as a Communist writer's nasal voice; Duvalier's drooping eyelids; a houngan's diarrhoea in the National Palace" to forge narratives about Haiti that are based both on actual knowledge and "the imaginative accumulation of unsavoury details" (112). The parallels to gossip—with its love of the detailed, the personal, the revelatory—are readily apparent in such texts, a point Greene himself makes in the foreword to Diederich and Burt's volume, which he asserts contains "material [. . .] for a Suetonius" (vii).[28] Just as apparent, though, is the explicitly adversarial approach through which such details are marshaled to puncture the public image of Duvalier and his regime: the gossip of writers such as Greene and Diederich is not simply a narrative flourish but rather a critical source of information, and therefore a weapon in a battle to define Duvalier (and Haiti) in the global public sphere.

Duvalier and Graham Greene: *Démasqué*

Part of the reason that Greene's words were so effective at riling Duvalier, in fact, was that they served as a reputational attack, operating on a register that Duvalier understood only too well: the deliberate leveraging of the personal, the gossipy, the scandalous. Gossip, in the Haitian context, is often understood as a calculated act. The Creole word *zin* (also written as *zen*), which broadly refers to news circulated through gossip, is understood, according to Michel S. Laguerre, as a pliable form that serves many uses in many contexts, not least the realm of military intelligence gathering (*Military and Society* 139–42). Crucially, Laguerre makes clear, *zin* is less concerned with its own truthfulness than with advancing an agenda: it can be circulated to test the loyalty of the listener, to spread misinformation, to disseminate accurate information, or as a means of luring the listener into disclosing information of their own. The boundaries between gossip and related forms such as rumor and slander here grow indistinct: *zin* can be intimate gossip in the classic sense, but it can also be a politically motivated act of slander, a deliberate effort to mislead, or the circulation of rumors for personal gain.

These, certainly, were among the roles that gossip played for François Duvalier: as Paul Christopher Johnson notes, Duvalier actively encouraged gossip about his more outlandish activities, real or imagined, as a means of controlling his public image. Did Duvalier really commune with spirits from a bathtub in the presidential palace or receive intelligence from the severed head of a former enemy? The point is moot, Johnson argues. "All of this is spectacular rumor. But what is clear is that Duvalier himself fomented the circulation of these kinds of rumors through gossip networks," he writes (427). "Even Duvalier's actual violence, usually perpetrated by the VSN [Volontaires de la Sécurité Nationale], was spectacular and staged, designed to generate stories. Even killing was *zin*, designed not merely to eliminate opponents but to foment the circulation of stories about the gruesome fates that awaited dissidents" (433). Gossip also allowed Duvalier to refract his own public image and to be different things to different people; he could publicly present himself as a Catholic, for instance, while also "circulating by reputation and gossip his implicit and well-established support of Vodou and his vehement opposition to the anti-superstition campaigns of the Church," Johnson notes (430).[29]

Gossip, therefore, was both a tool and a weapon for Duvalier. This being the case, he felt all too acutely the risks of allowing Greene's novel—or, worse still, its 1967 film adaptation—to define him in the public sphere. To prevent this, Duvalier launched a reputational attack against Greene himself. In 1968, Duvalier's foreign ministry published a remarkable bilingual tract called *Graham Greene Démasqué: Finally Exposed* that sought to destroy Greene's reputation and to reveal his novel, and the subsequent film, as a CIA-sponsored plot aimed at building international support for a US invasion. On the orders of Foreign Minister René Chalmers, a series of cultural officers and other officials composed heavily researched essays purporting to show Greene "finally himself just as he is, and has always been" and alleging him to be an "unbalanced, perverted writer" with "sadistic instincts" (7), a "chimerical racist" (33) in the pay of other racists, a drug addict always "stuffing himself with opium, cocaine, and marijuana" (61), a spy and "former torturer" (77), and a communist "little stool pigeon" (9) with "money problems" (13) and a "bent for lucre" (9).

While the personal attacks in *Démasqué* are presented, breathlessly, as hot gossip, many of its supposedly damning anecdotes are actually lifted directly from Greene's own autobiographical writings. One essay promises to "underline some traits of the character inherited from a consanguinity and a rather loaded heredity" based on Greene's own comment that he "was a Greene on both sides" because his parents were cousins (9). Another dives into Greene's drug use, reporting that while writing one of his novels he "would begin his day by swallowing a benzedrin tablet to be followed by another one at noon" and quotes Greene's own work to note that he was rendered "totally impotent" for months, and resorted to habit-forming "sexual experiments" that ultimately wrecked his marriage (13, 17). The pamphlet also dredges up a libel suit brought against Greene by 20th Century Fox over a 1937 movie review commenting on the sexualization of Shirley Temple; Greene saw Temple as "a woman-child fit for kindling the evanescent desire of aging gentlemen" and was bankrupted by the subsequent lawsuit, the pamphlet claims (17).[30] Another essay, written by protocol officer Yves Massillon, relays gossip from double agent and defector Kim Philby, noting that over caviar and cognac, Philby passed on "new fascinating revelations," including details of his past work with "such unheralded British spies as novelist Graham Greene" (61). Other attacks are unsourced: we learn that Greene had a "morbid" adolescence and obsession with death and that during the 1920s he indulged "daily in a game of Russian roulette" (9).[31] His brief membership in the Oxford Communist Party is also made the subject of eager speculation: "Who knows? He may have done so in view of some spying activities!" (9). A similar tone marks the pamphlet's treatment of Greene's conversion to Catholicism: "For some time he becomes the talk of a group of acquaintances. They wonder at his conversion. A bothering of his conscience, some say. Heresy, others retort. Self-advertisement and impudence, the most clearsighted whisper" (11).

The pamphlet's aim, clearly, is to stir up scandal: *Démasqué* is, above all, a reputational attack. Throughout, its writers draw direct contrasts between the "infamous name" of Greene (27) and the "eminently intelligent" leadership of "the Chief of the nation, Physician, Ethnologist, and Sociologist, Dr. François Duvalier" (19). Greene's novel is held up as an attempt to "slander a nation" (75) and "blemish the reputation of a country" (77)—an attempt the pamphlet insists has failed. "Graham Greene's work [. . .] far from besmirching the transcendent personality of the Leader of the Duvalierist Revolution, has increased the love of the Haitians for their chief," one essay asserts (77). *The Comedians* is presented as revealing only Greene's personal depravities: "Greene defines only himself" and "reveals only the Greenian sensibility, that of the unsatisfied" (57). One essay explicitly deals with Greene's reputation and "appreciable audience" abroad, reporting that "a discreet inquiry made among bookshop-keepers, professors, students, and quite a few members of the Haitian intelligentsia—reputed for their insight as well as their rather exacting judgment and critical minds— revealed that such audience in Haiti was confined within very narrow limits; only to the few who would think that the moon was made of blue cheese" (59). It further reports, in a gossipy aside, that Greene made an egotistical tour of Port-au-Prince bookshops trying to spot copies of his own works, only to be bitterly disappointed when none were to be found. "Anyway, in Haiti, Graham Greene was noticeably humiliated by the merely polite welcome he was given on purpose," the author claims (61).

The Duvalier government's extraordinary document bears numerous similarities to Cabrera Infante's literary assault on Greene: it uses Greene's religion to diminish the credibility of his work, cites his connection to Philby, lingers over his having played Russian roulette, and so forth. But Cabrera Infante, as we have seen, never takes his reader's acquiescence for granted; he works to earn it and to seduce his reader into complicity. The Duvalier pamphlet makes no such attempt: it is gossip without seduction, without charm, and thus ultimately without much ability to generate the sense of complicity upon which gossip relies. Drawing so heavily on recycled gossip taken from Greene's own memoirs, the pamphlet couldn't claim to be delivering much in the way of inside information either. Certainly, the assault proved easy for Greene—an outsider with no personal ties to Haiti and no specific reason to fear Duvalier—to shrug off; indeed, he evidently welcomed the publicity the pamphlet engendered and actively worked to disseminate it. "The first I heard of Duvalier's literary assault was in a letter from Graham dated 20 February 1969, which I received in Mexico City," Diederich reports. "He could hardly conceal his excitement and mirth. 'Have you seen his book about me in French and English called *Graham Greene Démasqué (Finally Unmasked)*? If you haven't seen it get somebody to ask for it from the embassy in Mexico City. It's a treasure'" (124).

Facing mockery in the foreign press over his government's pamphlet, Duvalier next sought legal remedy, launching a 10-million-franc libel suit in France against the producers of the film adaptation of Greene's novel. A report in a state-controlled Haitian newspaper made clear just how personally Duvalier had taken Greene's text: damages were due, it reported, for harm done "to Duvalier, admired as a man of letters and ethnologist. To Duvalier, as a learned doctor. To Duvalier, as an eminent statesman to whom the great personages of this world [. . .] have paid visits. To Duvalier, the president of Haiti, incarnation of the Haitian state" (qtd. in Diederich 134). In an unusual move, the Haitian foreign ministry circulated memos, both to its own diplomats abroad and to the heads of foreign diplomatic missions in Haiti, condemning the "frankly hostile character" of the film version of *The Comedians*. The memos further warned that "the acrimonious tone of each sequence in which the most unlikely facts are supposedly true to life, [and] the high price paid for the staging of the film permit to infer that Graham Greene's novel and the film drawn from it are part of a vast plan tending to prepare international public opinion for an action that might be carried out on a larger scale against the Republic of Haiti" (*Démasqué* 97). Even allowing the film to be screened, the memos warned, would be considered an act of indirect aggression against Haiti.

The libel suit was a modest victory for Duvalier: a court in Paris prevented the screening of *The Comedians* in France but mockingly awarded him a single franc in compensation. Still, the Haitian press declared the ruling a "Great National Victory" in front-page headlines, with an editorial pronouncing the ruling "a political and moral victory" against "an organized defamatory action" based on "slanderous propaganda." The editorial, surely published with the oversight of the presidential palace, continued: "Graham Greene and his accomplices managed to get off cheap, because on a simple order from President Duvalier he (Greene) could have been shot down like a wretch in any corner of the universe. As was said by a man greater than we in a memorable circumstance: 'For that we need only a stout-hearted man, and we have thousands of them'" (qtd. in Diederich 136–37). Duvalier's regime shows less subtlety than Arenas and Cabrera Infante attribute to Castro's government, which they portray as having a clearer strategy and a sophisticated propaganda machine. Duvalier, by contrast, uses cruder and more forceful methods: threats, diplomatic pressure, and lawsuits, with slanderous gossip serving as a secondary and less skillfully executed aspect of his approach.

Despite this, the Duvaliers were largely successful at silencing gossip in the literature of Haitian writers both on and off the island, leaving it to foreign "comedians" such as Greene to fill the gaps. While Greene, like Arenas and Cabrera Infante, may have somewhat overestimated the power of his words, it is undeniable that he did at least manage to anger and unsettle the Haitian dictator. In a speech rejecting foreign interference in Haitian affairs, Duvalier famously declared: "They know that bullets and machine guns capable of scaring Duvalier do not exist. [. . .] I am already an immaterial being. No foreigner is going to tell me what to do" (qtd. in Jallot and Lesage 28). Later, in his *Mémoires d'un leader du Tiers Monde* (1969), Duvalier links the film adaptation of *The Comedians*—screened across the Western hemisphere "with the exception of General Francisco Franco's Spain," he carefully notes—to a "shadowy maneuver" that led to criticism of Haiti's human rights record before the United Nations (135). "Napoleon used to say: 'No ifs and no buts; one must succeed.' I myself have triumphed over a vast international conspiracy," Duvalier insists (138). Despite his claims of victory, however, Duvalier revealed through his embittered and very public literary battle with Greene that even an immaterial being could be roused to anger by reputational attacks. And despite Duvalier's efforts, Greene's words helped shape the enduring public image of Papa Doc and his regime. They succeeded, in short, in scandalizing Haiti's recent history and thereby bringing a new understanding of the country's plight to a global audience. In a fitting postscript to the saga, a few months after Jean-Claude Duvalier fled Haiti, the film adaptation of *The Comedians* finally opened in Port-au-Prince cinemas. Gossip, in a sense, returned to Haiti, if it ever left; indeed, as will be shown in the next chapter, Haitian writers are now beginning to recognize gossip as a valuable narrative resource for engaging with the legacy of the Duvalier dynasty, and the long silences that have marked their literature and national history.

4 "Páginas en Blanco"
The Legacy of the Caribbean Gossip State

> Tú ves condenado, te maté por un chisme.
> —Juan Bosch

In 1964, a year after the military coup that ended his brief tenure as the Dominican Republic's first democratically elected president, Juan Bosch wrote an essay lamenting that "in the Dominican Republic, politics consists in turning gossip into official State business."[1] During Rafael Leónidas Trujillo's dictatorship, gossip could easily bring about a person's downfall; through the use of state-endorsed gossip columns (sometimes written, it was said, by Trujillo himself) and networks of neighborly informants, it also became a key resource for policing dissent and maintaining the state's monopoly on public discourse. The Trujillo regime, Bosch argues, sustained itself in large part through gossip: "Trujillo magnified the importance of gossip in national politics," he writes. "Gossip, given its mendacious nature, always engendered calumny, and Trujillo made calumny the habitual form of political struggle" (80). Trujillo's dangerous propensity for gossip was known not just within the Dominican Republic but across the Caribbean. Pedro Estrada, the infamous Venezuelan national security chief, recalls that Trujillo "was a man of great passions, an extremely dangerous man whose actions were often based on gossip." He continues: "I have never seen a country in which gossip gained the currency it did in the Dominican Republic. And that was the terror and the fear in which everyone lived. Gossip could cause a person's disappearance. People rose and fell because of a piece of gossip" (292).[2] Bosch, a left-wing politician still angling for a return to power, presents the Dominican obsession with gossip in terms of class struggle. The bourgeoisie, he writes, had "an abnormal psychological nature and could not live without the daily nourishment of gossip; they were—and are—a perpetual source of gossip; they create and consume gossip." By contrast, he somewhat implausibly claims, "the People, those without work, the peasants, the workers—and a portion of the small middle class—neither produce nor consume gossip" (54). In writing against the establishment figures and military factions that orchestrated his overthrow, Bosch seeks to define his own political project as a counterblast against Trujillo's gossip.[3] His party, he writes, "brought to the country a completely new political propaganda technique. [. . .] There was discussion of national problems, not of people; of the solutions to those problems, not of anyone's virtues or vices" (80). Gossip, in Bosch's post-Trujillo republic, was something to be exorcized from public life: a discourse tainted by association with the Trujillato and explicitly and irrevocably linked to the fallen dictator's corrupt, personalist approach to government.

Still, Bosch's condemnation of political gossip stands at odds with the approach taken by many other Dominican writers, for whom gossip has been a tool with which to manipulate the historical record or a means of probing the historical silences born of authoritarianism. In this chapter, I begin by reading the memoirs of Bosch's long-standing rival, the poet, essayist, and three-time president Joaquín Balaguer, who used gossip as a political tool with which to distance himself from the Trujillo regime and shape his own historical legacy. I next turn to Viriato Sención's 1992 novel *Los que falsificaron la firma de Dios,* which found a wide readership because of the political gossip it promised, and was perceived by many—including Balaguer himself—as a direct reputational attack on the then president. Many subsequent Dominican writers have been fascinated by the use of gossip in narrative battles over history and identity, a theme I trace in Marcio Veloz Maggiolo's *El hombre del acordeón* (2003), which pitches a gossipy merengue star against a revisionist historian, and Junot Díaz's *The Brief Wondrous Life of Oscar Wao* (2007), which both stages the uses of gossip in the Trujillo era and deploys gossip to rescue the stories of those silenced by the regime. Finally, I turn to Kettly Mars's 2010 novel *Saisons sauvages* to explore the way that a new generation of Haitian writers are similarly pushing back against the silence that has long marked their country's production and using gossip to come to terms with the abuses of the Duvalier regimes.

The Failings of Others: *Memorias de un cortesano de la "era de Trujillo"*

Where Bosch saw gossip as a moral failing, and perhaps a national character flaw, Balaguer—a more pragmatic and ultimately more successful politician—saw it simply as a means to an end. During the Trujillo years, gossip had allowed the dictator to monopolize public discourse and excise unflattering perspectives or dissenting voices from the historical record. Now Balaguer, having learned from Trujillo's methods, sought to deploy gossip to shape his own historical legacy. It was gossip, or the promise thereof, that drove Dominicans to flock to buy Balaguer's memoirs: *Memorias de un cortesano de la "era de Trujillo"* (1988) was reprinted ten times within thirteen months of its first publication. The book is now in its sixteenth edition, its continuing popularity a testament to the public's enduring curiosity about the "era de Trujillo." According to Giovanni Di Pietro, Dominicans "saw in the book what they wanted to see: a collection of the juiciest gossip of public and private life by a man who, thanks to his personality and longevity, practically summarizes the entire history of contemporary Dominican society" (96–97). The whitewashing of history, orchestrated in real time by Trujillo and ably abetted by Balaguer, had created a vacuum that Dominicans longed to see filled. With his autobiographical volume, Balaguer exploited Dominicans' thirst for knowledge to shape his own public image, preserving his legacy but also ensuring the continuing viability of a political career that would last for well over a decade after the publication of *Memorias*.

The allure of Balaguer's gossipy memoir derived, as reviewers in the Dominican Republic and elsewhere were quick to recognize, from its author's claim to having exclusive knowledge of the workings of the Trujillo government. Readers open the book, Delfín Garasa writes, in the "expectation of knowing what he said about himself and those who had surrounded him in more than sixty years of political life" (460). Garasa views the volume's title, with its promise of privileged insights into the Trujillo era, as a challenge to which Balaguer largely rises. "In this brave reckoning he does not evade his own responsibility, but leaves the final judgment to history," he writes (460). Balaguer evidently understood his readers' desire to penetrate the secretive fortress of Dominican politics, and makes a point of both flaunting and sharing his knowledge. In so doing, he focuses on people, not events, exhaustively cataloging, and at times simply listing, the key figures in Dominican politics since Trujillo's ascent. This appeared to satisfy many of his readers; after decades of personalist politics, Dominicans were primed for Balaguer's personality-driven attempt at a first draft of history.

Still, Garasa's second point, about Balaguer's deference to the judgment of history, is more problematic. Throughout *Memorias,* Balaguer presents himself as a marginal figure: a witness to the inner workings of government, but not the power behind the throne. He repeatedly evades questions about his own culpability by pointing fingers at others, most notably Trujillo, his family, and his military allies. In this way, Balaguer panders to his readers' appetite for gossip, and stokes his readers' desire for intimate, unauthorized revelations, even as he uses gossip about others to deflect attention from his own role in the events he describes. Discussing the Haitian massacre of 1937, which he calls a "slaughter" and a "holocaust," Balaguer claims that Trujillo ordered the genocide after downing "great quantities of Carlos I, his favorite cognac" and while surrounded by courtiers and beautiful women (*Memorias* 63). Balaguer's prim inclusion of personal details about Trujillo's decadence exploits gossip's presumption of ideological alignment between speaker and listener: the more we give in to Balaguer's invitation to condemn Trujillo's excesses, the harder it is to find fault in Balaguer himself. Balaguer lays it on thick, writing that Trujillo remained unrepentant even after more than a week of anti-Haitian violence. In a remarkable attempt to distance himself from Trujillo, Balaguer goes on to blame Trujillo's "instinct" and "crude passion" on "the precariousness of his culture, typical of a man who attended only the first years of elementary school" (64). The death of thousands of people in a genocidal massacre, in Balaguer's telling, resulted from Trujillo's character flaws and lack of education, not from any systemic logic of violence in which Balaguer—himself a refined and educated man—could reasonably be deemed complicit.[4]

This tone, more denunciatory than confessional, runs through much of Balaguer's volume. Balaguer insists that he had minimal influence over Trujillo and presents himself as a fly on the wall, privy to but not party to the excesses of the regime. Balaguer's self-description as a *cortesano* is significant: as Lauren Derby notes, Trujillo cultivated an inner circle of courtiers bound together by ambition, prestige, and mutual suspicion, with "the courtesans' distinction from those outside the inner circle becoming the crucial boundary maintaining the social formation" (*Dictator's Seduction* 8). Balaguer downplays the influence enjoyed by such courtiers, but promises to draw back the curtain and allow the Dominican people retroactive admission to Trujillo's court. This sense of insider knowledge, of intimate secrets being exposed for public scrutiny, is further bolstered by Balaguer's inclusion of a vast number of facsimiles of private letters and personal photographs. This is more than just the performance of disclosure: for Trujillo's courtesans, the personal details of one another's private lives was a form of currency and a critical means of orienting themselves within the idiosyncratic politics of Trujillo's inner circle. Derby writes that Trujillo embraced the "symbolic politics" of slavish allegiance to etiquette, "enforcing proper conduct under threat of denunciation," with people who wore the wrong jacket, picked up the wrong napkin, or lived in the wrong neighborhood liable to find themselves falling precipitously from grace (8). In such a context, gossip was not just idle talk: it was a dangerous but necessary tool, a means of survival, and one that Balaguer—the ultimate political survivor—learned to use well.

In *Memorias,* Balaguer repeatedly emphasizes the degree to which the Trujillo regime's authoritarian aspects were concomitant with a profound sense of paranoia that demanded immediate responses to every new piece of information about, or shadow of suspicion cast upon, either friend or foe. "Any piece of gossip whatsoever, even if only a social intrigue or a simple caprice typical of Trujillo's character, would serve as a pretext for revoking gains that had seemed firm and political positions that the public had judged well-established," Balaguer writes. "All Dominicans knew this weakness of Trujillo" (216). Gossip, if it reached Trujillo, could spell the end of political careers; equally, however, Trujillo was an active perpetrator of gossip, using it to precipitate the downfall of former intimates. In discussing Virgilio Alvarez Pina's fall from grace, Balaguer reports that Trujillo's shifting affections found their expression in the gossip columns:

> Alvarez Pina was often a victim of those changes in the whim and will of the one man who dispensed all official privileges. When that happened, the news was announced in the long-running "Foro Público" section of the newspaper "El Caribe." During one of those falls, Alvarez Pina, like others before and after him who fell from the ruler's favor, suffered vexing denigrations, which were made public in malicious commentaries prepared in the government's own offices. All Dominicans read the "Foro" every day. It allowed the entire country to follow the course of Trujillo's mood and the degree of favor then enjoyed by each and every one of his collaborators. The destitution of functionaries and the fall of those who once enjoyed the greatest degree of official favor was announced, in ominous tones, in that odious column in "El Caribe." Social gossip, born for the most part out of badmouthing and opprobrium, was taken to the "Foro Público" without the least consideration for the honor of distinguished families, regardless of whether or not they belonged to the palace cliques. (216)

Despite his theatrical disdain for the *Foro Público,* Balaguer describes a practice that loomed large in the paranoid squabbling and power struggles of Trujillo's inner circle, and that still weighs on the Dominican imagination.[5] Indeed, Balaguer's project in writing *Memorias* can be read as an extension of the cynical and deliberate deployments of gossip that took place in the state-sanctioned gossip column. With the Trujillo clan mostly dead or exiled, and an eye on his own legacy, Balaguer gleefully reveals the excesses and intimate secrets of the Trujillo family and its allies, essentially turning the gossip machine they cultivated against them.

In the fourth section of *Memorias*, "Trujillo's Relatives and Collaborators," Balaguer systematically offers intimate details about a long list of prominent members of the Trujillo-era elite. The section opens with a description of Ramfis Trujillo's "intimate encounters with several of the most famous Hollywood stars, such as Debra Paget, Kim Novak and Joan Collins," and the way his "bacchanals and excesses" adversely impacted his physical appearance (166). Later Balaguer describes Ramfis as "a vindictive being, dominated by an insatiable desire for retaliation" (173). Throughout his memoirs, Balaguer offers an unsparing account of the character and actions of the sprawling Trujillo family, including their having amassed "considerable wealth, sometimes by means not entirely legal" (181); their "psychic imbalance" and "lack of guts" (182); their obsession with "sex and money" (186); and even their "dreadful writing" and poor spelling (183). Other public figures are similarly exposed: Balaguer reports that Roberto Despradel, who in 1938 negotiated the Dominican debt in the United States, showed him a check for $50,000 given as payment for his services (219). Elsewhere, Balaguer states that Trujillo's secretary, Tirso Rivera, turned over to Ramfis Trujillo $10 million deposited for his father in offshore accounts (224). *Memorias* is full, in fact, of passages in which Balaguer sheds light on the network of allies that helped Trujillo to embezzle public funds. Trujillo's allies are also described as facilitating the dictator's sexual excesses: Balaguer tells his reader that two senior officials, Rafael Paíno Pichardo and José María Bonetti Burgos, arranged orgies at Trujillo's behest. Even crimes as egregious as those imputed to Trujillo's intelligence chief, Johnny Abbes García, are framed in terms of gossip: Balaguer writes archly that Abbes García grew so "fond of his role as executioner" that he would wander the palace reading a history book about torture methods. Balaguer reports that "many times I heard him read those pages and accompany the reading with a biting comment or a laugh that was somewhere between sardonic and jovial" (224).[6]

Through these and other anecdotes, the corruption, debauchery, and violence of the Trujillo era are portrayed as stemming from the actions and character flaws of individuals, rather than from institutional failures in which Balaguer himself could be deemed complicit. Balaguer presents his memoirs as a work of history, but in fact offers a novelistic collection of vignettes that, taken in the aggregate, understand Dominican politics as shaped by the moral and psychological failings of its protagonists.[7] Systemic problems are here subsumed in character assassination, with Balaguer using gossip to disperse responsibility for the regime's excesses among a panoply of individual targets. Balaguer thus uses gossip as a historiographic strategy and also a means of absolving himself of responsibility for the wrongdoings he describes. This is most apparent in Balaguer's broken promise to reveal what Di Pietro calls "the biggest gossip of all": the identity of the killers of the journalist Orlando Martínez (97). Above a photograph of Martínez, Balaguer writes:

> This page is left blank. For many years it will remain silent, but one day it will speak, so that its voice can be gathered by history. Quiet, like a tomb whose open secret will rise, accusingly, when the time comes to lift the headstone beneath which the truth lies.
>
> Its content is left in the hands of a friend who, for reasons of age, is expected to outlive me and whom I have charged with making it public some years after my death. (295)

Balaguer claims to have inside knowledge about the murder, but refuses either to share what he knows or to explain why he cannot. The blank page taunts its reader and invites speculative gossip: Who might the "friend" be? Why can't the facts be disclosed now? As Di Pietro comments, "The biggest gossip of all was thus replaced by another piece of gossip, a finer and crueler one: a blank page showing only that Dominicans, fooled by their own good faith as inveterate consumers of gossip, and dissatisfied in their ardent desire, would now have a long wait for the delivery of the goods for which they paid" (97). Balaguer positions himself explicitly as a gossip broker, introducing the blank page by writing: "One of the biggest frustrations that I will take to my tomb is that of dying without having known with certainty the name of the functionary, military or civil," who ordered the 1973 assassination of the journalist Gregorio García Castro. "In his case, contrary to what happened with Orlando Martínez Howley [...] there was a confabulation of silence at work that I was unable to defeat" (292). Balaguer here mockingly performs the frustration bequeathed to his readers by his blank page: the rhetorical resonance between the promise of secrets rising from a tomb and the frustration of answers withheld even unto the grave is perhaps not coincidental.

For Dominicans, Balaguer's blank page stands as a powerful symbol of historical whitewashing. It is also a symbol of Balaguer's larger project: Balaguer uses the structures of gossip to create the anticipation of full disclosure, but in the end offers only a carefully redacted account, seeking to fill past silences with tales that suit his own agenda and preempt accusations he might otherwise face.[8] The blank page fuels speculation by suggesting a secret too juicy to share, thereby diverting attention from Balaguer's own involvement in the murder of Martínez (who, it should be remembered, was killed after writing a column criticizing Balaguer). A similar exercise can be seen in the poem "Mujeres en mi Vida," a nostalgic sonnet about Balaguer's past loves—"I remember them all, and loved them all deeply" (335)—that ends with a poignant lament for the women's happy homes and the children who "might otherwise have been my children" (335). The poem's curious placement—constituting an entire chapter and set in an ornate frame unlike anything used elsewhere in the text—seems intended to signal a key, if cryptic, revelation about Balaguer's life, and to encourage speculation about his past romances. This is a nod, perhaps, to the fact that Balaguer's sexuality was the subject of considerable gossip; as Ana S. Q. Liberato notes, Balaguer was rumored to have bedded everyone from domestic servants to political appointees, and tales of his purported homosexuality and sexual deviance "circulated through gossip networks" (91). Balaguer offers gossip to preempt more hostile chatter, but as with the blank page, his gossip is once more notably devoid of content: it promises juicy details but delivers remarkably little.

This is an effective strategy in part because of the silence against which Balaguer writes: besides a few hostile whispers, there is little to contradict the versions he offers. As Balaguer well knows, in the absence of more reliable sources, the "open secrets" to which he gives voice become a crucial source for reconstructing Dominican history. The blank page is thus also a taunting reassertion of Balaguer's enduring narrative authority, a facet of the power dynamic inherent in gossip: the reader knows only what he chooses to tell them. This is underscored by Balaguer's remarkable epilogue, in which he looks back on his career in mock humility and blames the "irremediable moral deformity of men" for the wrongdoings he has witnessed (364). For himself, Balaguer claims a higher moral ground: "The very acts of betrayal and ingratitude to which we fell victim in the course of our existence are the result of our lack of foresight and our excessive faith in the decency of others. The greatest of the great have erred in this way more than once. Napoleon did not overlook the fact that Talleyrand sold secrets of State to his enemies and that his minister of police also played with marked cards" (366). Balaguer parodies his own tone of modest self-reflection by comparing himself to Napoleon and lacing his final words with references to scripture, Shakespeare, Goethe, and Aristotle. Nobody is infallible, he writes, but his own faults consist

"Páginas en Blanco" 167

in having been too trusting: "Many times, it might even be better to say almost always, the mistakes and errors of a Chief of State are due to a bad report or an intrigue perpetrated by his collaborators" (366). The moral wreckage of the Trujillo regime, and of Balaguer's own, is recast as the inevitable upshot of the moral failings of others, something for which Balaguer himself accepts little responsibility. Gossip functions not simply as an accusation or a way to fill the empty spaces of Dominican history, but also as a means of self-exoneration. Like his blank page, the text's overwrought closing is intended as a reminder: Balaguer's gossip may be partial and self-serving, but after decades of authoritarianism during which diverging accounts were ruthlessly erased, there is little left with which to contradict him.

Power and Titillation: *Los que falsificaron la firma de Dios*

Balaguer was not the only prominent member of the Trujillato to seek to shape his public image through gossipy memoirs. In the years since Trujillo's death, a literary cottage industry of exiled family members and other insiders sprang up, bringing the publication of numerous works promising the "true" account of the Trujillo years. Among the most notable is *Trujillo: The Last Caesar* (1963), by Arturo Espaillat, Trujillo's chief of intelligence, a breathless, tabloidy account that Russell H. Fitzgibbon describes as "anecdotal, 'confessional' (without confessing what really would be worth the effort), scandal-mongering, and highly revealing," though he concludes that Espaillat "tells little that could not be gained by a thorough reading of the New York Times" and "knows far more than he tells" (551–52). Angelita Trujillo's 2010 memoir *Trujillo, mi padre en mis memorias* is a celebration of the Trujillo years, currently banned from Dominican libraries, in which the dictator's daughter seeks to absolve her father of his regime's most notorious crimes. The novelist Aida Trujillo Ricart, the daughter of Ramfis Trujillo, has likewise written semiautobiographical works including *A la sombra de mi abuelo* (2008), which combines affection for her grandfather with a relatively clear-eyed view of his actions. The politician and diplomat Mario Read Vittini similarly promises an insider account in his 2007 memoir *Trujillo de cerca*, as does the diplomat and industrialist Hans Paul Wiese Delgado in his 2000 work *Trujillo: Amado por muchos, odiado por todos, temido por todos*.

Such texts raise questions about the reliability of memoirs that purport to reveal the truth about authoritarian regimes. To some extent, the fallibility of such memoirs is a given. "If memoirists didn't lie their heads off, what would biographers do with themselves?" asks Lidiia Ianovskaia in a 2008 issue of *Russian Studies in Literature* exploring gossip and slander in Soviet-era memoirs and archival accounts (76). Still, the nature of Trujillo's gossip state, with its aggressive policing of dissent and its establishment of gossip as a means of enforcing the state's narrative monopoly, makes Dominican memoirs especially complex, and represents a broader challenge for both Dominican readers and writers as they seek to engage with their nation's whitewashed history. Deprived of a commonly agreed or even plausibly reliable account of their society and their past, Dominicans often resort to gossip and rumor to resurface suppressed truths, or simply as a means of acknowledging the insufficiency of sanctioned public discourses. They do so, however, in the awareness that the state has not only strenuously policed such gossip, but also successfully used gossip of its own to shape and control public discourse. Gossip is thus both a contested and a compromised form of discourse: arguably the best or only option available to those who have lost faith in official discourses, but one still tainted, perhaps irrevocably, by the interventions of official figures, and successfully coopted—by Balaguer, by Trujillo—to shape their historical legacies.

One of the earliest writers to engage with this conundrum was Viriato Sención, whose *Los que falsificaron la firma de Dios* (1992) became a hit in the Dominican Republic after winning the country's Premio Nacional de Novela, only to be stripped of the prize after drawing vocal criticism from then president Balaguer.[9] The controversy surrounding Sención's novel stemmed from its denunciatory nature: the novel features characters easily recognizable as stand-ins for Trujillo, Balaguer, a string of military chiefs, and numerous members of Balaguer's family and entourage. Through these thinly veiled proxies, the text depicts both the Trujillo and Balaguer regimes as corrupt, authoritarian, and cruel. Many Dominican novels portray the two administrations in similar terms, but Sención's text is a straightforward roman à clef and was widely assumed by Dominican readers to be based on actual events and grounded in firsthand knowledge of Balaguer's actions and character.

In short, Dominicans readily recognized Sención's project not just as fiction but as gossip—a fact that likely contributed to the novel's popularity. In an article published shortly after *Falsificaron*, Di Pietro condemns Sención's work as a "gossip novel" of limited aesthetic significance (97), and argues that it "does little more than collect the gossip that everyone already knows and repeats about Balaguer" (107). Sención's novel, in this reading, operates rather like Balaguer's *Memorias,* in that it plays on people's suspicions to generate excitement and interest, but in the end offers little in the way of new information. Despite this, Ignacio López-Calvo notes that Sención's text has been read as a powerful act of artistic defiance in response to Balaguer's efforts to control Dominican public discourse.[10] Either way, it is hard to escape the conclusion that for the nation's readers, to participate in Sención's antagonistic and potentially dangerous act of public gossip was both exciting and meaningful.

Like Balaguer's *Memorias*, Sención's novel bases its claim to gossip-worthiness on its author's insider status: Sención had, for several years, administered a charity alongside Balaguer's sister and could plausibly claim a privileged view of the workings of the regime. This perceived betrayal may have contributed to Balaguer's outrage: Balaguer reportedly blamed his sister's death from a heart attack on her disappointment at Sención's text, and had the Premio Nacional withdrawn on the basis that *Falsificaron* was "a work injurious" to Balaguer and his family (qtd. in Encarnación Jiménez 10). Balaguer's public condemnation of Sención's novel, however, only increased Dominicans' interest in the gossip it contained, especially given the president's reclusiveness and refusal to make any but the most carefully controlled public appearances.

Sención did his best to cater to Dominicans' appetite for intimate gossip, offering countless details designed more to personally embarrass Balaguer than to provide insight into his regime's excesses. The youthful Ramos—a thinly veiled stand-in for Balaguer—is mocked for his limp handshake and effeminate mannerisms, and the narrator carefully traces the impact that people's jibes have on the young man. After being told by a group of classmates that "faggots never win glory," Ramos takes to concluding his poems with the line "Glory is there"—a "premonitory sentence" that contrives to suggest that the barbed anecdote has portentous psychological significance (89–90). Other lurid episodes are similarly arrayed: Ramos is shown seducing anonymous women on the outskirts of town, or even in cemeteries, finally becoming a "consummate master of surreptitious conquests" (91). After he wins power, an aide is tasked with procuring women, "younger every time," for the lascivious leader (91). Another popular piece of gossip—the suggestion that Balaguer was forewarned of the conspiracy to kill Trujillo—is similarly indulged: "One of the best-kept secrets is that one of the masterminds met privately with Doctor Mario Ramos," the text asserts. "The conspirator updated Doctor Ramos on the plan [. . .] and in turn invited him—as soon as the elimination was realized—to take the reins of power" (180–81).

Even superstitions are given an airing: toward the end of *Falsificaron*, Sención includes a solitary footnote recording the clairvoyant Doña

Muñinga's outlandish claim that Ramos "has a pact with the Devil," and that his youthful vigor is the result of "magico-erotical rites" conducted with adolescent victims supplied by Satan (314). The footnote allows Sención's narrator a degree of deniability—he doesn't directly endorse the psychic's allegations—but the very act of setting it apart from the text, both giving it space and assigning it a named source, serves to perpetuate and legitimize the swirling rumor.

The novel's fascination with gossip appears in other ways, too. The first third of the novel shows Frank Bolaño and several other characters living in a seminary, under the watchful eyes of the institution's leader, in an allegory of daily life under authoritarianism:

> Arturo perceived a state of extreme tension in the Seminary: there were whispers in every corner and surveillance had doubled. It had always been difficult there to find out what was going on, but this time there was no denying that the center of attention was Antonio Bell: that in July he had been imprisoned for political reasons; that he had been caught setting bombs in public buildings; that they were not bombs, but that early one morning he tried to set on fire, with gasoline and matches, all of the buildings in la Feria; that he had been tortured in Tyrant's prisons: la Victoria, la Cuarenta, the Government Palace itself; that he was mad. It was an underground rumor, a morbid one: a wasp of mystery transmitted through the tongue, through gestures, through glances, through the pencil.
>
> The communication among seminarians was always thwarted by the proximity of some teacher, and either way, a strict rule prohibited any talk of politics. They were all fearful. (102–3)

Despite the discrepancies in the accounts they hear, the youths rely on gossip—forbidden, but ubiquitous—to keep up with the politics of the day, to toy with the idea of resistance, and to make sense of their own place in their community. Gossip is defined by the surveillance that seeks its prohibition: it is a power struggle between the seminarians and their overseers, with the seminarians' whispers and furtive looks necessitated by their awareness of the illicit nature of their communication and of the penalties they would face if caught.

Later, Bolaño's perception of gossip as a resource for self-empowerment becomes more explicit: he taps phones, gathers information about others, and leverages it to his own advantage. Di Pietro reads Bolaño's character, and his passion for "collecting gossip," as an extension of Sención's own (107). But Bolaño is a complex character, concerned not just with amassing gossip but also with the political power he gains thereby. Gossip here is less a subversive force than an exercise in influence and control: Bolaño seeks not to overthrow the government but to insinuate himself into its workings. Though inspired to start tapping phones by his experiences as a jilted and jealous lover, Bolaño evolves into a political spy and becomes one of Ramos's most powerful allies. His ability to marshal intimate knowledge about others enables him to outmaneuver Ramos's advisers, including the less sophisticated gossips that populate the Great House, where Ramos's sisters live. But for Bolaño, power and prurience are inseparable, as is evident in a scene in which he arrives at Ramos's house:

> Frank did not hide the small package that he carried in his hands: he fanned himself with it. Everyone knew that the recorder was inside. . . . And Frank would half smile to the builder, who would soon bury himself in Albricia's room to settle accounts in dollars, and give accounts of love; would half smile to the functionary who waited, uneasy, for a late-night meeting with the President; would half smile to them all, pointing to them with the edge of the hidden tape where—who knew?—any of their indiscreet voices might be found.
>
> It was a dark weapon, and Frank stroked it between his hands like a sinister toy. (285–86)

Bolaño's "passion for spying" is motivated not only by a lust for power and knowledge but also by something more primal and perverse (285). Bolaño is presented less as a dangerous spy than as a lecherous voyeur, eager to violate the intimacy of others. The sexual undertones of the narrative—the penetration, the caresses—make clear that Bolaño's interest is less in espionage than in gossip: he seeks not just information but also titillation and social capital. The same is true when, earlier, he amuses himself by inviting friends to listen to recordings of his girlfriend's telephone conversations. It is through violating intimacy, and flaunting his power to do so, that Bolaño obtains pleasure.

In this, *Falsificaron* emphasizes a view of gossip as driven simultaneously by its power to thrill and its power to expose. As the novel progresses, the seminarians' desperate need to know gives way to a more cynical vision of surveillance and spying as methods of control that are effective, and seductive, because of the private spaces they invade. The power Bolaño gains through gossip is real and widely recognized, in part because gossip is already a critical component of the brutal logic of Ramos's terror state. People fear not only exposure but also its consequences: Bolaño "soon found fame for his powers of extermination" and "became the man most feared by government functionaries" (292). But if Bolaño's political enemies understand his gossip in terms of the threat it represents, Bolaño himself views his rise to power, and his ability to entrance Ramos with gossip, in passionate, sexual terms. Bolaño comes to spend "hours in the President's private room, enrapturing him with the almost musical charm of the freshly recorded phone conversations" (189). In Ramos, it becomes apparent, he has found a kindred spirit, one equally aroused by penetrating the privacy of others: "One of the aspects that the spy exploited the most, in his frequent evenings with President Ramos, was the President's weakness for *chismes de comadre* that so vehemently traversed the tapes; but especially the conversations about sex, of the most varying intensity, that some of the recordings captured. Frank, smacking his lips in success, would observe the way that Doctor Ramos would convulse from head to toe, struggling to control his moans, always in absolute silence, whenever eroticism appeared in the machine" (291–92). Ramos's own voyeuristic instincts thus find an outlet in the *chismes de comadre,* or intimate womanly gossip, that Bolaño's tapes reveal, as well as in the sexual conversations they contain. Eroticism and power are presented as sides of the same coin: the intrusions that so arouse Bolaño and Ramos are also the source of their power, and it is perhaps the power itself that makes the gossip so tantalizing.

The relationship between power and titillation runs through Sención's "gossip novel," and mediated both its commercial success and its official condemnation. Di Pietro approaches this fact when he writes that the novel is representative of a broader "gossip culture" (96)—but Dominican gossip culture is not, or not only, the decadent amalgam of trivia and falsehoods that Di Pietro suggests. Rather, it is the upshot of decades of highly politicized gossip, deployed by both Trujillo and Balaguer, and of an authoritarianism that left gossip as one of the few discourses still available to Dominicans even as it sought to regulate and limit opportunities for gossip. In such a context, gossip becomes both thrilling and potent: risky, but also explicitly engaged with questions of power.[11]

There is, moreover, a significance to the act of transcribing, or converting into literature, gossip already circulating from mouth to mouth. The paradox of the Dominican gossip state is that historical whitewashing has left historians more willing than they might otherwise be to accept gossip as a legitimate source of information. In such a context, the recording of gossip becomes a historicizing gesture; certainly, both Balaguer's and Sención's texts have been read as such. Derby, for instance, quotes Sención's novel as straightforward evidence of Balaguer's abilities as a "silver-tongued orator" ("Shadow" 331); Liberato, meanwhile, cites Sención in discussing Balaguer's "mysteriousness" and notes that Ramos, as a stand-in for Balaguer, is portrayed in Sención's text as "enigmatic" and a "master of surreptitious sexual conquest" (214). Likewise, in a profile published as Balaguer was ending his seventh term in office, the *New York Times* quoted at length from *Falsificaron* in search of insight into the president's personality and the workings of his inner circle.[12] Even fictionalized gossip, it seems, can add valuable detail and color to the postauthoritarian historical record.

A similar impulse led Dominicans to devour both Balaguer and Sención's texts, which promised, by revealing private or silenced information, to shed new light on the country's murky past. We may wonder how uncritically readers approached the gossip they read: few Dominicans, it seems safe to assume, took Balaguer's self-serving anecdotes as actually absolving him of culpability in Trujillo's excesses, or Sención's supernatural footnote as evidence of an actual diabolical streak in their then president. Sención, in fact, engages directly with gossip's reliability in his short story "La Marimanta," which is spliced somewhat awkwardly into the text of *Falsificaron*. In the tale, a civic-minded young man attempts to catch the "marimanta"—a kind of hobgoblin with long purple nails and a white shawl—that is terrifying his town.[13] The demonic creature's appearance is greeted with riotous, perversely joyful gossip, with the townsfolk chattering about the "mixture of scandal and mystery" unfolding before them (270). The hobgoblin is revealed to be a grotesquely costumed but beautiful woman who is having an affair with the town's priest; the gossip proves utterly inaccurate, but by stirring up the townsfolk, it helps unearth a real scandal. The gossipy anecdotes of *Falsificaron*, likewise, may not be literally true, but they serve the dual function of whetting the Dominican people's appetite for inside knowledge about the stage-managed, personalist regimes they have endured, and of calling attention to the countless real excesses of those regimes. The details in Sención's text may or may not be accurate, but few Dominicans would question the notion that scandals of some kind lie hidden behind their nation's sanitized official accounts. Even if the true history of the regime is unknowable, Sención's gossip insists that it is as plausible an account as any other, and a valuable counterbalance to the equally partial, agenda-driven gossip of Balaguer's memoirs.

Rival Versions: *El hombre del acordeón*

The interplay of gossip and history can similarly be traced in Marcio Veloz Maggiolo's 2003 novel *El hombre del acordeón,* which centers on Honorio Lora, a composer of pro-Trujillo merengues who breaks with the regime—and meets an untimely death—in the aftermath of the Haitian massacre. Lora is modeled upon, and shares a surname with, the real-life *merenguero* Ñico Lora, whose music was similarly co-opted by Trujillo, but who never attempted the kind of resistance shown by his fictional namesake. From its earliest days, merengue, like many of the Caribbean's other popular music forms, was an important part of the oral grapevine, a kind of sung gossip.[14] Merengue singers were not just musicians: they were tellers of stories and brokers of public knowledge. The musician "became also a chronicler of his time," writes Rafael Chaljub Mejía. "Witnessing an event or hearing about an occurrence that set in motion his talent, he would throw his instrument on his shoulder, and set off to tell people about it" (168).[15] In the Trujillo era, this aspect of merengue was embraced by the state, with officially sanctioned merengue becoming at once a potent nationalist symbol, a means of tapping into and manipulating class-based social tensions, and a way of substituting acceptable gossip and laudatory pro-Trujillo lyrics for potentially subversive musical messaging. Julie A. Sellers remarks that merengue's "capacity for criticism and social control infused it with both danger and potential," and was behind Trujillo's decision to have a merengue group join him on the campaign trail (13). With merengue, as with gossip, Trujillo sought to co-opt and control a popular narrative form, exploiting it for his own purposes while simultaneously curbing its utility as a potential space for dissent.[16]

Veloz Maggiolo's novel is fundamentally a text about contested spaces: not just the borderlands themselves but also the popular discourses through which resistance and subjugation are performed. As Maria Cristina Fumagalli writes, *El hombre* is committed to "a rejection of Dominican Hispanophilism and its Eurocentric and exclusionary notion of civilization" and explicitly engaged with "aspects of popular culture which are the product of the complicated history of the island but have traditionally been occluded or appropriated by dominant discourses (Vodú; magic; popular 'tales and legends'; *merengue*)" (*On the Edge* 167). Gossip, too, in the Dominican Republic is an "occluded or appropriated" discourse, and one that Veloz Maggiolo deploys throughout *El hombre* to stage both domination and dissent, and to explore the challenges that face the writer in authoritarian or postauthoritarian contexts. Much like *Falsificaron*, Veloz Maggiolo's text acknowledges and even embraces these challenges. *El hombre* opens with the admission that the text has been assembled in pursuit of narrative coherence rather than strict fidelity to the facts, which are elusive and perhaps unreachable:

The versions of this case are many and, in truth, the most relevant thing about them is that through them one can in some way organize the story of what happened. Therefore I make no pretension that everything is as ordered as it should be. [. . .]

If I had set out to write expecting to discern truth from falsehood I would have never achieved a more or less coherent tale, so the reader must accept my sometimes using voices out of sequence, phrases that I imagine were once logical, street stories that reached me in various ways and that I cannot justify without making reference to the stages of a common magic that is still being practiced. (11)

The story around which the narrative spirals, inching closer without ever quite reaching a definitive version, is that of the events surrounding Lora's death, which are told and retold in incomplete and contradictory versions. Lora, once a favorite of Trujillo's, appears to have fallen from grace after singing of the Haitian massacre, the narrator states, but whether Lora actually fell from grace, and how much that had to do with his death, is unknown and unlikely to be fully resolved. The narrator's goal, he warns, is not to determine the truth but merely to draw together the divergent accounts of Lora's death into a coherent account. Seeking a final version, and trying to fully separate truth from falsehood, the narrator suggests, would be an impediment to that goal. In his methodical reconstruction of what could plausibly have happened—or, rather, of what is said to have happened—the narrator relies on "many fragmentary versions" gathered through testimony and gossip from those who knew Lora. The narrator stresses the impossibility of cutting through the chatter to find a single true account: "'It is said that . . . , they affirm that . . . , I have heard that . . .' Doubts, many doubts" (45). A handful of accounts can be corroborated: four, in fact, "like the gospels" (45). The scriptural reference highlights the possibility of continuing contradictions between the accounts but also the sense that the aggregation of diverging accounts speaks to a kind of higher truth. Though it is impossible to pick between them, they reflect the community's collective understanding, scrappy and unresolved but still meaningful, of the events in question.

Much of *El hombre* deals with questions of self-definition, and of communities' efforts to determine which accounts will shape their collective understanding of the events that define them. In engaging with the Haitian massacre and the borderlands where the genocide took place, the novel is necessarily a study in liminality: an exploration of the negotiated boundaries between Haiti and the Dominican Republic and between Haitians and Dominicans. The inhabitants of the border region, the *rayanos,* slip between identities and resist easy categorization; like the resolution of the narrative itself, the drawing of a line separating one from the other is shown as a fraught and arbitrary act. The narrator warns: "It might bother the reader that the narrator never becomes convinced of anything, because within the cluster of contradictions about how he was killed, how he was buried, how he was moved to another location after he died, and other calamities that would end up in revenge and in various deaths, the only clear line to reconstructing events where the magical may reach beyond reality was the political influence that predominated among the inhabitants of the border and the *rayanos* who survived there deciding to be, as of that moment, Dominicans" (13). The narrator and the dictator are shown as conducting similar acts of narrative recomposition: perhaps necessary if the text (or the nation) is to exist in any coherent way, but morally ambiguous and even capricious, and given final shape only by the will of the writer or the leader.[17]

Given the text's focus on the ways in which scattered anecdotes cohere into the stories through which communities define themselves, it is notable that so much of the gossip in *El hombre* is described as *leyendas,* or legends, rather than simply idle chatter.[18] The narrator reflects on this in discussing Tantán's falling out with Lora. "As a journalist very well-versed in legends, I believe that Tantán's betrayal has other reasons. It is said that Tantán was madly in love with Remigia, and that she had given him hope, so that that night at the cockfighting pit [. . .] Tantán could not take his eyes off Remigia's breasts," he states. "From which it is inferred that there was jealousy getting in the way[. . . .] One cannot trust, of course, that which is sold as a sailor's legend" (74–75). The fragmented tale's origins in spoken accounts are clearly signposted, and much of what is described—the man "madly in love" with the woman, his ogling of her breasts—is quintessential gossip. In other passages, too, the narrator describes legends passing through the grapevine in a manner suggestive of gossip: "Legends run, they fly from rooftop to rooftop, they slide down *aleros* and fall to the ground as big drops of sticky water that wet the few passersby," he asserts (39–40).[19] The narrator's fusing of gossip and legend speaks to the journalistic desire to turn chatter into a first draft of history. Still, he makes clear that such legends have their origins in gossip: writing of the community's belief in a phantasmal voice that repeats the words "this man sure does know merengues," the narrator notes that they are "words legitimized by tradition and gossip" (46). Gossip and legend are cast as a continuum: words and stories shared through gossip cohere—or are curated—into the legends and traditions through which the community understands itself.[20]

This is not an entirely organic process: throughout *El hombre* we see people intervening to shape the stories that percolate through their community. The conversion of gossip into legend mirrors Vetemit Alzaga's efforts to forge respectable genealogical narratives for the inhabitants of the border region—a project that Alzaga claims was initiated by Trujillo himself, who "needed an official historian to give the region something like a lineage" (17).[21] Tellingly, Alzaga is not only a pro-Trujillo historian but also an informant channeling what the narrator calls "pasquinades and denunciations" back to the government (67). Alzaga denies this, claiming that he "has kept secret" an incriminating statement made to him by Tocay, but then admits: "Captain González found out about this phrase between domino games because, without any malice whatsoever, I mentioned it to him. [. . .] He told me that in the end Tocay was a traitor, and that anyone could have known what I, without malice and after a few drinks, had told him" (96). Alzaga disingenuously casts his betrayal merely as indiscreet chatter, justified by alcohol and lack of malice. Under Trujillo, however, such gossip is dangerous. The captain with whom Alzaga gossips is described as "always searching for those who criticized the government" (83); in such a context, Alzaga's words carry far more weight than he suggests, and in fact bring about Tocay's death.

Alzaga also appears to play a key role—depending on whose version one believes—in informing the authorities about Lora's subversive lyrics, which criticized Alzaga's bogus biographical work and mocked the pretentious Spanish surnames he granted to favored locals. Alzaga complains to the narrator that giving Tantán an aristocratic last name was "a serious mistake," because Lora knew his true origins and immediately composed a merengue mocking the pair. "Honorio was skeptical about my creations," Alzaga laments. "Every time I managed to persuade these peasants, for their own good, that they were descended from people of lineage, he would pull out his accordion and bombard me with improvised verses" (72). Alzaga's betrayals can be read as part of an adversarial back-and-forth between the conservative historian and the subversive merengue singer: Lora sings back against Alzaga's historicizing, just as Alzaga gossips back against Lora. Much like gossip, Lora's merengues are highly adversarial acts of verbal violence: they stage animosities, criticize, mock, and reveal the affairs of others. When Panchito Mejía attempts to seduce Lora's lover, she warns him: "Don't go looking for trouble with Honorio, because he can ruin your reputation by speaking about you in a merengue" (61). Indeed, upon hearing of the episode, Lora immediately improvises a merengue:

> Anyone who eats donkey-meat
> like Panchito Mejía
> retains something of the beast
> and can't keep from braying. (61)

Lora's sung gossip is as effective as a real weapon: Mejía responds by trying to kill Lora but is so enraged by the song that he winds up shooting himself in the leg.[22]

Merengue performances are shown as confrontational, testosterone-driven clashes: it is no coincidence that musical duels between singers typically follow cockfights. This becomes increasingly evident as Lora's songs grow more political; his accordion, the narrator notes, "transforms itself almost into a .30–30 caliber carbine, or a .44 Magnum revolver" (29).[23] Like taking up arms against Trujillo, singing against the regime is a risky business: the novel suggests that the ill-fated Lora "screwed himself with his numerous verses against the General" (81). Still, Lora takes pleasure in using merengue, the same form used as a propaganda tool by those in power, to record his enmities and preserve the history of La Línea and its inhabitants.[24] As Rita De Maeseneer notes, Veloz Maggiolo understands that popular music "can serve as a medium of rebellion and of submission" (236). As with gossip, merengue is a tool deployed by both conservative and radical forces, and a weapon available both to those in power and those fighting against them. This is not just a casual congruence between discursive forms: much of merengue's power stems from the degree to which it functions as gossip, disclosing and circulating an adversary's transgressions and challenging the narratives they themselves have put forth.

This is the central tension at the heart of *El hombre:* from its cockpit merengue duels to the confusion surrounding Lora's death, the text deals in clashing narratives and rival versions of events. Lora pushes back against the narratives preferred by the Trujillo regime—the "authors of so much death" (88)—just as the regime and its supporters seek, through gossip and denunciation, and perhaps also through actual violence, to suppress the singer's counternarratives. The result of these vying accounts is an inescapable narrative instability, in which even fiction and falsehoods are better than silence. "Forgetting is the worst thing," Alzaga argues. "And the worst thing is also to say 'I do not remember' when one can invent history without there being anyone able to rebut it" (91).[25] The narrator rejects Alzaga's narrative relativism but also acknowledges that his fabrications—as proxies for the regime's sanctioned self-narrative—"serve to collect certain versions that might be true" (71). In the gossip state, Veloz Maggiolo suggests, there can be no certainty, no firm historical ground upon which to stand: gossip can resurface different versions of events, but to forge a unitary account, to craft a narrative from the silences and lies and distortions that remain, is the domain of fiction rather than of conventional historiography.

Words as Weapons: *The Brief Wondrous Life of Oscar Wao*

History is a phenomenon that comes more clearly into focus with time and distance. Balaguer and Sención, writing contemporaneously, sought to influence a still unfolding process of public judgment and to sway the course of as-yet-unwritten histories. Veloz Maggiolo, more temporally removed but—unlike Sención—still writing from the Dominican Republic, grapples with the difficulties inherent in making sense of the sparring versions of history left to the nation by the gossip state and its discontents. Diasporic writers face similar challenges, as can be seen in Junot Díaz's 2007 novel *The Brief Wondrous Life of Oscar Wao,* a text that is itself saturated with gossip. Its characters gossip and are revealed through gossip; its Dominican American narrator, Yunior, gossips; even Trujillo is shown as both gossiped about and gossiping. The novel's proliferating gossip frames an account of the twentieth-century Dominican experience: Yunior's attempt to write a biography of his friend, the eponymous Oscar, spirals out to incorporate, through succeeding layers of gossip, the broader story of Oscar's family and, more obliquely, of the Dominican people, the Trujillo regime, and the Dominican diaspora. Yunior deploys gossip both as an essential source of information and as a narrative strategy that allows him to disseminate previously silenced or suppressed stories, in a manner that titillates the reader even as it subtly draws him or her into ideological complicity with him, and seduces them into accepting, and even adopting, the ideological stance on which Yunior's telling of the events is founded. In so doing, however, Yunior also reveals gossip's status as a contested medium, capable both of comforting Dominicans and of serving as a tool for their oppression. Gossip, in Díaz's text much as in Veloz Maggiolo's, grants a measure of narrative power to those denied a place in official discourses, but is also readily harnessed and largely monopolized by the Trujillo regime, which repeatedly used it to suppress dissent and strengthen its grip on power.

In *Oscar Wao*, gossip is neither condemned nor vindicated but is rather presented as a malleable, pervasive, and potent narrative form that can be marshaled to very different ends by those seeking to resist or to sustain established hierarchies of power. It is gossip's malleability, and its ability to be co-opted and deployed by both the powerful and the disenfranchised, after all, that makes it so ubiquitous in Díaz's Dominican Republic, and perhaps in other societies similarly marked by the authoritarian impulse for narrative control. This recalls the totalitarian aspects of gossip—as a narrative form that denies alternative discourses and seeks to establish its own primacy—explored in chapter 1. Michael Taussig writes that "all societies live by fictions taken as real. What distinguishes cultures of terror is that the epistemological, ontological and otherwise philosophical problem of representation—reality and illusion, certainty and doubt—becomes infinitely more than a 'merely' philosophical problem. [. . .] It becomes a high powered medium of domination" (121). Díaz's novel traces the construction and deconstruction of such fictions, describing gossip's development as precisely such a medium of domination, but also its ability to be used, post facto, to destabilize the dominant narratives of the past.

Much of *Oscar Wao*, in fact, can be read as an attempt to reconstruct the counterpublic of gossip, to borrow Dalleo's term, from the safety of temporal and geographical distance. In recounting his family saga, Yunior excavates both the gossip that furtively circulated during the Trujillo era and the many stories that would have been fodder for gossip had there been more scope to speak freely. He frequently does so, moreover, by emulating the cadences and structures of gossip, inserting himself into a Caribbean tradition of gossip as a potent and frequently political form of discourse. This is a culturally appropriate way to tell his story, but also a way to foreground the subversive and revisionary nature of the tales he recounts, and to revivify and lay claim to a counterpublic to which Dominicans had, at best, very limited access under authoritarianism. Gossip, in this sense, maps precisely onto the fraught representational space that Taussig describes: it is a means to challenge the Dominican Republic's sanitized official narrative but also a tool whereby such challenges can be suppressed. It is, as in *El hombre*, a space in which a society can negotiate which of its fictions will be taken to be real and which narratives will come to dominate its discourses. Ultimately, *Oscar Wao* proposes that gossip's fundamental promise to deliver hidden truths, and its ability to either undermine or reinforce narratives, makes it a narrative battleground over which both the downtrodden and those who would keep them so must vie for control.

Cozarinsky suggests that gossip concerns itself with either exceptional people or exceptional events, and we can see both forms at play in *Oscar Wao*. In telling his story, Yunior offers up countless tales of the private lives of senior members of the Trujillo regime: some scandalous and some relatively banal, but all made worthy of the telling by the power and prominence of the people they concern. The impetus to discuss the intimate peccadillos of the powerful is driven, in part, simply by prurient curiosity; in the context of a personalistic and authoritarian regime, however, such tales carry more weight. If the leader is the state, then the minutiae of the leader's life become a matter of genuine importance, and apparently trivial gossip becomes complex and politically charged. More broadly, gossip renders judgment: the complicity and shared moral framework presumed by gossip is leveraged by Yunior to convince his reader of the validity of his opinion of the powerful individuals he describes. Yunior, in gossiping, seeks not just to inform the reader, but to enlist him or her in a revisionary process that will continue as they repeat and recirculate the tantalizing tidbits they have heard—and, in so doing, perpetuate the moral judgments implicit in the gossip they share.

This is apparent when Díaz's text introduces Ramfis Trujillo, the dictator's son, "born while his mother was still married to another man, un cubano" (99). Yunior dwells on the most titillating elements of Ramfis's biography, fusing familial discord, sex, celebrity, and bizarre private habits: "It was only after the cubano refused to accept the boy as blood that Trujillo recognized Ramfis as his own. (Thanks, Dad!) [. . .] As an adult Ramfis was famed for being a polo player, a fucker of North American actresses (Kim Novak, how could you?), a squabbler with his father, and a frozen-hearted demon[. . . .] (In a secret report filed by the US consul [. . .] Ramfis is described as 'imbalanced,' a young man who during his childhood amused himself by blowing the heads off chickens with a .44 revolver)" (99). Yunior attributes some of his biographical snapshot to a historical document, but the details purportedly plucked from diplomatic papers lack the gravitas of history. They are, rather, a collection of private episodes from Ramfis's misspent youth, stories circulated through gossip and now mobilized to reveal and tarnish Ramfis's character. Yunior displays a similar predilection for provocative details in an early footnote describing Trujillo as "a portly, sadistic, pig-eyed mulato who bleached his skin, wore platform shoes, and had a fondness for Napoleon-era haberdashery" and was famous for, among other things, "fucking every hot girl in sight, even the wives of his subordinates, thousands upon thousands upon thousands of women" (2).[26] Similarly juicy details abound throughout *Oscar Wao,* and it is easy to see them as gossip mobilized to influence the reader's view of its target: made salient by Trujillo's standing, and exploited both to reinforce claims about his character and to mockingly domesticate the larger-than-life dictator and his accomplices. In these dramatically staged stories, the content, complicity, and structures of gossip are readily recognizable. Yunior provides secrets about third parties, using oral cadences and joking, faux-shocked asides, while taking evident pleasure (and anticipating the reader's pleasure) in skewering and diminishing his powerful subjects. Through such gossip, Yunior presents a ribald Who's Who of the Trujillato, painting each new crony and henchman in vivid detail, and spending as much time cataloging their personal foibles and sexual proclivities as explicating their role in the regime.

Yunior also gossips about Oscar and his family members, and about other ordinary Dominicans, focusing less on exposing their character flaws and private indiscretions than on revealing the unspeakable abuses and terrors they endured under the Trujillato. Using similar cadences and structures, Yunior once more shares the secrets of absent others—but in this instance, the driving emotional force is not salacious pleasure taken in transmitting tales of debauchery, but rather sympathy spiked with an appalling, unavoidable fascination at hearing the family's experience of state terror. While Oscar's family members are ostensibly the subject of the gossip in question, there is a sense in which Yunior's tales are built less around their victims than around their perpetrators. The "fukú stories" (6) Yunior tells are reflections of the regime's excesses, and as such speak to Trujillo's character and his purportedly evil nature. If they are gossip about Oscar and his family, then they are also gossip about Trujillo, and about the extent and consequences of his perceived perversities.

It might seem surprising that Yunior, a hypermasculine figure who brags about spending his days "out chasing the pussy" or "out with the boys" (184), should deploy gossip so freely. Still, as discussed elsewhere in this volume, the gossip of the Caribbean is not (or not only) a gendered practice; it can be the talk of disenfranchised women, but it can equally be the chatter of marginalized men, or a tool used by powerful figures of either gender as they participate in the public sphere. Díaz's text presents gossip as an adversarial and revisionary practice: Yunior frequently gossips with the explicit intent of subverting or undermining the discourses imposed by the Trujillo and Balaguer regimes. Gossip here stands not as a gendered phenomenon but a fundamentally political one, available to both men and women and rooted in the dynamics of power and narrative control.

Not all of the gossip in *Oscar Wao* lends itself easily to such readings; the novel portrays and deploys multiple forms of gossip, including gossip as a means for intimates to construct and transmit social knowledge. It is through this more conventional gossip that it is revealed—via "a whisper in La Inca's ear" (254)—that Belicia, La Inca's second cousin, is still alive. The "astonishing tale" (255) of a girl horribly beaten and burned by her adopted family is not simply relayed to the reader, but is explicitly staged through revelatory gossip, with Yunior re-creating the very moment of its transmission:

> And the wildest part of the story? Rumor had it that this burned girl was a relative of La Inca!
> How could that be possible, La Inca demanded.
> Do you remember your cousin who was the doctor up in La Vega? The one who went to prison for saying the Bad Thing about Trujillo? Well, fulano, who knows fulano, who knows fulano, said that that little girl is his daughter! (255–56)

Yunior transcribes the gossip, relishing its performative aspects as he re-creates its speech patterns and even its claimed provenance. In so doing, he depicts it as a tool that allows La Inca to receive information about her extended family and thereby navigate the landscape of her terrorized community. There is little that can be done for Abelard, who, now imprisoned, is almost entirely defined by the "Bad Thing" he supposedly said. However, it is the information delivered by gossip that allows La Inca to come to his daughter's rescue and, in some small way, push back against the indifferent brutality of the terror state.

Díaz portrays the circulation of information as a double-edged sword: through the chatter of prying neighbors, La Inca learns about and rescues Belicia, but this swirling gossip also presents risks. To reveal a secret, even to a close friend, is to risk its broader dissemination and the attendant consequences. When, as a child, Lola is assaulted, the news becomes known by "a sizable section of Paterson, Union City, and Teaneck," unleashing an "urikán of pain, judgment, and bochinche" (25). A similar episode occurs when Belicia falls pregnant with the Gangster's child and ignores La Inca's pleas for discretion: "Please don't tell anyone, La Inca begged, but of course she whispered it to her friend Dorca, who put it out on the street. [. . .] The bochinche spread through their sector of Baní like wildfire" (136). A shared moment of intimacy becomes *bochinche*—vicious, fast-spreading gossip—as it is relayed and relayed again, until inevitably, fatally, it reaches Trujillo's sister, the Gangster's wife, with disastrous consequences for Belicia and her unborn child.

If such danger can arise from a simple moment of unguarded intimacy, then it becomes easy to understand the risks inherent in giving voice to more subversive gossip. After all, Abelard's plight, and all the suffering endured by his family, springs only from his having spoken a little too freely about Trujillo's government. Gossip, though a useful source of information, was dangerous, the text insists; to speak out of turn was to place yourself entirely at your neighbor's mercy:

> It wasn't just Mr. Friday the Thirteenth you had to worry about, either, it was the whole Chivato Nation he helped spawn [. . .]. It was widely believed that at any one time between forty-two and eighty-seven percent of the Dominican population was on the Secret Police's payroll. Your own fucking neighbors could acabar con you just because you had something they coveted or because you cut in front of them at the colmado. [. . .] (You wonder why two generations later our parents are still so damn secretive, why you'll find out your brother ain't your brother only by accident.) (225–26)

The final parenthetical reveals the bitter cost of the discord sown by the Trujillo regime: not just tales of the regime's excesses but even family gossip was all but silenced. Indeed, the wariness of unguarded speech became so ingrained that for some the practice remains effectively taboo two generations later. Decades after Trujillo's fall, *Oscar Wao* suggests, to reconstruct lost stories, of the family or of the nation, remains a difficult and sometimes impossible task.

The resurfacing of such gossip, as we have seen, is a critical piece of the narrative project underpinning both Yunior's tale and *Oscar Wao* itself. If gossip, despite its risks, is shown as providing valuable information for the characters of *Oscar Wao*, it is also shown as preserving at least some of that information, despite Trujillo's efforts, and making it accessible to Yunior as he seeks to piece together the family saga. Time and again, crucial episodes from the family's history can be reconstructed only because of the gossip they generated. Beli's affair with the Gangster is a prominent example:

> This was the affair that once and for all incinerated Beli's reputation in Santo Domingo. No one in Baní knew exactly who the Gangster was and what he did (he kept his shit hush-hush), but it was enough that he was a man. In the minds of Beli's neighbors, that prieta comparona had finally found her true station in life, as a cuero. Old-timers have told me that during her last months in the

> DR Beli spent more time inside the love motels than she had in school—an exaggeration, I'm sure, but a sign of how low our girl had fallen in the pueblo's estimation. (127)

Yunior draws on old gossip to propel his narrative, presenting it as a useful tool for making sense of both the facts and the social dynamics of the past. The gossip itself may not be strictly accurate, he suggests, but it captures something of the lived experiences of the community in which it circulates.

It is telling, too, that Yunior refers to reconstructing the social knowledge of the period from tales recalled by "old-timers"—essentially, through resurfaced gossip. This is a strategy to which Yunior returns as he slips between his two narrative projects: the reconstruction of a family saga and the reconstruction of a nation's history. Consider the following passage:

> Ask any of your elders and they will tell you: Trujillo might have been a Dictator, but he was a Dominican Dictator, which is another way of saying he was the Number-One Bellaco in the Country. [. . .] It's a well-documented fact that in Trujillo's DR if you were of a certain class and you put your cute daughter anywhere near El Jefe, within the week she'd be mamando his ripio like an old pro and *there would be nothing you could do about it!* Part of the price of living in Santo Domingo, one of the Island's best-known secrets. (216–17)

Oscar Wao is explicitly concerned with the challenges of constructing (or reconstructing) a family's story in a postauthoritarian nation in which both historical facts and private tales of human suffering have been ruthlessly effaced. Yunior tells his reader to ask his or her "elders," framing what follows as a reconstruction from temporal or geographic exile: the reader is cast alongside the narrator as a young, post-Trujillo Dominican, a child of diaspora. Yunior's suggestion that Trujillo's taste for rape is "a well-documented fact," meanwhile, is an ironic nod to the lack of any adequate historical record of the regime's excesses. Despite official efforts to eliminate them, rumor and gossip—those "best-known secrets"—were among the few means available to circulate, and later preserve, the memory of the abuses that took place.

This preoccupation with gossip's status as a potential salve for the historiographic and narrative scars left by authoritarianism further reveals itself in the defining image of *Oscar Wao:* Balaguer's aforementioned blank page. In another of the novel's many footnotes, Díaz's narrator offers a portrait in miniature of Balaguer: "Balaguer was a Negrophobe, an apologist to genocide, an election thief, and a killer of people who wrote better than himself, famously ordering the death of journalist Orlando Martínez. Later, when he wrote his memoirs, he claimed he knew who had done the foul deed (not him, of course) and left a blank page, a página en blanco, in the text to be filled in with the truth upon his death. (Can you say *impunity?*) Balaguer died in 2002. The página is still blanca" (90). This is a pivotal moment in *Oscar Wao*'s deployment of gossip: Díaz calls out Balaguer's gossip as a political stratagem and insists that his real legacy is a blank page, a silence. In this, Díaz suggests, the promise of gossip gives way to threat: the wordless page is a pointed reminder of the enduring silence imposed by the regime, and an attempt to assert and perpetuate the regime's monopoly on gossip. Yunior's outrage at Balaguer's silence is palpable in the searing revelations, obtained through the revival of old gossip, with which he seeks to challenge Balaguer and deface or annotate the blank page. Instead of silence, Yunior chooses *bochinche:* he aims to resurrect and unleash tales that survived through gossip, and to stir up an unrestrained, uncontrollable *urikán* of moral judgment rather than cede to the regime the narrative control and consequent impunity that it sought.

It is in this context, and against Balaguer's *página en blanco,* that Yunior's many lurid tales must be read. Where the Trujillo and Balaguer regimes sought to eradicate unsanctioned gossip and impose a monolithic national narrative, Yunior seeks to look beyond the blank page, and resurrect and reinscribe the rumors and gossip that were once suppressed. Discussing another Trujillo official's excesses, Yunior returns to this motif, ironically noting the difficulties inherent in telling the full story of a nation whose people still feel a "lingering unease when it comes to talking about the regime." He adds: "I'll give you what I've managed to unearth and the rest will have to wait for the day the páginas en blanco finally speak" (119).[27] In a nation where history is incomplete and obscured by blank pages, Yunior falls back on the Dominican Republic's "best-known secrets"—which is to say, secrets spread and preserved through furtive gossip. The "well-documented fact" of the harm caused by Trujillo's runaway libido will not be found in official records (217); it derives its truth status not from documentary evidence but from rumor and gossip—or, rather, the recollection thereof, from the safety of exile, by "any of your elders" (216). Whether such gossip is historically true or false is generally unknowable, and hardly the point: what matters, from the standpoint of the regime's survivors, is that it is told at all.

Plausibility here matters as much as, or perhaps more than, the historical record; indeed, for a nation recovering from a regime that routinely erased all record of its misdeeds, the absence of direct evidence can come to bolster the credibility of the gossip in question. If it was worth covering up, the logic goes, then the story must have been true. The tenuous relationship of gossip to verifiable fact is wryly acknowledged by Yunior throughout the text: we see it, for instance, in his account of Abelard's torture and imprisonment. Though ostensibly persecuted for gossiping about Trujillo, Abelard was also rumored to have been working on a book-length exposé of the dictator's demonic, supernatural nature. Yunior dismisses the notion as "a figment of our Island's hypertrophied voodoo imagination" (246), but as Tim Lanzendörfer remarks, the manuscript's disappearance after Abelard's arrest lends the laughable rumors a credibility they would not otherwise merit. "The implication that Trujillo must have been after something is obvious, and in the broader context Yunior's disavowal [. . .] becomes a backhanded affirmation," he writes (134–35). This recalls Sención's footnote about Balaguer's supposed Satanic orgies: where Sención provides a source to hint that his tantalizing gossip might be true, Yunior's denials serve as a kind of ironic validation. The gossip is unverifiable, but so too, in Trujillo's Dominican Republic, is history itself. In cultures of terror, paradoxically, the very impossibility of confirming gossip's claims can serve to render them all the more convincing.

In reconstructing Dominican history from tenuous, secondhand sources, Yunior's goal is necessarily to persuade as much as to inform or educate. In this, too, narrative strategies that approximate gossip play a vital role. As a narrative form, gossip both stages a story and presumes the listener's acquiescence with the judgments it asserts. By emulating the formal structures of gossip, Yunior's narrative similarly presumes and seeks to ensure the reader's acceptance of the text's perspective and value system. Writing of the Gangster, Yunior tells his reader that "our young villain [. . .] dabbled in forgery, theft, extortion, and money laundering" and adds that it "was even rumored, never substantiated, that our Gangster was the hammerman who slew Mauricio Báez in Havana in 1950" (120). The thrilling, if speculative, details, along with the repeated use of the word *our* to describe the subject while calling him a "villain," draws the reader into the complicity typical of gossip.

Yunior embraces the relational aspect of gossip, just as he embraces its content and cadences: he revels in and parades his own bias against the Trujillo regime, and in doing so seeks to seduce his reader into accepting the moral framework he proposes. Crucially, however, this seduction occurs not through polemic or persuasion but rather through the simple assumption and performance of a shared perspective: Yunior does not seek to convince his reader of his position, but rather assumes that they already share it, and makes their full enjoyment of the details he shares conditional upon that fact, just as gossip depends upon the nodding complicity of its audience. Gossip is grounded, after all, in its own moral charge, and often comes from a place of moral absolutism: it seeks not to parse or persuade but rather to pronounce judgment.[28] By channeling and emulating gossip, Yunior thus simultaneously imbues his narrative with a compelling moral clarity and seeks to ensure his reader's unquestioning acceptance of the moral framework through which his tale is told.

Inasmuch as Yunior succeeds in winning over his reader, and reinscribing a plausible story onto history's blank page, his tale stands as a narrative triumph and a cathartic reclamation of power. Indeed, as Guillermo B. Irizarry notes, *Oscar Wao*'s descriptions of state violence, portrayed "unflinchingly, and at length," come to serve "as an exorcism" (116), seeking to purge a historical trauma that has hung over the island and its people since the fall of the Trujillato. As Yunior makes clear, under Trujillo the Dominican people had few formal opportunities to express themselves, either in public or in private. A poorly judged joke or comment could bring down an individual or an entire family; faced with such consequences for speech, many Dominicans retreated into silence. In using gossip both to publicly disseminate private or silenced stories and to frame them in clear moral terms, *Oscar Wao* casts the practice as an effective narrative means of coming to terms with and overcoming the silences and betrayals of history. Gossip, in this context, must necessarily often be a retrospective process of reconstruction: not the restoration of words once spoken but the reclamation of things known but left unsaid. "Ask any of your elders," Yunior tells his reader, for only now, from exile and decades later, will they finally be able to speak.

The notion that gossip can mediate a valuable and even necessary reconfiguration of official discourses stands in stark contrast to the way in which the interplay of gossip and history has generally been considered. Some scholars, such as Søren Kierkegaard, see gossip as ephemeral froth on history's still-churning waters; as time passes and the waters settle, Kierkegaard suggests, gossip evaporates into nothing. He writes: "If we could suppose for a moment that there was a law which did not forbid people talking, but simply ordered that everything which was spoken about should be treated as though it happened fifty years ago, the gossips would be done for, they would be in despair" (52–53). Others, equally troubled by gossip as a form of discourse, are less convinced that its babble will inevitably fade into silence. D. A. Miller writes: "One way not to have a story is to tell one about somebody who does: narration is a solid protection against the narratable. It is easy to see how the logic of gossip makes it the inevitable practice of a community that would remain unhistorical" (124). In this reading, gossip is corrosive to both historical and literary endeavors; it is, in fact, the sound of a society turning away from self-knowledge, the very opposite of the view that *Oscar Wao* defends.

Such criticisms weigh the effervescent, moralizing chatter of gossip against more ponderous and supposedly unbiased discourses and find it wanting. It is precisely gossip's partiality and judgmentalism, however, that makes it so appealing to Díaz's narrator. There is a redemptive power to moral outrage in the face of oppression, and in offering a one-sided account Yunior views himself as placing a restorative finger on a set of scales historically weighted firmly against the silenced Dominican people. By showcasing gossip's ability to reconfigure narratives of power and to surface and circulate private or previously suppressed stories, Díaz's novel reveals the practice's value to those excluded from supposedly objective historical accounts. In this sense, gossip provides more than a merely nominal triumph: for those excluded from their societies' official narratives, gossip can function—even if only retrospectively—as a powerful tool of self-assertion. Indeed, in *Oscar Wao* the power of gossip is so clearly recognized by the Trujillo regime that it seeks not just to silence gossip but also to co-opt it: officials use the practice not only to reinforce moral values and behaviors but also to affirm and strengthen state-sanctioned narratives. Gossip in this sense emerges not as ahistorical chatter but rather as a sharply contested medium—as is the case in Veloz Maggiolo's novel—through which public narratives are at once reinforced and challenged: a potent weapon for both sides in their constant struggle for narrative control.

This has historically been a key, if largely unacknowledged, aspect of the social experience of gossip: both a resource for the disenfranchised and a "medium of domination" deployed by the powerful to assert and sustain their narrative monopoly.[29] This duality is clearly shown in *Oscar Wao*, where the Trujillo regime maintains its grip on Dominican society through a sophisticated spy system, itself a network of gossip and insinuation that channels information back to Trujillo. In so doing, the regime regulates private behaviors and conversations with almost supernatural efficiency. Yunior writes: "You could say a bad thing about El Jefe at eight-forty in the morning and before the clock struck ten you'd be in the Cuarenta having a cattleprod shoved up your ass. [. . .] Mad folks went out in that manner, betrayed by those they considered their panas, by members of their own family, by slips of the tongue. [. . .] It was whispered that he did not sleep, did not sweat, that he could see, smell, feel events hundreds of miles away, that he was protected by the most evil fukú on the Island" (225–26). In fact it is gossip, not *fukú,* that protects Trujillo. By harnessing the furtive chatter of intimates, the Trujillo regime is able to infiltrate private spaces and rob gossip of much of its oppositional power. Gossip here comes to corrode trust in the private sphere and to strengthen the terror state. Indeed, gossip itself becomes a tool for bolstering Trujillo's reputation as an all-seeing and all-powerful leader: rather than whispering about the regime's transgressions, people are reduced to whispering about El Jefe's power and his preternatural ability to overhear malicious gossip and root out his foes.

In Trujillo's hands, gossip becomes not just a source of intelligence but also an instrument for humiliating and isolating those who step out of line. The state's use of gossip goes beyond mere character assassination: as Balaguer's *Memorias* also makes clear, government-planted gossip in the *Foro Público* was widely and correctly recognized as a harbinger of calamities to come. Indeed, after deflecting Trujillo's lascivious advances on his nubile daughter, it is gossip itself that Abelard most fears. Yunior explains: "For the next three months Abelard waited for the End. Waited for his name to start appearing in the 'Foro Popular' section of the paper, thinly veiled criticisms aimed at a certain bone doctor from La Vega— which was often how the regime began the destruction of a respected citizen such as him—with disses about the way your socks and your shirts didn't match" (223). Trujillo's spies may themselves inspire gossip— they're tasked with recruiting sexual partners for their master, Yunior repeatedly reminds his reader—but they also turn the practice to their own ends. As Abelard knew, the gossip column that Díaz dubs the "Foro Popular" mattered not because of the specific information it contained but rather because it indicated who had fallen from grace: it was the first step on a road that led, inexorably, not simply to the loss of one's reputation but to the destruction of one's entire life.

Abelard's fear is well warranted. When the hammer finally falls, he is accused not of denying Trujillo his daughter but rather of "slander and gross calumny against the Person of the President" (233).[30] Ironically, the accusation is itself based on gossip: "hidden 'witnesses'" claim that Abelard jokingly said there were no corpses hidden in his car's trunk because *"Trujillo must have cleaned them out for me"* (235). Abelard denies having uttered the words, and Yunior, narrating the tale, makes it clear that the real facts of the matter are not only unknown but unknowable:

"What's certain is that nothing's certain. We are trawling in silences here. Trujillo and Company didn't leave a paper trail[. . . .] A whisper here and there but nothing more. Which is to say if you're looking for a full story, I don't have one" (243). Once more, Yunior underscores the insufficiency of the historical record, whose gaps can only be filled with whispered gossip. But his retrospective reclamation of Abelard's story is of little consolation for its subject, who is sentenced to eighteen years in the notorious Nigüa death camp. There, Abelard's jailers turn slander, presented and received as truthful gossip, into an instrument of punishment, spreading malicious stories to ensure Abelard's mistreatment at the hands of his fellow detainees: "The guards then proceeded to inform the other prisoners that Abelard was a homosexual and a Communist—That is *untrue!* Abelard protested—but who is going to listen to a gay comunista?" (239). The text once more insists that gossip can be as much a tool of oppression as a comfort for the oppressed. Gossip, as much as torture or imprisonment, ultimately consumes Abelard: following a makeshift lobotomy, he is left unable to recall his past life, reduced to a subject of gossip even for his fellow inmates. The regime's narrative victory, its eradication of Abelard's version of his own life story, is complete.

Abelard's fate casts a long shadow over *Oscar Wao*'s narrative. Yunior asks his reader to consider the incident as exemplifying the Dominican Republic's broader history of violence and of silence: Abelard, robbed of memory and narrative agency, echoes the condition of the nation as a whole. His family, trying to reconstruct its story, always begins with an account of the "Bad Thing" that Abelard said about Trujillo. As Yunior notes, "There are other beginnings certainly, better ones, to be sure—if you ask me I would have started when the Spaniards 'discovered' the New World— . . . but if this was the opening that the de Leóns chose for themselves, then who am I to question their historiography?" (211). The suggestion that the family's story should truly begin with Columbus's arrival on the island once more suggests a reading of the family as a synecdoche of the nation, and underscores the novel's attempt to foreground the private stories of individuals—the "brief, nameless lives" of its epigraph—within the larger context of the national history.[31]

It is telling that Yunior defends the family's right to construct its history against, or regardless of, Yunior's own views. Yunior's writing can be read as an attempt to reinscribe the blank pages imposed on history by the Trujillato, but as Yunior's tolerance of the family's historiography reveals, his project is not to replace the regime's blank page with a univocal and final alternative account. Monica Hanna contends that Yunior "maintains his freedom from the onus of telling the definitive, authoritative version of Oscar's history and Dominican history" and instead probes the gaps and silences that result from the Trujillato's drive for narrative control (501).[32] There is space in this project for divergent voices, viewpoints, and historiographies. Indeed, Yunior grants himself a sort of gleeful poetic license that frees him from the rigors of academic histories, and allows him to creatively exploit and write into the gaps and silences. Hanna writes that Yunior "does quite a bit of traditional research, reading a variety of primary sources and conducting interviews, yet he still gives himself license to imaginatively recreate elements of the story that are otherwise inaccessible" (501). Through this process, Díaz's text marks its distance from traditional narrative practices that claim to offer definitive accounts of Dominican history.[33] Díaz asserts that he deliberately broke with the historical register in order to avoid being seduced by the larger-than-life figure of Trujillo and to present a demythologized account of Dominicans' recent past. "The power of Trujillo perpetuates itself in the histories written about him. My book tries to erect a counterhistory," he states ("Pesadillas"). In this view, the Trujillato's revisionism presents an all but insurmountable obstacle for the traditional historian, who must rely on the regime's own sanctioned and sanitized paper trail.[34] Gossip, however, operates according to different rules: by definition it deals in the unofficial and unsanctioned, and is not necessarily rendered less convincing by the paucity of evidence for its claims.

The travails of the scholar of Dominican history are memorably staged in Yunior's tale of "Basque supernerd" and Columbia University doctoral student Jesús de Galíndez, the author of a "rather unsettling" dissertation (96):

> The topic? Lamentably, unfortunately, sadly: the era of Rafael Leónidas Trujillo Molina. [. . .] Long story short: upon learning of the dissertation, El Jefe first tried to buy the thing and when that failed he dispatched his chief Nazgul (the sepulchral Felix Bernardino) to NYC and within days Galíndez got gagged, bagged and dragged to La Capital, and legend has it when he came out of his chloroform nap he found himself naked, dangling from his feet over a cauldron of *boiling oil,* El Jefe standing nearby with a copy of the offending dissertation in hand. (And you thought *your* committee was rough.) (97)[35]

Díaz, much like Veloz Maggiolo, describes as legend an anecdote that is recognizable—in the names named, the specificity of the grisly imagery, the bone-dry gallows humor, and the perverse pleasure taken in its narration—as tracing the formal structures of gossip.[36] Yunior shows the limited capacity of the historian to cope with or accurately depict the actions of a regime that shows no compunction in violently silencing those who promulgate unauthorized versions of the past. There is an absurdity in Yunior's comparison of Trujillo to a dissertation committee, yet Yunior is serious in his portrayal of the dictator as the self-appointed arbiter of historical accounts and gatekeeper of the historical record. In staging history's failure, Díaz's text shows gossip's enduring utility: it is through gossip, after all, that Yunior is now able to rescue the memory of the murdered history student and to ensure the page is not left entirely blank.

History, in this view, is limited by its own insistence on objectivity and factual accuracy. In contrast, the gossip Yunior offers—tendered from history's margins, by its victims—is not necessarily diminished by the fact that its truth status is indiscernible. In a discussion of Trujillo's sister, "known affectionately as La Fea" (138), he elaborates: "There are those alive who claim that La Fea had actually been a pro herself in the time before the rise of her brother, but that seems to be more calumny than anything, like saying that Balaguer fathered a dozen illegitimate children and then used the pueblo's money to hush it up—wait, that's true, but probably not the other—shit, who can keep track of what's true and what's false in a country as baká as ours" (139). Yunior, like the narrator of *El hombre*, is aware of gossip's epistemological limitations: to begin tugging at threads by asking which gossip is true and which is not is to risk unraveling the entire narrative. As the text shows, trading history for gossip does not necessarily leave the reader any closer to the truth. Still, *Oscar Wao* is marked by the sharp awareness that the public narratives of authoritarian regimes frequently do not even aspire to the truth, but instead perpetuate sanitized and monolithic versions of the events in question. To "keep track of what's true and what's false" is impossible, but unbiased truth isn't the only goal for which to strive. What matters, when those in power have twisted the truth to breaking point, Díaz suggests, is the freedom to approximate what happened or may have happened and to consider a multiplicity of versions. Part of what makes gossip powerful is precisely that even at its most extreme, it is couched in self-righteous terms as the unearthing of hidden truths, the revelation of secrets. Indeed, the relationship between gossip and truth, which has (understandably, perhaps) been largely unexplored by scholars of literature, is a fundamental one.[37] Gossip, after all, is one of the few narrative forms where the immediate indiscernibility of the truth it purports to reveal is presupposed. It is notoriously hard to prove, but difficult to disprove; it is usually plausible, not final. Gossip, in fact, foregrounds its own lack of narrative monopoly:

while each kernel of gossip promises to reveal a definitive truth, it does so by offering to revise an existing narrative, against which it is itself defined. To participate in an act of gossip is inherently to judge between, or at least to acknowledge, divergent viewpoints and versions of events; where authoritarianism seeks to impose a unitary account, gossip depends upon plurality.[38]

In its attempt to leverage gossip to establish the Dominican people's collective narrative, then, *Oscar Wao* asks for its reader's credulity, but does not insist upon its own finality. As Roger Sell notes, gossip implicitly recognizes that each story contains its own truth and that each teller's perspective on a given event may be different. "We participate in gossip, not *despite* our scepticism, but *because* we are sceptical," Sell writes. "If gossip were ever to arrive at an absolute truth about the people it takes up for discussion, it would cease" (221). The will to gossip is not the will to arrive at a single version of any given event but rather the will to test many versions, to hear many accounts, and to construct from them a narrative that seems plausible to the listener, on the understanding that another listener may come to entirely different conclusions. The search for truth ultimately matters more than the truth itself, a point Irit Rogoff echoes in writing that "gossip, by its troubled relation to historical realism, has been postmodern all along" (60). The power of gossip rests not primarily in its ability to provide new historical truths, but rather in its assertion that truth itself is pliable, multiple, and fleeting.[39]

This aspect of gossip is especially valuable in nations marked by authoritarianism. The narratives that Yunior spins are intended to serve as a collective self-narrative for a fractured people—an alternative to the corrupted, univocal history imposed by the Trujillo regime. In writing *Oscar Wao,* Díaz says, he sought to look beyond the flattering lie of Dominican unity and to acknowledge the country's splintered, ahistorical reality. The book, Díaz explains, was conceived of as "an archipelago [. . .] a textual Caribbean. Shattered and yet somehow holding together" ("Questions"). It is by acknowledging and writing into the gaps and contradictions in their nation's history, rather than passing them over in silence, Díaz suggests, that Dominicans can hold their nation together and finally begin to exorcise the lingering ghosts of the Trujillato. It is in this sense that the true cathartic power of *Oscar Wao* reveals itself: not an act of narrative aggression meant to replace one hegemonic historical account with another, but rather an attempt to acknowledge the insufficiency of the historical record and allow countless individual versions and private stories, the lived experiences of the regime's victims, to flow free.

In probing gossip's utility for those who live under authoritarianism, *Oscar Wao* mounts an effective defense of the practice, while also acknowledging its potential dangers. In Díaz's text, gossip lacks the gravitas of historical discourse but never devolves into mere chatter; it may be vapid or vindictive or vicious, but it is also purposeful, an act committed with a specific intent and in opposition to a specific adversary. It stands, in fact, as a weaponized narrative form: capable of being used and abused by those in power, but also of providing those who live in cultures of terror with a vital means to navigate and make sense of their fractured collective identity. In this way, gossip is revealed as a valid and even essential form of knowledge, an epistemological tool capable of transcending rigidly binary notions of truth and falsehood, and of exploring the analog: plausibility, plurality, shades of gray. Gossip, for all its moralizing, rejects the Manichean dichotomies insisted upon and used to silence dissent by totalitarian regimes; it occupies a more liminal space, scribbling in the margins of supposedly fixed narratives and irreverently defacing the blank pages of official histories. For the dispossessed and disenfranchised people of *Oscar Wao*'s Dominican Republic and its diaspora, gossip traces the fault lines in monolithic discourses and serves as a defense—partial, in both senses of the word, but still valuable—against the imposition of narrative hegemony.[40]

Complicity and Shame: *Saisons sauvages*

It is not just in the Dominican Republic that gossip has provided a means for writers to delve back into traumatic periods of their countries' history. As described in the preceding chapter, Haitian novelists, both on the island and in exile, have tended to approach the trials of the Duvalier regimes obliquely: allegory and temporal distancing have offered both emotional insulation against the period's unthinkable horrors and much-needed cover for authors who feared political reprisals. More recently, however, a new generation of Haitian writers have sought to probe the silences bequeathed to them by authoritarianism. One remarkable such attempt is Kettly Mars's 2010 novel *Saisons sauvages,* which graphically portrays a single family's suffering at the hands of François Duvalier's fictionalized police chief. While Duvalier himself appears only fleetingly, Mars's novel has, as John P. Walsh remarks, been correctly read as a "a kind of *roman de dictature*" (68); certainly, the dictatorship itself and the state's security apparatus are a constant presence in Mars's harrowing text. As Yves Chemla writes, Mars is one of several recent Haitian writers who have sought "to take charge of that which appeared unnamable" and to "untangle the knots" of Haiti's conflicted history. Still, Chemla notes, while Mars's novel may be a *roman de dictature,* it is not "a pure fiction: it is also a roman à clef." The family story that Mars tells is a cipher: a fiction that, Mars asserts, is "inspired by real facts." She explains: "This situation happened more than once [. . .] often, after the book was published, people would come to me asking me to confirm if the story concerned such or such family" ("Interview"). The horrors she reveals speak not just to the fictional family she portrays but to the suffering of the Haitian national family as a whole, in much the same way that the horrors uncovered by Díaz's family saga serve to frame and memorialize the abuses suffered by all Dominicans.

Saisons sauvages is a tale, then, about the impact of the Duvalier dictatorship in the private lives of a single family—an immediacy that Nirvah, the main protagonist and sometime narrator, presents as a vital part of coming to terms with the legacy of the Duvalier era: "Month after month, we have seen dictatorship's tentacles tighten around people's lives, but it has always been the lives of others. We only take the true measure of its horror in the moment in which we are seized in the jaws of this absurd madness of power. Before that, they are rumors, whispers, a hell far removed from our daily lives, which we prefer to forget or deny" (37). Still, as the novel makes clear from its earliest pages, rumors and gossip remain an urgent and acutely felt part of the experiences of those who are entangled in the regime's "tentacles." When Nirvah's husband, a dissident journalist named Daniel, is arrested, she learns of his whereabouts through hearsay: "They tell me that he is still alive. They, meaning anyone with a crumb of information, a sliver of hope. They, meaning an acquaintance whose cousin, imprisoned at Fort-Dimanche, was able to slip a piece of paper outside giving the names of a few survivors—that was a week ago. They, meaning a gardener at the prison, the cousin of my cleaner's husband, who found out that Daniel is being kept in the right wing of the building" (11).

Armed with this tentative information, Nirvah uses a personal connection to win a brief audience with Raoul Vincent, the secretary of state in charge of Duvalier's secret police. There, she tells him that she doesn't know for sure where her husband is and that all she has to go on are rumors. He replies: "Rumors in our country, you see, Madame, are a double-edged sword, a merciless weapon. They liberate and condemn you. They cost you money. They can make you happy, but never for long. They make you vulnerable" (16–17). Daniel's disappearance makes him the stuff of gossip and rumor, and to try to ascertain his exact whereabouts is a risky business. But Nirvah's biggest concern is less the risk she runs by asking questions than simply the inscrutability of the Duvalier regime: swallowed up by the state security apparatus, Daniel is now knowable only through secondhand stories. After leaving the secretary of state—who warns her once more not to trust rumors—Nirvah walks out into the sunlight, where behind her "the somber mass of the Dessalines Barracks emerges like a sphinx from a background of shadows" (18). The impenetrable building is packed with prisoners, Nirvah reflects; clearly, her husband is now one of these unknowable people, reachable only through the murky networks of hearsay that serve as a substitute for reliable public information.

While Raoul, who swiftly moves to seduce Nirvah, insists that rumor and gossip are fundamentally unsound, he also makes a point of asserting his own knowledge of and power over the intimacies of Haitians' private lives. His overtures to Nirvah are presented as a breaking of boundaries: like Sención's Bolaño and Ramos, he seeks to "assault her daily life," feeling that he has thereby "penetrated the intimate life of the dissident called Daniel Leroy" and affirmed his own power and authority (63). Later, he makes clear the extent to which his own invasion of private spaces parallels a state-led effort to infiltrate, scrutinize, and control Haitians' public and private lives: "Our agents are there at cockfights, in stadiums, in brothels. Every day more men and women of every social class join the ranks of the VSN to infiltrate homes, bedrooms, medical clinics, and so forth. They work night and day" (133). The most intimate spaces are under government scrutiny, and Raoul describes the state's informants in sinister terms as being like a vast and ruthless "flock of guinea fowl" that scours the country for suspicious activity. Raoul's strange simile hints at the preternatural efficiency of the state gossip networks, recalling Díaz's discussion of Trujillo's *fukú* or even the flying witches of Veloz Maggiolo's Dominican Republic. "It would be wrong to underestimate their efficacy," Raoul warns. "Like those stocky birds that nonetheless move quickly, they're the real sentinels of the revolution" (133).

Nirvah seeks to reassert some measure of control over her situation by gossiping with her friend Maggy. It is through interpretive, analytic exchanges with her friend that she ponders the significance of Raoul's epilepsy, considers whether to keep the jewelry he sends, and speculates about whether Raoul will free Daniel if she succumbs to his advances (105–8). Still, she is essentially powerless in the face of Raoul's decision to possess her and unable to learn anything about her husband beyond the scant information that Raoul provides. "I only have his word to confirm that my husband is still alive. Even the rumors seem already to have forgotten his existence," she says (166). Nirvah knows she is being toyed with but gives in to Raoul; perhaps unsurprisingly, however, she never manages to secure Daniel's release, visit him, or even find out much about his situation.

Mars presents gossip, despite its limitations, as a key resource for people living under the Duvaliers, and a source of power and status for those who use it effectively. Nirvah's next-door neighbor, Solange, despite being "not well regarded in the neighborhood," uses gossip about Daniel's disappearance to force Nirvah to perform neighborliness with her, telling her "about her life for close to an hour" and pointedly addressing her as "neighbor" before finally revealing how, from her stoop, she saw the Tontons Macoutes taking Daniel away (42). Solange's gossip is portrayed as a more appropriate and potent form of discourse than Daniel's essays and diaries, which lead him only to disaster. "Praise the lord! I don't know how to read or write," she laughs when she hears of the reason for Daniel's arrest, warning Nirvah that literariness is "discomfiting to people" (43) before plunging into a gossipy account of her life as a prostitute and *manbo*. This is a critical point: Daniel writes against Duvalier's falsified account of Haiti's history, which he insists is a mere fiction. But as Walsh notes, when Daniel seeks to expose Duvalier in the public sphere, "his truth is immediately silenced because the public justice sought by the journalist no longer exists" (74).[41] As Daniel learns to his cost, the public sphere is no longer a space for resistance or even for the assertion of memory; only through informal discourse, such as Solange's gossip, can Haitians preserve an authentic identity of their own.

But if gossip offers something of Dalleo's counterpublic to Haitians, *Saisons sauvages* also shows it as intrusive and even violent. Nirvah soon comes to fear Solange's knowledge of her private life: "Is Solange spying on me? Does she have a way of knowing what is happening inside my house? [. . .] All my determination is melting beneath the impression of being surrounded on all sides by inquisitive looks. I no longer control my life, a sensation that is slowly giving way to panic" (142). Solange uses gossip to reinforce the frayed ties of her community, but for Nirvah, wracked by guilt, gossip serves instead to stage the failure of such bonds. Much as discussed in chapter 1, pervasive gossip comes to highlight Nirvah's awareness of being watched and judged by those around her, in a manner that recalls the claustrophobia of Roger Mais's short stories or even the panoptic surveillance society depicted by Antonio José Ponte.

Under Duvalier, *Saisons sauvages* suggests, the intimate communities associated with gossip grew strained to the point of collapse, and neighborly interactions devolved into a parody or perversion of the friendly camaraderie with which they are more usually associated.

Gossip, in this context, also serves as a weapon, and one readily turned against Nirvah by those who resent her newfound political connections. Her sister-in-law, Arlette, comes to Nirvah with gossip about the reasons for their street being paved; the other women join in, crediting it to the "new mistress" of the secretary of state (128). Nirvah, quite rightly, perceives their gossip as "a frontal attack" (127) and promises herself that henceforth she will be far more guarded. "From today, I'm going to learn to say the opposite of what I think, and to build a screen around my life," she thinks (127). Later, in a remarkable moment, Nirvah takes on Arlette's gossip about her directly: "She tells everyone that I'm sleeping with a macoute in Daniel's bed. Easy. For starters, Raoul has changed the bed and the bedroom furniture, at my request, and next, she's never lifted a finger to get her brother out of that hellhole. It seems that her lover, the major, has gone into exile" (164). Nirvah here uses insinuations about Arlette's own influential lover as a weapon of self-defense, while rebutting the specific content of Arlette's gossip—that she's having sex with Raoul in Daniel's bed—by essentially bragging about one of the perks of her infidelity. One suspects that Arlette would not feel that Nirvah's acquisition of new bedroom furniture diminishes the validity of her attack.

Despite claiming that she can fence herself off from gossip, Nirvah processes her guilt by collectivizing it—Port-au-Prince is "a city with two faces, a treacherous city," she says (162)—and by imagining herself gossiping about a friend in a similar situation. "I would surely have called her cowardly, a gold-digger, and lots of other things too. It's true that I'm cowardly," she admits (154). In fact, gossiping about other women would be scant consolation, she reflects. "I don't take any relief or satisfaction in knowing that others have a similar lot to mine," she says. "This is about me. [. . .] It's me who has to close my eyes, my skin, my ears to the condemnation of public opinion" (154–55). It is gossip that, as time passes, affirms Nirvah's conflicted identity as a victim made dependent upon her victimizer. Her affair with Raoul is common knowledge, she realizes, and her social network has dramatically changed as a result. "The whole city knows it [. . .]. I've joined the club of macoute mistresses," she thinks (162–63). "I leave behind me a trail of intoxicating perfume and swagger. The women who condemn me must surely fantasize about my relations with Raoul-the-Beast" (163). In imagining the jealousy of her former friends, Nirvah also seeks to shrug off her own responsibility, claiming a little too glibly that Daniel, in his "presumptuousness" and "thoughtlessness," is responsible for the situation in which she now finds herself (164). This is a rehearsed self-justification, an attempt to construct her own image more favorably both to herself and to those who gossip against her. This stresses the degree to which Nirvah's torment is grounded in shame and the fear of public judgment rather than in the specifics of her situation: if nobody knew or talked about Nirvah's actions, the text suggests, her self-justification would go unchallenged, and her guilt would be far easier to bear.

Mars's text returns to the image of the purged bedroom, as a metaphor for both Nirvah's shame and her attempts to gloss over her transgressions, when Nirvah admits to quietly removing from the room everything that reminds her of her husband. In a moment of insight, she realizes that she is doing the government's work by adjusting to her new life and removing any trace of her husband from her home: "I finally understood that for this government, forgetting is a tactic for getting rid of opponents" (168). The regime forces its opponents into mute, sphinxlike prisons as a way of avoiding the scandals that executions would spark, Nirvah reflects, but also as a way of making them the subjects of an inexorable amnesia. Detention, Nirvah suggests, is a process of zombification that breaks the will of the captive but also leads to him or her being forgotten and thus rendered powerless. This scrubbing away of even the memory of resistance recalls Nirvah's repeated claim that her "sex is like fine china; it retains no trace of infamy; once I wash it, it's like new" (155). Nirvah insists that if and when Daniel returns, she will be able to scrub away her infidelities and compromises. In the end, however, the only things scrubbed away are the traces of her absent husband: Nirvah's claim that her innocence is retrievable, that her sins can be forgiven, is finally revealed as wishful thinking or downright self-deception.[42]

This is most clear when Nirvah burns Daniel's books, and later his diaries, as a way of preventing them from falling into official hands but also of obliterating her husband's continuing presence in her life. This act of destruction, of willful and irrevocable forgetting, is an attempt to redact her family's narrative—a gesture that recalls the conflagration through which Gloria seeks to draw a line under the swirling narratives of *Maldito amor,* and also echoes Balaguer's cynical attempt to substitute blank pages and silences for continuing discussion of his regime's actions. Nirvah seeks not just to destroy the physical pages of Daniel's diaries but also to cauterize the wound left by their memory: "This small notebook never existed; I didn't read these words," she insists (145). She justifies the decision as a way of erasing Daniel's absence, or reclaiming for a moment the "insipid, predictable, marvelous" life they shared before his writing made him a target of the regime (145). But she cannot help but realize that she has also destroyed what little of her husband's life and liberty still remained, and left him without voice or legacy. "Daniel's story ends here," she says. "These ashes make me a widow" (146). Where Díaz sees the regime papering over its own history, Mars delves into the complicity of Haitians in establishing and accepting silence: Nirvah silences Daniel as a way of coping with her pain and guilt, and of seeking to free her children from the memory of their father's dissidence and detention. This is a resonant gesture that Mars manages to render as both transparently self-serving and emotionally relatable; in this episode, as elsewhere in *Saisons sauvages,* the reader is given both access to the protagonist's tortured interior monologue and sufficient distance to view her claims with a degree of ironic detachment. The result is that the reader is invited at once to condemn Nirvah's selfish actions, and to relate to her suffering and her lack of options.

Despite Nirvah's insistence that she is fighting for her children, it is they who pay the highest price for her compromises—a significant plot detail in a text so explicitly engaged with the legacy of Duvalierism for subsequent generations. Nirvah first learns about her children's plight from Maggy, her friend, who tells her people are saying "odd things" about her family. Nirvah claims to have "become numb to gossip" and resents Maggy's efforts to "disturb the serenity of my Sunday afternoon with gossip" (185, 186). Maggy persists: "Even though my beauty salon is a hotspot for gossip, I always keep these stories at arm's length. It doesn't amuse me anymore to see these ladies smear each other with bile and shit, but this time . . . I think you should pay attention. It's about your kids . . ." (186). Nirvah is alarmed, and Maggy finally explains: "They're saying that . . . Raoul . . . abuses Marie and maybe even . . . Nicolas . . . in your house. [. . .] At least, that's what I heard very clearly from the conversation of two clients who were getting manicures" (186). Nirvah dismisses the gossip as calumny: "Do you see how far Haitians' perversity can go? Deep down, that's what they would like. They'd like to see me destroyed," she says. "That's why they are attacking my children, the thing dearest to me. My God!" (187). Maggy tries to engage her friend in interpretive metagossip, noting that Raoul has a reputation as a sexual predator and plenty of opportunities to be alone with the children. Nirvah rejects her attempts at solidarity and collaborative analysis, instead diving into an almost jealous reverie about Raoul's sexual possession of her, a thought that recalls her previous claim that her various enemies were simply envious of her new lover. Nirvah's initial response, in fact, is outrage less at the rape of her children than at Raoul's violation of their transactional arrangement and apparent disregard for the reputational sacrifices she has made. "I accepted the tarnishing of my reputation, the loss of close friends, becoming a renegade in the eyes of society," Nirvah thinks. "Why does he also need to profane my children's innocence?" (189).

With Maggy forgotten, Nirvah tries to make sense of what she has heard, swinging between rejecting the news and giving it credence. "These stories are just gossip, spitefulness, badmouthing, lies, dirty tricks, nothing more," she thinks. "Who could know what takes place in my home? That information could only come from Raoul himself" (190). Still, she quickly realizes that Raoul's penetration of her home has created the opportunity for gossip:

> There's also the hired help. Maybe Tinès, Auguste's replacement? Raoul brought him in to keep the generator running, among other things. I knew that he wanted, above all, to have ears and eyes inside my home, to know the ins and outs, the visitors. I've acted like I didn't get it. But you could expect nothing else from the Secretary of State for Defense and Public Safety, the chief of the government's secret police. Tinès is quiet enough, he works and the house is clean, but he has a shifty look. Any leak must have come from him. Yva is devoted to me, I'm sure. The children themselves—would they let it slip . . . ? But what am I saying? It's pointless to give credence to the spitefulness of sour people. Marie and Nicolas are fine. Raoul respects my children. (190–91)

In the end, however, Nirvah cannot bring herself to fully reject the gossip: overwhelmed, she vomits on the floor. Her emesis is a visceral reaction; like her involuntary urination after her first meeting with Raoul, it is a physical response more direct and honest, and certainly less conflicted, than her emotional one.

When Nirvah subsequently confronts Raoul, demanding to know the truth of the matter, he rages at her, using the accusation's roots in gossip to cast it as inherently untrustworthy. "Don't come crying to me today because some gossip reached you," he warns (217).[43] Nirvah insists, and he unleashes a torrent of obscene, contradictory stories: that he prostituted himself with men to gain power; that Nicolas is unappealing to him; that Marie is willing, unwilling, lascivious, innocent, inexperienced, or a better lover than Nirvah. With so many stories swirling around, Raoul suggests, the truth of the matter is unknowable and can only be a construction, a choice. "How could you not have seen a thing this huge happening here, right before your eyes? Or is it that there's nothing to see?" he asks. "What's your decision? To believe me, or not to? What is your truth?" (218). Nirvah is horrified but succumbs, telling herself: "He's a master of the art of confusion. Maybe he no longer even knows what the word truth means" (218–19). I have traced the epistemological frailties of gossip in previous chapters; in this instance, however, the truth of the matter is well understood, at least by the reader. By the time Nirvah hears the gossip, Mars has already staged Raoul's assault of Nicolas and Marie in grotesque detail, making the reader assume the role of the prying eyes Nirvah imagines impassively watching the abuse of her children. While Raoul seeks to obfuscate the truth by peppering Nirvah with alternative accounts of what has happened, the gossip that runs through *Saisons sauvages* is actually remarkably accurate: it records and circulates unspeakable horrors, yes, but the horrors themselves are real.

Despite Raoul's efforts to convince Nirvah that "truth" is a meaningless abstraction, the family's friends and neighbors have no doubts about the facts of the matter. When Marie becomes pregnant and tries to convince her boyfriend to support her, he resorts to gossip—"words that one shouldn't say, that mark you like a branding iron," Marie thinks (234)—to disavow responsibility for the pregnancy. "There were at least two of us shooting you full of sperm, darling Marie," he says, continuing: "You're screwing that macoute secretary of state, the so-called family friend. They say he's also your mother's lover. What a family you make!" (234). Marie, like her mother, seeks to use sex to gain some vestige of control over her own life; gossip, however, outpaces her, tripping up her attempts at self-assertion before they can begin.[44]

In fact, gossip is shown as tripping up virtually everyone in *Saisons sauvages,* without regard for their status in Duvalier's Haiti. Raoul's own downfall is brought about through gossip, with his affair with Nirvah, and even his assault on Marie, becoming known to his political rival, Maxime Douville, who bitterly refers to him as "the lover of Nirvah Leroy." Dressing up his political rivalry in moral outrage, Douville continues: "People claim he's even doing it with Leroy's daughter. It's too much! Raoul Vincent will pay dearly for this" (224). It is through gossip, along with some arm-twisting, that Douville convinces Duvalier's ministers to recommend freeing Daniel, in a gambit intended to embarrass Raoul and force him to end his affair with Nirvah. In the event, however, Raoul miscalculates and urges Duvalier not to free Daniel. As Douville rightly perceives, Raoul's motives are too transparent and dramatically diminish his standing. "They all knew the modesty of the chief of state, who in the heart of the national palace had kindled a passionate affair—in secret, he believed—with his private secretary, but who would certainly never condone such a flagrant sex scandal," Douville asserts (226). Duvalier's own indiscretions are scrutinized through gossip, Mars suggests, and even he is unwilling to jeopardize his reputation by helping Raoul to survive the scandal in which he is embroiled.

Raoul's downfall comes about, in fact, because he misreads the degree to which gossip is eroding his political capital. Only too late does he realize the limits of his own relationship with Duvalier: "François Duvalier would not cut him loose, it was simply unthinkable. He, who had given his life and sold his soul for the revolution. But he also knew of the vicious gossip that his enemies were feeding the president. Duvalier wouldn't touch him, but he would let his lackeys finish him off" (249). Raoul tries to limit the gossip: when his government slush fund dries up, he decides against taking a loan from one of his contacts because "the news would travel too fast" (249), and stops short of telling his wife because "she might panic, say too much, and do a lot of harm" (263). Still, Raoul's political decline has already begun, and is mapped by his increasing conversion into a subject of gossip. Nirvah's brother, Roger, advises her to flee the country, saying: "The Secretary of State . . . is in a bad place. [. . .] The rumors are gaining force" (259). Raoul's wife perceives that he is in trouble; from her worried looks, he determines that the "rumor-mill must have appraised her of his setbacks" (263). Eventually, Raoul announces that he plans to seek asylum: "I'm sure that the rumors have reached you," he tells Nirvah, who only replies, "'Yes . . . they are talking about it'" (276). Finally, as they attempt to flee the country, Roger tells Nirvah that he has heard that Raoul was arrested, dressed as a woman, while trying to seek asylum at the Venezuelan ambassador's home. As before, when gossip revealed Raoul's abuse of her children, Nirvah's first response is to laugh. "What a pitiful end for His Excellency" she reflects (293). Nirvah's laughter is not of victory—within pages she herself has been apprehended—but signals, rather, a moment of clarity: she sees now that even the "Beast" who has toyed with and possessed her is ultimately ensnared in, and subject to, the same forces by which she herself has been afflicted. This is arguably the key to the gossip that saturates Mars's text: gossip is simultaneously relied on and feared by everyone in Duvalier's Haiti, becoming an allegory both of Haitians' suffering and of the compromises so many Haitians were forced to make in order to survive.

With its unflinching account of Haitians' complicity in their own suffering, *Saisons sauvages* is a significant literary response to the Duvalier era, and all the more so when considered against the silences and allegorizations that have typified prior Haitian literary engagement with the period. As Munro notes, "Mars's work confirms that fiction is a highly potent means of revisiting the apocalyptic past, bringing it to life and working against the kind of forgetting that allows dictatorship and tyranny to exist" (*Tropical Apocalypse* 63). It is precisely against such forgetting that Mars writes. When Nirvah seeks to console Marie—and perhaps, in the process, herself—she offers not a reckoning or a restoration but rather a wiping clean of the slate: "We'll leave these hostile years behind us. We'll learn to forget, forget the land of Haiti, Port-au-Prince, Rue des Cigales, the *macoutes,* and everything that causes pain in our country" (233). This is the best future that Nirvah—and by extension, in Mars's reading, many of the Haitians who lived through the Duvalier era—can envision: not rebirth or reconciliation but rather denial and the release that comes with amnesia. It is with this postauthoritarian ahistoricity, this lack of self-narrative—imposed, but also desired—that Mars's text grapples: by tracing the ubiquity of gossip (and thus also of guilt and shame) she seeks to reconstruct the widespread complicity she perceives in the silences and compromises of the past. Unlike many other postdictatorship states, as Munro notes, Haiti has largely failed to grapple with the legacy of the Duvalier years in any formal or organized way. In such circumstances, Munro argues, novels such as *Saisons sauvages* "become means of testifying to individual and general suffering, and of keeping memories alive and thereby validating experiences that would otherwise never be spoken about" (64). This resurfacing of suppressed trauma, clearly, is among the chief aims of Mars's novel, inspired, she claims, by "real facts," and her text, with all its gossip, tells a family story intended to be taken as speaking to a more general national trauma. In so doing, the text stages the complicity and compromises—facilitating survival, but leaving so much unsaid and unsayable—that marked the nation's decades of dictatorship.

This recalls Patricia A. Turner's assertion that for African Americans, rumor is like scar tissue: a marker of past pain and betrayal but also of "historical ignorances" and suspicions born of unresolved trauma (220). In Caribbean nations marked by authoritarianism and state-sponsored violence, gossip plays a similar role. Crucially, though, as the texts examined in this chapter show, gossip is grounded in the specific and the personal: where rumor (in Turner's reading) festers amid ignorance, gossip promises to repopulate the blank spaces of history with first- or secondhand accounts of suppressed events. This has a claim to be the most urgent, and perhaps most enduring, of gossip's uses in the Caribbean: that it whispers into silent spaces, reinscribes memories where amnesia might otherwise prevail, and forces confrontations with the compromises and conveniently forgotten sins—the uncomfortable, unacknowledged realities—of the past. It is, after all, by acknowledging their conflicted pasts that the fractured, conquered, and colonized nations and peoples of the Caribbean are beginning to forge futures, and construct coherent identities, for themselves. The Haitian novelist Gary Victor writes that Mars, like Victor and a handful of others, belongs to a "generation of Haitian writers whose destiny is to bear a too-heavy past, to dissect a painful and incoherent present, to invent an already compromised future" (61). The challenges Victor describes are not uniquely Haitian: across the Caribbean, writers are wrestling with unresolved pasts, unstable presents, and uncertain futures. As this volume has shown, gossip—in its many forms, its many deployments, its many uses—has emerged as a singularly potent narrative form for those who have taken up the challenge of addressing these questions and writing for, and about, the contemporary Caribbean.

Conclusion
Radical Gossip

Idle Talk, Deadly Talk is a book about gossip in the literature of the Caribbean, and about a strand of adversarialism and narrative conflict that I take to be especially palpable therein. This is not to say that all Caribbean gossip is marked by such tensions: as I have stressed, the region's gossip can also be as idle, harmless, or salutary as the "good gossip" that Spacks and other scholars trace in Anglo-American literature. So, too, of course, can the gossip of England or the United States (or any other place) contain latent or overt adversarialism, narrative struggle, and even violence. My contention in this book is not that adversarial gossip is unique to the Caribbean, but only that it is often foregrounded in the region's literature because of specific historical and political challenges that make narrative conflict and social division pressing concerns for the region's inhabitants. Many other places in the world—including subaltern regions, of course, but also, increasingly, the old and new colonial powers, and the centers of cultural production—are similarly marked by conflict and by unresolved questions of power and identity; it should not surprise us, then, if writers from such places use gossip in ways similar to those described in this book. Such gossip may be particularly easy to spot in the contemporary Caribbean, but if we care to look, we should expect to find gossip similarly deployed in the literature of many other periods and places.

Nonetheless, my focus in this study has been squarely upon the Caribbean, where gossip has played, and continues to play, a critical role in the region's narratives. Gossip's ubiquity and evident narrative significance in the Caribbean admits a number of plausible explanations, perhaps the most obvious of which is that gossip is prototypically oral, and the Caribbean is a region steeped in oral traditions. The sung or spoken word constitutes a thread—frayed, but not severed—that links the region's peoples back to Africa, and has often served as a battleground between slave and master, colonizer and colonized, in ways that mirror the tensions I have here mapped through gossip. The role of orality in the Caribbean and the connections between this orality and the broader Caribbean drive to gossip are easy to comprehend and hard to deny. Writers who seek to capture the oral cadences of the Caribbean will, quite naturally, frequently find themselves depicting acts of gossip.

Beyond this, one might also suspect that there exists a kind of Caribbean sensibility that makes gossip a readily available and appropriate means of expressing culturally or personally significant ideas. The "comic principle" and "élan of the raconteur" that Walcott identifies, grudgingly, as the "assigned role" of the Caribbean writer resonates, one might suppose, with the effervescent mischievousness of gossip (130). How better to give voice to this aspect of the Caribbean character than through delightful, ribald, pretension-skewering, and altogether unauthorized gossip?

Such claims, however, skew too close for comfort to the exoticizing, othering supposition that the gossip of the Caribbean stems from some specific peculiarity of the peoples of the Caribbean. In this study, I have sought to suggest the opposite: that gossip is not an emergent phenomenon springing from some quintessentially "Caribbean" trait or sensibility, but rather a malleable tool used in different ways and to different ends in different times and places. It thus admits uses in the literature of the contemporary Caribbean that vary significantly in form and emphasis from its uses in texts from, for instance, nineteenth-century Britain or mid-twentieth-century America—or, for that matter, the Caribbean of the early colonial period. The gossip of the Caribbean, I argue, must be read not as speaking to some intrinsic quality of the Caribbean peoples but rather as a response to the historicized contexts in which such gossip occurs.

Throughout this book I have sought to characterize some of these responses, offering a vision of gossip as a narrative practice prevalent in Caribbean literature and essential to a full understanding of the Caribbean more generally. I have emphasized both gossip's complexity and its potentiality, which lie in its resistance to easy categorization. But I have also stressed a deeper radicalism that I take to lie at the heart of gossip: a sense not just of individual stories being reframed or revised, but also of a deeper and more insidious destabilization that seeps into and subverts our understandings and constructions of the world around us. To gossip is to challenge not just a specific previous account of the world but also, in so doing, to acknowledge the fragility of discourse itself: what once was certain and stable must, in the face of gossip, give way to a discomfiting but inescapable doubtfulness.

Gossip's resistance to categorization, then, must be understood as one of its defining traits—and if I have not sought to reduce gossip to a simple category or label (be that narrative strategy, social phenomenon, source of information, or epistemological method), it is because gossip encompasses or slips between all such categories. Gossip is fascinating precisely because it admits so many uses; to explore it most fruitfully, we must read it in context, embrace its nuances, and recognize the impossibility of reducing it to a single universally applicable definition. This being the case, it should go without saying that the foregoing chapters are not an exhaustive accounting of gossip's uses, nor even of gossip's uses in the contemporary Caribbean. Rather, I have highlighted aspects of gossip that I take to be especially significant in the literature of the Caribbean, and to have been generally overlooked by scholars exploring gossip's role in the Anglo-American and European traditions.

In general, I have sought to make the case that gossip deserves to be taken seriously—which is not to say that all gossip is serious. Much gossip is ostensibly trivial, marked by gaiety and good humor, and playfully mischievous rather than openly antagonistic. There is, as Rosario Ferré notes, joy to be found in such gossip: "A good bit of Puerto Rican gossip has more entertainment potential than twenty Mexican or Venezuelan telenovelas, especially when it is seasoned with a little truth, which, like pepper in stew, brings out the lie's subtlest flavors," she writes ("Clara y Julia" 999). In Caribbean literature, gossip is often used in this way. Caribbean gossip is not *always* deadly or divisive; oftentimes, it is used to strengthen intimate bonds and neighborly relations, with its adversarial aspects downplayed or harnessed to reinforce communal ties. Still, even in these moments, writers use gossip to reflect and interrogate both tensions within their communities, and the viewpoints that are asserted or suppressed in the forging of group memberships. As Barthes recognizes, gossip's ludic quality depends upon the transformation of the other into an object of amusement: gossip's exuberance, in other words, comes at someone else's expense. Even in its playful or lighthearted manifestations, gossip is weaponized—albeit with widely varying degrees of actual malice—and even jocular or breezy gossip typically has an agenda, and seeks to increase the social capital of the person who gossips by positioning them as a well-connected informant.

Caribbean writers who stress gossip's more intimate and communitarian aspects typically still recognize the adversarialism at its core, an aspect that becomes more apparent in contemporary Caribbean narratives because of the social divisions that persist in the region, born variously of colonialism, slavery, globalization, migration, and authoritarianism. Caribbean history is defined, after all, by collisions—cultural, political, linguistic—that often give way to entrenched inequalities and the domination of one group by another. This fraught history has created social fractures, and fostered mistrust and adversarialism. It is this, more than anything, that makes gossip such a fertile narrative form for the region's writers. As these struggles play out in Caribbean narratives, gossip—itself a discourse of collision, defined by the domination of one narrative by another—is often marshaled as a uniquely effective form of counterdiscourse, or embraced as a means of staging and highlighting the tensions that persist in the region. Recognizing gossip's role in mediating such struggles helps us to understand how narratives are constructed and deployed in the Caribbean, and illuminates key aspects of Caribbean cultural dynamics: the relationships between the public and the private, between the center and the periphery, between the written and the spoken word, and between the writer and her society. It likewise sheds important light on the political uses of literature in the Caribbean, on the region's troubled epistemologies, and on the struggles faced by communities seeking to assert and sustain themselves in colonial or postcolonial settings.

Such gossip can be empowering. For Arenas and Kincaid, for instance, gossip is a valuable narrative form precisely because it provides catharsis and allows official narratives to be challenged and corrected. But adversarialism is a two-way street: gossip is not used exclusively by underdogs seeking to subvert or undermine established narratives, nor by marginalized peoples seeking to establish counterpublics in opposition to spaces from which they are excluded. Gossip can and does fill this role, as I have shown, and is frequently deployed as a form of resistance, though more often as a critique of power than as a remedy to its abuses. But gossip is also readily co-opted by those in authority: it can serve as a rebuke to the excesses of the powerful, but can just as readily be used to reinforce narratives of power and to suppress alternative or unauthorized narratives. In texts by Veloz Maggiolo, Díaz, or Mars, gossip is a weapon deployed both by and against those in power—and if these writers present a more favorable view of gossip when it is used by underdogs and rebels, they still frame gossip as essentially violent, and present it with palpable ambivalence. Indeed, many of the works examined in *Idle Talk, Deadly Talk* offer a view of gossip from the perspective of its victims, foregrounding the vulnerabilities of individuals and communities in thrall to gossip's seductive power. In so doing, such texts foreground gossip's power but also the risks inherent in its use.

In the Caribbean, these risks are real, and gossip can be literally deadly: reputations matter, and casual speech can have lethal consequences. Though clearly true for texts grappling with the region's authoritarian regimes, this is a more general point; in the texts of Rhys, Sánchez, and Sylvain, for instance, idle yet malicious gossip swiftly leads to bloodshed. Still, gossip does not usually threaten violence directly, offering instead a more subtle means of negotiating conflicts and power struggles. Often gossip exerts power by privately undermining its subjects, who are diminished (at least in the eyes of its participants) without necessarily realizing that they have been targeted. Indeed, by thematizing discrepancy and doubt, gossip frequently offers a way to rethink or recalibrate existing discourses without the need for direct confrontation: it typically corrects public narratives privately, without allowing the challenged party to immediately rebut its claims.

Gossip emerges as a resource for the marginalized, allowing them to challenge or comment on existing narratives, but also as a transgressive practice that questions the boundaries between the public and the private and that, like voyeurism, suggests a desire to take possession of something held privately by another. Yet it is also, despite or because of this veiled violence, a powerful means of knowledge production, and one especially well suited to the uncertainties and contested narratives of the Caribbean. This collision of the private and public spheres (or of the public and counterpublic) is made more vivid by the fact that those in power have repeatedly appropriated private spaces, and the discourses or registers associated with them, in the service of their own public narratives. The power of small, intimate interactions, and the intersection of such private spaces with public ones, is thus explicitly a part of Caribbean political and public life.

This is true in large part because the narratives of the Caribbean are deeply inscribed with questions of doubt and suspicion. Behind every shared story lies a constellation of private interpretations and analyses intended to ascertain the true facts of the matter. This process of testing and questioning is often mediated through gossip, which is, after all, an exercise in faith and uncertainty: a challenging of established narratives and a test of the listener's willingness to give credence to an alternate version of events. This is an especially critical process in the Caribbean, where so many narratives are contested and so many truths have been silenced by history's victors. It is telling, in this sense, that the texts examined in this book tend to sidestep the question of gossip's truth status or even its reliability. Sometimes gossip is true, sometimes it isn't, and sometimes it's impossible to tell; despite this, gossip remains a key aspect of knowledge production in the Caribbean.

In ducking the thorny question of gossip's epistemological validity, the texts discussed herein suggest that gossip in the Caribbean is more an act of faith than a rigorous means of approaching or discovering definitive truths. It is an assertion, not of certainty but of plausibility, that feeds upon skepticism about purportedly truthful accounts. This applies, certainly, to official narratives, with news heard through the grapevine being taken as valid precisely because it is unauthorized, unverified, and exists at a remove from untrustworthy official versions of events. But it also admits a more radical doubtfulness: the corrosion of faith in established narratives leads to a profusion of voices, a hubbub in which all stories are open to question, and therefore all are potentially true. Knowledge production, in such circumstances, is not a positivist progression toward objective fact but rather a messier process of deliberating between countless plausible yet contradictory accounts—precisely the kind of operation, in fact, at which gossip excels.

Gossip is powerful because it exists in relation to other versions of events; it is revisionary, and always itself at risk of being revised or corrected. What we gain in reading Caribbean texts in terms of gossip, then, is a sense of narrative struggles *as* narrative struggles: gossip contextualizes and reveals the conflicts underpinning the fragile, contested narratives of the Caribbean. Gossip both stages and helps to navigate these struggles, but in the process brings risks of its own. The gossip of the Caribbean is grounded upon narrative skepticism, but demands a faith in its claims that is not always well founded, with fabricated or distorted gossip often taken as accurate and accepted as such because it is compelling rather than because it is true. For both participants and subjects, such gossip—such belief, marked by narrative paranoia and unmoored from verifiable fact—can be a dangerous and even deadly thing.

This is the paradox of gossip: it can be a democratizing force, but also a dangerous one that frequently leaves individuals disempowered or in the sway of larger social and political currents. Gossip is ubiquitous because it places a measure of narrative self-assertion within reach of man and woman, rich and poor, powerful and subjugated. But gossip enacts and performs narrative battles that crystallize other resentments, other power struggles, and in which facts are often secondary to the speaker's agenda and allegiances. Gossip, in short, is a weapon available to all, and one frequently used to brutal effect in a region marked and marred by division, struggle, betrayals, and violence. In its ubiquity, moreover, gossip threatens not simply to allow the weak to challenge the narratives of the powerful, but to foster a kind of narrative nihilism in which notions of truth and falsehood are subsumed by a deeper current of suspicion and unanswerable doubt. Gossip is not merely difficult to categorize: it is a discourse that challenges the very notion of categorization, for in its radical uncertainty it undermines, revolutionizes, and threatens to destroy every other discourse that it touches.

This ontological instability, or destabilization, is fundamental to gossip and fundamental to its place in Caribbean literature and culture. Edward Kamau Brathwaite argues that to understand the Caribbean's catastrophic history requires a *"literature of catastrophe"*—a broken mirror to reflect the Caribbean's broken reality and to account "for our persisting literary characteristic (which is also our persisting cultural characteristic), the contradiction, the dichotomy, the paradox" that leaves innocents obsessed with corruption, islanders dreaming of the wider world, and exiles dreaming of home ("Metaphors" 457, 459). The gossip studied in this book is a product of this same historic and still-unfolding Caribbean catastrophe, and marked by much the same fraught and paradoxical obsessions. It is far from the only such response to the historical phenomena that Brathwaite describes; still, it is a potent one. The gossip of the Caribbean is revisionary yet frequently powerfully conservative; obsessed with truth, yet seldom entirely reliable; demanding of intimacy and trust, yet serving to foster suspicions and equivocacy; refractive and plural, yet driven by the will to narrative domination. It is, in short, a charged and fundamentally conflicted discourse—a reflection of, as much as a solution to, the region's troubled reality.

This study is only a first look at gossip's role and uses in the contemporary Caribbean, and much remains to be explored. Questions of periodization and geographical variation remain to be answered, the gossip of earlier periods remains to be studied, and many other instances of gossip in the region's literature, culture, and politics remain to be considered, especially with regard to the way that globalization and new technologies are facilitating new, less geographically bounded forms of gossip. As this book has illustrated, the uses of gossip are seldom distinct: this messy, organic practice invites deployments that overlap, crisscross, and interact with or resist one another in complex and subtle ways. Critically, too, it remains to be seen how the gossip of the Caribbean can inform the study of gossip's role in other regions—including but not limited to the Anglo-American tradition on which most scholarship has hitherto focused. Armed with a better understanding of gossip's epistemological challenges and possibilities, or of its totalitarian and conservative aspects, how might we read the gossip of Proust or James, Austen or Atwood?

Such questions lie beyond the scope of this book, in which I have sought simply to show that contemporary Caribbean texts and writers use gossip in rich and interesting ways, and thereby reveal an overarching preoccupation with gossip's role in their societies. Gossip is an essential part of the stories we tell in the Caribbean, and of the way we tell them: it is entwined with what we know, how we know, and the ways in which we speak about and evaluate knowledge. To overlook the gossip of the Caribbean is thus to miss a vital component of the region's culture and thought. The study of narrative in the Caribbean necessitates an engagement with the gossip that shapes and informs it, for only by recognizing gossip's place as a prevalent and potent narrative form can we hope to fully understand the peoples and literatures of the Caribbean.

Notes

Introduction

1. Unless otherwise noted, all translations are my own.
2. Bracketed ellipsis points indicate editorial omissions; unbracketed ellipsis points are in original of quoted texts.
3. Translated and quoted by Abraham P. Bloch (150).
4. Gossip has received more critical attention in fields such as anthropology, sociology, and folklore than in literary studies. In these fields, the dynamics of gossip are commonly understood as deeply rooted in its social context; see, for instance, Max Gluckman's pioneering "Gossip and Scandal" (1963), which casts gossip as a deeply social practice; Robert Paine's 1967 response to Gluckman, which insists on the importance of viewing gossip through the lens of the individual rather than the community; the folklorist Sally Yerkovich's 1977 exposition of gossip as "the strategic management of information" based upon a shared moral code (192); Jörg Bergmann's *Discreet Indiscretions: The Social Organization of Gossip* (1993), which focuses on the structure and logic of gossip rather than its specific content; or, more recently, cultural anthropologist Niko Besnier's *Gossip and the Everyday Production of Politics* (2009), which frames gossip as a communicative practice fundamentally engaged with questions of power. Such readings approach gossip from different angles, but coincide in treating gossip not simply as idle chatter but rather as an active social endeavor that can be either salutary or corrupting according to the nature of its deployment. Similarly utilitarian approaches are followed by psychologists such as Robin Dunbar, who views gossip as a means of maintaining social ties, much like the grooming practices of primates, and by a number of philosophers: see, for instance, Karen C. Adkins's 2002 reading of gossip in terms of feminist epistemology, or C. A. J. Coady's 1994 interrogation of gossip's validity as a form of testimony. The diversity of such readings contrasts with the more circumscribed approaches taken by literary scholars, who have largely adhered to Patricia Meyer Spacks's reading of gossip as a benign, empowering practice.

5. Agnes Lugo-Ortiz similarly connects Puerto Rican literary output during the 1960s to the cultural, political, and economic convulsions of the period—a time, she writes, "when established models of authority appeared to be shaken or crumbling, and dominant discourses of 'identity'—sexual, gender, or national—underwent significant disturbances" (117).

6. See Sylvia Molloy's examination of Onetti's use of gossip, and of gossip as a transactional practice, in her 1979 essay "El relato como mercancía."

7. And so too, of course, may instances of the "good gossip" that Spacks traces in Austen or James be readily found in the Caribbean. As Hope Munro writes, apropos of Trinidadian gossip, "People lime in different contexts for various reasons, but essentially the activity renews social networks and offers a performance space for participants to share knowledge and daily experiences. While it appears to be 'the art of doing nothing,' liming is an important way to reinforce social bonds or create new ones" (16). The texts of Ana Lydia Vega, Olive Senior, and many other Caribbean writers often feature or reflect upon this kind of intimate, socially rewarding gossip.

8. Gossip and related forms have been the subject of numerous popular nonfiction works since the turn of the millennium, perhaps in part due to the increasing cultural significance of gossip blogs, social networks, and related media. Joseph Epstein's *Gossip: The Untrivial Pursuit* (2012) and Roger Wilkes's *Scandal: A Scurrilous History of Gossip* (2002) offer engaging overviews, while Jeannette Walls's *Dish: How Gossip Became the News and the News Became Just Another Show* (2000) focuses on the interplay of gossip and the news media—a topic that has only grown more timely since her volume's publication. See also Cass R. Sunstein's *On Rumors: How Falsehoods Spread, Why We Believe Them, What Can Be Done* (2009) for an exploration of the effects (predominantly negative, in Sunstein's reading) of rumor and gossip in American politics and society.

9. Interestingly, Spacks's view of gossip has filtered back into the field of sociology: a 1994 study by Diego Gambetta offers a nuanced sociological reading of gossip informed by Spacks's work. Gambetta's approach to gossip is also informed by sociological research on the practice, allowing him to incorporate Spacks's notion of "good" gossip into a more comprehensive framework. Riffing on the Italian notion of gossip as a trivial but pleasurable activity—the Italian word *pettegolezzo* derives from *peto*, or "fart," Gambetta notes—he argues that gossip's myriad uses are subsidiary to its ability to both satisfy curiosity and broker "emotional complicity" between participants. This is a valuable insight and a notion to which I will return in the pages that follow.

10. The question of the extent to which lexicographical and etymological divergences reflect real differences in the lived experiences of gossip across different cultures is tantalizing but far beyond the scope of this study; neither do I propose to explore the reasons for such apparent divergences. (It is, however, interesting to note that many of the early English sources—Chaucer, Spenser, and so forth—clearly view gossip and backbiting in negative terms, more in keeping

with the connotations found in Spanish and French.) Rather, I suggest that literary gossip scholarship on Anglo-American texts has been significantly influenced by the etymological felicities of *gossip*'s roots in the intimate bonds of kinship, and has at times overlooked readings of gossip that might more readily suggest themselves to scholars of *bochinche* or *cancan*.

11. Spacks does go on to offer a "minimal definition" of gossip as "idle talk about other persons not present" (26), although she readily admits such a reductive definition misses much of the nuance and power of gossip. In the introduction to *Potins, cancans et littérature,* Solomon likewise insists on the difficulties of defining gossip, which she traces to gossip's complex origins in both the chatter of women and the *quanquam* of (male) university scholars (8).

12. The pleasures of gossip are manifold and rather underrated, at least by recent literary scholarship: as Gambetta notes, Spacksian gossip scholars, in pushing back against prior condemnation of gossip in moral terms, at times become almost puritanical in stressing gossip's functions rather than its delights. "One of the few safe things we can say about gossip is that if we indulge in it so painstakingly it is because gossip is pleasurable. But the pioneers in the study of gossip, driven by an urge to stress its positive functions against the standard morals which disapprove of it, kept this elementary reality concealed," Gambetta writes (201–2). Solomon makes a similar point, noting that the pleasure taken in gossip is both a part of the reason it is so easily dismissed as "unimportant chatter" and a part of the reason that gossip is so powerful: "Gossip is defined first and foremost by the pleasure it gives: the pleasure of transmitting, the pleasure of knowing," she writes. "It is this desire that drives and justifies the circulation of words exchanged because their content is scandalous, secret, or simply concerns a third party. This is the reason why perpetrators of gossip like to deal in sexuality, slander, and unpublished information about their neighbors" (8). The thrill of gossip, as will be seen throughout this book, is often the driving force that provides it with such charge and potency, and allows it to admit so many uses, both for good and ill.

13. See also Roger D. Abrahams on the performative nature of casual interactions in St. Vincent. "While there would be no confusion in the minds of the community between a Carnival song and an everyday argument, they would be recognized as being related to each other as controlled contest forms and evaluated as performances," he writes. "Gossip is therefore seen as simply one of the many inevitable performances of everyday life" (81). Abrahams further argues that the power of gossip rests in large part upon its performative appropriation of the names (and thus reputations) of the people gossiped about. "Someone who is always talking about others is described as having a *fas' mout'*. The term is significant, for being *fas'* means being thievish, and having a fas' mout' is thus regarded as *t'iefin* someone's good name; that is, betraying trust," he asserts (83).

14. Similarly, the *Oxford English Dictionary* defines rumor as "talk or hearsay" that is "not based on definite knowledge," and also as "an unverified or unconfirmed statement or report." In Spanish, the *Real Academia* dictionary

defines *rumor* as a "voice that runs among the public," a "confused noise of voices," and a "vague, dull, and continuing noise"—all definitions that suggest the imprecise murmuring of a circulating rumor, as opposed to the more precise act of gossip. The French word *rumeur* suggests buzzing confusion rather than specific information; *Larousse* offers three definitions describing *rumeur* as "a confusion of noises, sounds, and voices," an "indistinct noise of any origin," and a "confused murmuration of disapproval," before conceding that the word can also suggest "news [. . .] of which the origin is unknown or uncertain and the veracity doubtful."

15. Carrión, a Mexican writer and conceptual artist, systematically explored the practice of gossip through collective practices, "experiments," filmic projects, and more formal theorizations in conference talks, particularly in the 1980s. His engagement with gossip was explored in a 2017 retrospective in Museo Jumex, Mexico City.

16. Indeed, Spacks continues, gossip derives its power from the residual traces of a primitive belief in the practice's potency. "Like the notion that taking a photograph of someone endangers his spirit, the view that saying something bad has the force of *doing* something bad wells from pre-rational depths," she asserts (30). This sense of gossip as a harmless, if transgressive, practice, seems reasonable for Spacks's gossipers, who are drawn chiefly from English literature. Spacks's view is easy to understand, too, when read against her cataloging of the medieval and other early writers who describe gossip in terms of murder and manslaughter, and demand physically violent reprisals against those who commit acts of verbal violence against them. Reading the violence of the early English sources against the mannered restraint of nineteenth-century gossips, it is easy to allow oneself to be convinced that a process of evolution—even of civilization—is at work.

17. Brian Johnson's reading of Margaret Atwood's *The Handmaid's Tale* is instructive in this context: Johnson perceives in Offred's gossip, and her narrative as a whole, "the ultimate form of productive gossip," in keeping with Spacks's concept of gossip as an intimate and empowering practice. But Johnson also acknowledges that for Atwood's oppressed handmaids, gossip's power "often proves to be illusory," with the Mayday gossip network cast as being almost as oppressive as the authoritarian regime against which it stands (48). It is tempting to suggest that the dystopian imaginary here provides a space for engaging with gossip on terms not entirely dissimilar to those found in the lived realities of the authoritarian Caribbean.

18. It is not only in the Caribbean that writers have looked beyond framings of gossip as "women's talk." Cozarinsky, writing in 1973 about Jorge Luis Borges and Marcel Proust, recognizes gossip as a practice traditionally associated with women but used, needed, and feared by both men and women (18–21). More recent scholarship, such as Phillips's study; Martin's edited journal issue; and Cara Cilano's *Contemporary Pakistani Fiction in English,* which includes a section on gossip in Pakistani novels, has similarly begun to question the understanding

of gossip as an inherently feminine practice. Note, too, the recent effort to consider male gossip in the British context, of which Amy Milne-Smith's 2009 study of gossip in the gentlemen's clubs of nineteenth-century London is a fascinating example.

19. Martínez Alvarez published his novel *La ciudad chismosa y calumniante* under the pen name Martín Alva.

20. Clearly, gossip has played a far larger role in the broad sweep of Caribbean history and letters than I can address in this book. A study of gossip's role in mediating representations of the Caribbean during the early colonial period, for instance, could be both rich and fascinating. The literary spat between Bartolomé de Las Casas and Gonzalo Fernández de Oviedo offers a rich vein of ad hominem attacks and gossipy anecdotes; Las Casas notably criticizes Fernández de Oviedo for writing "as if he had witnessed all that he writes about this island" while in fact seldom leaving Santo Domingo (102), accuses him of defaming the indigenous peoples in order to justify their abuse and enslavement, and alleges that the only parts of Fernández de Oviedo's writings, "and of all his gossip," that are trustworthy are his descriptions of the local flora (104). Another worthy subject, in a similar vein, might be the historian Peter Martyr, whose 1530 work *De Orbe Novo*, as Herbert W. Krieger notes, is based on "pure gossip, for he admits that everyone who had been to the Indies visited him" (33). More recently, Édouard Glissant tantalizingly hints at gossip's role in mediating (and controlling) narratives surrounding emancipation in the Francophone Caribbean, reproducing Louis Thomas Husson's "odious, hypocritical, smarmy" (72) 1848 notice to Martinique field slaves warning them to reject "evil gossip" (80) and "comply with the orders of your masters" (79). Martínez Alvarez's 1926 novel *La ciudad chismosa y calumniante,* meanwhile, laments San Juan's obsession with gossip, and ends with the claim that a city populated entirely by blind, deaf, and mute people would be "a city without gossip, without intrigue, without calumny, and happier, far happier" than a place where people can see, speak, and gossip freely (Alva 234). Other examples, from the early colonial period to the present day, surely abound.

1. "A Mouthful of Dynamite"

1. Orality is not, of course, solely a concern for the Anglophone Caribbean. Hispanic Caribbean writers such as Guillermo Cabrera Infante and Luis Rafael Sánchez draw heavily on the spoken word in constructing their narratives—and also, not coincidentally, freely weave gossip into their texts. Much the same might also be said of Patrick Chamoiseau, Maryse Condé, and many other Francophone Caribbean writers. As Glissant and others have noted, it is impossible to conceive of Francophone Caribbean production without orality, not least with reference to Creole oral production. Importantly, for writers from across the Caribbean traditions and their diasporas, orality can be a way of rescuing memories from silence or of giving space to marginalized voices (often those of women and minorities),

as seen for instance in the work of the Haitian exile writer Marie-Célie Agnant. In such cases, orality becomes not (or not just) a locus of resistance but also a way of processing loss: the ephemeral spoken word can be preserved through its transposition into writing, and the writer's engagement with orality can become a means of reaching back to lost or near-forgotten people, periods, and places. This has been true, for instance, of writers such as the anthropologist and poet Lydia Cabrera, who deploys orality to capture Afro-Cuban dislocations born both of slavery and of more recent displacements. For Cabrera, the spoken word is a supplement to the incomplete historical record. Her story "Historia verdadera de un viejo pordiosero que decía llamarse Mampurias," for instance, begins with the assertion that "there are events that do not appear in written history, that escape a people's knowledge for one reason or another, because they were willfully erased, or were not contemplated or understood, or they occurred in the present of a time outside time itself, and the true reality, in all its unreality, disappears behind closer and more evident realities" (72). Gossip, so concerned with narrative corrections and revisions, plays an important part in this process of challenging and expanding upon monolithic official or historical accounts, a theme to which I return in later chapters.

2. The role of gossip in the colonies, from the colonizers' perspective, would make a fascinating comparative study in its own right. See, for instance, Emily J. Manktelow's 2015 study of gossip in a South Seas missionary outpost, Kirsten McKenzie's 2004 exploration of scandals in nineteenth-century colonial port cities, or Michael K. Walonen's brief acknowledgment in *Writing Tangier in the Postcolonial Transition* (2013) of gossip's role in creating community among British expatriates.

3. I here follow Cliff's use of male pronouns for Harry/Harriet, who later in the text becomes simply Harriet.

4. Another possibility: perhaps Harry/Harriet is even better read than he appears and is familiar with Barthes's suggestion, in *Fragments d'un discours amoureux*, that the *Symposium* is "not only a 'conversation' (we are speaking about something) but also a gossip (we are speaking amongst ourselves, about others)" (217).

5. Like orality, gossip has been at the core of diasporic writers' nostalgia for their lost home country. The African American writer Audre Lorde, the daughter of Caribbean immigrants, writes lyrically of "West Indian voices in the supermarket and Chase Bank, and the Caribbean flavors that have always meant home. Healing within a network of Black women who supplied everything from a steady stream of tender coconuts to spicy gossip to sunshine" (119).

6. In this, I follow in the footsteps of post-Gluckman sociologists who have sought to read gossip as a means not just of binding communities together, but also of furthering individual interests and mediating intra- and intergroup conflicts. Robert Paine, writing in 1967, views Gluckman's communitarian thesis as "unsatisfactory because it makes the community the center of attention instead of the

individual" and argues instead for a conception of gossip rooted in participants' individual goals and private agendas. "I would hypothesize that gossipers also have rival interests; that they gossip, and also regulate their gossip, to forward and protect their individual interests," he writes (280). As both Sally Engle Merry and Niko Besnier note, the debate between Gluckman's "structural-functionalist" and Paine's "transactionalist" followers dominated anthropological and sociological gossip scholarship for many years; still, more recent studies have sought to reconcile the two readings, exploring both the nature of the society in which gossip occurs and the needs and goals of the individual actors therein. "Gossip occupies a pivotal position between the sociopolitical structure of the group and the agency of particular members of the group," Besnier asserts. "Studying gossip is thus tantamount to investigating the relationship between individual action and the structure of society in which the individual is embedded" ("Gossip" 547). In this chapter, I explore precisely this nexus between the community and the individual.

7. Efforts to regulate gossip are by no means unique to the Caribbean, nor indeed a recent innovation. In sixteenth-century England and Scotland, male and female gossips were punished using the scold's bridle, which physically kept the wearer's tongue from wagging; the practice endured in parts of Europe until the nineteenth century. In 1913, Wisconsin passed a "criminal gossip law" making it illegal to gossip about an absent third party in a way that "shall injure or impair the reputation of such person for virtue or chastity or which shall expose him to hatred, contempt or ridicule," with Wisconsin attorney general Walter C. Owen writing: "I cannot find where there is any law like it in any other state. [. . .] Its purpose, evidently, is to suppress gossip" (219). A century later, in 2016, Saskatoon's municipal leaders considered an antibullying law that would have allowed police to ticket people they caught gossiping. Efforts to suppress gossip can also be intended to curb dissent; in 1973, for instance, Filipino dictator Ferdinand Marcos issued a decree calling gossip "one of the most insidious means of disrupting [. . .] peace, order and tranquility" (44) and ordering the imprisonment of anyone caught spreading gossip; a 2013 Chinese law, meanwhile, allowed officials to jail people who posted gossip online.

8. See also Michael Wood's discussion of García Márquez's "borrowing from talk or oral tradition" in *Cien años de soledad;* Wood perceives "the ribbon development of gossip" in the deceptively simple flow of the narration (*García Márquez* 17).

9. In García Márquez's work, in other words, gossip becomes a kind of counterpoint to the wandering storytellers described by Mario Vargas Llosa as "taking and bringing anecdotes, lies, fabulations, *chismografías* [gossip], and jokes that make a community out of a town of dispersed beings, and that keeps alive among them the feeling of being together, of constituting something fraternal and compact" (*El hablador* 234).

10. As a form, the *pasquín* is fundamentally connected to gossip: the original "talking statue" of Rome was supposedly named for Pasquino, a domestic

worker (in some tellings a tailor or a barber) whose trade gave him insights into the behind-the-scenes happenings at the Vatican. Pasquino became famous for the gossip he circulated, and after his death people honored his legacy by posting gossip, in the form of lampoons and sarcastic poetry about the political leaders of the day, at the base of his statue. The gossip at the heart of *La mala hora* has perhaps been obscured in the Anglophone scholarship by the tendency to translate *pasquines* as "lampoons"; as Robert Coover notes, "Though an accurate enough translation of pasquines or 'pasquinades,' the word is somewhat misleading, for the wall posters are merely gossipy, not satirical."

11. Scholars have noted the class divisions highlighted by the pasquinades' reception. William Rowe and Vivian Schelling perceive "a sharp contrast between the notables of the town, preoccupied with scandals which undermine their pretension to gentility, and the poor," who struggle with more tangible losses (206). The pasquinades, Stephen Minta writes, "only become a problem [. . .] when the élite families in the town recognize that the existence of the lampoons, and the apparent inability or unwillingness of the authorities to do anything about them, is undermining their own position of authority and control" (86). More broadly, see James C. Scott's *Weapons of the Weak* for a discussion of the ways in which gossip allows the poor to insert themselves into public discourse while subtly reinforcing the norms of the society in which they operate.

12. Sims also reads the pasquinades as undermining the mayor's authority: "The fact that the pasquinades appear and disappear at will exposes at once the fragility of the official world and the irrepressible vitality of the carnivalesque space," he argues (56). The pasquinades, he continues, "function as subversive elements" that produce "a series of spreading waves that shake the official world" (56). Regina Janes would agree: "The pasquins are not in themselves political, but [. . .] symbolize resistance to the order imposed upon the town [. . .] the pasquins suggest that writing itself is subversive, especially the sort of writing that tells aloud what everybody already knows and does not say" (34).

13. With some notable exceptions: the dentist, who as the corrupt and despotic mayor's political enemy stands for courage and integrity, does not fear the pasquinades, for example.

14. The mayor's response to the pasquinades has been widely read as opportunistic: he uses or co-opts the circulating gossip to justify a wave of repressive violence against the townspeople. While correct, such readings risk minimizing the power of the pasquinades themselves. It is the violence already sparked by the *pasquines,* after all, that allows the mayor to unleash the force he claims is necessary to halt them.

15. In fact, Nora de Jacob seems eager to have her secret revealed: she is frustrated to be secretly engaged in a love affair with "a man who might have been made to be talked about by a woman," and half-jokingly threatens to tell everyone about their affair. "I'm quite capable of putting up my own *pasquín*," she warns (172).

16. In this sense, *La mala hora* can be seen as delving into the same territory—speech and writing, authorized and unauthorized discourse—previously discussed in relation to orality in the Anglophone Caribbean. The boundaries between the spoken and the written have been well explored in Caribbean literature, particularly with reference to colonial and postcolonial tensions. As Kaiama L. Glover notes in connection with Francophone Caribbean literature, the "perception of an embattled oral tradition overcome by an oppressive written culture dominates postcolonial theory" (217). It is reasonable to read García Márquez's project, in part, as a subversion of this trope, with an oral form, gossip, appropriating or slipping into the written word in order to upend existing power structures.

17. The pasquinades emulate forms of scandalous, expository gossip seen elsewhere in the Caribbean. As S. Elizabeth Bird notes, following Gluckman, the *simidors*, or leaders, of the scandal songs sung in Haitian villages use gossip to lampoon the indiscretions of their neighbors (31). Herskovits, in his classic study, quotes one Haitian as saying: "The *simidor* is a journalist, and every *simidor* is a Judas!" (74). (Tellingly, as Elizabeth A. McAlister writes, the Creole word *jouda*, derived from "Judas," is used to denote a gossip.) Much like the pasquinades of *La mala hora*, it is from the public exposition of acts already privately gossiped about that the *simidors*' songs derive their power. "It is not so much the song itself that is feared, but rather the way the story now becomes the public property of the village, and source for endless speculation," Bird writes (31).

18. As Vargas Llosa points out, by the end of *La mala hora* the violence has recommenced, the prison is full of dissidents, and men are fleeing to the mountains to join the rebels. "The mendacious peace has ended: the 'people' return to their quotidian hell," he writes. "Who started all this? That anonymous and proliferating agent: the implacable 'papelitos'" (*Historia de un deicidio* 454).

19. The doctor comes close to acknowledging as much when he remarks that the pasquinades say "what everyone already knows, which by the way is almost always the truth" (104). Similarly, Benjamin's assertion that the pasquinades are a symptom of social breakdown is rebuffed by the dentist's assertion that they are simply "a sign that sooner or later, everything becomes known" (124).

20. See, among many other examples, Dieter Janik's 1994 essay positioning *La mala hora* as part of a broader genre of "literature of *la violencia*" and Carmenza Kline's discussion, in *Los orígenes del relato* (2003), of *La mala hora*'s mapping of Colombian communities' experiences of violence.

21. Gossip generates a similar inexorable apathy in *Zohara* (1961), by the Barbadian writer Geoffrey Drayton, in which a peasant village is gripped by the gossip of María, its sinister, soothsaying midwife, eventually leading to the death of Manrique, a mute boy whose innocence stands in counterpoint to María's malicious chatter. María's gossip becomes a means of manipulating those around her: her gossip sessions are described as séances, or as enchanting those who participate, with gossip shown as governing the villagers' lives. "The news of events invariably preceded the events themselves. But for the fact that those concerned

were thus forced into action, there would [. . .] have been neither births, marriages, nor deaths in the village," reflects Don Gumersindo (103). María's gossipy prognostication becomes a self-fulfilling prophecy: "The Marías of this world both foretold disaster and initiated the steps that made disaster inevitable," Gumersindo thinks (92). María's calumnies, which focus upon Satanic rituals supposedly being carried out in the mountains, eventually lead the villagers to murder Manrique in an act described as a collective sin. "It was all the men in the village, you know—every last one of them," Ana says (184). Unlike *Crónica,* Drayton's novel pairs communal inertia with a single, almost supernatural gossip—a gesture that, interestingly, mirrors the doom-mongering prophecies of the midwife in *Presagio* (1974), a film scripted by García Márquez.

22. Yolanda Martínez San Miguel points to "gossip and social reputation as key places in the public representation of masculinity" and suggests that "El Venao" must be read as a reassertion of traditional Dominican values in the face of migration and other community-eroding factors. "Here gossip functions as a means of re-establishing and maintaining the coherence of a community," Martínez San Miguel writes (198).

23. This recalls Jean-Luc Nancy's notion of the community's role in the transfiguration of death via an "an immortal communion where death at last loses the senseless sense that it would otherwise have had" (*Communauté désœuvrée* 39). In Nancy's conception, communities vindicate individual deaths by framing them in terms of salvation or martyrdom. In *Crónica,* this process is perverted: the death of Nasar is meaningless, with the sacrifice serving only to sustain a self-justifying system of hollow morality.

24. Mais's short stories circulated in magazines and self-published manuscripts during the 1940s but found a broader audience with the publication of *Listen, the Wind,* which collected his scattered published works along with previously unpublished manuscripts held in the archives of the University of the West Indies. His stories' use of gossip serves as a reminder that the trends I explore in post-1960s Caribbean literature are rooted in earlier cultural and literary currents. This is, in Mais's case, perhaps unsurprising: Mais was deeply concerned with the independence of the West Indies and, in criticizing the region's present and imagining its future, anticipated some of the chief literary themes and practices addressed in this study. As Alison Donnell and Sarah Lawson Welsh note, as early as the 1940s, Mais's texts constituted "demands for serious cultural development in the region's creative consciousness," thus anticipating "the 'protest [. . .] against or about ourselves' which Brathwaite calls for in the early 1970s" (113). Welsh similarly notes that Mais's *The Hills Were Joyful Together* (1953) and *Brother Man* (1954)—the latter, especially, significantly marked by the gossip of its community—anticipated works of the 1960s such as John Hearne's *Land of the Living* (1961) and Sylvia Wynter's *The Hills of Hebron* (1962).

25. The stigmatization of gossiping women is a recurring theme in the Caribbean. In 1994, the Trinidadian calypso artist Winston Bailey, known as

the Mighty Shadow, put out a track called "Gossiping" that depicts a woman gossiping endlessly—about neighbors but also about ducks, dogs, cats, and even her food. The gossip is shown as a hypocrite—she gossips about everyone else's flaws but "would never, ever say she husband / Sneakers stink"—and also as an object of ridicule, so caught up in a frenzy of disclosure that she can't keep track of the secrets she has learned. "She tell and she tell till she fuh get / Who she tell," Bailey sings. "She fuh get is you who give her de news." Not all Caribbean writers think this way about women's gossip, of course. Reading Opal Palmer Adisa's *It Begins with Tears* (1997), Donna Weir-Soley notes that the riverside can become "a site of therapeutic recreation" for women as they gather to do their laundry: "A place for the exchanging of news, gossip, and story-telling for the women and children. While they wait for the clothing to dry, the women and children cook, eat, talk, laugh, enjoy a swim [. . .]. Thus, the harshness of physical labor is often transcended by a sense of community, playfulness, and female bonding" (248).

26. Mais's view of community echoes Maryse Condé's suggestion, in *La civilisation du bossale* (1978), that in African societies "individualism is viewed with contempt." Condé perceives the community's need to subsume the individual in the collective, writing that "one should insert oneself harmoniously into the community and not do anything to harm its cohesion." Still, she casts gossip as a blow against that process, a means of throwing grit into the wheels of community. "The gravest faults are slander, the calumny that, in these societies without writing, where the spoken word is the only representation, is considered as the negation, the destruction of the personality of those they attack," she writes. "The greatest virtues are those of tolerance, of patience, which contribute to appease the tensions of communal life" (28). Condé suggests that African communities depend upon passive processes of ritual and respect to sustain themselves; Mais, in contrast, envisions gossip as a more active process whereby communities can subjugate individuals and demand their acquiescence.

27. As Roger Mais's tales show, gossip—in the Caribbean as elsewhere—is often bound up in a poetics of place: there are specific locations, such as Mais's riverbanks and backyard fences, where people go to gossip and where gossip flows as people come together to work, relax, or socialize. Often, these spaces have, or acquire, a deeper significance and color the gossip exchanged therein: Mais uses the yard to emphasize neighborly relations (and encroachments), just as Luis Rafael Sánchez, in *La importancia de llamarse Daniel Santos* (1988), uses the billiard hall to suggest virility. One thinks also of Émile Ollivier's *La discorde aux cent voix* (1986), in which neighborhood cafés and groceries become microcosms, allowing the text to interrogate and juxtapose the many different ranks and kinds of people who populate the town. This is especially true of the Leclerc grocery: "The place where passersby and loafers never failed to stop for their daily dose of extravagant rumors. It was there the thousand flavors of Cailles were distilled: lovers' trysts, esoteric discussions, political questions, health problems, bedroom stories, open secrets. All passed by the arbor of Leclerc's grocery," Ollivier writes

(232). These spaces are typically unsanctioned and unauthorized, if not actually unruly: places where people talk freely, and that are in turn colored and defined by the oral exchanges that take place therein. Dash makes a similar point regarding the marketplace and bar in Patrick Chamoiseau's *Chronique des sept misères* (1986), noting that a "stream of gossip, rumor, and stories" serves to contrast "these spaces of exuberant orality with the regimented world of the written" (*Other America* 144).

28. Mrs. Ramage's trip is presented as an attempt to evade the prying eyes of the people in the town: "When asked why she had left so secretly—she had taken a fishing boat from the other side of the island—she answered sullenly that she didn't want anyone to know her business, she knew how people talked. No, she'd heard no rumours about her husband, and the Gazette—a paper written in English—was not read in Guadeloupe" (21). Here again, an individual's desire to avoid gossip proves intolerable to the community, with brutal consequences for those who seek privacy.

29. Thorunn Lonsdale argues that "Sleep It Off, Lady" is partly autobiographical, citing letters written by Rhys to her editor, Francis Wyndham, about her prying neighbors: "What I *can't* is to be left alone in a place like Cheriton Fitz which has to be seen to be believed," Rhys writes. "It is completely isolated yet not peaceful—full to the brim of very stupid gossip. Unkind too" (Lonsdale 147). Lonsdale notes that Rhys also complains of mice scurrying around her cottage walls—another link to the plight of the protagonist of "Sleep It Off, Lady" (147).

30. Sánchez also deploys gossip to notable effect in his novels. He refers to *La importancia de llamarse Daniel Santos* as a "fabulación," alluding to the gossip from which it is woven, and offers up an "invented reality" that has "swum through seas of gossip" en route to the reader (26). In this, Sánchez uses gossip to perpetuate what Jason Cortés terms "a flight from the tyranny of ontology" (80); in Sánchez's text, this narrative ambiguity allows "rumors of genital anarchy" to blossom into a mythos of "deafeningly macho prestige" (*Importancia* 9). Santos's very celebrity is founded upon a reputation for virility grounded in, and serving to fuel, acclamatory gossip about his nocturnal adventures. This gossip is participated in equally by men and by women: the pool hall, a "guy thing" described as the "male response to the beauty salon," is a venue where "gossip is uncovered, slander exercised, reputations paraded, and cuckolds' horns scrupulously accounted for" (126). Gossip's "oral graffiti" is everywhere, Sánchez suggests, and is embraced avidly by both men and women (26).

31. All citations from "¡Jum!" refer to Rose M. Sevillano's translation, "Hum!" (1997).

32. For this final line of the story, I follow Suzanne Jill Levine's translation.

33. The interpretive quality of gossip is one that Spacks and others view as underpinning the process of constructing intimate communities. While not an aspect of gossip that I substantively explore in this volume, this is, of course, still present in both the Caribbean and its literature. Consider, for instance, Kamau

Brathwaite's transcription of positive, community-building gossip in "The Dust," a Creole poem from *Rights of Passage* (1967). Women meet at a corner store and chat about the groceries they are buying, but soon begin seeking to understand the world around them through gossip. Talk turns to the bizarre volcanic dust choking the land, and existential questions arise: "Without rhyme / without reason, all you hope gone / ev'rything look like it comin' out wrong. / Why is that? What it mean?" (69).

34. Nancy is dismissive of gossip: in *La communauté désavouée* he singles out "chatty speech," or *discours bavard* (73), as the only form of "thought that is not experience," while in *Une pensée finie* he approvingly quotes Heidegger's condemnation of "idle talk"—both in spoken gossip and written "scribbling"—as a curtailing or closing off (*fermeture* in Nancy's term, or *Verschliessen* in Heidegger's) of understanding (120).

35. As Todd May notes, "totalitarianism" in the work of Nancy and other philosophers of community relates not strictly to political authoritarianism but rather to "the project of constraining people's lives and identities within narrowly defined parameters" and by extension "the attempt to capture all of reality within a narrow conceptual framework" (4). It is a term that "refers to narrow constraints placed upon individual and social identity and behavior rather than just to a type of state" (23); still, May continues, "although this way of thinking of totalitarianism is more conceptual than political, its links with political totalitarianism are not far to seek" (4). This is a theme to which I return in subsequent chapters.

36. The politicization of gossip and its uses both by and against the state are more fully explored in chapters 3 and 4; here, I concentrate instead on Ponte's writing as reflecting the individual experience of gossip-mediated state surveillance.

37. Gossip is similarly institutionalized elsewhere in the Caribbean and Latin America, most notably in the Dominican Republic under Trujillo. See also Olga M. González's account, in *Unveiling Secrets of War in the Peruvian Andes*, of the use of gossip by Shining Path guerrillas, who both punished the *soplones* who gossiped about them, and enlisted legions of gossiping informants to help them monitor and control local populations: "Gossip was more dangerous than ever before. There were snoops who supported or belonged to the Shining Path and who enacted a terrifying apparatus of the senses. Known simply as the *mil ojos y mil oídos*, 'thousand eyes and thousand ears,' this surveillance apparatus managed to keep the population in check and generated a state of paranoia. Gossip as Sarhuinos had experienced it before the Shining Path seemed inoffensive in contrast to the politicized *chismosos* who, in their allegiance to the Shining Path, hunted *soplones*, the *chismosos* who opposed the party. Gossip had become a deadly weapon" (56).

38. Philippe Zard describes Kafka's *The Trial* as being built upon a "totalitarisme cancanier" (55), or gossip-based totalitarianism, that is strikingly similar to the suffocating surveillance portrayed by Ponte. *The Trial*'s Tribunal stands, Zard argues, as "a sort of Panopticon" into which everything feeds, "from the old lady

at the window to the little girl in the building's courtyard" (59). This ultimately creates a surveillance society in which "neighbors and even one's own children can become either spies or witnesses for the prosecution" (59).

39. The dispersion of surveillance has been widely studied, from Simone Browne's exploration of New York's eighteenth-century "lantern laws," which mandated that black people out after dark should carry lit candles, to recent work by scholars such as Anders Albrechtslund and Robert Tokunaga on peer-to-peer surveillance using social-media platforms such as Twitter and Facebook.

40. Ponte's focus on the watched city recalls Tönnies's focus on the city as the antithesis of *Gemeinschaft*, which he sees as rooted in the family and the home, and growing increasingly untenable as social groups swell and develop into sprawling and complex urbanizations.

2. "Parallel Versions"

1. Patrick Chamoiseau similarly riffs on the markers that accompany the fictions of the Caribbean in his detective novel *Solibo magnifique* (1988), in which Solibo's dying words—"Patat'sa"—prompt the audience to interpret his death as a performance and to respond formulaically with "Patat'si." The crime goes unsolved, with the tropes of Euro-American detective fiction proving unable to account for what Wendy Knepper terms Chamoiseau's framing of "the Caribbean mystery as a third consciousness, an irreducible Otherness" (92).

2. Gossip features in many of Ferré's other works. *The House on the Lagoon* (1995) shows its protagonist, Isabel, encountering layer upon layer of gossip as she attempts to write her family's story. As in *Maldito amor*, this sparks a battle for narrative control: Isabel's words are read and corrected by her husband, but her storytelling in turn serves as a mechanism for rebellion, denunciation, and finally emancipation. In *Flight of the Swan* (2001), likewise, Ferré shows a metaphorical family unit, a Russian ballet troupe visiting Puerto Rico, torn apart by gossip. Masha, the narrator, gains power through her insights into the private life of the troupe's leader: "I knew all of her secrets [. . .]. This knowledge gave me power, and the other dancers respected me for it," she insists (7). Ferré's short stories also explore gossip's uses and risks: in "El collar de camándulas" the protagonist's erratic behavior is viewed in terms of the harm it could do to her husband's reputation (*Papeles de Pandora* 124), while "Cuando las mujeres quieren a los hombres" shows the degree to which women use gossip to mediate relationships. Gossip also drives the plot of "La bella durmiente," in which a husband receives anonymous gossip about his wife along with the warning that "it isn't enough to be decent; above all, one had to seem to be so" (150). In "Isolda en el espejo" (*Maldito amor y otros cuentos* 191), meanwhile, gossip becomes institutionalized: the wives of the town's bankers declare themselves to be "arbiters of public decorum," and use gossip to enforce a "law of respectability" (192).

3. Dany Laferrière's 1991 novel *L'Odeur du café* similarly highlights the contradictory versions of events that circulate in a small Haitian town. The

protagonist, a young boy, sits at his grandmother's feet and listens to passersby's accounts of different happenings, from theories about the identity of a madwoman to an episode in which a man claims to have had his arm bitten off by a "sea-dog" (149). Repeatedly, contradictory accounts—labeled with the speaker's name, such as "Zette's version" or "Willy Bony's version" (150–51)—are presented. The text is largely passive, like a child overhearing adults' conversations, with the versions allowed to come and go without being challenged. The ordering of the passages, however, does lend weight to some versions: the accounts of Sylphise's death variously claim that the girl is still alive, that she levitated before she died, that she was turned into a zombie and sold, or that the "entire business was made up by jealous people" (66). Still, by the end of the chapter, two versions converge, with the final account—presented with the words "I owe you the truth" (69)—allowed to stand as the definitive version of events. Similarly, in the sea-dog tale, a succession of lurid accounts give way to a more plausible version, with Love Léger using gossip about a mutual acquaintance to explain the beast's attacks. "There's always a reason, if you only listen out for it," he concludes (152). Gossip here provides little epistemic certainty—even Sylphise's death is waved off rather than satisfactorily explained—but that failure does not generate the anxiety present in Ferré's text. Rather, the repetition of versions becomes almost soothing: a passive acknowledgment that definitive truths are unreachable and that the gathering together of stories is the only consolation that remains.

4. Where possible, I have followed Ferré's own translation of *Maldito amor*, published as *Sweet Diamond Dust* in 1988. However, Ferré's translation differs, at times significantly, from the original. I use the abbreviations *SDD* and *MA* in citations throughout this chapter to indicate whether I am quoting from *Sweet Diamond Dust* or, using my own translation, directly from *Maldito amor*.

5. By violating Nicolás's privacy and dragging his purported transgressions into the open, Arístides also wins a more direct victory over his brother. There is an inherent power, beyond the shaping of narrative, in the violation that comes with revealing things others would keep secret and in the exposure of people's private lives to scrutiny, moral judgment, and ridicule.

6. The original Spanish is more vividly persecutory than Ferré's English rendition: "Las malas lenguas la tienen pelada, y dicen que hasta está loca, y que es y que correntona con los hombres," Titina says (*MA* 128)—literally, "Wicked tongues have trashed her, and even say she's crazy, and that she's loose with men."

7. Ferré's English version speaks only of the rumors coming from "unreliable sources" (24).

8. The Spanish original has Arístides say of Gloria: "no será ella quien desate sobre el pueblo esa madeja de intrigas con que intenta hoy arruinarnos"— literally, "it will not be she who unleashes upon the town this web of intrigue with which she is now trying to ruin us" (*MA* 142).

9. This use of gossip has been noted by Spacks and others. In an essay on Virginia Woolf and Toni Morrison, Jane Lilienfeld states that gossip constitutes

"an effective language for those who are silenced in the dominant culture," given her belief "that some white women's voices, often muffled in the family and by cultural practices and institutions, could, through gossip, break free of the control of official stories" (51).

10. María Inés Lagos discusses this issue, writing that "even if Gloria tries to break with the world of the past by sparking a fire, and expresses her desire for change in altering the lyrics of the song that Elvira used to sing when she fell in love with Julio Font, she still keeps singing the song as she modifies it, indicating that not even the flames can erase completely the history and the culture of past generations" (99).

11. In this, she attempts a reversal of the situation José Luis González describes in his essay "El país de cuatro pisos." González writes: "If Puerto Rican society has always been a society divided by class, and if [. . .] in every society divided by class two cultures coexist, that of the oppressors and that of the oppressed, and if what is known as 'national culture' is generally the culture of the oppressors, then we must recognize that what in Puerto Rico we have always understood as 'national culture' is the culture produced by the class of landowners and professionals" (18). Gloria's actions would correspond to the attempt by the oppressed to impose their story, or, following González's terminology, to produce culture on their own terms.

12. This is not the primary concern of Spacks's study, and in this respect her views are not as fully developed as Cozarinsky's. Still, Spacks notes that "much gossip delights by an aesthetic of surfaces. It dwells on specific personal particulars. People and their concerns preoccupy gossipers, by definition, but the special way in which they matter evolves from belief in the importance of the small particular" (15). In this, Spacks perhaps thinks of the kernel of information that hints at larger, hidden truths, the logical conclusion of which, one might argue, would be the shattering of Cozarinsky's "realist illusion."

13. The idea of destructive conflict within the idealized Puerto Rican *gran familia* is a recurring theme in Ferré's fiction. See, for instance, *The House on the Lagoon* (which, incidentally, also ends with the family's son Manuel burning down the family home), *Flight of the Swan* (where the family is a metaphorical one, a ballet troupe), and the *Papeles de Pandora* stories "De tu lado al paraíso" and "Amalia." As María Acosta Cruz remarks, "This explosive end to the familiar allegory for the nation (the house) runs entirely parallel with Ferré's knack for blowing up the metaphorical house of Puerto Rican literature" (93).

14. This contrasts with Enrico Mario Santí's notion of gossip as "a peculiar national allegory, or else a microcosm of Mexico" in Juan Rulfo's *Pedro Páramo* (1955) and Elena Garro's *Los recuerdos del porvenir* (1963). Santí, following Spacks, reads gossip as "a metaphor for the reconstitution of communal life outside the reaches of the State, a kind of collective salvation 'through the grapevine'" (134). Ferré's text, evidently, suggests a rather less generous view of gossip's role in communal and familial life.

15. Ferré anticipates, perhaps, the exhausted détente that Frances Negrón-Muntaner traces in Puerto Rico's recent political life, with voters preferring to accept uncertainty rather than commit to the thankless pursuit of definitive solutions. According to Negrón-Muntaner, "Within this ambiguous space, there are undoubtedly tremendous conflicts, inequities, and frustrations," and "yet there is a place for many contradictory versions of community and self" (10). Ferré also stands as a precursor of the recent intellectual and literary trend, identified by Acosta Cruz, that has seen "newer generations of culture producers [. . .] stake the claim that they are free from the monomaniacal search for national identity" (104). Such writers reject the "nationalist dictum" that literature should aspire to forge a unitary national identity, and instead come to embrace plural and contradictory viewpoints: "The island's paradoxical and conflicted feelings about dependency versus independence are the mix, the brew, the *burundanga* from which rise stories, themes, and images that power up the culture" (178). *Maldito amor,* in vividly tracing the consequences of that "monomaniacal search," highlights the tensions that gave rise to such sensibilities and the risks inherent in seeking to replace one story with another.

16. See Lizabeth Paravisini-Gebert in *The Cambridge Companion to Gothic Fiction* (253). Gutiérrez Mouat also writes lucidly of the thematic and structural congruences between the texts, noting that there is an irony to the way that the "crisis of the process of Caribbean decolonization" in Rhys's text echoes "a historical moment of recolonization in *Maldito amor*" (304).

17. Although this evidence may be less conclusive than typically assumed; as Carine M. Mardorossian shows, Rhys portrays Christophine's Obeah with marked ambivalence. Christophine's threats of magical retribution go unheeded, her potion fails to work, and she herself refers to the practice as "foolishness" and a "tim-tim story," and warns that her practices have no power over white people (67–68). Despite the space Rhys gives to Obeah as a theme and plot element, "the black creoles in her fiction are neither shown standing in fear of it, nor are they shown really practicing it," Mardorossian writes (73).

18. Arnold E. Davidson offers an incisive reading of the tiff between Tia and Antoinette, noting that it "so subtly parallels Antoinette's subsequent treatment at the hands of Edward Rochester that it is easy to overlook the point of the earlier episode" (23). The transactions at play—pennies for the girls, a £30,000 dowry for Rochester's bride—require both Tia and Rochester to redefine Antoinette (as a "properly penniless ragamuffin," as "Bertha") in order to profit while retaining their own sense of self-worth. "Even though the stakes are then higher, the principle remains the same," Davidson argues (24).

19. Cosway's personal history is itself the subject of gossip. Asked whether his name is really Cosway, Amélie says, "Some people say yes, some people say no," and recalls seeing photographs of his black parents. "They say one time he was a preacher in Barbados, he talk like a preacher," she adds (72).

20. As Homi Bhabha notes, gossip is of a piece with the seething energy of Caribbean life, one of the "signs of a culture of survival that emerges from the

other side of the colonial enterprise, the darker side" (xii–xiii). In Bhabha's reading of Naipaul, gossip—along with humor, aspirations, and fantasies—is a result of the hybrid, in-between status of Naipaul's Caribbean characters.

21. Condé's work is marked by her ambivalence toward both the Caribbean and her own status as an exile, and her abiding suspicion of the Caribbean's histories and myths. Writing of *La vie scélérate,* Marie-Denise Shelton remarks that "everything is gnawed by the virus of inauthenticity or failure, even the myths produced by popular imagination [. . .]. Condé has entered, as it were, into an 'era of suspicion.' In the postcolonial world she describes, language, myth, and ideas are infused with ambiguity. The idea which prevails at the end is that in the Caribbean today a crisis of the spirit, a crisis of meaning, exists" (719).

22. In *Célanire,* witchcraft and Célanire's implied status as a "horse" also serve as a bridge back across the Atlantic Ocean: a common thread of gossip and superstition connecting the African and Afro-Caribbean experience.

23. Nunez's text describes gossip's role in 1950s Trinidad in terms remarkably similar to V. S. Naipaul's 1957 novel *The Mystic Masseur.* Like Nunez, Naipaul describes word of mouth as surpassing conventional media in its reach and rapidity. When Ganesh, the titular masseur, began to manifest his healing powers, there "was no report of this incident in the newspapers, yet within two weeks all Trinidad knew," Naipaul writes (125). Naipaul, like other Caribbean writers, stresses both gossip's extraordinary efficacy and its tendency to exaggerate or corrupt the information it transmits. News of Ganesh's talents "went about on the local grapevine, the Niggergram, an efficient, almost clairvoyant, news service," he writes. "As the Niggergram noised the news abroad, the number of Ganesh's successes were magnified, and his Powers became Olympian" (125).

24. The tale of the haunted room is more rumor than gossip, in that it concerns a place, not a person. Many of the stories that bubble through *Célanire* tread the line between rumor and gossip, not least because they are seldom staged directly: the narrator reports what is said but seldom shows the speech act. Though firmly grounded in gossip about specific characters, many of the episodes thus relayed are deprived of the performative aspect of gossip.

25. Condé's description of the doctor as "Papa Doc" carries a "Duvalier echo," presumably deliberate, that fuses a little Caribbean Vodou with the Frankenstein motif running through *Célanire,* notes Carolyn Duffey (74).

26. Sociologists and anthropologists have frequently noted the interplay of gossip and witchcraft; see, for instance, Wolf Bleek's 1976 study of gossip's role as a mechanism of accusation in Ghana; E. E. Evans-Pritchard's pioneering work examining witchcraft as a means of probing the unknowable; Christiane Bougerol's *Une ethnographie des conflits aux Antilles* (1997); and Pamela J. Stewart and Andrew Strathern's *Witchcraft, Sorcery, Rumors and Gossip* (2003).

27. Condé's treatment of supernatural rumors and gossip recalls Derek Walcott's sonnet "Le Loupgarou," from the sequence "Tales of the Islands" (1962), which tells the "curious tale that threaded through town / through greying women

sewing under eaves" of Le Brun, a fruit peddler who, gossip has it, is secretly a "slathering lycanthrope." Walcott dwells on the gory details of the tale—the werewolf "lugged its entrails, trailing wet / With blood"—but also makes clear that the story is just something that "these Christian witches said" about an outsider greeted by "slowly shutting jalousies" as he tottered through the town (*Green Night* 30). Once more, superstitious and bloodcurdling tales fuel gossip that is used to mark the exclusion of its target.

28. In *Rire haïtien* (2006), Georges Anglade also casts gossip as an evaluative process but shows final consensus being arrived at through the intervention of external authority figures. His tale "Le cabri à la dent d'or" tracks a scandal that flares in a Haitian marketplace after a butcher's arrest: "It is whispered that he is supposed to have sold a young goat's head that had one gold tooth. It is on this fabric that Quina's rumors will embroider all day long" (99–100). New details emerge, and the townsfolk bicker over whether it was really a gold tooth—implying an upper-class victim—or merely an amalgam filling. The stories proliferate; finally, a magistrate intervenes, ruling that the gossip was started as an act of revenge by a girl conducting an affair with the butcher. The reputational sabotage might have succeeded, the magistrate adds, had the butcher not been caught making love with a boy the previous evening. The tale ends with a bang of the magistrate's gavel—dismissing the gossip, but also marking its final transformation from groundless rumor into a tale that will be repeated and remembered long after market day is over. In another tale, "Lincoln, Churchill et le contremaître," Anglade shows gossip's use by Port-au-Prince's conservative elites. Gossip swirls freely, with people stirring up trouble and waiting to see which of their calumnies will stick. "Three people, two telephones, and a day are all that is necessary to launch a substantial rumor in the small, interconnected society of Port-au-Prince," Anglade writes. "By the next day, it is possible to verify whether people are willing or not to subscribe to the plot[. . . .] The third day, the zen, the plausible lie, has taken on a life of its own" (322). But the gossips defer to outside authority: the tale's narrator becomes the arbiter of gossipy complaints made against one of his employees and ultimately sees through the gossips' self-serving slander. Despite this, an unspoken anxiety underpins many of Anglade's tales. The gossip shown as circulating in Haitian society seldom provides access to the truth—and in the absence of an organic consensus, truth emerges simply as whatever those in power determine it to be.

29. The fluctuating racial divisions and differences of opinion in the community underscore Célanire's rejection by both white and black society, an interesting point given that Célanire is repeatedly depicted as monstrous and cannibalistic. As Patricia A. Turner notes, accusations of cannibalism are racially charged: from their earliest encounters, both white Europeans and black Africans described one another as cannibalistic, with each using alleged anthropophagy as a vivid shorthand for amorality and barbarism. Turner dryly remarks: "When the belief that a given people eat the bodies of others is perpetuated, we can be sure that relations

between the parties in question are, at the very least, strained" (*Grapevine* 31). In depicting Célanire as cannibalistic—through acts of specific gossip, rather than the vaguer rumors that Turner describes—both blacks and whites thus position her as the other, morally and socially distinct from their own racial identity.

30. Gossip is used in a similar fashion in Émile Ollivier's 1986 novel *La discorde aux cent voix,* in which circulating stories about a town's residents are carefully inventoried. Consider, for example, the competing stories about Cyprien Anselme: various bits of gossip are explicitly pitched against one another, with their sources—from the senator's "political enemies" to the "goldsmiths of rumors" (45)—tracing the divisions in the town itself. Many other sparring scraps of gossip and rumor are similarly arrayed in the text, without any attempt to discern their veracity. Much like Estévez's Havana, it seems, Ollivier's fictional town can only be fully represented through an accounting of its gossip and rumors.

31. The seemingly definitive resolution of Torres's text is in keeping with the traditional detective story, which Brooks describes as claiming "that all action is motivated, causally enchained, and eventually comprehensible as such to the perceptive observer" (*Reading for the Plot* 269), and which Geoffrey Hartman notes is inextricable from the "the ritual persistence of the problem-solving formula" (171). The novel's resolution, however, is at odds with many of Torres's other novels: *Doña Inés contra el olvido* (1992) and *Los últimos espectadores del acorazado Potemkin* (1999) both eschew definitive versions, suggesting that *La fascinación* owes its clear resolution, at least to a degree, to the conventions of the classic detective story.

32. See Maryann Ayim's essay "Knowledge through the Grapevine: Gossip as Inquiry" for a discussion of gossip as a positivist investigative framework in Christie's Marple stories.

33. As Forrester states, "The practice of psychoanalysis involves speaking what sounds often remarkably like gossip, rumour and—that extraordinary word so close to the analytic process itself—*hearsay*" (10). The patient, at least in the popular imagination, does not look directly at the analyst but reclines: analysis is thus a speech act without an object, allowing an unusual slippage of identity. "One consequence of this peculiar stance of the analyst is that the patient finds it possible to gossip about him- or herself—something that in everyday life is impossible" (247). The similarity between the speech act of gossip and the speech act of therapy is more than merely structural: gossip, in Forrester's reading, is a key piece of the analytic process and mediates subtle leakages between analytic discourse and real-world happenings. This is a profound and rich, if sometimes troubling, connection: "Gossip is the underbelly of analysis," Forrester asserts (253), elaborating that gossip functions as a common thread linking individual analytic dyads back to the founders of the field, and coming to serve as "the cultural unconscious of psychoanalysis" (259).

34. Latin American writers such as Jorge Luis Borges, Juan José Saer, and Ricardo Piglia, among many others, have mined the tropes of detective fiction.

In the Caribbean, meanwhile, see Persephone Braham's *Crimes against the State, Crimes against Persons* (2004); Stephen Wilkinson's *Detective Fiction in Cuban Society and Culture* (2006), which is grounded in a reading of the works of Leonardo Padura; and Jane Bryce's "'Who No Know Go Know': Popular Fiction in Africa and the Caribbean" on the use of crime fiction as a vehicle for "gritty realism" in the popular fiction of the Anglophone Caribbean (232). The investigations shown in Caribbean crime fiction often take place against a backdrop of official apathy and inaction, a point that John D. Erickson explores with reference to Chamoiseau's aforementioned *Solibo magnifique*, Raphaël Confiant's *Le meurtre du Samedi-Gloria*, and Condé's *Traversée de la mangrove*. Jason Herbeck also offers an insightful take on the nature of detective fiction in the Francophone Caribbean, which he terms an "undercover operation" (63), arguing that the failure, in works such as *Traversée de la mangrove*, to offer definitive resolutions to the texts' central mysteries speaks not to a definitive break with the paradigmatic conventions of the detective novel but rather to an attempt to bring the norms of the format into dialogue with the historical, narrative, and epistemological idiosyncrasies and instabilities of the region. Condé, he suggests, gives each of her witnesses' stories "equal bearing on the investigation" (71)—a betrayal of generic readerly expectations that speaks to the lived reality of the "(neo)colonial French Caribbean." Similarly, reading Chamoiseau, Herbeck suggests that "the inherent opacity and countless crimes of the colonial period render it [. . .] impossible to discount any particular narrative as false" (76).

35. Although, as previously discussed, outsider status can be narratively useful; recall Forrester's notion that the analyst's distance allows the patient to gossip about him- or herself. Standing apart from Venezuelan society gives Madigan an ability to tease apart and weave back together the countless narrative threads she hears through gossip, much as the detached analyst can help a patient find coherence and clarity in his or her own story.

36. Lorraine Code makes a similar point about the value of social knowledge derived from gossip. "If knowing other people were recognized as knowledge without which it would be virtually impossible to negotiate the world successfully, then it would not be so difficult to demonstrate the epistemic worth of gossip," she notes (147). Gossip's focus on the inner lives of others makes it a powerful investigative tool but also reveals its epistemic fragility. "In knowing other people, no one can claim absolute authority, not even the people who are allegedly known," Code concedes (xvi).

37. Brooks's thesis takes on a special charge in the Caribbean, where the body—and the desire to know, biblically and epistemically, the body—has so often been the locus of questions of power and domination. The Caribbean itself was viewed by Europeans, from the first moments of the discovery, with exoticizing and eroticizing eyes; this tendency, as Guillermina De Ferrari notes, left deep marks in the region's troubled history: "After all, much like conquest itself, sex often seeks to justify appropriation on the basis of knowledge of the Other, or

at least on the basis of the desire for such knowledge" (145). In the Caribbean, to speak of the body is necessarily to speak of colonialism, of slavery, and of the body's role in authoritarian power politics of punishment and domination.

3. "An International Scandal"

1. Besnier's *Gossip and the Everyday Production of Politics* (2009) proposes a focus on gossip's consequences rather than its mechanisms and structures, an approach that he argues "leads us to return to problems of power, resistance, and agency" (17). Gossip is "above all dangerous" (97) and can have consequences that include "ridicule, ostracism, or even death" (17); still, Besnier argues, it can also be co-opted and used by those with power and wealth, or those already so marginalized that gossip holds little fear for them.

2. As James Scott notes, "The character of gossip that distinguishes it from rumor is that gossip consists typically of stories that are designed to ruin the reputation of some identifiable person or persons" (*Domination* 142). Such a differentiation applies chiefly to the content disclosed; the rumormonger could still conceivably use the performative or linguistic markers of gossip.

3. Dalleo engages fruitfully with this point, describing the Caribbean public sphere as "part of a transnational negotiation of power relations" and exploring the tensions between globalization theory, empire studies, and postcolonial studies (227–28). Such theorizations are valuable but beyond the scope of this project; I will note only that I conceive of the Caribbean, and approach the question of the Caribbean public sphere, from a perspective more in keeping with Benítez-Rojo's notion of the Caribbean as a "meta-archipelago" that "has the virtue of lacking either boundary or center." Benítez-Rojo writes: "Thusly, the Caribbean outgrows and overflows its own ocean, and its ultima Thule can be found in Cádiz or Seville, in a Bombay suburb, in the low and rumor-filled shores of Gambia, in a Cantonese tavern of the 1850s, in a Balian temple, in a blackened Bristol dock, in a windmill by the Zuiderzee, in a warehouse of Colbert-era Bordeaux, in a Manhattan discotheque, and in the existential saudade of a Portuguese song" (18). This—globalized and without limits in its self-conception—is the Caribbean of which I write.

4. I follow Dolores M. Koch's translation, *Before Night Falls,* to which all parenthetical citations refer.

5. Arenas hews close to Sylvia Molloy's notion of the "autobiographer as gossip." As with Lucio V. Mansilla, of whom Molloy writes, there is "nothing self-effacing" about Arenas's literary persona. Molloy argues that Mansilla's first-person "I" is a gossip who "unremittingly commands attention; the substance of his story, while certainly not meaningless, pales before the display of the storyteller" (183). Much the same, clearly, could be said of Arenas.

6. Many critics have pointed out the falsehoods and exaggerations in Arenas's text. Delfín Prats, depicted as Hiram Pratt (or Hiram Prado in Koch's translation) in *Antes que anochezca,* calls Arenas "a great fabulist" whose work

cannot be read as truthful: "The things he attributed to me were really something. In his writing, everything is hyperbolized. [. . .] As testimony his writing fails" ("Yo tengo" 26). Names—real and pseudonymous—are used inconsistently across Arenas's work, both in the original and in Koch's translation: Arenas's text changes some names (the writer Miguel Barnet, for instance, is "Miguel Barniz" in *Antes que anochezca* but Miguel Barnet once more in Koch's translation), while leaving others (including Virgilio Piñera, José Lezama Lima, Alejo Carpentier, and Severo Sarduy). Interestingly, Arenas attributes Delfín Prats's *Lenguaje de mudos* (1969) to "Delfín Prats" and not to "Hiram Pratt," to whom Arenas refers on the same page.

7. Arenas describes his conviction as itself grounded in a kind of gossip: the *castrista* law under which homosexual acts are prosecuted, he writes, allows convictions to be made based on a single denunciation—essentially, on the basis of gossip rather than hard evidence. Similarly, the regime uses gossip to locate dissidents: it is Arenas's friend Hiram who, by chatting with acquaintances, seeks to learn his whereabouts in order to inform the authorities.

8. The use of gossip to construct and defend queer identity is not confined to the Caribbean. Lisa Kahaleole Chang Hall asserts that "gay identity is really founded on storytelling and gossip" and that to become part of a queer community is to become "embedded in a legendary network of gossip, tale-telling, and multiple interpretations of the same events" in which identity is continually performed and reasserted (229). See, too, Ryan Linkof's intriguing study of queer writers' co-option of the fledgling gossip columns of Edwardian England; Linkof suggests that privileged but marginalized gay men used their conflicted status to gain entry to, but also criticize and stand apart from, English high society.

9. Arenas's defiant sexual exuberance, commingled with gossip, in the face of an ossified authoritarian reality recalls Magdalena Perkowska-Alvarez's reading of gossip in *Margarita, está linda la mar* (1998), by the Nicaraguan writer Sergio Ramírez, as a carnivalesque exercise in narrative resistance. "Gossip can become an art of resistance, and a transgressive element, destabilizing official discourses and eternal and unquestionable truths," she writes. "Seen through this lens, the small stories of gossip contain enormous transgressive—which is to say, festive—potential" (266).

10. Throughout *Antes que anochezca,* however, Arenas insists that the works of "counterrevolutionary" writers circulated freely among Castro's allies and senior government officials. During his stay in the home of writer Norberto Fuentes—a stay orchestrated, if we are to believe Arenas, by the Seguridad del Estado—he is able to read Cabrera Infante's *Vista del amanecer en el trópico,* as well as "all kinds of literature unavailable to anyone in Cuba except officials in Fidel Castro's government" (225).

11. Arenas feared not just friends who became informants but all those whose loose tongues could cause trouble: "Even if he was not an informer," he writes about Reinaldo Gómez Ramos, "he was prone to gossip" (238).

12. Arenas comes to see Miami's exile community in particular as equivalent to "the worst of Cuba: the eternal gossip, the chicanery, the envy" (292) and to feel himself "surrounded by gossip and difficulties" (292) and living "in a state of constant paranoia" (293).

13. It would not have been the first time that US officials took note of Arenas's efforts; in a 1983 letter, Elliott Abrams, then assistant secretary of state for human rights and humanitarian affairs, urged the Immigration and Naturalization Service to allow Arenas to travel: "Given Arenas' demonstrated ability to speak and write about his life in Cuba and his new life in America, I believe that there is a strong public interest argument for his case. It is in our national interest that he be able to travel."

14. As Cabrera Infante notes, *Antes que anochezca* was transcribed, not typed, and is highly oral in its delivery, a last flurry of gossip before the light fades: "Written in a race against death, frequently not badly written but barely written: dictated, spoken, shouted, this book is his masterpiece" (*Mea Cuba antes y después* 922).

15. Not all gossip is testimony, and not all testimony is gossip. John Beverley defines *testimonio* as "a novel or novella-length narrative in book or pamphlet (that is, printed as opposed to acoustic) form, told in the first person by a narrator who is also the real protagonist or witness of the events he or she recounts, and whose unit of narration is usually a 'life' or a significant life experience" (30–31); such a reading would admit *Antes que anochezca* but exclude much if not all of Cabrera Infante's gossip. Axel Gelfert's *A Critical Introduction to Testimony* offers a reading of gossip as a "pathology of testimony" that can, but does not always, ascend to the level of true testimony (213); see also C. A. J. Coady's 2006 study, which informs Gelfert's reading.

16. Cabrera Infante cotranslated many of his works from Spanish into English, or vice versa, frequently changing details and adding puns. I use my own translations, with page references to *Mea Cuba antes y después* (MCAD), the latest and most authoritative edition of Cabrera Infante's essays, which includes *Mea Cuba* and *Vidas para leerlas*. Where Cabrera Infante's translations vary from the Spanish, I quote from Kenneth Hall's cotranslation of *Mea Cuba* (MC), which also incorporates essays originally published in *Vidas*. I also cite from the *London Review of Books*, where two of Cabrera Infante's essays—"Bites from the Bearded Crocodile" (BC) and "Infante's Inferno" (II)—were originally published in English; the latter is not to be confused with *Infante's Inferno* (1984), Cabrera Infante and Suzanne Jill Levine's cotranslation of *La Habana para un Infante difunto* (1979). These essays were subsequently translated into Spanish and included in *Mea Cuba* as "Mordidas del caimán barbudo" and "Los poetas a su rincón."

17. Will Corral makes a similar point in a review of *Mea Cuba,* noting that the text is "full of information, insight, and gossip" that adds up to a "Who's Who, What's What, Where's Where of contemporary Cuban letters"—not a work that everyone will agree with or approve of, but one that demonstrates that

"Cabrera Infante's knowledge of Cuban literariness is the broadest, liveliest, and nastiest to date" (342–43).

18. Hall's cotranslation holds that Cabrera Infante arranged Greene's "final" meeting with Castro, not his first (*MC* 295); Greene, for his part, denies that Cabrera Infante played any part in arranging his sole meeting with Castro, which took place in 1966. Cabrera Infante excuses the error with more name-dropping and another insult, stating that while Greene may not have been present on "that Havana night in 1959," he did introduce Castro to Alec Guinness, Carol Reed, and Noel Coward. "I must have confused them with each other and all of them with Graham Greene. But I have an excuse for that embarrassing gaffe. You see, for me then, all Englishmen looked alike," Cabrera Infante writes ("Letters: Cain's Cuba"). For a detailed overview of Greene's stay in Cuba while researching *Our Man in Havana* in 1957, and while preparing to shoot the subsequent film in 1959, see Peter Hulme's article "Graham Greene and Cuba: Our Man in Havana?" (2008).

19. In the Spanish, "*con su más cara máscara de pez abisal que nunca*"—literally, with a more expensive deep-sea fish mask than ever.

20. The use of gossip in oratory is neither a Caribbean innovation nor a modern one. Susan Phillips notes that medieval English priests "used gossip as a teaching tool, a device for holding the attention of their chattering congregations" (207).

21. Here and throughout, I follow Anglade's English text, given alongside the French, from *Rire haïtien* (2006).

22. For another famous example of the enduring power of silence both during and after Duvalier's rule, consider Marie Vieux Chauvet's decision to publish *Amour, colère et folie* in Paris in 1968. "Persecuted, terrorized by a hideous dictatorial regime, we find ourselves constrained to ruse in order to cry out the truth!" she wrote to Simone de Beauvoir. "It has been 10 years that we have waited, choked; it has been 10 years that Haitian novelists and poets have been silenced. Help me break this silence, please" (qtd. in Joseph 32). Chauvet's writing was intended as a blow against a regime that had already robbed her of a cousin (the poet Antonio Vieux, whom Duvalier boasted of having personally executed in Fort Dimanche) and two nephews (killed randomly in 1963 in the wake of a botched kidnapping attempt against Jean-Claude Duvalier). After the detention of other family members in 1968, Chauvet's family convinced her to withdraw and suppress *Amour, colère et folie*—and to continue to do so even after the end of the Duvaliers' rule, effectively reducing Chauvet's masterpiece to fodder for literary gossip. "Rumors circulated of family intrigues and political dramas that led to the persistent censorship of the trilogy," Thomas Spear writes. "Facts and anecdotes about this silencing generated contradictory myths" (14).

23. Anthony Phelps argues that young Haitians "close themselves off" by writing in Creole. "When they use Creole, they move themselves away from America, they shut themselves off from the rest of the new continent," he warns ("Anthony Phelps" 381).

24. See, for instance, Madelaine Hron's assertion that zombification is only possible because of a global cultural relativism due to which "the world refuses to recognize the horrors of Duvalier's regime" (164).

25. As Bernard Diederich notes, Greene protests too much: many of the characters in *The Comedians* are directly modeled upon real people and, Diederich claims, remain instantly recognizable to any reader—of whom, admittedly, there would have been very few—who moved in the Haitian and expatriate circles that Greene describes (107–11).

26. Greene names no names, but the account clearly refers to army rifleman François Benoit, who was accused on little evidence of mounting an attack on Duvalier's children, triggering brutal reprisals and an international crisis that came close to toppling Duvalier's regime, a story Greene recounts in "Nightmare Republic."

27. There is a knowingness and even an irony to Greene's use of such local color: Joseph, for instance, dryly proclaims himself an "ignorant man" (134) when pressed on locals' belief in Duvalier's use of corpses in religious rites, while the foreigners, who are largely shielded from Haiti's national tragedy, are presented as vain, inauthentic, and naive.

28. In this, Greene recalls Cabrera Infante who, as Kenneth E. Hall notes, channels classical gossips in his biographical works. "Plutarch and Suetonius, for example, are significant to *Mea Cuba*," he writes (394).

29. Duvalier's regime vested much of its claim to power in its embrace of folk religion, which served some of the same roles fulfilled by gossip in Cuba and the Dominican Republic, coming to constitute a two-way system of communication and surveillance. "Voudou is everywhere in Haiti. Penetrating the religion in a systematic manner was, therefore, a guaranteed way of communicating to or receiving information from the people," R. Anthony Lewis notes (46). See also Laguerre's assertion that Duvalier used gossip to circulate religious gossip about himself: "This served to enhance the regime's power. In a country like Haiti, what is important is not the veracity of these stories but whether they effectively project a certain image and perception of the government" (*Voodoo and Politics* 119).

30. Fox won £3,500 in the case, of which Greene had to pay £500 personally; the case didn't break the bank but did prompt Greene's flight to Mexico, where he wrote *The Power and the Glory* (1940). Greene's review, though scandalous at the time of its publication, has more recently been read as a perceptive early commentary on the risks associated with representing childhood in film; see, for instance, Kristen Hatch's *Shirley Temple and the Performance of Girlhood* (2015).

31. Another exaggeration: as Cabrera Infante notes, Greene told Castro he played Russian roulette only four times.

4. "Páginas en Blanco"

1. Bosch attributes the insight to Eugenio María de Hostos, the nineteenth-century Puerto Rican intellectual.

2. The tendency of political leaders to gossip, and thereby bolster their grasp on power, is a common thread running through the Caribbean's authoritarian regimes. Pedro Estrada records that under the dictator Marcos Pérez Jiménez, Venezuela was "a country of gossips." He continues: "Gossip in Venezuela has brought great problems, tragedies, catastrophes. It is far easier to handle gossip than information. It is easier to propagate, to repeat. I have seen many political heads fall as a result of gossip" (141). As described in chapter 3, the revolutionary government in Cuba also used gossip to gather intelligence and repress dissidents, while in Duvalier's Haiti gossip helped shape the regime's public image. The authoritarian preoccupation with gossip is not a uniquely Caribbean phenomenon: Augusto Pinochet used gossip and other "mysterious channels of information" to keep aides on their toes (see Pamela Constable and Arturo Valenzuela's *A Nation of Enemies*, 81), and even Napoleon, writing in 1809, urged his police chief to arrest rumormongers and plant agents to shape the gossip swirling on the streets (see E. K. Bramstedt's *Dictatorship and Political Police*, 22). Such gossip also leaves marks in dictatorship fiction from beyond the Caribbean: Augusto Roa Bastos's *Supremo* frets over pasquinades and gripes about "malignant rumors, gossip, chatter [. . .] which whispering scribes will repeat prolifically through the centuries" (56), while Daniel Sada's *Porque parece mentira la verdad nunca se sabe* (1999) shows an authoritarian regime crumbling until little remains but gossip.

3. Bosch continued to condemn gossip throughout his career. In 1993, he wrote: "Gossip is a Dominican invention not found in any other country in the world, and gossip consists in thinking false things and making them circulate, saying them, as though they are true or legitimate" (qtd. in Di Pietro 94).

4. Balaguer's irreverent tone contrasts with the hagiographies he perpetrated during Trujillo's lifetime. In his *Two Essays on Dominican History* (1955) Balaguer wrote that the "providential hand of Trujillo" had led to a period in which "the wonders of legends have been undone by the marvels of objective reality," with Trujillo working "miracles that are as portentous as those which, during the preceding four centuries, were worked solely through the intervention of supernatural powers in the nation's life" (22). Note, however, Derby's assertion that Balaguer's skill as a writer and orator allowed him to combine praise with subtle—yet, to his audience, pointed—criticism of Trujillo, using techniques such as substitution and synecdoche to raise concerns about the caudillo's actions ("Shadow" 331–33). The temptation to read Balaguer's gossip as his breaking silence after decades of restraint should be avoided: as his calculated contemporary criticism of Trujillo shows, Balaguer was acutely self-aware, and not given to making off-the-cuff comments or rattling off anecdotes without an ulterior motive.

5. For a more detailed reading of the role of the *Foro Público* and its successor, Radio Caribe, see the work of Lipe Collado, who brands the *Foro* a "monument of gossip" (55). Derby also notes that the *Foro Público* published not just denunciations but also retaliatory letters in defense of those accused. She further

records the use of anonymous government-published books attacking individuals, anonymous pasquinades sent to individuals by mail, and a cohort of "pens for hire" employed by Trujillo specifically to praise or slander people as they rose or fell in his favors ("Shadow" 298).

6. Abbes García, one of Trujillo's most brutal allies, published his own gossipy memoir, *Trujillo y yo: memorias de Johnny Abbes García*, in 2009.

7. Balaguer's stylized use of gossip is far from trivial; as Derby remarks, the official gossip of the Trujillo era became a kind of self-justifying practice, gaining potency through its own ambiguity: "As Vicente Rafael has said, 'Rumors . . . work by separating seeing from believing.' Indeed, denunciation wreaked havoc by doing just that: forging ruinous hearsay of unknown provenance and unlikely veracity that was believable only by virtue of its everyday style. [. . .] Denunciation gave gossip an official imprimatur and created the illusion that the accused were actually at fault" ("Shadow" 305–6). Balaguer's memoirs seek to replicate, through gossip, the rituals of denunciation deployed by Trujillo's regime.

8. At the time that *Memorias* was published, Balaguer was himself beginning to be the focus of confessional, tell-all accounts by former colleagues; see, for instance, *Balaguer y yo* (1986) by Ramón A. Font-Bernard, a former functionary in Balaguer's first administrations. Subsequent examples include *Balaguer y yo: La historia* (2006) by Víctor Gómez Bergés, a former minister of external affairs, and *Balaguer y yo: Testimonio de una amistad* (2003) by lawyer and ambassador Zoila Martínez de Medina. The similar titles, though coincidental, speak to the memoirists' drive to assert inside knowledge of the events they describe.

9. Néstor Rodriguez calls this episode "a dramatic example of the continuity of paternalism tied to the historic figure of Balaguer" and "an unprecedented decision in Dominican literary history" (15–16). As Silvio Torres-Saillant notes, the slight to Sención serves as a reminder that under Balaguer conservative social forces "had the power to name reality and to render the opposition mute[. . . .] There is no question as to who really has the last word" (*Dominican Blackness* 48).

10. Another warning against dismissing Sención's novel comes from Junot Díaz, who notes that the text "tangled with the legacies of Trujillo directly and explored the nightmare brought about by Joaquín Balaguer's regime. Sención is phenomenally important" (*Conversations with Ilan Stavans* 49).

11. Though, as Derby notes, such engagement was not always to the people's advantage. The *Foro Público,* she writes, "empowered citizens, since it appeared to include them in a new disciplinary apparatus that gave them the power to judge others, even while their participation in the Foro enabled the state to better police them as well." Though experienced as empowering, Derby argues, the *Foro Público* in fact served as what Foucault terms a "technology of power" or "mode of suspicion" ("Shadow" 316).

12. The *Times* also quotes Sención directly, noting his past access to Balaguer's family home. Sención seizes the opportunity to gossip: "It was a most strange and curious household," he recalls. "There were two female dwarfs, kept as

mascots but who to this day are part of his retinue, and a pair of aggressive collies that, when they bit you, you had no choice but to sit there and smile" (Rohter).

13. In *La mosca soldado* (2004), Marcio Veloz Maggiolo describes marimantas as "beings of indefinite form who emerge from the darkness of the night wrapped in a white sheet; slowly approaching spoiled children to cover them and take them away" (9). The parallels between the social-policing aspect of gossip and the disciplinary invocation of the marimanta are perhaps not coincidental. A further resonance lies in the derivation of Tonton Macoute from a Haitian folk tale, as Edwidge Danticat notes in her 1994 novel *Breath, Eyes, Memory:* "In the fairy tales, the *Tonton Macoute* was a bogeyman, a scarecrow with human flesh. [. . .] *If you don't respect your elders, then the Tonton Macoute will take you away.* Outside the fairy tales, they roamed the streets in broad daylight, parading their Uzi machine guns" (137). Gossip, both for Dominicans and Haitians, allegorizes risks that are very real.

14. An entire book could be dedicated to the connection between music and gossip in the Caribbean: as Gordon Rohlehr notes, the typical calypso protagonist is "a peeping Tom, a gossip or simply a reporter of incidents which he always claims to have personally witnessed. [. . .] The stereotype of the inquisitive and contentious neighbor becomes soundly established by calypsoes" (215). And gossip is a common thread running through not just calypso and merengue but also the mento of Jamaica, the tumba of Curaçao, the parang of Carriacou, the plena of Puerto Rico, the benna of Antigua, the combite songs of Haiti, and many of the region's other folk and popular musical forms. Given the profound role such music plays in Caribbean society—"it is only in the calypso that the Trinidadian touches reality," notes Naipaul (*Middle Passage* 66)—it is unsurprising that musical gossip often filters back into the region's literature. See, for instance, references to scandalous benna in Jamaica Kincaid's 1978 story "Girl"; Naipaul's *Miguel Street* (1959), which Kamal Mehta describes as "calypsos in prose, dealing with the local social life in Trinidad. [. . .] Like many real calypsos, these stories are based on anecdotes" (282); Earl Lovelace's *Is Just a Movie* (2011), which features a "true-true kaisonian" who boasts of being a "maker of confusion, recorder of gossip, destroyer of reputations, revealer of secrets" (5); and even Alejo Carpentier's conflation, in *El reino de este mundo* (1949), of "the symphonies of violins and the murmurations of slander, the gossip of their beloveds and the trilling of their captive birds" (14).

15. This was especially true for the working classes, for whom merengue served as a gateway to political news and public discourse. "The lyrics [. . .] served as news for people in poor neighborhoods," write Elizabeth Gackstetter Nichols and Timothy R. Robbins. "Merengue lyrics often communicated the reality of what was happening, people and events, to people too poor to afford a newspaper or a radio" (30).

16. As Fernando Valerio Holguín writes, Trujillo used merengue as a propaganda tool and means of revenging himself against Dominican elites. "From its

beginnings, merengue always had an epic character, and therefore a political one, as it narrated an anecdote, a heroic act, or an important event. [. . .] Trujillo made the most of the epic character of merengue and thus had merengues composed that extolled his deeds as though they were *cantares de gesta,*" or epic romances (103).

17. Danticat's *The Farming of Bones* (1998) also explores the Haitian massacre, using rumor to stage the uncertainty and powerlessness of the Haitian border dwellers. As Pramod K. Nayar notes, rumor maps the distrust between Haitians and Dominicans; a group of cane workers initially refuse an invitation to drink coffee with Señora Valencia, for example, because it is rumored that Dominicans are poisoning Haitians. Both threats and victims are "constructed within the fugitive discourse of hearsay, rumours and stories," Nayar writes (6). But Danticat's text also uses rumor and "talk" to stage the Haitians' disbelief and loss of agency: "I keep hearing it, but I don't know if all of it is true," says Sebastien (127). Later, Amabelle is warned that soldiers are approaching her home. "It couldn't be real. Rumors, I thought. There were always rumors, rumors of war[. . . .] This could not touch people like me," she insists (140). It is telling that the episodes are framed as unsourced rumors rather than gossip about specific individuals: the sense is of people caught up in historical currents they cannot fully fathom, with little ability to escape the approaching crisis. "I'd never let the rumors engage me. If they were true, it was something I could neither change nor control," Amabelle reflects (147). Only in hindsight do the rumors cohere into concrete testimonies: Amabelle reclaims a measure of agency by accepting a secondhand story as the truth about Sebastien's death. "I believed it because of what I had seen [. . .] because of what I had heard [. . .] because of what the people said" (241). After the uncertainty that marks the text's treatment of the massacre, her credulity is poignant and potent—a gesture against ahistoricity and an insistence that these stories, preserved through hearsay and testimony, can memorialize those who would otherwise "vanish like smoke into the early morning air" (280).

18. The word *leyenda* is also used in a different sense, to allude to stories pertaining to Vodou or magic, such as that of the dark rider who appears at the time of Lora's death. In such cases the word *leyenda* adheres more closely to its more typical Spanish association with the fantastical.

19. The notion of gossip flying from rooftop to rooftop recalls Veloz Maggiolo's 2006 short story "Nido de volanderas," which describes "flying witches" who reproduce without male assistance and carry political gossip around the Dominican Republic. Even though "they were excellent messengers," with the end of the country's internal wars they disappeared and "no longer go from province to province spreading gossip" (73–74).

20. The lack of clear distinction between rumor and other narrative forms has been acknowledged by other scholars. Patricia A. Turner writes that folklorists "often place rumors on a continuum with myth, folktale, contemporary legends, memorates as the genres within which they are considered. Sociologists often place rumor in conjunction with gossip, hearsay and anecdote" (Introduction 169).

21. Alzaga is modeled on Eulogio León, who conducted a similar exercise in genealogical manipulation at Trujillo's behest, and of whom Veloz Maggiolo writes in *La memoria fermentada* (2000). In a 2001 interview with José Carvajal, Veloz Maggiolo admits: "I never met Eulogio, so I invented him on the basis of fragmentary biographies and things that happened to several inhabitants of Villa Francisca" ("Memoria fermenta"). Veloz Maggiolo's admission to inventing parts of León's story dovetails with his comment elsewhere in *La memoria fermentada* that "the invention of memory is [. . .] a way to erase stubborn and squalid authentic memories. A novelist always tries to invent memories" (134). The act of writing fiction, in the narrative monopoly it implies and the imaginative liberties the author takes, echoes the pseudohistorical revisionism perpetrated by León and by the Trujillo regime more broadly. See Rita De Maeseneer's 2008 study for further discussion of this point.

22. Mejía learns his lesson and seeks revenge through gossip of his own: "It is said that he too was among those who carried reports to the authorities about Honorio's lyrics" (61).

23. Given merengue's ability to disseminate criticism, Sellers writes, "Both musician and instrument become dangerous weapons for the dictator as well as those who oppose him in the novel. For Lora, his accordion is his weapon of choice" (14).

24. Music allows the transmutation of street gossip into something more durable. Jeremy Verity notes the preservation of centuries-old gossip in still-current songs: "There are mentos that go back over 200 years, and the news and gossip in them is sometimes very old. I've heard one in the Jamaican Blue Mountains that I am told is about Admiral Lord Nelson's affair with Lady Hamilton, which must have been on every lip in late eighteenth-century Jamaica. British governors and administrators, lawyers and preachers, good and bad, are all pictured in these songs" (185).

25. Alzaga's attack on forgetting offers a counterpoint to Renan's claim, examined in chapter 2, that forgetting is critical for constructions of nation. Of course, Alzaga's revisionism is itself a form of forgetting, designed to unify the nation around a state-approved version of the past and of Dominican identity.

26. It is telling that so much of *Oscar Wao*'s gossip is transmitted through footnotes. For T. S. Miller, the footnotes provide "an outlet for Yunior's historiographical impulse: his secret history becomes marginal in multiple ways, a history told from the margins and in the margins" (96). This impulse, though introduced in gossipy footnotes, comes to dominate the text. Miller continues: "The whole novel becomes a sort of not-so-secret history, complete with all the scandalous gossip and outrageous hyperbole of the original *Anecdota (Secret History)* by Procopius" (97).

27. Yunior alludes not only to the challenges of historicity in the post-Trujillo era but also to the limits of narration itself. La Inca and Belicia never discuss the girl's abuse, which becomes their "very own página en blanco" (78), a veil behind

which Yunior cannot peer. More intriguingly, Beli's bizarre, otherworldly mongoose vision is also presented as beyond the scope of Yunior's narratorial authority. "Even your Watcher has his silences, his páginas en blanco," he admits (149).

28. Erica Wickerson notes a similar process at work in Thomas Mann's *Doktor Faustus,* suggesting that the novel's style of narration "implicitly resembles the dialogic form of gossip," with the reader "unavoidably" becoming Zeitblom's confidant (212–13). Wickerson also ponders the destructive and adversarial aspects of gossip in relation to Germany's troubled history; in revealing "gossip as a tool for revenge and for blame" (224), she suggests, Mann presents literature itself as "more useful as a mode of working through conflicting interpretations of a traumatic past than it is as a reliable representation of that past" (225). For a fuller exploration of the seductions of Yunior's slippery narrative strategy, see T. S. Miller (100) and Elena Machado Sáez (162, 175).

29. Rafael Rojas argues that all states—democracies and authoritarian regimes alike—rely for their legitimacy upon "historiographic consensuses" ("Legitimidad e historia" 21); the difference is that in free societies consensus emerges from a plurality of sources, while in totalitarian states the government enforces a predetermined consensus derived only from approved sources. In such contexts, acts of political dissent, as well as moral offenses, are brought into the spectrum of transgressions scrutinized and regulated by gossip. See also Helen Lima de Sousa for a discussion of state-sponsored gossip in Brazil.

30. In *The Spiral of Silence,* political scientist Elisabeth Noelle-Neumann interrogates the connections between slander and gossip: "The boundary between slander and gossip is fluid. When does talking with disapproval about someone who is absent cease to be mere opinion? Reputations are destroyed, characters assassinated, honor brought into disrepute and disgrace; it becomes taboo to be seen in that person's presence" (120–21). Derby explores similar ground, noting that "during the Rafael Trujillo regime in the Dominican Republic, slander against regime insiders was used as a means of social control" ("Beyond Fugitive Speech" 125).

31. As Dorrit Cohn points out, historical accounts tend to be concerned with broad trends and epic battles, not the details and drudgery of daily lives or even the specific terrors and tragedies experienced by individuals as historically momentous events unfurl. "History is more often concerned with collective 'mentalities' than with individual minds," Cohn notes, giving rise to "the massive prevalence of summary over scene in historical narration" (121). Díaz's deployment of gossip, in concerning itself with individuals and their actions, clearly favors, and meticulously stages, what Cohn calls scenes.

32. The role of literature in the reclamation of the Dominican Republic's deleted histories has been remarked elsewhere. Mónica G. Ayuso suggests that the 1937 massacre was so thoroughly purged from the historical record that it "was an event reduced to silence and imprecision" until it was reclaimed and restored to public consciousness in the 1990s by writers such as Edwidge Danticat, Rita Dove, and Julia Álvarez (47).

33. Díaz breaks with the authoritative mode of storytelling used by Mario Vargas Llosa in *La fiesta del chivo* (2000) and aligns himself with the "narrative fragmentation and uncertain allegory" that Adam Lifshey traces in works such as Freddy Prestol Castillo's *El Masacre se pasa a pie* (1973) and Bosch's 1960 short story "La mancha indeleble" (436). Díaz himself notes, in *Oscar Wao* and elsewhere, that the all-powerful author resembles a dictator, and his suspicion of definitive versions is surely marked by this awareness. As Lifshey writes, "a text that slips out of discursive control, that offers itself willingly to interpretation, that is self-contradictory and ruptured, and uncertain rather than consistent and coherent and comprehensive—this may be the most fundamental disputation of any dictator's dominance over word and thought" (454–55).

34. In this, Díaz's narrative project resonates with Derby's call for the admittance of "fugitive speech such as rumor, gossip, and hearsay as primary sources for Caribbean historical research" ("Beyond Fugitive Speech" 124). "Bringing unsanctioned speech forms into the writing of Caribbean history could help put back into history-writing popular agency and instrumentality," Derby writes. "More than that, everyday speech genres such as rumor, gossip, and hearsay also enable one to capture a staple of everyday experience that in all of its disorderly interruption challenges the 'univocity of statist discourse'" (139).

35. The historiography of the Galíndez incident would make a compelling study in its own right: the details surrounding Galíndez's abduction remain hazy, and much of what has gradually entered the public record has done so through rumor and gossip. After the event, Dominicans "whispered the details of Galíndez's torture," notes Stuart A. McKeever in *The Galíndez Case,* and these rumors entered the historical record circuitously through, for example, the relayed gossip of FBI informers. "You pick these stories up bit by bit; you ask no questions for fear of your life," one such informer told the bureau, along with a detailed account of Galíndez's final moments (87).

36. That what is presented as legend contains traces of or structural similarities to gossip recalls the significant body of research, chiefly in the field of social psychology, that suggests legend itself can be understood as calcified rumor, and as a form in dialogue with less fixed discourses such as rumor and gossip. See, for instance, Gordon W. Allport and Leo Postman's framing of legend as "solidified rumor" (162) or Patrick B. Mullen's suggestion that "some legends become rumors and some rumors become legends" (98). Derby, meanwhile, perceptively notes that both "gossip and rumor are rough drafts of what *might* become a genre—an autobiography, a story, a legend, or a tale—and they are conveyed with hesitancy so that they are not taken as codified statements of fact" ("Beyond Fugitive Speech" 131).

37. Although, as seen in the second chapter, the connection between gossip and epistemology has been explored by scholars in other fields—notably philosophy—and has also been fruitfully explored by Caribbean writers. Indeed, there are resonances between Yunior's project and Gloria's attempt, in *Maldito*

amor, to supplant a master narrative with her own account. Still, where Gloria seeks to impose her own univocal narrative, Yunior is more open to accepting the need for plurality and multivocality.

38. Jan Gordon hints at this, noting that gossip is "a semiotic reminder that all information is in a sense already mediated, that all listeners are prey to a previous dialogic encounter to which all are late, whose sources we can never recover[. . . .] Gossip is always belated, always attempting to recover some original information, or an original account, yet hopelessly bound to the intransitive domain of the self-supplanting 'version'" (59). In the Dominican context, gossip's secondhand, revisionary striving becomes a means of troubling monolithic or totalitarian narratives: in emphasizing its own truth status at the expense of an existing narrative, gossip reveals the fragility of such claims and foregrounds the possibility and necessity of other versions of the past.

39. This aspect of gossip resonates with Linda Hutcheon's concept of historiographic metafiction, which "like postmodernist architecture and painting, is overtly and resolutely historical—though, admittedly, in an ironic and problematic way that acknowledges that history is not the transparent record of any sure 'truth'" (10).

40. There are parallels in this to the all-seeing "Public Eye"—a kind of counterpoint to Díaz's eye of Sauron—that Glen Perice discerns as shaping public discourse and mediating violent reprisals in post-Duvalier Haiti. "The Public Eye in Haiti is the memory of political violence. The Public Eye is an allegorical reference to seeing and remembering. [. . .] In the stories and rumors of the killings, memories were ignited and fanned. [. . .] People had kept accounts and revenge in their heads for many years" ("Public Eye" 255).

41. Walsh perceives that the "conceit of the journal allows Mars to inflect the fiction of her novel with historical facts" (73); true, but the novel as a whole is written with a similar aim, with gossip about events that Mars suggests really happened serving to blur the lines between fact and fiction. The same "crossing of boundaries [. . .] from private to public, past to present, and from psychological to allegorical modes" that Walsh perceives as "central to the idea of literature as a means of reconstruction" (72) is also, after all, a critical aspect of the mechanics of gossip.

42. This motif is interesting when read in relation to Mars's *L'heure hybride* (2005), which similarly explores the interplay between the personal and the political. The protagonist, Rico, foregrounds a secret that he keeps from the reader until the last pages of the novel, in a move that Lindsey Scott reads as establishing "a tension between the intimacy and seduction of the first-person voice and the mistrust engendered through the keeping of secrets" (546). The keeping of secrets becomes a gesture of both narrative and sexual agency in the face of authoritarianism, much as it is gossip, *télédiol,* that ultimately affirms for Rico "that the beautiful dictatorial machine is breaking down" (*L'heure hybride* 106). The destabilization of the state finally allows Rico to assert his own homosexuality; as with

Nirvah, his body is a contested space over which he struggles to assert control. "Since the Duvaliers used sexual violence so extensively during their regimes, the body became a unique place for resistance," Scott writes (548).

43. It is significant that Nirvah's initial use of gossip to track down Daniel is described in transactional terms: "Each item of information is paid for with cash or with insomnia" (11). All the characters in Mars's novel—Nirvah and Raoul, but also Arlette, Marie, Solange, and the gossiping neighbors—are presented as compromised and self-serving. Duvalier's revolution, in Mars's telling, corrodes the bonds of community and makes Haitians into cynical survivors, for whom even basic acts of neighborliness come with a price tag.

44. The parentage of Marie's baby is an open question. Both Anthony and Raoul use gossip about Marie's sexual partners to absolve themselves of responsibility for the pregnancy. When Nirvah, assuming Raoul to be the father, asks Marie whose baby it was, she considers the question a critical test: "Will she tell me the truth? [. . .] Who is this young woman, the fruit of my loins?" (283). In fact, Marie tells Nirvah that the father was Ziky, her imaginary friend.

Works Cited

Abbes García, Johnny. *Trujillo y yo: memorias de Johnny Abbes García*. Edited by Orlando Inoa. Santo Domingo: Letra Gráfica, 2009.
Abrahams, Roger D. *The Man-of-Words in the West Indies: Performance and the Emergence of Creole Culture*. Baltimore: Johns Hopkins University Press, 1983.
Abrams, Elliott. Letter to the US Immigration and Naturalization Service, January 11, 1983. Reinaldo Arenas Papers, box 23, folder 1. Manuscripts Division, Department of Rare Books and Special Collections, Princeton University Library.
Acosta Cruz, María. *Dream Nation: Puerto Rican Culture and the Fictions of Independence*. New Brunswick, NJ: Rutgers University Press, 2014.
Adkins, Karen C. "The Real Dirt: Gossip and Feminist Epistemology." *Social Epistemology* 16, no. 3 (2002): 215–32.
Agard, John. "Listen Mr Oxford Don." In *Mangoes and Bullets: Selected and New Poems, 1972–1984*. 1985. Reprint, London: Serpent's Tail, 1990. 44.
Albrechtslund, Anders. "Online Social Networking as Participatory Surveillance." *First Monday* 13, no. 3 (2008). http://dx.doi.org/10.5210/fm.v13i3.2142.
Allatson, Paul. *Latino Dreams: Transcultural Traffic and the U.S. National Imaginary*. Amsterdam: Rodopi, 2002.
Allport, Gordon W., and Leo Postman. *The Psychology of Rumor*. New York: Henry Holt, 1947.
Alonso, Carlos. "Writing and Ritual in *Chronicle of a Death Foretold*." In *Gabriel García Márquez: New Readings*, edited by Bernard McGuirk and Richard Andrew Cardwell. Cambridge: Cambridge University Press, 1987. 151–68.
Alva, Martín [Rafael Martínez Alvarez]. *La ciudad chismosa y calumniante*. San Juan: Imprenta Venezuela, 1926.
Anglade, Georges. *Rire haïtien: Les Lodyans de Georges Anglade / Haitian Laughter: A Mosaic of Ninety Miniatures in French and English*. Bilingual edition translated by Anne Pease McConnell. Coconut Creek: Educa Vision, 2006.
Arenas, Reinaldo. *Antes que anochezca*. 1992. Reprint, Barcelona: Tusquets Editores, 2010.

———. *Before Night Falls.* Translated by Dolores M. Koch. 1993. Reprint, New York: Penguin, 1994.
Asturias, Miguel Ángel. *El señor presidente.* Edited by Alejandro Lanoël-d'Aussenac. 8th ed. Madrid: Cátedra, 2009.
Avila, Leopoldo. "Las respuestas de Caín." *Verde olivo* 6, no. 44 (November 3, 1968): 17–18. Reprint in *El caso Padilla: Literatura y revolución en Cuba, Documentos,* edited by Lourdes Casal. Miami: Ediciones Nueva Atlántida, 1971. 20–24.
Ayim, Maryann. "Knowledge through the Grapevine: Gossip as Inquiry." In *Good Gossip,* edited by Robert F. Goodman and Aaron Ben-Ze'ev. Lawrence: University Press of Kansas, 1994. 85–99.
Ayuso, Mónica G. "How Lucky for You That Your Tongue Can Taste the 'R' in 'Parsley': Trauma Theory and the Literature of Hispaniola." *Afro-Hispanic Review* 30, no. 1 (2011): 47–62.
Bailey, Carol. "Performing 'Difference': Reading Gossip in Olive Senior's Short Stories." In *Constructing Vernacular Culture in the Trans-Caribbean,* edited by Holger Henke and Karl-Heinz Magister. Lanham, MD: Lexington Books, 2008. 123–38.
Bailey, Winston. "Gossiping." *Dingolay!* Kiskidee Records, 1994.
Balaguer, Joaquín. *Memorias de un cortesano de la "era de Trujillo."* 10th ed. 1988. Reprint, Santo Domingo: Papelería Impresora Sierra, 1989.
———. *Two Essays on Dominican History.* Ciudad Trujillo: Editora del Caribe, 1955.
Barros, Sandro. "The Self as an Act of Message and Reinaldo Arenas's *Antes que anochezca.*" *Dissidences: Hispanic Journal of Theory and Criticism* 2, no. 4 (2008): 1–19.
Barthes, Roland. *Fragments d'un discours amoureux.* Paris: Éditions du Seuil, 1977.
Bejel, Emilio. *Gay Cuban Nation.* Chicago: University of Chicago Press, 2001.
Benítez-Rojo, Antonio. *La isla que se repite.* Barcelona: Editorial Casiopea, 1998.
Benjamin, Walter. "Karl Kraus." In *Walter Benjamin: Selected Writings,* vol. 2, part 2, 1931–1934, edited by Michael W. Jennings, Howard Eiland, and Gary Smith, translated by Rodney Livingstone and others. Cambridge, MA: Harvard University Press, 1999. 433–58.
Bennett, Louise. "Bed-Time Story." In *Selected Poems,* edited by Mervyn Morris. 1982. Reprint, Kingston: Sangster's Book Stores, 1983. 6.
———. "Colonisation in Reverse." In *Jamaica Labrish.* Kingston: Sangster's Book Stores, 1966. 179–80.
Bercoff, Brigitte. "Le tout premier cancan du monde." In *Potins, cancans et littérature: Actes du colloque de Perpignan, 24 au 26 novembre 2004,* edited by Nathalie Solomon and Anne Chamayou. Perpignan: Presses Universitaires de Perpignan, 2006. 17–30.

Bernard, Louise. "Countermemory and Return: Reclamation of the (Postmodern) Self in Jamaica Kincaid's *The Autobiography of My Mother and My Brother.*" *Modern Fiction Studies* 48, no. 1 (2002): 113–38.

Bertolotti, Tommaso, and Lorenzo Magnani. "An Epistemological Analysis of Gossip and Gossip-Based Knowledge." *Synthese* 191, no. 17 (2014): 4037–67.

Besnier, Niko. "Gossip." In *Encyclopedia of Cultural Anthropology*, vol. 2, edited by David Levinson and Melvin Ember. New York: Henry Holt, 1996. 544–47.

———. *Gossip and the Everyday Production of Politics*. Honolulu: University of Hawai'i Press, 2009.

Beverley, John. *Testimonio: On the Politics of Truth*. Minneapolis: University of Minnesota Press, 2004.

Bhabha, Homi K. *The Location of Culture*. 1994. Reprint, New York: Routledge, 2009.

Bird, S. Elizabeth. *Audience in Everyday Life: Living in a Media World*. New York: Routledge, 2003.

Birkenmaier, Anke. "La Habana y sus otros: Presencias fantasmagóricas en *La fiesta vigilada* de Antonio José Ponte y *La neblina del ayer* de Leonardo Padura." In *Cultura y letras cubanas en el siglo XXI*, edited by Araceli Tinajero. Madrid: Iberoamericana Vervuert, 2010. 245–58.

Bleek, Wolf. "Witchcraft, Gossip and Death: A Social Drama." *Man* 11, no. 4 (1976): 526–41.

Bloch, Abraham P. *A Book of Jewish Ethical Concepts: Biblical and Postbiblical*. New York: KTAV, 1984.

Boisseron, Bénédicte. "The Indirect Language of Love: Creole Fragments of a Lover's Discourse." *Australian Journal of French Studies* 47, no. 3 (2010): 253–65.

Borges, Jorge Luis. *Obras completas*. 4 vols. Barcelona: Emecé Editores, 1996.

Bosch, Juan. *Crisis de la democracia de América en la República Dominicana*. 1964. Reprint, as supplement to *Panoramas*, no. 14. Mexico City: Centro de Estudios y Documentación Sociales, 1965.

Bougerol, Christiane. *Une ethnographie des conflits aux Antilles: Jalousie, commérages, sorcellerie*. Paris: Presses Universitaires de France, 1997.

Bouson, J. Brooks. *Jamaica Kincaid: Writing Memory, Writing Back to the Mother*. Albany: State University of New York Press, 2005.

Braham, Persephone. *Crimes against the State, Crimes against Persons: Detective Fiction in Cuba and Mexico*. Minneapolis: University of Minnesota Press, 2004.

Bramstedt, E. K. *Dictatorship and Political Police: The Technique of Control by Fear*. 1945. Reprint, Abingdon: Routledge, 2007.

Brathwaite, Edward Kamau. *The Arrivants: A New World Trilogy*. Previously published as *Rights of Passage*, 1967; *Islands*, 1968; and *Masks*, 1969. Oxford: Oxford University Press, 1973.

———. "Metaphors of Underdevelopment: A Proem for Hernan Cortez." In "The Caribbean." Special issue, *New England Review and Bread Loaf Quarterly* 7, no. 4 (1985): 453–76.

———. *The Development of Creole Society in Jamaica, 1770–1820*. Oxford: Oxford University Press, 1971.

Britten, Benjamin, and Montagu Slater. *Peter Grimes*. Compact disc. Performed by the Royal Opera House Chorus and Orchestra, Covent Garden. 1958. Reissued, Decca, 2001.

Britton, Celia M. *Edouard Glissant and Postcolonial Theory: Strategies of Language and Resistance*. Charlottesville: University Press of Virginia, 1999.

———. *The Sense of Community in French Caribbean Fiction*. Liverpool: Liverpool University Press, 2010.

Brooks, Peter. *Body Work: Objects of Desire in Modern Narrative*. Cambridge, MA: Harvard University Press, 1993.

———. *Reading for the Plot: Design and Intention in Narrative*. 1984. Reprint, Cambridge, MA: Harvard University Press, 1992.

Browne, Simone. *Dark Matters: On the Surveillance of Blackness*. Durham, NC: Duke University Press, 2015.

Bryce, Jane. "'Who No Know Go Know': Popular Fiction in Africa and the Caribbean." In *The Novel in Africa and the Caribbean since 1950*, edited by Simon Gikandi. Oxford: Oxford University Press, 2016. 217–35.

Butterworth, Emily. *The Unbridled Tongue: Babble and Gossip in Renaissance France*. Oxford: Oxford University Press, 2016.

Cabrera, Lydia. *Anagó: vocabulario lucumí. (El yoruba que se habla en Cuba.)* Miami: Ediciones Universal, 1986.

———. "Historia verdadera de un viejo pordiosero que decía llamarse Mampurias." In *Cuentos para adultos niños y retrasados mentales*. Miami: Colección del Chicherekú en el exilio, 1983. 72–88.

Cabrera Infante, Guillermo. "Bites from the Bearded Crocodile." *London Review of Books* 3, no. 10 (June 4, 1981). Accessed May 10, 2016. https://www.lrb.co.uk/v03/n10/g-cabrera-infante/bites-from-the-bearded-crocodile.

———. *La Habana para un Infante difunto*. Barcelona: Editorial Seix Barral, 1979.

———. "Infante's Inferno." *London Review of Books* 4, no. 21 (November 18, 1982). Accessed May 10, 2016. https://www.lrb.co.uk/v04/n21/g-cabrera-infante/infantes-inferno.

———. *Infante's Inferno*. Translated by Guillermo Cabrera Infante and Suzanne Jill Levine. 1984. Reprint, Champaign, IL: Dalkey Archive, 2005.

———. Letter to Alberto Cellario, January 3, 1968. Guillermo Cabrera Infante Papers, box 13, folder 1. Manuscripts Division, Department of Rare Books and Special Collections, Princeton University Library.

———. Letter to Emir Rodríguez Monegal, July 10, 1981. Emir Rodríguez Monegal Papers, series 1, box 4, folder 3–4. Manuscripts Division, Department of Rare Books and Special Collections, Princeton University Library.

———. "Letters: Cain's Cuba." *London Review of Books* 5, no. 2 (February 3, 1983). Accessed May 5, 2016. https://www.lrb.co.uk/v05/n02/letters#letter10.

———. *Mea Cuba*. 1992. Reprint, Madrid: Alfaguara, 1999.

———. *Mea Cuba*. Translated by Kenneth Hall with Guillermo Cabrera Infante. New York: Faber and Faber, 1994.

———. *Mea Cuba antes y después*. Vol. 2 of *Obras Completas*, edited by Antoni Munné. Barcelona: Galaxia Gutenberg, 2015.

———. *Vidas para leerlas*. 1992. Reprint, Madrid: Extra Alfaguara, 1998.

———. *Vista del amanecer en el trópico*. 1981. Reprint, Madrid: Mondadori España, 1987.

Caistor, Nick. "Recovering the Power of Words." *Index on Censorship* 17, no. 3 (1988): 7–9.

Carpentier, Alejo. *El reino de este mundo*. 1949. Reprint, San Juan: Editorial de la Universidad de Puerto Rico, 2006.

Carrión, Ulises. *Lilia Prado superestrella (y otros chismes)*. Edited by Juan G. Agius. Translated by Heriberto Yépez. 2nd ed. Mexico City: Tumbona Ediciones / Consejo Nacional para la Cultura y las Artes, 2015.

Cervantes Saavedra, Miguel de. *El coloquio de los perros*. Barcelona: Red ediciones, 2017.

Chaljub Mejía, Rafael. "El valor del Merengue Típico y la importancia nacional de su preservación." In *El merengue en la cultura dominicana y del Caribe: Memorias del Primer Congreso Internacional Música, Identidad y Cultura en el Caribe*, edited by Darío Tejeda and Rafael Emilio Yunén. Santo Domingo: Instituto de Estudios Caribeños, 2006. 165–72.

Chamoiseau, Patrick. *Chronique des sept misères*. Paris: Gallimard, 1986.

———. *Solibo magnifique*. Paris: Gallimard, 1988.

Chaucer, Geoffrey. *The Canterbury Tales*. Translated by Burton Raffel. New York: Modern Library, 2008.

Chemla, Yves. "Kettly Mars, *Saisons sauvages*." *Le Nouvelliste*, January 6, 2010. Accessed January 16, 2017. http://lenouvelliste.com/lenouvelliste/article/80158/Kettly-Mars-Saisons-sauvages.

Cilano, Cara N. *Contemporary Pakistani Fiction in English: Idea, Nation, State*. Abingdon: Routledge, 2013.

Cliff, Michelle. *No Telephone to Heaven*. 1987. Reprint, New York: Plume, 1996.

Clifford, James. *The Predicament of Culture: Twentieth-Century Ethnography, Literature, and Art*. Cambridge, MA: Harvard University Press, 1988.

Coady, C. A. J. "Pathologies of Testimony." In *The Epistemology of Testimony*, edited by Jennifer Lackey and Ernest Sosa. Oxford: Oxford University Press, 2006. 253–71.

Code, Lorraine. *Rhetorical Spaces: Essays on Gendered Locations*. New York: Routledge, 1995.

Cohn, Dorrit. *The Distinction of Fiction*. Baltimore: Johns Hopkins University Press, 2000.

Collado, Lipe. *El Foro Público en la Era de Trujillo: De cómo el chisme fue elevado a la categoría de asunto de estado*. 2nd ed. Santo Domingo: Editora Collado, 2000.
Collins, Merle. "Crick Crack." 1992. Reprint, *Conjunctions* 27 (1996): 193–96.
Condé, Maryse. *Célanire cou-coupé: roman fantastique*. Paris: Robert Laffont, 2000.
———. *La civilisation du bossale: réflexions sur la littérature orale de la Guadeloupe et de la Martinique*. Paris: Éditions L'Harmattan, 1978.
———. "A Conversation at Princeton with Maryse Condé." In *Feasting on Words: Maryse Condé, Cannibalism and the Caribbean Text*, edited by Vera Broichhagen, Kathryn Lachman, and Nicole Simek. Translated by Katherine Lachman and Nicole Simek. Princeton, NJ: PLAS Cuadernos, 2006. 1–28.
———. *Traversée de la mangrove*. Paris: Mercure de France, 1989.
Confiant, Raphaël. *Le meurtre du Samedi-Gloria*. Paris: Mercure de France, 1997.
Constable, Pamela, and Arturo Valenzuela. *A Nation of Enemies: Chile under Pinochet*. New York: Norton, 1991.
Cooper, Carolyn. "'Something Ancestral Recaptured': Spirit Possession as Trope in Selected Feminist Fictions of the African Diaspora." In *Motherlands: Black Women's Writing from Africa, the Caribbean, and South Asia*, edited by Susheila Nasta. New Brunswick, NJ: Rutgers University Press, 1992. 64–87.
Coover, Robert. "The Gossip on the Wall." *New York Times*, November 11, 1979. Accessed September 17, 2016. http://www.nytimes.com/books/97/06/15/reviews/marque-evil.html.
Coromines, Joan. *Breve diccionario etimológico de la lengua castellana*. 3rd ed. Madrid: Editorial Gredos, 2008.
Corral, Will H. "Review: Mea Cuba by Guillermo Cabrera Infante." *World Literature Today* 67, no. 2 (1993): 342–43.
Cortázar, Julio. Letter to Cabrera Infante, March 10, 1967. Guillermo Cabrera Infante Papers, box 12, folder 12. Manuscripts Division, Department of Rare Books and Special Collections, Princeton University Library.
Cortés, Jason. *Macho Ethics: Masculinity and Self-Representation in Latino-Caribbean Narrative*. Lewisburg, PA: Bucknell University Press, 2015.
Counter, Andrew J. *The Amorous Restoration: Love, Sex, and Politics in Early Nineteenth-Century France*. Oxford: Oxford University Press, 2016.
Cozarinsky, Edgardo. *Nuevo museo del chisme*. Buenos Aires: La Bestia Equilátera, 2013.
Cudjoe, Selwyn. "Jamaica Kincaid and the Modernist Project: An Interview." *Callaloo* 12, no. 2 (1989): 396–411.
Dabove, Juan Pablo. "Los pasquines como alegoría de la disolución de la ciudadanía en *La mala hora* de Gabriel García Márquez." *Revista de Crítica Literaria Latinoamericana* 26, no. 52 (2000): 269–87.
Dalleo, Raphael. *Caribbean Literature and the Public Sphere: From the Plantation to the Postcolonial*. Charlottesville: University of Virginia Press, 2011.

Danticat, Edwidge. *Breath, Eyes, Memory.* 1994. Reprint, New York: Soho, 2015.
———. *The Farming of Bones.* 1998. Reprint, New York: Penguin, 1999.
Dash, J. Michael. "Engagement, Exile and Errance: Some Trends in Haitian Poetry 1946–1986." *Callaloo* 15, no. 3 (1992): 747–60.
———. "Exile and Recent Literature." In *A History of Literature in the Caribbean,* vol. 1, *Hispanic and Francophone Regions,* edited by A. James Arnold, Julio Rodríguez-Luis, and J. Michael Dash. Amsterdam: John Benjamins, 1994. 451–61.
———. *Haiti and the United States: National Stereotypes and the Literary Imagination.* 2nd ed. Basingstoke: Macmillan, 1997.
———. *Literature and Ideology in Haiti, 1915–1961.* London: Macmillan, 1981.
———. *The Other America: Caribbean Literature in a New World Context.* Charlottesville: University Press of Virginia, 1998.
Davidson, Arnold E. *Jean Rhys.* New York: F. Ungar, 1985.
De Ferrari, Guillermina. *Vulnerable States: Bodies of Memory in Contemporary Caribbean Fiction.* Charlottesville: University of Virginia Press, 2007.
De Maeseneer, Rita. "¿Cómo (dejar de) narrar el (neo)trujillato?" In *Aproximaciones a la literatura dominicana,* edited by Rei Berroa. Santo Domingo: Banco Central de la República Dominicana, 2008. 221–49.
De Moya, E. Antonio. "Power Games and Totalitarian Masculinity in the Dominican Republic." In *Interrogating Caribbean Masculinities: Theoretical and Empirical Analyses,* edited by Rhoda Reddock. Kingston: University of the West Indies Press, 2004. 68–102.
Derby, Lauren. "Beyond Fugitive Speech: Rumor and Affect in Caribbean History." *Small Axe* 18, no. 2 (2014): 123–40.
———. *The Dictator's Seduction: Politics and the Popular Imagination in the Era of Trujillo.* Durham, NC: Duke University Press, 2009.
———. "In the Shadow of the State: The Politics of Denunciation and Panegyric during the Trujillo Regime in the Dominican Republic, 1940–1958." *Hispanic American Historical Review* 83, no. 2 (2003): 295–344.
Devonish, Hubert. "The Decay of Neo-colonial Official Language Policies: The Case of the English-Lexicon Creoles of the Commonwealth Caribbean." In *Focus on the Caribbean,* edited by Manfred Görlach and John A. Holm. Amsterdam: J. Benjamins, 1986. 23–51.
Díaz, Junot. "Driven: Junot Díaz." Interview with Ilan Stavans. In *Conversations with Ilan Stavans,* by Ilan Stavans. Tucson: University of Arizona Press, 2005. 47–51.
———. *The Brief Wondrous Life of Oscar Wao.* New York: Riverhead Books, 2007.
———. "*The Brief Wondrous Life of Oscar Wao:* Questions for Junot Díaz." Interview with Meghan O'Rourke, *Slate,* November 8, 2007. Accessed October 5, 2014. http://www.slate.com/articles/news_and_politics/the_highbrow/2007/11/the_brief_wondrous_life_of_oscar_wao.html.

———. "'EE UU tiene pesadillas en español.'" Interview with Eduardo Lago. *El país,* May 1, 2008. Accessed October 19, 2014. http://elpais.com/diario/2008/05/01/cultura/1209592801_850215.html.

Dictionary of Caribbean English Usage. Edited by Richard Allsopp, with a French and Spanish supplement edited by Jeannette Allsopp. 1996. Reprint, Kingston: University of the West Indies Press, 2003.

Diederich, Bernard. *Seeds of Fiction: Graham Greene's Adventures in Haiti and Central America, 1954–1963.* London: Peter Owen, 2012.

Diederich, Bernard, and Al Burt. *Papa Doc: The Truth about Haiti Today.* New York: McGraw-Hill, 1969.

Di Pietro, Giovanni. *Lecturas de novelas dominicanas.* Ciudad Universitaria: Publicaciones de la Universidad Autónoma de Santo Domingo, 2006.

Donnell, Alison, and Sarah Lawson Welsh. "1930–49: Introduction. Creative Disturbances." In *The Routledge Reader in Caribbean Literature,* edited by Alison Donnell and Sarah Lawson Welsh. London and New York: Routledge, 1996. 107–27.

Drayton, Geoffrey. *Zohara.* London: Secker and Warburg, 1961.

Duffey, Carolyn. "Ezili the Subversive: The Erotics of Maryse Condé's *Célanire cou-coupé.*" *MaComère* 6 (2004): 70–77.

Dunbar, Robin. *Grooming, Gossip, and the Evolution of Language.* Cambridge, MA: Harvard University Press, 1998.

Duvalier, François. *Mémoires d'un leader du Tiers Monde. Mes négociations avec le Saint-Siège; ou, Une tranche d'histoire.* Paris: Hachette, 1969.

Encarnación Jiménez, Pedro. *Joaquín Balaguer y Juan Bosch: Principio y fin de un liderazgo politico.* Santo Domingo: Editora El Nuevo Diario, 1997.

Epps, Brad. "Proper Conduct: Reinaldo Arenas, Fidel Castro, and the Politics of Homosexuality." *Journal of the History of Sexuality* 6, no. 2 (1995): 231–83.

Epstein, Joseph. *Gossip: The Untrivial Pursuit.* New York: Houghton Mifflin Harcourt, 2011.

Erickson, John D. "Creole Identity in Chamoiseau's *Solibo magnifique* and Confiant's *Le meurtre du Samedi-Gloria.*" *Journal of Caribbean Literatures* 4, no. 2 (2006): 1–15.

Espaillat, Arturo R. *Trujillo: The Last Caesar.* Chicago: H. Regnery, 1963.

Espina Pérez, Darío. *Diccionario de cubanismos.* Barcelona: Impr. M. Pareja, 1972.

Esteban, Ángel. "Santiago Nasar y Cristo Bedoya: Los nombres que anuncian la muerte." *Revista de crítica literaria latinoamericana* 35, no. 69 (2009): 329–41.

Estévez, Abilio. "Between Nightfall and Vengeance: Remembering Reinaldo Arenas." Translated by David Frye. *Michigan Quarterly Review* 33, no. 3/4 (1994): 859–67.

———. *Inventario secreto de La Habana.* Barcelona: Tusquets Editores, 2004.

Estrada, Pedro, and Agustín Blanco Muñoz. *La dictadura: Pedro Estrada habló.* Caracas: Universidad Central de Venezuela, Consejo de desarrollo científico y humanístico, 1983.

Evans, Lucy. *Communities in Contemporary Anglophone Caribbean Short Stories*. Liverpool: Liverpool University Press, 2014.
Evans-Pritchard, E. E. *Witchcraft, Oracles and Magic among the Azande*. 1937. Reprinted in abridged form, Oxford: Oxford University Press, 1976.
Fatton, Robert, Jr. "African Diaspora and Political Science." In *The African Diaspora and the Disciplines*, edited by Tejumola Olaniyan and James H. Sweet. Bloomington: Indiana University Press, 2010. 161–72.
Ferré, Rosario. "Entre Clara y Julia (Dos poetas puertorriqueñas)." *Revista Iberoamericana* 52, no. 137 (1986): 999–1006.
———. *Flight of the Swan*. 2001. Reprint, New York: Plume, 2002.
———. *The House on the Lagoon*. 1995. Reprint, New York: Plume, 1996.
———. *Maldito amor y otros cuentos*. 1986. Edited by Dianna Niebylski. Reprint, Mexico City: Fondo de Cultura Económica, 2006.
———. "Memorias de Maldito amor." In *Maldito amor y otros cuentos*, edited by Dianna Niebylski. 1986. Reprint, Mexico City: Fondo de Cultura Económica, 2006. 107–12.
———. *Papeles de Pandora*. 1976. Reprint, New York: Vintage Español, 2000.
———. *Sweet Diamond Dust and Other Stories*. Translated by Rosario Ferré. 1988. Reprint, New York: Plume, 1996.
Fitzgibbon, Russell H. "Review: *Trujillo: The Last Caesar* by Arturo Espaillat." *Western Political Quarterly* 17, no. 3 (1964): 551–52.
Font-Bernard, Ramón A. *Balaguer y yo*. Santo Domingo: Editora Taller, 1986.
Forrester, John. *The Seductions of Psychoanalysis: Freud, Lacan, and Derrida*. Cambridge: Cambridge University Press, 1990.
Foucault, Michel. *Society Must Be Defended: Lectures at the Collège de France, 1975–76*. Translated by David Macey. Edited by Mauro Bertani, Alessandro Fontana, Arnold I. Davidson, and François Ewald. New York: Picador, 2003.
———. *Surveiller et punir: Naissance de la prison*. Paris: Gallimard, 1975.
Franco, Jean. *The Decline and Fall of the Lettered City: Latin America in the Cold War*. Cambridge, MA: Harvard University Press, 2002.
Frankétienne. *Les affres d'un défi*. Port-au-Prince: Henri Deschamps, 1979.
———. *Dézafi*. Port-au-Prince: Fardin, 1975.
Franqui, Carlos. *Retrato de familia con Fidel*. Barcelona: Seix Barral, 1981.
Fraser, Nancy. "Transnationalizing the Public Sphere: On the Legitimacy and Efficacy of Public Opinion in a Post-Westphalian World." *Theory, Culture & Society* 24, no. 4 (2007): 7–30.
Fulton, Dawn. *Signs of Dissent: Maryse Condé and Postcolonial Criticism*. Charlottesville: University of Virginia Press, 2008.
Fumagalli, Maria Cristina. "Names Matter." *Journal of Caribbean Literatures* 3, no. 3 (2003): 123–32.
———. *On the Edge: Writing the Border between Haiti and the Dominican Republic*. Liverpool: Liverpool University Press, 2015.

Gackstetter Nichols, Elizabeth, and Timothy R. Robbins. *Pop Culture in Latin America and the Caribbean*. Santa Barbara, CA: ABC-CLIO, 2015.

Gambetta, Diego. "Godfather's Gossip." *European Journal of Sociology / Archives Européennes de Sociologie / Europäisches Archiv für Soziologie* 35, no. 2 (1994): 199–223.

Garasa, Delfín L. "Joaquín Balaguer, escritor." *Boletín de la Academia Argentina de Letras* 56, no. 221–22 (1991): 447–61.

García Márquez, Gabriel. *Crónica de una muerte anunciada*. Bogotá: Editorial La Oveja Negra, 1981.

———. *El general en su laberinto*. Bogotá: Editorial La Oveja Negra, 1989.

———. *La hojarasca*. 1955. Reprint, Barcelona: Random House Mondadori, 1998.

———. *La mala hora*. 1962. Reprint, Barcelona: Random House Mondadori, 2010.

———. *El otoño del patriarca*. 1975. Reprint, Barcelona: Random House Mondadori, 2011.

García Márquez, Gabriel, and Luis Alcoriza. *Presagio*. Directed by Luis Alcoriza. Mexico City: Conacine and Producciones Escorpión, 1974.

Gelfert, Axel. *A Critical Introduction to Testimony*. London: Bloomsbury Academic, 2014.

Gelpí, Juan. "La cuentística antipatriarcal de Luis Rafael Sánchez." *Hispamérica* 15, no. 43 (1986): 113–20.

Glissant, Édouard. *Le discours antillais*. Paris: Gallimard, 1997.

Glover, Kaiama L. *Haiti Unbound: A Spiralist Challenge to the Postcolonial Canon*. Liverpool: Liverpool University Press, 2010.

Gluckman, Max. "Papers in Honor of Melville J. Herskovits: Gossip and Scandal." *Current Anthropology* 4, no. 3 (1963): 307–16.

Gómez Bergés, Víctor. *Balaguer y yo: la historia*. 2 vols. Santo Domingo: Cuesta-Veliz Ediciones, 2006.

González, José Luis. "El país de cuatro pisos." 1979. Reprinted in *El país de cuatro pisos y otros ensayos*. Río Piedras, Puerto Rico: Ediciones Huracán, 1989. 11–42.

González, Luis Eduardo. "Por decreto prohíben volver a echar chisme." *El Tiempo*. May 17, 2005. Accessed February 6, 2016. http://www.eltiempo.com/archivo/documento/MAM-1627148.

González, Olga M. *Unveiling Secrets of War in the Peruvian Andes*. Chicago: University of Chicago Press, 2011.

Gordon, Jan B. *Gossip and Subversion in Nineteenth-Century British Fiction: Echo's Economies*. New York: Palgrave Macmillan, 1996.

Graham Greene Démasqué: Finally Exposed. Port-au-Prince: Imprimerie Theodore, 1968.

Greene, Graham. *The Comedians*. New York: Viking, 1966.

———. Foreword to *Papa Doc: The Truth about Haiti Today*, by Bernard Diederich and Al Burt. New York: McGraw-Hill, 1969. vii–x.

---. "Letters: Cain's Cuba." *London Review of Books* 5, no. 1 (January 10, 1983). Accessed May 10, 2016. https://www.lrb.co.uk/v05/n01/letters#letter3.
---. "Nightmare Republic." *New Republic*, November 16, 1963, 18–20.
---. *The Power and the Glory*. 1940. Reprint, London: Heinemann, 1950.
Gregg, Veronica Marie. *Jean Rhys's Historical Imagination: Reading and Writing the Creole*. Chapel Hill: University of North Carolina Press, 1995.
Guerra, Lillian. *Visions of Power in Cuba: Revolution, Redemption, and Resistance, 1959–1971*. Chapel Hill: University of North Carolina Press, 2012.
Guha, Ranajit. *Elementary Aspects of Peasant Insurgency in Colonial India*. Durham, NC: Duke University Press, 1999.
Gutiérrez Mouat, Ricardo. "La 'loca del desván' y otros intertextos de *Maldito amor*." *Modern Language Notes* 109 (1994): 283–306.
Habermas, Jürgen. *The Structural Transformation of the Public Sphere: An Inquiry into a Category of Bourgeois Society*. Translated by Thomas Burger in 1989. 1962. Reprint, Cambridge: Polity, 2011.
Hall, Kenneth E. "Cabrera Infante as Biographer." *Biography* 19, no. 4 (1996): 394–403.
Hall, Lisa Kahaleole Chang. "Bitches in Solitude: Identity Politics and Lesbian Community." In *Sisters, Sexperts, Queers: Beyond the Lesbian Nation*, edited by Arlene Stein. New York: Plume, 1993. 218–29.
Hall, Stuart. "Negotiating Caribbean Identities." In *New Caribbean Thought: A Reader*, edited by Brian Meeks and Folke Lindahl. Kingston: University of the West Indies Press, 2001. 24–39.
Handley, George. "'It's an Unbelievable Story': Testimony and Truth in the Work of Rosario Ferré and Rigoberta Menchú." In *Violence, Silence and Anger: Women's Writing as Transgression*, edited by Deirdre Lashgari. Charlottesville: University Press of Virginia, 1995. 62–79.
---. *Postslavery Literatures in the Americas: Family Portraits in Black and White*. Charlottesville: University Press of Virginia, 2000.
Hanna, Monica. "'Reassembling the Fragments': Battling Historiographies, Caribbean Discourse, and Nerd Genres in Junot Díaz's *The Brief Wondrous Life of Oscar Wao*." *Callaloo* 33, no. 2 (2010): 498–520.
Hartman, Geoffrey. *The Geoffrey Hartman Reader*. Edited by Geoffrey Hartman and Daniel T. O'Hara. New York: Fordham University Press, 2004.
Hatch, Kristen. *Shirley Temple and the Performance of Girlhood*. New Brunswick, NJ: Rutgers University Press, 2015.
Hayes, Jarrod. "Créolité's Queer Mangrove." In *Music, Writing, and Cultural Unity in the Caribbean*, edited by Timothy J. Reiss. Trenton: Africa World Press, 2005. 307–32.
Heidegger, Martin. *Being and Time*. Translated by Joan Stambaugh. Revised by Dennis J. Schmidt. Albany, NY: SUNY Press, 2010.
Herbeck, Jason. "Detective Narrative Typology: Going Undercover in the French Caribbean." In *Detective Fiction in a Postcolonial and Transnational World*,

edited by Nels Pearson and Marc Singer. 2009. Reprint, Abingdon: Routledge, 2016. 63–80.

Herskovits, Melville J. *Life in a Haitian Valley*. New York: Alfred A. Knopf, 1937.

Higdon, David Leon. *Shadows of the Past in Contemporary British Fiction*. London: Macmillan, 1984.

Holguín, Fernando Valerio. "El orden de la música popular en la literatura dominicana." *Céfiro* 8, no. 1 (2009): 101–18.

Hron, Madelaine. *Translating Pain: Immigrant Suffering in Literature and Culture*. Toronto: University of Toronto Press, 2009.

Hulme, Peter. "Graham Greene and Cuba: Our Man in Havana?" *NWIG: New West Indian Guide / Nieuwe West-Indische Gids* 82, no. 3/4 (2008): 185–209.

———. "The Locked Heart: The Creole Family Romance of *Wide Sargasso Sea*." In *Colonial Discourse / Postcolonial Theory*, edited by Francis Barker, Peter Hulme, and Margaret Iversen. Manchester: Manchester University Press, 1994. 72–88.

Hutcheon, Linda. "Historiographic Metafiction: Parody and the Intertextuality of History." In *Intertextuality and Contemporary American Fiction*, edited by Patrick O'Donnell and Robert Con Davis. Baltimore: Johns Hopkins University Press, 1989. 3–32.

Ianovskaia, Lidiia. "Are All Memoirs Credible?" *Russian Studies in Literature* 45, no. 1 (2008): 64–81.

Inoa, Orlando. *Diccionario de dominicanismos*. Santo Domingo: Letra gráfica, 2010.

Irizarry, Guillermo B. "Literatura de violencia para tiempos de paz: *Nuestra Señora de la noche* de Mayra Santos y *The Brief Wondrous Life of Oscar Wao* de Junot Díaz." *Chasqui: revista de literatura latinoamericana* 43, no. 2 (2014): 110–22.

Jallot, Nicolas, and Laurent Lesage. *Haïti: Dix ans d'histoire secrète*. Paris: Editions du Félin, 1995.

James, Marlon. *The Book of Night Women*. 2009. Reprint, New York: Riverhead, 2010.

Janes, Regina. *Gabriel García Márquez: Revolutions in Wonderland*. Columbia: University of Missouri Press, 1981.

Janik, Dieter. "La experiencia de la violencia: Problemas de su transposición estética." In *Literatura colombiana hoy: Imaginación y barbarie*, edited by Karl Kohut. Frankfurt: Iberoamericana Vervuert, 1994. 139–45.

Jaramillo Zuluaga, J. E. "El deseo y el decoro en la novela colombiana del siglo XX." *Boletín cultural y bibliográfico* 29, no. 30 (1992): 3–31.

Johnson, Brian. "Language, Power, and Responsibility in *The Handmaid's Tale*: Toward a Discourse of Literary Gossip." *Canadian Literature* 148 (1996): 39–55.

Johnson, Paul Christopher. "Secretism and the Apotheosis of Duvalier." *Journal of the American Academy of Religion* 74, no. 2 (2006): 420–45.

Joseph, Régine Isabelle. "The Letters of Marie Chauvet and Simone de Beauvoir: A Critical Introduction." In *Revisiting Marie Vieux Chauvet: Paradoxes of the Postcolonial Feminine,"* edited by Kaiama L. Glover and Alessandra Benedicty-Kokken. Special issue, *Yale French Studies* 128 (2015): 25–39.

Kakar, Sudhir. "Rumors and Religious Riots." In *Rumor Mills: The Social Impact of Rumor and Legend*, edited by Gary Alan Fine, Véronique Campion-Vincent, and Chip Heath. New Brunswick, NJ: Aldine Transaction, 2005. 53–85.

Kanzepolsky, Adriana. "¿Yo no soy el tema de mi libro? *La fiesta vigilada* de Antonio José Ponte." *Abehache* 1, no. 1 (2011): 59–69.

Kierkegaard, Søren. *The Present Age and Two Minor Ethico-Religious Treatises*. Translated by Alexander Dru and Walter Lowrie. Oxford: Oxford University Press, 1940.

Kincaid, Jamaica. "Girl." *New Yorker* 54, no. 19 (June 26, 1978): 29.

———. "Interview with Jamaica Kincaid." Interview with Donna Perry. In *Reading Black, Reading Feminist: A Critical Anthology*, edited by Henry Louis Gates. New York: Penguin, 1990. 493–509.

———. *A Small Place*. New York: Farrar, Straus and Giroux, 1988.

Kline, Carmenza. *Los orígenes del relato: Los lazos entre ficción y realidad en la obra de Gabriel García Márquez*. Bogotá: Ceiba Editores, 1992.

Knepper, Wendy. *Patrick Chamoiseau: A Critical Introduction*. Jackson: University Press of Mississippi, 2012.

Krieger, Herbert W. *Archeological and Historical Investigations in Samaná, Dominican Republic*. Smithsonian Institution: United States National Museum, Bulletin 147. Washington, DC: United States Government Printing Office, 1929.

Kurosawa, Akira, dir. *Rashomon*. Produced by Jingo Minoura. Tokyo: Daiei. 1950.

Laferrière, Dany. *L'Odeur du café*. 1991, Reprint, Paris: Zulma, 2016.

La Fountain-Stokes, Lawrence M. *Queer Ricans: Cultures and Sexualities in the Diaspora*. Minneapolis: University of Minnesota Press, 2009.

Lagos, María Inés. "Subjetividades corporalizadas: 'Maldito amor' de Rosario Ferré y *Jamás el fuego nunca* de Diamela Eltit." *Nomadías* 10 (2011): 87–110.

Laguerre, Michel S. *The Military and Society in Haiti*. Basingstoke: Macmillan, 1993.

———. *Voodoo and Politics in Haiti*. 1989. Reprint, New York: Palgrave Macmillan, 1989.

Lamming, George. "The Legacy of Eric Williams." *Callaloo* 20, no. 4 (1997): 731–36.

Lanzendörfer, Tim. "The Marvelous History of the Dominican Republic in Junot Díaz's *The Brief Wondrous Life of Oscar Wao*." *MELUS: Multi-Ethnic Literature of the United States* 38, no. 2 (2013): 127–42.

Larkin, Philip. "Annus Mirabilis." In *Collected Poems,* edited by Anthony Thwaite. London: Faber and Faber, 1988. 167.

Las Casas, Bartolomé de. *Historia de las Indias*. Vol 5. Madrid: Imprenta de Miguel Ginesta, 1876.

Latham, Sean. *The Art of Scandal: Modernism, Libel Law, and the Roman à Clef*. Oxford: Oxford University Press, 2012.

Laviera, Tato. "juana bochisme." In *Bendición: The Complete Poetry of Tato Laviera*. Houston: Arte Público, 2014. 95–96.

Lewis, R. Anthony. "Language, Culture and Power: Haiti under the Duvaliers." *Caribbean Quarterly* 50, no. 4 (2004): 42–51.

Liberato, Ana S. Q. *Joaquín Balaguer, Memory, and Diaspora: The Lasting Political Legacies of an American Protégé*. Lanham, MD: Lexington Books, 2013.

Lifshey, Adam. "Indeterminacy and the Subversive in Representations of the Trujillato." *Hispanic Review* 76, no. 4 (2008): 435–57.

Lilienfeld, Jane. "'To Have the Reader Work with the Author': The Circulation of Knowledge in Virginia Woolf's *To the Lighthouse* and Toni Morrison's *Jazz*." *Modern Fiction Studies* 52, no. 1 (2006): 42–65.

Lima de Sousa, Helen. "Playing Chinese Whispers: The Official 'Gossip' of Racial Whitening in Jorge Amado's *Tenda dos Milagres*." In "Literature and Gossip," edited by Nicholas Martin. Special issue, *Forum for Modern Language Studies* 50, no. 2 (2014): 196–211.

Lindroth, Colette. "Whispers Outside the Room: The Haunted Fiction of Jean Rhys." In *Critical Perspectives on Jean Rhys*, edited by Pierette M. Frickey. Washington, DC: Three Continents, 1990. 85–91.

Linkof, Ryan. "'These Young Men Who Come Down from Oxford and Write Gossip': Society Gossip, Homosexuality, and the Logic of Revelation in the Interwar Popular Press." In *British Queer History: New Approaches and Perspectives*, edited by Brian Lewis. Manchester: Manchester University Press, 2013. 109–33.

Lock, Helen. "Rhys's Epistemological Background." *Journal of Commonwealth and Postcolonial Studies* 6, no. 1 (1999): 96–103.

Loichot, Valérie. *Orphan Narratives: The Postplantation Literature of Faulkner, Glissant, Morrison, and Saint-John Perse*. Charlottesville: University of Virginia Press, 2007.

Lonsdale, Thorunn. "Literary Foremother: Jean Rhys's 'Sleep It Off, Lady' and Two Jamaican Poems." In *Telling Stories: Postcolonial Short Fiction in English*, edited by Jacqueline Bardolph. Amsterdam: Rodopi, 2001. 145–54.

López-Calvo, Ignacio. *"God and Trujillo": Literary and Cultural Representations of the Dominican Dictator*. Gainesville: University Press of Florida, 2005.

Lorde, Audre. *I Am Your Sister: Collected and Unpublished Writings of Audre Lorde*. Edited by Rudolph P. Byrd, Johnnetta Betsch Cole, and Beverly Guy-Sheftall. Oxford: Oxford University Press, 2009.

Lovelace, Earl. *Is Just a Movie*. 2011. Reprint, Chicago: Haymarket Books, 2012.

Lowe, Lisa. *Immigrant Acts: On Asian American Cultural Politics*. Durham, NC: Duke University Press, 1996.

Luchting, Wolfgang A. "Lampooning Literature: *La mala hora.*" *Books Abroad* 47, no. 3 (1973): 471–78.

Lugo-Ortiz, Agnes. "Community at Its Limits: Orality, Law, Silence, and the Homosexual Body in Luis Rafael Sánchez's '¡Jum!'" In *¿Entiendes? Queer Readings of Hispanic Writings,* edited by Emilie L. Bergmann and Paul Julian Smith. Durham, NC: Duke University Press, 1995. 115–36.

Machado Sáez, Elena. *Market Aesthetics: The Purchase of the Past in Caribbean Diasporic Fiction.* Charlottesville: University of Virginia Press, 2015.

Mais, Roger. *Listen, the Wind.* Edited by Kenneth Ramchand. Harlow: Longman, 1986.

Majumdar, Saikat. "Modernism in the Basement: Subversive Discourse in *Wide Sargasso Sea.*" *Sargasso: A Journal of Caribbean Language, Literature, and Culture* 2 (2002): 105–14.

Mallarmé, Stéphane. *Œvres complètes de Stéphane Mallarmé.* Edited by Bertrand Marchal. Paris: Gallimard, 1998. Bibliothèque de la Pléiade.

Manktelow, Emily J. "Thinking with Gossip: Deviance, Rumour and Reputation in the South Seas Mission of the London Missionary Society." In *Subverting Empire: Deviance and Disorder in the British Colonial World,* edited by Will Jackson and Emily Manktelow. Basingstoke: Palgrave Macmillan, 2015. 104–25.

Marcos, Ferdinand E. "Presidential Decree No. 90: Declaring Unlawful Rumor-Mongering and Spreading False Information." In *Proclamation No. 1081, and Related Documents,* compiled by F. D. Pinpin. Mandaluyong, Philippines: Cacho Hermanos, 1973. 42.

Mardorossian, Carine M. *Reclaiming Difference: Caribbean Women Rewrite Postcolonialism.* Charlottesville: University of Virginia Press, 2005.

Mars, Kettly. *L'heure hybride.* La Roque d'Anthéron: Vents d'ailleurs, 2005.

———. "An interview of Kettly Mars by her Translator Jeanine Herman." *French Culture Books: French Embassy in the United States.* November 29, 2016. Accessed January 30, 2017. http://frenchculture.org/books/interviews/interview-kettly-mars-her-translator-jeanine-herman.

———. *Saisons sauvages.* Paris: Mercure de France, 2010.

Martin, Nicholas. "Literature and Gossip—An Introduction." In *"Literature and Gossip,"* edited by Nicholas Martin. Special issue, *Forum for Modern Language Studies* 50, no. 2 (2014): 135–41.

Martínez de Medina, Zoila. *Testimonio de una amistad: Balaguer y yo.* Santo Domingo: De colores, 2003.

Martínez San Miguel, Yolanda. "Off-Beat Migrancies: Musical Displacements in the Hispanic Caribbean." In *Displacements and Transformations in Caribbean Cultures,* edited by Lizabeth Paravisini-Gebert and Ivette Romero-Cesareo. Gainesville: University Press of Florida, 2008. 188–214.

Mauriac Dyer, Nathalie. "Portrait du romancier en 'Potinière': Proust." In *Potins, cancans et littérature: Actes du colloque de Perpignan, 24 au 26 novembre*

2004, edited by Nathalie Solomon and Anne Chamayou. Perpignan: Presses Universitaires de Perpignan, 2006. 253–68.

Mawby, Spencer. *The Transformation and Decline of the British Empire: Decolonisation after the First World War.* Basingstoke: Palgrave Macmillan, 2015.

May, Todd. *Reconsidering Difference: Nancy, Derrida, Levinas, and Deleuze.* University Park: Pennsylvania State University Press, 1997.

McAlister, Elizabeth A. "'The Jew' in the Haitian Imagination: Pre-Modern Anti-Judaism in the Postmodern Caribbean." In *Black Zion: African American Religious Encounters with Judaism,* edited by Yvonne Chireau and Nathaniel Deutsch. Oxford: Oxford University Press, 2000. 203–27.

McKeever, Stuart. *The Galindez Case.* Bloomington: AuthorHouse, 2013.

McKenzie, Kirsten. *Scandal in the Colonies: Sydney and Cape Town, 1820–1850.* Carlton: Melbourne University Press, 2004.

Mehta, Kamal. "Naipaul as a Short Story Writer." In *V. S. Naipaul: Critical Essays,* vol. 3, edited by Mohit Kumar Ray. New Delhi: Atlantic, 2005. 279–94.

Méndez, José Luis. *Cómo leer a García Márquez: Una interpretación sociológica.* 1989. Reprint, San Juan: Editorial de la Universidad de Puerto Rico, 2000.

Merry, Sally Engle. "Rethinking Gossip and Scandal." In *Toward a General Theory of Social Control,* vol. 1, edited by Donald J. Black. New York: Academic, 1984. 271–302.

Miller, D. A. *Narrative and Its Discontents: Problems of Closure in the Traditional Novel.* Princeton, NJ: Princeton University Press, 1989.

Miller, T. S. "Preternatural Narration and the Lens of Genre Fiction in Junot Díaz's *The Brief Wondrous Life of Oscar Wao.*" *Science Fiction Studies* 38, no. 1 (2011): 92–114.

Milne-Smith, Amy. *London Clubland: A Cultural History of Gender and Class in Late Victorian Britain.* New York: Palgrave Macmillan, 2011.

Minta, Stephen. *Gabriel García Márquez: Writer of Colombia.* London: Jonathan Cape, 1987.

Molloy, Sylvia. *At Face Value: Autobiographical Writing in Spanish America.* 1991. Reprint, Cambridge: Cambridge University Press, 2005.

———. "El relato como mercancía: *Los adioses* de Juan Carlos Onetti." *Hispamérica* 8, no. 23/24 (1979): 5–18.

Monsiváis, Carlos. "Ustedes que jamás han sido asesinados." *Revista de la Universidad de México* 7 (1973): 1–11.

Moreno, Marisel C. "Family Matters: Revisiting *la gran familia puertorriqueña* in the works of Rosario Ferré and Judith Ortíz Cofer." *Centro Journal* 22, no. 2 (2010): 75–105.

Mouffe, Chantal. "Artistic Activism and Agonistic Spaces." *Art & Research* 1, no. 2 (2007): 1–5.

Mullen, Patrick B. "Modern Legend and Rumor Theory." *Journal of the Folklore Institute* 9, no. 2/3 (1972): 95–109.

Munro, Hope. *What She Go Do: Women in Afro-Trinidadian Music.* Jackson: University Press of Mississippi, 2016.

Munro, Martin. *Exile and Post-1946 Haitian Literature: Alexis, Depestre, Ollivier, Laferrière, Danticat.* Liverpool: Liverpool University Press, 2007.

———. *Tropical Apocalypse: Haiti and the Caribbean End Times.* Charlottesville: University of Virginia Press, 2015.

Naipaul, V. S. *Miguel Street.* 1959. Reprint, New York: Vanguard, 1960.

———. *The Middle Passage: Impressions of Five Colonial Societies.* 1962. Reprint, London: Picador, 2011.

———. *The Mystic Masseur: A Novel.* 1957. Reprint, New York: Vintage Books, 2002.

———. *A Writer's People: Ways of Looking and Feeling.* New York: Alfred A. Knopf, 2008.

Nair, Rukmini Bhaya. "Text and Pretext: History as Gossip in Rushdie's Novel." *Economic & Political Weekly* 24, no. 18 (1989): 994–1000.

Nancy, Jean-Luc. *La communauté désavouée.* Paris: Éditions Galilée, 2014.

———. *La communauté désœuvrée.* Nouvelle édition revue et augmentée. Paris: Christian Bourgois, 1999.

———. *Une pensée finie.* Paris: Galilée, 1990.

Natarajan, Nalini. "Modes of Discourse and the National Imaginary in Two Caribbean Texts." *Caribbean Studies* 27, no. 1/2, (1994): 128–37.

Navia, José. "El día en que el chisme hizo famoso a Icononzo." *El Tiempo,* May 22, 2005. Accessed February 6, 2016. http://www.eltiempo.com/archivo/documento/MAM-1692372.

Nayar, Pramod K. *Human Rights and Literature: Writing Rights.* New York: Palgrave Macmillan, 2016.

Negrón, Luis. *Mundo cruel.* 2010. Reprint, San Juan: Agentes Catalíticos, 2014.

———. *Mundo cruel: Stories.* Translated by Suzanne Jill Levine. New York: Seven Stories, 2013.

Negrón-Muntaner, Frances. Introduction to *None of the Above: Puerto Ricans in the Global Era,* edited by Frances Negrón-Muntaner. New York: Palgrave Macmillan, 2007. 1–17.

Noelle-Neumann, Elisabeth. *The Spiral of Silence: Public Opinion, Our Social Skin.* 2nd ed. Chicago: University of Chicago Press, 1984.

Nunez, Elizabeth. *Bruised Hibiscus.* 2000. Reprint, New York: Ballantine Books, 2003.

Oates, Joyce Carol. "Romance and Anti-Romance: From Brontë's *Jane Eyre* to Rhys's *Wide Sargasso Sea.*" *Virginia Quarterly Review: A National Journal of Literature and Discussion* 61, no. 1 (1985): 44–58.

Ocasio, Rafael. "Queering the Cuban Exile: Reinaldo Arenas's Memoirs as a Sexual Outlaw." In *Dictatorships in the Hispanic World: Transatlantic and Transnational Perspectives,* edited by Patricia L. Swier and Julia Riordan-Goncalves. Madison, NJ: Fairleigh Dickinson University Press, 2013. 185–213.

Ollivier, Émile. *La discorde aux cent voix*. Paris: Albin Michel, 1986.
Onetti, Juan Carlos. *Los adioses*. In *El pozo: Novelas breves 1*. Mexico City: Penguin Random House, 2016. 39–104.
Ortega, Julio. "Rosario Ferré y la voz transgresiva." In *Reapropiaciones: Cultura y nueva escritura en Puerto Rico*. Río Piedras: Editorial de la Universidad de Puerto Rico, 1991. 87–92.
Owen, Walter C. *Opinions of the Attorney General of the State of Wisconsin*. Vol. 3. Madison, WI: Wisconsin Attorney General's Office, 1915.
Paine, Robert. "What Is Gossip About? An Alternative Hypothesis." *Man* 2, no. 2 (1967): 278–85.
Paravisini-Gebert, Lizabeth. "Colonial and Postcolonial Gothic: The Caribbean." In *The Cambridge Companion to Gothic Fiction*, edited by Jerrold E. Hogle. Cambridge: Cambridge University Press, 2002. 229–57.
Parry, Benita. "Problems in Current Theories of Colonial Discourse." *Oxford Literary Review* 9, no. 1/2 (1987): 27–58.
Pavel, Thomas G. "Literary Criticism and Methodology." *Dispositio* 3, no. 7/8 (April 1978): 145–56.
Penuel, Arnold M. "The Sleep of Vital Reason in García Márquez's *Crónica de una muerte anunciada*." *Hispania* 68, no. 4 (1985): 753–66.
Pereira, Manuel. "Reinaldo antes del alba." *Quimera* 111 (1992): 54–58.
Pérez, Mario Emilio. "El chisme: Pasatiempo nacional." *Estampas dominicanas: Primera Entrega*. 1971. Reprint, Santo Domingo: Publicaciones América, 1981. 57–59.
Perez Sarduy, Pedro. "Letters: Cain's Cuba." *London Review of Books* 4, no. 24 (December 30, 1982). Accessed May 5, 2016. https://www.lrb.co.uk/v04/n24/letters#letter1.
Perice, Glen. "Political Violence and the Public Eye." In *Cultural Shaping of Violence: Victimization, Escalation, Response*, edited by Myrdene Anderson. West Lafayette, IN: Purdue University Press, 2004. 249–57.
———. "Rumors and Politics in Haiti." *Anthropological Quarterly* 70, no. 1 (1997): 1–10.
Perkowska-Alvarez, Magdalena. "La fiesta oficial y el chisme festivo en *Margarita, está linda la mar* de Sergio Ramirez." *América: Cahiers du CRICCAL* 28 (2002): 261–70.
Phelps, Anthony. "Anthony Phelps." Interview and poems. *Callaloo* 15, no. 2 (1992): 381–83.
———. *Mon pays que voici . . . suivi de Les dits de fou-aux-cailloux*. Honfleur: Oswald, 1968.
Phillips, Susan E. *Transforming Talk: The Problem with Gossip in Late Medieval England*. University Park: Pennsylvania State University Press, 2007.
Pino-Ojeda, Walescka. *Sobre castas y puentes: Conversaciones con Elena Poniatowska, Rosario Ferré y Diamela Eltit*. Santiago: Editorial Cuarto Propio, 2000.

Plutarch. *Moralia*. Vol. 6 (Loeb Classical Library no. 337), translated by W. C. Helmbold. Cambridge, MA: Harvard University Press, 1939.
Ponte, Antonio José. *La fiesta vigilada*. Barcelona: Editorial Anagrama, 2007.
Prats, Delfín. *Lenguaje de mudos*. 1969. Reprint, Madrid: Editorial Betania, 2013.
———. "Yo tengo un mal karma: Entrevista a Delfín Prats." Interview with Leandro Estupiñán Zaldívar. *La gaceta de Cuba* 3 (2006): 22–26.
Preble-Niemi, Oralia. "Polyphony and Heteroglossia in Narratives with Ulterior Motives in Rosario Ferré's *Sweet Diamond Dust*." *Label Me Latina/o* 2 (Spring 2012): 1–22.
Puig, Manuel. *Boquitas pintadas*. 1968. Reprint, Buenos Aires: Booket, 2005.
———. Letter to Cabrera Infante, June 29, 1980. Guillermo Cabrera Infante Papers, box 12, folder 25. Manuscripts Division, Department of Rare Books and Special Collections, Princeton University Library.
Rama, Angel. "García Márquez entre la tragedia y la policial o Crónica y pesquisa de la crónica de una muerte anunciada." *Sin nombre* 13, no. 1 (1982): 7–27.
Ramchand, Kenneth. Introduction to *Listen, the Wind*, by Roger Mais. Harlow: Longman, 1986. vi–xxx.
Read Vittini, Mario. *Trujillo de cerca*. Santo Domingo: San Rafael, 2007.
Renan, Ernest. *Qu'est-ce qu'une nation? Conférence faite en Sorbonne le 11 mars 1882*. 2nd ed. Paris: Calmann Lévy Éditeur, 1882.
Rhys, Jean. *Sleep It Off, Lady: Stories*. New York: Harper and Row, 1976.
———. *Wide Sargasso Sea*. 1966. Edited by Judith L. Raiskin. Reprint, New York: Norton, 1999.
Riley, Nerea. "Reinaldo Arenas' Autobiography *Antes que anochezca* as Confrontational 'Ars Moriendi.'" *Bulletin of Latin American Research* 18, no. 4 (1999): 491–96.
Roa Bastos, Augusto. *Yo, el Supremo*. Caracas: Biblioteca Ayacucho, 1986.
Rodríguez, Néstor E. *Escrituras de desencuentro en la República Dominicana*. Mexico City: Siglo Veintiuno Editores, 2005.
Rodríguez Monegal, Emir. Letter to Cabrera Infante, September 8, 1972. Cabrera Infante Papers, series 2, subseries 2A, box 12, folder 26. Manuscripts Division, Department of Rare Books and Special Collections, Princeton University Library.
Rogoff, Irit. "Gossip as Testimony: A Postmodern Signature." *Generations and Geographies in the Visual Arts: Feminist Readings*. Edited by Griselda Pollock. London: Routledge, 1996. 58–65.
Rohlehr, Gordon. *Calypso & Society in Pre-independence Trinidad*. Port of Spain, Trinidad: G. Rohlehr, 1990.
Rohter, Larry. "A Dominican Institution Exiting, Aura Intact." *New York Times*, May 18, 1996. Accessed September 10, 2016. http://www.nytimes.com/1996/05/19/world/a-dominican-institution-exiting-aura-intact.html.
Rojas, Rafael. "Legitimidad e historia en Cuba." In *El otro paredón: Asesinatos de la reputación en Cuba*. Miami: Eriginal Books, 2011. 19–34.

———. *Tumbas sin sosiego: Revolución, disidencia y exilio del intelectual cubano.* Barcelona: Editorial Anagrama, 2006.

Romay Chacón, Tomás. "Sobre la murmuración y los chismes." In *Obras completas,* vol. 2. Havana: Academia de Ciencias de la República de Cuba and Museo Histórico de las Ciencias Médicas "Carlos J. Finlay," 1966. 226–27.

Ross, Karl. "Merengue Hit Fuels Passion, Maybe Murder, in Caribbean." *Billboard* 107, no. 40 (October 7, 1995): 14, 121.

Rowe, William, and Vivian Schelling. *Memory and Modernity: Popular Culture in Latin America.* London: Verso, 1993.

Rushdie, Salman. *Midnight's Children.* New York: Knopf, 1981.

Sada, Daniel. *Porque parece mentira la verdad nunca se sabe.* Mexico City: Tusquets, 1999.

Sánchez, Luis Rafael. *En cuerpo de camisa.* 1966. Reprint, Río Piedras, Puerto Rico: Editorial Cultural, 1984.

———. "Hum!" Translated by Rose M. Sevillano. *Grand Street* 61 (1997): 130–35.

———. *La importancia de llamarse Daniel Santos: Fabulación.* 1988. Reprint, San Juan: Editorial de la Universidad de Puerto Rico, 2005.

Sánchez-Eppler, Benigno. "Reinaldo Arenas, Re-writer Revenant, and the Repatriation of Cuban Homoerotic Desire." In *Queer Diasporas,* edited by Cindy Patton and Benigno Sanchez-Eppler. Durham, NC: Duke University Press, 2000. 154–82.

Santí, Enrico Mario. *Ciphers of History: Latin American Readings for a Cultural Age.* New York: Palgrave Macmillan, 2005.

Santos, Lidia. "Melodrama y nación en la narrativa femenina del Caribe contemporáneo." *Revista Iberoamericana* 69, no. 205 (2003): 953–68.

Savory, Elaine. *The Cambridge Introduction to Jean Rhys.* Cambridge: Cambridge University Press, 2009.

Schantz, Ned. *Gossip, Letters, Phones: The Scandal of Female Networks in Film and Literature.* Oxford: Oxford University Press, 2008.

Scott, James C. *Domination and the Arts of Resistance: Hidden Transcripts.* New Haven, CT: Yale University Press, 1990.

———. *Weapons of the Weak: Everyday Forms of Peasant Resistance.* New Haven, CT: Yale University Press, 1985.

Scott, Lindsey. "Selling Sex, Suppressing Sexuality: A Gigolo's Economy in Kettly Mars's *L'Heure hybride.*" *Contemporary French and Francophone Studies* 19, no. 5 (2015): 543–50.

Sell, Roger D. "Literary Gossip, Literary Theory, Literary Pragmatics." In *Literature and the New Interdisciplinarity: Poetics, Linguistics, History,* edited by Roger D. Sell and Peter Verdonk. Amsterdam: Editions Rodopi B. V., 1994. 221–42.

Sellers, Julie A. "Nebulous Boundaries: Geographies of Identity in *El hombre del acordeón.*" *Studies in 20th & 21st Century Literature* 39, no. 1 (2015): 1–22.

Sención, Viriato. *Los que falsificaron la firma de Dios*. 4th ed. 1992. Reprint, Santo Domingo: Taller, 1993.

Senior, Olive. *Dancing Lessons*. Ann Arbor, MI: Dzanc Books, 2014.

———. "The Story as *Su-Su*, the Writer as Gossip." In *Writers on Writing: The Art of the Short Story*, edited by Maurice Angus Lee. Westport, CT: Praeger, 2005. 41–50.

Shelton, Marie-Denise. "Condé: The Politics of Gender and Identity." *World Literature Today* 67, no. 4 (1993): 717–22.

Silva, María Guadalupe. "Antonio José Ponte: El espacio como texto." *Iberoamericana* 14, no. 53 (2014): 69–83.

Simek, Nicole. "The Politics of Parody in Patrick Chamoiseau's 'Solibo Magnifique' and Maryse Condé's 'Célanire Cou-Coupé.'" *Romance Notes* 46, no. 2 (2006): 253–62.

Sims, Robert L. "Periodismo, ficción, espacio carnavalesco y oposiciones binarias: La creación de la infraestructura novelística de Gabriel García Márquez." *Hispania* 71, no. 1 (1988): 50–59.

Sloan, Cynthia A. "Caricature, Parody, and Dolls: How to Play at Deconstructing and (Re-)constructing Female Identity in Rosario Ferré's *Papeles de Pandora*." *Pacific Coast Philology* 35, no. 1 (2000): 35–48.

Solomon, Nathalie. Introduction to *Potins, cancans et littérature: Actes du colloque de Perpignan, 24 au 26 novembre 2004*, edited by Nathalie Solomon and Anne Chamayou. Perpignan: Presses Universitaires de Perpignan, 2006. 1–14.

Souza, Raymond D. *Guillermo Cabrera Infante: Two Islands, Many Worlds*. Austin: University of Texas Press, 1996.

Spacks, Patricia Meyer. *Gossip*. Chicago: University of Chicago Press, 1985.

Spear, Thomas C. "Marie Chauvet: The Fortress Still Stands." In *"Revisiting Marie Vieux Chauvet: Paradoxes of the Postcolonial Feminine,"* edited by Kaiama L. Glover and Alessandra Benedicty-Kokken. Special issue, *Yale French Studies* 128 (2015): 9–24.

Spivak, Gayatri Chakravorty. "Three Women's Texts and a Critique of Imperialism." *Critical Inquiry* 12, no. 1 (1985): 243–61.

Stewart, Pamela J., and Andrew Strathern. *Witchcraft, Sorcery, Rumors and Gossip*. Cambridge: Cambridge University Press, 2003.

Stovel, Bruce. "*Tristram Shandy* and the Art of Gossip." In *Jane Austen & Company: Collected Essays*, edited by Nora Foster Stovel. Edmonton: University of Alberta Press, 2011. 21–34.

Sunstein, Cass R. *On Rumors: How Falsehoods Spread, Why We Believe Them, What Can Be Done*. New York: Farrar, Straus and Giroux, 2009.

Sylvain, Patrick. "Odette." In *Haiti Noir*, edited by Edwidge Danticat. New York: Akashic Books, 2011. 19–26.

Taussig, Michael. *Shamanism, Colonialism, and the Wild Man: A Study in Terror and Healing*. Chicago: University of Chicago Press, 1991.

Thelwell, Michael. *The Harder They Come*. 1980. Reprint, New York: Grove, 1988.

Tokunaga, Robert S. "Social Networking Site or Social Surveillance Site? Understanding the Use of Interpersonal Electronic Surveillance in Romantic Relationships." *Computers in Human Behavior* 27, no. 2 (2011): 705–13.

Tönnies, Ferdinand. *Community and Society*. 1887. Translated and edited by Charles P. Loomis, 1957. Reprint, Mineola, NY: Dover, 2002.

Torrents, Nissa, and Christopher Abel. "Letters: Bites from the Bearded Crocodile." *London Review of Books* 3, no. 12 (July 2, 1981). Accessed May 10, 2016. https://www.lrb.co.uk/v05/n02/letters#letter10.

Torres, Ana Teresa. *Doña Inés contra el olvido*. Caracas: Monte Ávila Editores, 1992.

———. *La fascinación de la víctima*. Caracas: Editorial Alfa, 2008.

———. *Los últimos espectadores del acorazado Potemkin*. Caracas: Monte Ávila Editores, 1999.

Torres-Saillant, Silvio. *An Intellectual History of the Caribbean*. New York: Palgrave Macmillan, 2006.

———. Introduction to *Dominican Blackness*. New York: CUNY Dominican Studies Institute, 1999.

Trujillo, Aída. *A la sombra de mi abuelo*. Santo Domingo: Norma, 2008.

Trujillo de Domínguez, María de los Ángeles. *Trujillo, mi padre: en mis memorias*. Miami: Ediciones Unicaribe, 2010.

Turner, Patricia A. *I Heard It Through the Grapevine: Rumor in African-American Culture*. Berkeley: University of California Press, 1993.

———. Introduction to *Rumor Mills: The Social Impact of Rumor and Legend*, edited by Gary Alan Fine, Véronique Campion-Vincent, and Chip Heath. 2005. Reprint, New Brunswick, NJ: AldineTransaction, 2009. 169–72.

Valoy, Christopher. "El Venao." On Los Cantantes' compact disc *El Virao*. Santo Domingo: Unidos Records, 1995.

Vaquero, María, and Amparo Morales, eds. *Tesoro lexicográfico del español de Puerto Rico*. San Juan: Academia puertorriqueña de la lengua española, 2005.

Vargas Llosa, Mario. *La fiesta del chivo*. Madrid: Alfaguara, 2000.

———. *García Márquez: Historia de un deicidio*. Barcelona: Barral Editores, 1971.

———. *El hablador*. Barcelona: Seix Barral, 1987.

———. "Pájaro tropical." *El País* (Madrid), June 15, 1992. Accessed July 1, 2016. http://elpais.com/diario/1992/06/15/opinion/708559208_850215.html.

Vega, Ana Lydia. *Falsas crónicas del sur*. San Juan: Editorial de la Universidad de Puerto Rico, 1991.

Veloz Maggiolo, Marcio. *El hombre del acordeón*. Madrid: Ediciones Siruela, 2003.

———. "Una memoria fermenta: Entrevista con el escritor dominicano Marcio Veloz Maggiolo." Interview by José Carvajal. March 2001. Accessed

September 3, 2016. http://web.archive.org/web/20010616121926/http:/www
.librusa.com/entrevista_velozmaggiolo.htm.
———. *La memoria fermentada: Ensayos bioliterarios*. Santo Domingo: Amigo
del Hogar, 2000.
———. *La mosca soldado*. Edited by Rafael Rodríguez-Henríquez. 2004. Reprint,
Buenos Aires: Stockcero, 2007.
———. "Nido de volanderas." In *Palabras de ida y vuelta: cuentos*. Santo
Domingo: Editora Cole, 2006. 73–81.
Venegas, José Luis. "Exile, Photography, and the Politics of Style in Guillermo
Cabrera Infante's *Tres tristes tigres*." *Latin American Literary Review* 36, no.
72 (2008): 107–33.
Verity, Jeremy. "The Roots of Reggae." *Listener* 101, no. 2596 (February 2,
1979): 185.
Victor, Gary. "Kettly Mars dit la vie, de mieux en mieux." *Notre librairie* 158
(2005): 60–61.
Voznesensky, Andrei. "Ode to Gossips." Translated by Stanley Moss. In *Antiworlds*. New York: Basic Books, 1966. 81–82.
Walcott, Derek. *In a Green Night: Poems, 1948–1960*. 1962. Reprint, London:
Jonathan Cape, 1969.
———. "The Gift of Comedy—West Indian Gaiety: Our Most Successful Role."
In *Derek Walcott: The Journeyman Years: Occasional Prose 1957–1974*, vol.
1, edited by Gordon Collier. Amsterdam: Editions Rodopi, 2013. 129–33.
———. "The Schooner Flight." In *Collected Poems, 1948–1984*. New York: Farrar, Straus and Giroux, 1986. 345–61.
Walford, Lynn. "America as a Community of Violence in Three Early Novels of
Gabriel García Márquez." *Hispanófila* 119 (1997): 31–45.
Walls, Jeannette. *Dish: How Gossip Became the News and the News Became Just
Another Show*. New York: Avon Books, 2000.
Walonen, Michael K. *Writing Tangier in the Postcolonial Transition: Space and
Power in Expatriate and North African Literature*. Farnham: Ashgate, 2011.
Walsh, John P. "Reading (in the) Ruins: Kettly Mars's *Saisons sauvages*." *Journal
of Haitian Studies* 20, no. 1 (2014): 66–83.
Weir-Soley, Donna. "Myth, Spirituality, and the Power of the Erotic in *It Begins
with Tears*." *MaComère* 5 (2002): 243–52.
Welsh, Sarah Lawson. "The Literatures of Trinidad and Jamaica." In *A History
of Literature in the Caribbean*, vol. 2. *English- and Dutch-Speaking Regions*,
edited by A. James Arnold. Amsterdam: John Benjamins, 2001. 69–95.
Wert, Sarah, and Peter Salovey. "Introduction to the Special Issue on Gossip."
In "Gossip," edited by Wert and Salovey. Special issue, *Review of General
Psychology* 8, no. 2 (2004): 76–77.
Wickerson, Erica. "Demonizing Gretchen through Gossip in Thomas Mann's
Doktor Faustus." In *"Literature and Gossip,"* edited by Nicholas Martin.
Special issue, *Forum for Modern Language Studies* 50, no. 2 (2014): 212–26.

Wiegmink, Pia. "Performance and Politics in the Public Sphere." *Journal of Transnational American Studies* 3, no. 2 (2011): 1–40.

Wiese Delgado, Hans Paul. *Trujillo: Amado por muchos, odiado por otros, temido por todos*. Santo Domingo: Editorial Letra Gráfica, 2000.

Wilkes, Roger. *Scandal: A Scurrilous History of Gossip, 1700–2000*. London: Atlantic Books, 2002.

Wilkinson, Stephen. *Detective Fiction in Cuban Society and Culture*. Oxford: Peter Lang, 2006.

Williams, Eric. "Massa Day Done (Public Lecture at Woodford Square, 22 March 1961)." *Callaloo* 20, no. 4 (1997): 725–30.

Wilson, Peter J. *Crab Antics: The Social Anthropology of English-Speaking Negro Societies of the Caribbean*. New Haven, CT: Yale University Press, 1973.

Wood, Michael. "The Claims of Mischief." *New York Review of Books*. January 24, 1980. Accessed July 27, 2016. http://www.nybooks.com/articles/1980/01/24/the-claims-of-mischief/.

———. *Gabriel García Márquez: One Hundred Years of Solitude*. Cambridge: Cambridge University Press, 1990.

Yerkovich, Sally. "Gossiping as a Way of Speaking." *Journal of Communication* 27, no. 1 (1977): 192–96.

Zard, Philippe. "Les concierges de l'Eternel: Esquisse d'une métaphysique du potin chez Franz Kafka." *Potins, cancans et littérature: Actes du colloque de Perpignan, 24 au 26 novembre 2004*, edited by Nathalie Solomon and Anne Chamayou. Perpignan: Presses Universitaires de Perpignan, 2006. 45–61.

Zephaniah, Benjamin. "The SUN." In *City Psalms*. Newcastle upon Tyne: Bloodaxe Books, 1992. 58–59.

Index

Abbes García, Johnny, 164, 242n6
Abel, Christopher, 132, 133
Abrahams, Roger D., 217n13
Abrams, Elliott, 238n13
accusations, 34, 53, 136, 139, 151, 165, 219n20, 233n29; against Arenas, 115, 117, 121; against Cabrera Infante, 130; in criminal investigations, 51, 101; in Cuban discourse, 121, 126, 130; and gossip, 167, 190, 202, 232n26, 242n7; by the government, 117, 121, 144, 190, 240n26, 241n5, 242n7; of infidelity, 43–44; of murder, 49, 101, 115, 121, 122. *See also* denunciation; scandal
Acosta Cruz, María, 230n13, 231n15
Adisa, Opal Palmer: *It Begins with Tears*, 225n25
Adkins, Karen C., 66–67, 215n4
adversarialism, 113, 207, 209–10; in *Antes que anochezca* (Arenas), 115, 122–23; in *The Brief Wondrous Life of Oscar Wao* (Díaz), 182, 195; in Cabrera Infante's texts, 21, 128, 135, 137; in *La fascinación de la víctima* (Torres), 101; of gossip, 10, 15, 18, 21, 24, 27, 29, 35, 68, 101, 115, 122, 137, 154, 177–78, 182, 195, 207, 209–10, 246n28; in Haiti, 145, 146, 154; in *El hombre del acordeón* (Veloz Maggiolo), 177–78; and language, 10, 15, 25–26; in *La mala hora* (García Márquez), 34, 35; in *Maldito amor* (Ferré), 68, 71, 78–79
African American culture, rumor and, 205. *See also* diaspora
African cultural influences: on Afro-Caribbean experience, 207, 232n22;

Ewe proverb used by Collins, 66; on individualism and community, 225n26; linguistic, 11–12, 26
Afro-Caribbean, 11–12, 23, 65, 220n1, 232n22. *See also* African cultural influences; Afro-Cubans
Afro-Cubans: orality of, 220n1; Yoruba vocabulary and, 12
Agard, John: "Listen Mr Oxford Don" (poem), 25–26
aggression, gossip as act of, 34, 46, 55, 168. *See also* adversarialism; violence
Agnant, Marie-Célie, 220n1
Albrechtslund, Anders, 228n39
Allatson, Paul, 75
Allport, Gordon W., 247n36
Allsopp, Richard: *Dictionary of Caribbean English Usage*, 12
Alonso, Carlos, 36, 41
Alva, Martin (Rafael Martínez Alvarez), 18; *La ciudad chismosa y calumniante*, 219nn19–20
Álvarez, Julia, 246n32
Alvarez Pina, Virgilio, 163
Anglade, Georges: "Le cabri à la dent d'or," 231n28; "Les couverts de trop," 143–44; "La galerie des huit portraits à grands traits," 144–45; "Lincoln, Churchill et le contremaître," 233n28; *Rire haïtien*, 233n28
Anglophone Caribbean: crime fiction in, 235n34; orality in, 25–29, 219n1, 223n16; terms for "gossip" in, 12. *See also* British West Indies; *specific countries and authors*

Antes que anochezca (Arenas), 21, 113, 114–25; attacks on Castro in, 117, 122–25; criticism of, 125–26, 236–37n6; gossip as means of challenging official narratives in, 210; gossip as means of revenge in, 116–17, 126; as self-gossip, 113, 114, 124–26, 236n5, 238n15; suicide note included in, 124–25; orality of, 238n14; prison in, 116, 120–21, 123; reputational pranks in, 115; sexuality in, 21, 113, 114–21, 122, 126, 237n7, 237nn9–10; slander in, 116; "War of the Anonymous Letters" and, 115

anthropology: cannibalism and, 233–34n29; gossip as field of study in, 8, 17, 23, 56, 215n4, 221n6; influence on literary scholarship, 2, 6; on witchcraft's relationship with gossip, 232n26

Antigua: benna, 243n14; in *A Small Place* (Kincaid), 113, 138–42, 146; in the works of Jean Rhys, 48, 50, 84

apathy, 36–37, 77, 106, 223–24n21, 235n34. See also *Crónica de una muerte anunciada* (García Márquez)

Arenas, Reinaldo: in exile, 117, 124, 130, 142, 238n12; literary persona of, 236n5, 236–37n6; public sphere and, 113, 122, 123–24, 137, 138; unpublished works of, 130. See also *Antes que anochezca*

Armando Fernández, Pablo, 122

Asturias, Miguel Angel, 4

Atwood, Margaret, 214; *The Handmaid's Tale*, 218n17

Austen, Jane, 3, 16, 214, 216n7

authoritarianism: in the Caribbean, 19, 23, 66, 101, 111–13, 121, 205, 210–11, 218n17, 235–36n37; in the Dominican Republic, 142, 159–61, 163, 167–68, 170, 172, 180–81, 185, 193–95; gossip and, 4, 22, 61–62, 139, 142, 159–60, 205, 221n7, 237n9, 241n2, 248n42; in Haiti, 147; literature of, 21, 22, 142, 145, 195–96, 205; narrative and, 247n33, 248n42; postauthoritarianism, 3, 20, 173, 174, 185, 205; sexuality and, 21, 117–21, 122, 131, 133, 237n7, 248n42; and totalitarianism, 61, 227n35, 246n29. See also totalitarianism; *specific countries and leaders*

autobiography, 155, 161, 226n29, 247n36; as self-gossip, 113, 114, 117, 124–25, 236n5. See also *Antes que anochezca* (Arenas); *Memorias de un cortesano de la "era de Trujillo"* (Balaguer)

Avila, Leopoldo, 130

Ayim, Maryann, 234n32

Ayuso, Mónica G., 246n32

Bailey, Carol, 8, 58–59

Bailey, Winston (the Mighty Shadow), 224–25n25

Balaguer, Joaquín, 22, 160–73, 179, 200, 240n8; in *The Brief Wondrous Life of Oscar Wao* (Díaz), 182, 185–87, 193; condemnation of Sención, 169, 242n9; in *Los que falsificaron la firma de Dios* (Sención), 168–69, 172–73, 242n10; *Two Essays on Dominican History*, 241n4. See also *Memorias de un cortesano de la "era de Trujillo"* (Balaguer)

Barbados, 12, 231n19

Barnet, Miguel, 122, 237n6

Barros, Sandro, 117, 119

Barthes, Roland, 2, 209, 220n4

Bejel, Emilio, 21, 118

Benítez-Rojo, Antonio, 19, 22, 236n3

Benjamin, Walter, 2

Bennett, Louise: "Bed-Time Story" (poem), 26; "Colonisation in Reverse" (poem), 26–27; *Jamaica Labrish*, 26

Benoit, François, 240n26

Bentham, Jeremy, 33, 61. See also panopticon

Bercoff, Brigitte, 11

Bergmann, Jörg: *Discreet Indiscretions: The Social Organization of Gossip*, 215n4

Bernard, Louise, 141

Bertolotti, Tommaso, 66

Besnier, Niko: *Gossip and the Everyday Production of Politics*, 110, 215n4, 221n6, 236n1

Beverley, John, 125, 238n15

Bhabha, Homi, 79–80, 231–32n20

billiard halls (or pool halls), as site of gossip, 225n27, 226n30

biography, 74–75, 168, 177, 179, 181, 240n28, 245n21. See also autobiography; memoirs

Bird, S. Elizabeth, 223n17

Birkenmaier, Anke, 63–64

Bleek, Wolf, 232n26

blogs. *See* internet

bochinche: as term for gossip, 9, 11, 15, 17, 183, 186, 217n10; as ruckus, 136
body, 95, 200; as corpse, 148, 151, 190, 240n27; desire to know, 108–9, 235–36n37; as site of resistance, 117, 248–49n42
Boisseron, Bénédicte, 8
Bolívar, Simón, 30
Borges, Jorge Luis, 4, 218n18, 234n34
Bosch, Juan, 159–60, 240n1, 241n3; "La mancha indeleble," 247n33
Bougerol, Christiane, 232n26
Bouson, J. Brooks, 139–40
Braham, Persephone, 235n34
Bramstedt, E. K., 241n2
Brathwaite, Edward Kamau, 25, 213, 224n24; *Rights of Passage,* 226–27n33
Brazil, 246n29
Brief Wondrous Life of Oscar Wao, The (Díaz): 160, 179–95; adversarial use of gossip in, 182, 195; Balaguer in, 182, 185–87, 193; blank page in, 185–86, 188, 191, 193, 195, 245n27; danger of unguarded speech in, 183–84, 189–90; footnote use in, 181, 185, 245n26; gossip and gender in, 182; gossip as intimate in, 183; gossip as malleable in, 180; gossip as performative in, 183, 187; and *El hombre del acordeón* (Veloz Maggiolo), 179, 180, 192, 193; moral framework of narrator, 186, 187–88, 189; narrative battles in, 160, 177, 180, 188–95, 210; plausibility in, 186–87, 188, 193–95; reconstruction of history in, 179, 184–85, 186, 187, 188, 191–93, 194; silence and, 179, 184, 186, 188–89, 191–92, 193, 194–95, 201, 246n27; suspicion of definitive accounts in, 192, 193–94, 247n33; Ramfis Trujillo as object of gossip in, 181; Trujillo regime's use of gossip in, 179–80, 189–90
British West Indies, 25, 218n5; independence of, 3, 224n24
Britten, Benjamin: *Peter Grimes,* 4
Britton, Celia, 60, 97
Brontë, Charlotte, 82; *Jane Eyre,* 3
Brooks, Peter, 100, 234n31; *Body Work,* 104, 107–9, 235n37; *Reading for the Plot,* 234n31
Browne, Simone, 228n39
Bryce, Jane, 235n34

Burt, Al, 153–54
Butterworth, Emily, 2

Cabrera, Lydia: *Anagó: vocabulario lucumí,* 12; "Historia verdadera de un viejo pordiosero que decía llamarse Mampurias" (short story), 220n1
Cabrera Infante, Guillermo, 21, 110, 113, 126–38; and Arenas, 21, 126, 133, 138, 142, 158, 237n10; on Casey, 131–32; Castro regime's reputational attacks on, 129–30; criticism of, 127, 128–29, 132; *Diccionario de la literatura cubana,* removal from, 130; Greene and, 134–36, 146, 153, 156, 158, 239n18, 240n28; as "king of gossip," 127; knowledge of Cuban affairs, 127, 131, 134, 238–39n17; *Lunes de revolución* (editor), 127; *Mea Cuba,* 125, 126, 132, 135, 137, 145, 238nn16–17, 240n28; orality and, 219n1; and public sphere, 126, 130, 132–38; *Tres tristes tigres,* 130; *Vidas para leerlas,* 125, 126–27, 238n16; *Vista del amanecer en el trópico,* 138, 237n10; and Williams, 138; wordplay of, 126, 238n16
calypso, 18, 224–25n25, 243n14. *See also* music and song
Canada, 23, 102
cancan, 10–11, 217n10, 227n38
cannibalism, 95, 233–34n29
Caribbean, the: connections to Africa, 4, 26, 207, 232n22; European views of, 30, 87, 153, 235n37; as globalized archipelago, 22, 111, 112, 194, 236n3; gossip's role in, 3–5, 6, 8, 16–19, 22–24, 29, 110, 113, 207–14, 219n20, 231–32n20; history of, 1, 5, 18–19, 22–24, 65–67, 138, 207–8, 210–11, 213, 219n20, 232n21, 235n34, 235n37, 247n34; identity in, 19, 23, 67, 97; language in, 5, 25–26; orality in, 25, 208, 219–20n1, 223n16; politics of, 1, 3–4, 5, 19, 24, 111–12, 207, 210, 211, 213, 241n2; public sphere and, 23, 110–13, 137, 182, 211, 236n3. *See also* colonialism; diaspora; postcolonialism; *specific countries*
Carpentier, Alejo, 237n6, 243n14
Carrión, Ulises, 15, 218n15
Casey, Calvert, 131–32

Castro, Fidel: and Reinaldo Arenas, 117–125, 146; and Guillermo Cabrera Infante, 126–37, 146, 239n18; gossip about, 122, 127–31, 133; meetings with Graham Greene, 134–35, 239n18, 240n31; "Palabras a los intelectuales" (speech), 121, 127; use of gossip by, 62, 121, 131. *See also* Cuba

Célanire cou-coupé (Condé), 21, 67, 89–99; and *Bruised Hibiscus* (Nunez), 91; collective voice in, 90, 97–98; and *La fascinación de la víctima* (Torres), 101, 103; gossip incited in, 94; gossip as seductive in, 92–99; gossip as speculative in, 89, 92–93, 94, 96–99; homosexuality in, 89, 94–95; knowledge in, 96–97, 103; monstrosity in, 94–95, 98, 232n25, 233–34n29; racial divisions in, 97, 233–34n29; rumor and gossip in, 232n24; witchcraft and superstition in, 94–96, 232n22

Cervantes, Miguel de: *El coloquio de los perros*, 2
Chaljub Mejía, Rafael, 174
Chalmers, René, 155
Chamayou, Anne: *Potins, cancans et littérature* (with Solomon), 7
Chamoiseau, Patrick, 219n1; *Chronique des sept misères*, 226n27; *Solibo magnifique*, 228n1, 235n34
Chaucer, Geoffrey, 2, 216n10
Chauvet, Marie Vieux, 239n22
Chemla, Yves, 195–96
Chile, 124
chisme, 1, 9–11, 15, 55, 110, 159, 172; *chismografías*, 221n9; *chismoso*, 9–10, 227n37
Christie, Agatha, 104, 234n32
Cilano, Cara: *Contemporary Pakistani Fiction in English*, 218–19n18
city: Port-au-Prince, 53–55, 199; and the public sphere, 111; St. Pierre, 50; as site of gossip or rumor, 102, 147, 151, 219n20; surveilled, 63–64, 144, 228n40
class divisions: challenged by gossip, 68; and merengue, 174; in Puerto Rico, 73, 75, 230n11; reinforced by gossip, 56; revealed by gossip, 58, 159–60, 222n11; transcended by gossip, 49, 84, 88, 197
Cliff, Michelle: *No Telephone to Heaven*, 27–28, 220n3
Clifford, James, 22

Coady, C. A. J., 92, 99, 215n4, 238n15
Code, Lorraine, 235n36
Cohn, Dorrit, 246n31
Collado, Lipe, 241n5
Collins, Merle: "Crick Crack" (poem), 65–66, 67
Colombia, 17, 29–30, 223n20. *See also violencia, la*
colonialism: and the body, 235–36n37; and Caribbean identity, 4, 19, 23, 60, 84–85, 111, 206, 210, 219n20; and gossip, 27–28, 58, 110–11, 137–39, 207–8, 220n2, 232n20; and knowledge, 23, 66, 82, 87, 89, 235n34; and language, 25–27, 207–8, 223n16; in Puerto Rico, 79, 81, 231n16; violence and, 83. *See also* neocolonialism; postcolonialism
Comedians, The (Greene), 21, 113, 142, 145–58; attacked by Duvalier's regime, 155–58; as exposé, 145–47, 153–54, 158, 240n25; film adaptation of, 155, 157–58; gossip as source of information in, 147–48, 149–50, 151–54; libel suit filed by Duvalier, 157–58; in relation to *Mea Cuba* (Cabrera Infante) and *Antes que anochezca* (Arenas), 145, 146, 153, 158
commérage, 10, 12, 15, 17
community: in African societies, 225n26; constructed through gossip, 2–3, 28–29, 99, 220–21n6, 226n33; failure of, 20, 25, 29, 36–37, 69, 87, 198–99; in *La fiesta vigilada* (Ponte), 61–64; gossip used to strengthen, 209, 230n14; in "Gravel in Your Shoe" (Mais), 48; and the individual, 20, 34, 39, 42, 44, 45–50, 53, 60, 61, 64, 97, 215n4, 220–21n6, 224n34, 225n26, 226n28; in "¡Jum!" (Sánchez), 51–53; and language, 26–29; in *Listen, the Wind* (Mais), 45; in *La mala hora* and *Crónica de una muerte anunciada* (García Márquez), 29–44; in "Odette" (Sylvain), 53–55; and the public sphere, 18, 42, 111; scholarship on, 6–7, 59–60; and Senior, 57–59; in *Sleep It Off, Lady* (Rhys), 44–50. *See also Gemeinschaft* and *Gesellschaft*
Condé, Maryse: and the Caribbean, 232n21, 235n34; *La civilisation du bossale*, 225n26; and detective fiction, 235n34; and Ferré and Rhys, 89; and Mais, 225n26; and orality, 219n1; and skepticism, 98–99; and the supernatural,

232n27; *La Traversée de la mangrove*, 98–99, 235n34; *La vie scélérate*, 232n21. See also *Célanire cou-coupé*
Confiant, Raphaël: *Le meurtre du Samedi-Gloria*, 235n34
confidentiality. *See* privacy
Conrad, Joseph, 152–53
Constable, Pamela, 241n2
Cooper, Carolyn, 82
Coover, Robert, 222n10
Corral, Will, 238–39n17
Cortázar, Julio, 127
Cortés, Jason, 17, 226n30
Counter, Andrew, 13
counterpublic, 18–19, 110–11, 180, 198, 210–11
Covarrubias, 9, 10
Cozarinsky, Edgardo: on Borges and gossip, 4, 218n18; on gossip, 8, 13, 14, 77–78, 80, 103, 181; on James and gossip, 77–78; on Proust and gossip, 77, 218n18; and Spacks's view of gossip, 230n12
Creole: Anglophone Caribbean writers' use of, 25, 227n33; and colonialism, 28, 84, 87; Haitian writers' use of, 145, 239n23; oral production, 219n1; and terms used for "gossip," 11–12, 154, 223n17
crime fiction, 105–6, 235n34. *See also* detective fiction
Crónica de una muerte anunciada (García Márquez), 36–44; failure of community in, 20, 29, 36–44, 224n21; fate and fatalism in, 36, 37, 41, 42; and "¡Jum!" (Sánchez), 53; and Kincaid, 141; and *La mala hora* (García Márquez), 29, 38, 44, 60; and "Odette" (Sylvain), 55; social cohesion and gossip in, 44, 60; unreliability of gossip in, 40–41; and *Zohara* (Drayton), 223–24n21. See also *violencia, la*
Cuba: under Batista, 134, 135; criticism of gossip in, 1, 99–100; gossip used by Castro regime in, 61–62, 121, 131, 241n2; *hombre nuevo* in, 21, 113, 118–19, 133; informants in, 61, 114–15, 122, 132, 237n7, 237n11; machismo in, 21, 113, 118–19, 133; missile crisis in, 131; public sphere in, 122–26; Radio Bemba in, 91; repression of intellectuals in, 121–22, 127, 130–31; and its revolution, 3, 117–20, 127–28, 131–34, 136–37; sexual politics in, 21, 113–22, 131–33, 237n7; as surveillance state, 29, 61–64, 122–23, 132; terms for gossip in, 11–12; totalitarian gossip in, 29, 61, 64. *See also* Afro-Cubans; *Antes que anochezca* (Arenas); Cabrera Infante, Guillermo; Castro, Fidel; Ponte, Antonio José
cuckolding, 30, 43–44, 55–56, 70, 151, 226n30
Cudjoe, Selwyn, 141
Curaçao, 243n14

Dabove, Juan Pablo, 8, 32, 33
Dalleo, Raphael, 18, 110–11, 180, 198, 236n3; *Caribbean Literature and the Public Sphere: From the Plantation to the Postcolonial*, 8–9
Danticat, Edwidge, 65, 246n32; *Breath, Eyes, Memory*, 243n13; *The Farming of Bones*, 244n17
Dash, J. Michael, 98–99, 142–43, 152–53, 226n27
Davidson, Arnold E., 231n18
De Ferrari, Guillermina, 235–36n37
De Maeseneer, Rita, 178, 245n21
de Moya, E. Antonio, 43–44
denunciation, 54, 117, 119, 129, 162, 168, 228; gossip as, 73, 126, 101, 122; by or to those in power, 63, 121, 163, 177, 178, 237n7, 241n5, 242n7. *See also* accusations; scandal
Depestre, René: *Le Mât de cocagne*, 143
Derby, Lauren: on Balaguer, 172, 241n4, 242n7; *The Dictator's Seduction: Politics and the Popular Imagination in the Era of Trujillo*, 9, 162–63; on *Foro Público*, 241–42n5, 242n11; on gossip and rumor, 246n30, 247n34, 247n36
Despradel, Roberto, 164
detective fiction, 100, 103–6, 108, 228n1, 234nn31–32, 234–35n34. *See also fascinación de la víctima, La* (Torres)
Devonish, Hubert, 25
diaspora: of the British West Indies, 25–27, 220n5; and Caribbean identity, 4, 111, 112; Dominican, 179, 185, 195; gossip networks and, 23; Haitian, 23, 142, 144; Jamaican, 26–27; language and, 25; Miami's exile community, 22, 236n12; outposts of, 22–23, 112; writers of, 28, 111, 142–45, 179, 219n1, 220n5. *See also specific authors*

Díaz, Junot, 4, 22, 192, 194, 210, 247n33; on Sención, 242n10. See also *Brief Wondrous Life of Oscar Wao, The*

Díaz, Porfirio, 134

Diederich, Bernard, 153–54, 157–58, 240n25

Di Pietro, Giovanni, 161, 165, 168, 170, 172

Dominica, 87

Dominican Republic, 3, 42, 43; criticism of gossip in, 159–60, 163, 241n3; gossip as resource in, 142, 159, 170, 189, 248n38; Haitian massacre (1937) and, 162, 174, 175, 244n17, 246n32; informants in, 159, 177, 189–90; institutionalization of gossip in, 22, 159–60, 163–64, 168, 172, 174, 179, 190, 227n37, 241–42n5; memoirs in, 22, 160, 161, 164, 167–68, 173, 186, 242nn6–8; terms for gossip in, 11. See also *Brief Wondrous Life of Oscar Wao, The* (Díaz); *hombre del acordeón, El* (Veloz Maggiolo); *Los que falsificaron la firma de Dios* (Sención); *Memorias de un cortesano de la "era de Trujillo"* (Balaguer); *venao, el*

Donnell, Alison, 224n24

doubt, 30, 70, 81, 135, 139, 175, 180, 218; gossip provoking, 46, 83, 86–87, 208; gossip thematizing, 24, 80, 83, 211–13. See also epistemology; narrative; skepticism

Dove, Rita, 246n32

Drayton, Geoffrey: *Zohara*, 223–24n21

Duffey, Carolyn, 232n25

Dunbar, Robin, 215n4

Duvalier, François, 3, 21, 22, 142–43, 147, 153–58, 195–96, 198, 203–4, 232n25, 239n22, 240n27; *Mémoires d'un leader du Tiers Monde*, 158; regime of, 113, 142, 145–47, 151–52, 154, 158, 160, 195, 240n24, 240n26; as subject of gossip, 152, 154–55, 204; use of gossip by, 142, 154–55, 240n29. See also *Comedians, The* (Greene); Haiti; *Saisons sauvages* (Mars)

Duvalier, Jean-Claude, 158, 239n22

dystopia, 60, 218n17

England. See United Kingdom

epistemology, 139, 180, 209–10, 235n34, 235n37; in *Célanire cou-coupé* (Condé), 67, 89, 98–99; in *La fascinación de la víctima* (Torres), 67, 99–100, 103–4; feminist, 67, 215n4; gossip and, 4, 18, 20–21, 24, 66–67, 104, 107–9, 193, 195, 203, 209, 212–13, 229n3, 235n36, 247n37; in *Maldito amor* (Ferré), 67, 69, 76–77, 80–81, 103, 247–48n37; in *Wide Sargasso Sea* (Rhys), 67, 82, 86–89, 103

Epps, Brad, 123

Epstein, Joseph, 114, 216n8

Erickson, John D., 235n34

Espaillat, Arturo: *Trujillo: The Last Caesar*, 167

Espina Pérez, Darío: *Diccionario de cubanismos*, 11

Esteban, Ángel, 38

Estévez, Abilio, 116; *Inventario secreto de La Habana*, 99–100, 234n30

Estrada, Pedro, 159, 241n2

Europe, 58, 87, 137, 174, 233n29; Caribbean diaspora in, 22, 23, 26–27, 127, 143; conception of Caribbean in, 30, 152–53, 235n37; gossip in, 88, 207, 221n7; literature of, 7, 16, 66, 209, 228n1

Evans, Lucy, 57–58

Evans-Pritchard, E. E., 232n26

exile, 23, 111, 113, 213; Arenas and, 117, 124, 142, 238nn12–13; Cabrera Infante and, 21, 113, 126–27, 129–31, 133, 142, 143; Condé and, 232n21; of Dominicans, 142, 164, 167, 185–86, 188; of Haitians, 142–45, 147, 195, 199, 220n1. See also diaspora; nostalgia

family, 102, 111, 230n9, 230n13, 239n22; Balaguer's, 168–69, 242n12; in *The Brief Wondrous Life of Oscar Wao* (Díaz), 180, 182–85, 190, 191; and community, 60, 228n40; in Ferré's texts, 67–81, 228n2; reputation, 38–39, 163; in *Saisons sauvages* (Mars), 195–96, 200, 201, 203, 205; secrets, 72, 80, 85–86, 88, 102, 141, 164, 184; Trujillo's, 162, 164, 167, 181. See also *gran familia*

fascinación de la víctima, La (Torres), 99–107; accessibility of truth in, 102–6, 234n31; as detective fiction, 100, 234n31; gossip as investigative method in, 21, 67, 100, 102–3; gossip, psychoanalysis, and detective work in, 21, 67, 100–107

Fatton, Robert, Jr., 22–23
femininity: effeminacy, 12, 17, 34, 169; gossip and, 1, 12, 17, 55, 73, 219n18
feminism, 66; epistemology and, 67, 215n4; *Maldito amor* (Ferré) and, 21, 67–68, 69, 72–73, 75
Fernández de Oviedo, Gonzalo, 219n20
Ferré, Rosario, 4, 70, 81, 209, 231n15; "La bella durmiente" (short story), 228n2; "El collar de camándulas" (short story), 228n2; "Cuando las mujeres quieren a los hombres" (short story), 228n2; feminism of, 21, 68, 69, 72–75; *Flight of the Swan*, 228n2, 230n13; *gran familia* as theme in, 228n13; *The House on the Lagoon*, 228n2, 230n13; "Isolda en el espejo" (short story), 228n2; *Papeles de Pandora*, 228n2, 230n13. See also *Maldito amor*
Fitzgibbon, Russell H., 167
Flaubert, Gustave: *Madame Bovary*, 108
folklore and folktales, 215n4, 243n13, 244n20
Font-Bernard, Ramón A., 242n8
footnotes, 169–70, 173, 181, 185, 187, 245n26
forgetting and amnesia, 46, 79–80, 100, 130, 206, 220n1, 245n25; in *The Brief Wondrous Life of Oscar Wao* (Díaz), 191; in *El hombre del acordeón* (Veloz Maggiolo), 178, 245n21, 245n25; in *Maldito amor* (Ferré), 76, 80; in *Saisons sauvages* (Mars), 196, 198, 200–201, 205. See also memory
Foro Público (Dominican newspaper column), 163–64, 190, 241–42n5, 242n11. See also news media
Forrester, John, 107, 234n33, 235n35; *The Seductions of Psychoanalysis*, 104
Foucault, Michel, 5, 61–62, 242n11
France, 124, 127, 143, 157, 239n22; literature of, 7. See also diaspora; Europe; Francophone Caribbean
Franco, Jean, 126
Francophone Caribbean, 3; detective fiction in, 235n34; emancipation in, 219n20; Haiti as part of, 145; orality in, 219–20n1, 223n16; *télédiol* in, 90–91; terms for gossip in, 12, 90. See also Creole; *specific countries and authors*
Frankétienne: *Les Affres d'un défi*, 145; *Dézafi*, 145

Franqui, Carlos: *Retrato de familia con Fidel*, 131
Fraser, Nancy, 111–12
Fuentes, Norberto, 237n10
fukú, 182, 190, 197
Fulton, Dawn, 98
Fumagalli, Maria Cristina, 82, 174

Galíndez, Jesús de, 192, 247n35
Gambetta, Diego, 216n9, 217n12
Garasa, Delfín, 161
García Márquez, Gabriel, 35, 223n16; *Cien años de soledad*, 221n8; *El general en su laberinto*, 30; *La hojarasca*, 30, 35; *El otoño del patriarca*, 30; *Presagio* (film), 224n21. See also *Crónica de una muerte anunciada*; *mala hora, La*
Garro, Elena: *Los recuerdos del porvenir*, 230n14
Garton Ash, Timothy, 62
Gelfert, Axel: *A Critical Introduction to Testimony*, 238n15
Gelpí, Juan, 52, 55
Gemeinschaft and *Gesellschaft*, 59–60, 64, 228n40
Germany, 62, 128, 132, 133, 137, 150, 246n28. See also Europe
Glissant, Édouard, 1, 219n1, 219n20; *Malemort*, 97
globalization, 23, 111–12, 210, 213, 236n3
Glover, Kaiama L., 223n16
Gluckman, Max, 6, 8, 23, 220–21n6, 223n17; "Gossip and Scandal," 6, 215n4
Gómez Bergés, Víctor, 242n8
Gómez Ramos, Reinaldo, 237n11
González, José Luis: "El país de cuatro pisos," 81, 230n11
González, Olga M.: *Unveiling Secrets of War in the Peruvian Andes*, 227n37
Gordon, Jan, 3, 248n38; *Gossip and Subversion in Nineteenth-Century British Fiction: Echo's Economies*, 7
gossip: adversarialism of (*see under* adversarialism); brokers of, 113, 127, 131, 151, 165, 174; columns (*see under* news media); as conservative force, 20, 29, 31, 39, 178, 213, 214, 233n28; definition of, 9–16, 17, 209, 217n11; etymology of terms for, 10–12, 216n9, 216–17n10,

gossip (continued)
223n17; and gender, 1, 4, 7, 8, 10, 16–18, 34, 49, 56, 67, 69, 73–74, 182, 218–19n18, 226n30; "good" gossip, 3, 6, 8, 59, 207, 216n7, 216n9; harmlessness of, 6, 207, 218n16; as idle talk, 2, 7, 9, 10–11, 15, 163, 217n11, 227n34; malleability of, 5, 13, 15, 180, 208; as performance, 13–14, 36–37, 41–42, 44, 53, 57, 71, 85, 92, 133, 183, 187, 198, 212, 217n13, 232n24, 236n2, 237n8; playfulness of, 100, 209, 225n25; and pleasure, 13–14, 16, 26, 31, 57, 73, 131, 171, 182, 192, 209, 216n9, 219n12; policing social norms, 6, 20, 29, 33, 39, 44, 46–48, 51–53, 57–59, 60, 121, 222n11, 228n2, 243n13; politicization of, 4–5, 17–18, 19, 21–22, 61, 110–13, 133, 136–38, 140, 143, 154, 159–60, 163, 170–72, 180–82, 186, 203–4, 212, 227nn36–37, 241n2; as radical force, 18, 77, 178, 207–8, 212–13; as resource for the marginalized, 3, 4, 5–6, 16–17, 27–28, 49, 59, 69, 74, 78, 88, 110–11, 182, 188–95, 210–11, 219n1, 229–30n9, 236n1; as resource for the powerful, 18, 24, 27, 149, 154, 163–64, 178, 179–80, 182, 189–95, 210–11, 212, 233n28, 236n1, 241n2; rumor and, 9, 14–15, 92, 110, 147–48, 151, 154, 205–6, 218n14, 232n24, 236n2, 244n17, 244n20; terms for, 1, 9–12, 15, 17, 28, 216n9, 217n13, 223n17; ubiquity of, 1, 4, 5, 9, 18, 34, 67, 80, 96, 170, 180, 205, 207, 212, 226n30. See also adversarialism; hearsay; men's talk; narrative; rumor; sociology; talk; women's talk
graffiti, 115, 226n30. See also pasquinades
Graham Greene Démasqué: Finally Exposed, 154–57
gran familia (Puerto Rico), 69, 79, 230n13
Great Britain. See United Kingdom
Greene, Graham: Cabrera Infante and, 134–36, 153, 156, 158, 239n18, 240n28; and Castro, 134–36, 239n18, 240n31; Duvalier's reputational attacks on, 21, 113, 142, 154–57; lawsuit against, 155, 240n30; "Nightmare Republic," 146–47, 240n26; Our Man in Havana, 62, 239n18; The Power and the Glory, 240n30. See also Comedians, The; Graham Greene Démasqué: Finally Exposed
Gregg, Veronica, 86–87
Grenada, 12, 65
Guadeloupe, 48, 89, 90, 94, 226n28
Guerra, Lillian, 119; Visions of Power in Cuba, 62
Guevara, Alberto, 120
Guevara, Che, 126, 133
Guha, Ranajit, 110
Guibert, Rita, 127–28
Gutiérrez Mouat, Ricardo, 79, 231n16
Guyana, 12, 25

Habermas, Jürgen, 32–33, 112–13
Haiti: combites, 18, 223n17, 243n14; Dominican relations, 175–76, 244n17; Duvaliers' rule in, 3, 113, 142–47, 150–60, 195–96, 198–99, 203–5, 239n22, 240n24, 240n26, 240n29, 241n2, 248n40; exile writers of, 142–45, 219–20n1; gossip and télédiòl in, 6, 12, 19, 22–23, 143–45, 149–52, 198, 203, 233n28, 241n2; literature of, 21, 22, 113, 142–45, 158, 160, 195–96, 206, 239nn22–23; music of, 18, 223n17, 243n14; public sphere in, 23, 248n40; terms for gossip in, 12, 154, 223n17. See also Comedians, The (Greene); Graham Greene Démasqué: Finally Exposed; Haitian massacre (1937); Saisons sauvages (Mars); Tontons Macoutes; zombification
Haitian Creole. See Creole
Haitian massacre (1937), 162, 175, 186, 244n17, 246n32
Hall, Kenneth E., 240n28
Hall, Lisa Kahaleole Chang, 237n8
Hall, Stuart, 18
Handley, George, 76, 86
Hanna, Monica, 191–92
Hartman, Geoffrey, 104, 234n31
Hatch, Kristin, 240n30
Hayes, Jarrod, 90–91, 99
Hearne, John, 224n24
hearsay, 96, 131, 132, 145, 217n14; and criminal investigation, 51, 104; and history, 22, 247n34; and information networks, 102, 148, 152, 153, 196, 197; and psychoanalysis, 234n33; and rumor, 217n14, 242n7, 244n17, 244n20

Heidegger, Martin, 2, 227n34
Herbeck, Jason, 235n34
Herodotus, 127
Herskovits, Melville, 6, 8, 23, 223n17
Higdon, David Leon, 82
Hinds, Justin, 25
history: authoritarianism and, 23–24, 63, 130, 132, 158, 160–61, 165–68, 172–73, 185–89, 191–95, 196, 198, 246n29; Caribbean, 1, 5, 18–19, 22–24, 65–67, 111, 138, 205–6, 207, 208, 210, 211, 213, 219n20, 235n37, 247n34; Cuban, 130, 132; Dominican, 22, 160–67, 168, 172–74, 178–79, 184–89, 191–95, 241n4, 242n9, 245n21, 247n35; gossip and, 2, 14, 16, 38, 110, 127, 137–38, 140, 176, 179, 184, 188–89, 191–95, 205–6, 245n26, 246n31, 247n34, 248n39; Haitian, 158, 196, 198, 201, 205, 244n17, 248n41; Puerto Rican, 73, 79–81; revision through gossip of, 8, 23–24, 73, 80–81, 82, 132, 160–61, 166–67, 168, 172–73, 179, 184, 186–89, 191–95, 205–6, 220n1, 244n17, 246n28, 247n34; whitewashing of, 22, 66, 161, 165–68, 168, 172, 173, 180, 192–94, 201, 205, 211, 220n1, 246n32; in *Wide Sargasso Sea* (Rhys), 82; Eric Williams and, 137–38, 140. See also *Brief Wondrous Life of Oscar Wao, The* (Díaz); *hombre del acordeón, El* (Veloz Maggiolo); *Los que falsificaron la firma de Dios* (Sención); *Maldito amor* (Ferré); *Memorias de un cortesano de la "era de Trujillo"* (Balaguer)
Holguín, Fernando Valerio, 243–44n16
hombre del acordeón, El (Veloz Maggiolo), 160, 173–79, 210; border region in, 174, 175–76; and *The Brief Wondrous Life of Oscar Wao* (Díaz), 182, 189, 192, 193; community and, 175–77; Haitian massacre (1937) in, 174, 175; *leyenda* (legend) in, 176–77, 192, 244n18; and *Los que falsificaron la firma de Dios* (Sención), 174; merengue in, 160, 173–74, 175, 176, 177–78; narrative in, 174–75, 176, 178–79, 180
homosexuality, 4, 12, 166; Arenas and, 21, 114–122, 237n7; in *The Brief Wondrous Life of Oscar Wao* (Díaz), 191; Castro's Cuba and, 21, 114–22, 131–32, 133, 237n7; in *Célanire cou-coupé* (Condé), 89, 94; gay identity and gossip, 21, 237n8; in "¡Jum!" (Sánchez), 51–52; in *Maldito amor* (Ferré), 70, 71, 73; in Mars's texts, 201–2, 248n42; in "Muchos o de cómo a veces la lengua es bruja" (Negrón), 57, 60
Hostos, Eugenio María de, 240n1
Hron, Madelaine, 240n24
Hulme, Peter, 83–84, 239n18
Husson, Louis Thomas, 219n20
Hutcheon, Linda, 248n39
hypocrisy, 36, 39, 51, 119–20, 133, 135, 219n20, 225n25

Ianovskaia, Lidiia, 168
identity: in the Caribbean, 5, 19, 23, 207; collective, 17, 27, 28, 41, 60, 79, 97, 195; gay, 21, 117, 118, 121, 237n8; gossip and, 17, 19, 20, 128, 160, 198, 199; knowledge and, 67, 97; memory and, 79–80, 113, 245n25; Puerto Rican nationhood and, 69, 79, 81, 216n5, 231n15; racial, 97, 234n29; of *rayanos*, 176; totalitarianism and, 227n35
idle talk: gossip as, 2, 7, 9–11, 34, 45, 207, 211, 217n11; gossip as more than, 1–2, 15, 19, 150, 163, 176, 215n4; Heidegger on, 227n34
inequality, 5, 23, 24, 210, 231n15. See also class divisions
informants. See denunciation; surveillance; *and under* Cuba; Dominican Republic
Inoa, Orlando: *Diccionario de dominicanismos*, 11
internet: and blogs or social media, 14, 216n8, 228n39; effect of, 23; regulation of, 221n7
Irizarry, Guillermo B., 188

Jamaica: gossip in, 19, 27–28, 45, 56, 57–58, 83–87; language and, 26–27, 28; music of, 243n14, 245n24; race in, 83–84
James, Henry, 3, 77–78, 108, 214, 216n7
James, Marlon: *The Book of Night Women*, 27
Janes, Regina, 222n12
Janik, Dieter, 223n20
Jaramillo Zuluaga, J. E., 35
Johnson, Brian, 218n17

Johnson, Paul Christopher, 154–55
Jolicoeur, Aubelin, 149

Kafka, Franz, 7; *The Trial*, 227–28n38
Kakar, Sudhir, 15
Kanzepolsky, Adriana, 63
Kierkegaard, Søren, 2, 188
Kincaid, Jamaica: and Arenas, 141, 210; and Cabrera Infante, 141; challenging official narratives through gossip, 210; "Girl" (short story), 243n14; and Greene, 142, 146; *A Small Place*, 113, 138–42
Kline, Carmenza, 223n20
Knepper, Wendy, 228n1
knowledge, 86–87, 235–36n37; as battleground, 80; and Cabrera Infante, 113, 127, 129, 134, 146, 239n17; common knowledge, 86, 90, 93, 199; and community, 93, 96–99, 100–101, 216n7; gossip and, 13, 15, 20, 28, 77, 103, 106, 107–8, 195, 197–98, 214, 220n1; gossip as depository of, 41, 66, 91, 102; gossip as means of transmitting, 13, 18, 32, 38, 82, 92, 93, 100–101, 110, 183, 216n7, 217n12; gossip and production of, 109, 211–12; inside, 22, 86, 129, 134, 153, 161–62, 165, 168, 171, 173, 242n8; and power, 101, 150–51, 171, 197, 228n2; public, 40, 174; rumor and, 217n14; social, 97, 107, 183, 185, 235n36; speculation and, 93, 96; subjugated, 5, 82. See also *Célanire cou-coupé* (Condé); epistemology; *fascinación de la víctima, La* (Torres); *Wide Sargasso Sea* (Rhys)
Krieger, Herbert W., 219n20
Kurosawa, Akira. See *Rashomon* (film)

Labra, Carilda Oliver, 114
La Fea (Trujillo's sister), 193
Laferrière, Dany: *L'Odeur du café*, 228–29n3
La Fountain-Stokes, Lawrence Martin, 53
Lagos, María Inés, 230n10
Laguerre, Michel S., 154, 240n29
Lamming, George, 138
lantern laws (New York), 228n39
Lanzendörfer, Tim, 187
Larkin, Philip, 4
Las Casas, Bartolomé de, 219n20

Latham, Sean, 7
Latin America, 23, 30, 66, 124; gossip's role in, 4, 227n37; literature of, 68, 105, 234–35n34; *telenovelas* of, 70, 209. See also specific countries
Laviera, Tato: "juana bochisme" (poem), 23
laws against gossip, 29–30, 188, 221n7. See also punishment
legends (*leyenda*), 174, 241n4; and gossip, 174, 176–77, 192, 244n18, 244n20, 247n36
León, Eulogio, 245n21
letters, 14, 19, 62, 82, 85–86, 162, 226n29, 238n13, 241–42n5; of Arenas, 115, 121, 123–25; of Cabrera Infante, 127–28, 129, 132, 133, 239n18; of Greene, 135, 142, 146, 157
Lewis, R. Anthony, 240n29
Lezama Lima, José, 237n6
libel, 155, 157–58. See also slander
Liberato, Ana S. Q., 166, 172
lies and lying, 66, 71, 78, 84, 87, 92, 103, 132, 179, 202, 221n9; false accusations, 43, 144; false testimony, 2
Lifshey, Adam, 247n33
Lilienfeld, Jane, 229–30n9
Lima de Sousa, Helen, 246n29
liming, 1, 216n7
Lindroth, Colette, 88
Linkof, Ryan, 237n8
Littré, Émile: *Dictionnaire de la langue française*, 11
Lock, Helen, 88
Loichot, Valérie, 97
Lonsdale, Thorunn, 226n29
Lope de Vega: *Fuenteovejuna*, 31
López, César, 122
López-Calvo, Ignacio, 169
Lora, Ñico, 174
Lorde, Audre, 220n5
Los que falsificaron la firma de Dios (Sención), 22, 160, 167–73; Balaguer's condemnation of, 160, 168, 169, 242n9; gossip and, 160, 168–173; as "gossip novel," 168, 172; and history, 168, 172–73, 179; and *Memorias de un cortesano de la "era de Trujillo"* (Balaguer), 168–69, 173; reception, 168; as roman à clef, 168; seminary in, 170, 171; superstition in, 169–70, 173, 187;

Index 285

surveillance and spying in, 170–72, 197; voyeurism in, 172
Lovelace, Earl: *Is Just a Movie,* 243n14
Lowe, Lisa, 110
Luchting, Wolfgang A., 31
Lugo-Ortiz, Agnes, 52, 216n5

Machado Sáez, Elena, 246n28
machismo, 17, 21, 73, 113, 118–19, 133, 226n30. *See also* masculinity
magic, 87, 95, 170, 174–75, 176, 231n17, 244n18. *See also* superstition; witchcraft
Magnani, Lorenzo, 66
Mais, Roger, 20, 29, 60, 198, 225n27; *Brother Man,* 224n24; and Condé, 225n26; "Gravel in Your Shoe," 46–50, 61; *The Hills Were Joyful Together,* 224n24; *Listen, the Wind,* 29, 45–46, 224n24; and Ponte, 61
Majumdar, Saikat, 82, 87
mala hora, La (García Márquez), 20, 29–36; class divisions in, 31, 222n11; community and, 30, 31–36, 44, 60; and *Crónica de una muerte anunciada,* 29, 38, 44, 60; orality and writing in, 32, 223n16; pasquinades in, 20, 30–36, 44, 221–22n10, 222nn11–15, 223nn16–19; public and private in, 32–33, 34, 223n17; violence in, 20, 29, 30, 33, 35, 222n14, 223n18, 223n20; *la violencía* and, 35–36, 223n20. *See also* pasquinades
Maldito amor (Ferré), 20–21, 67–81; class in, 68, 69, 73, 75; community and, 20, 230n14, 231n15; epistemology and, 21, 69, 76–77, 80–81, 103, 229n3, 247–48n37; family and nation in, 67–81, 231n15; and *La fascinación de la víctima* (Torres), 101, 103, 106; feminism and, 21, 67–68, 69, 72–73, 75; homosexuality and homophobia in, 70, 72, 73; "Maldito amor" (*danza*), 76, 230n10; narrative fragmentation in, 68–70, 71, 73–74, 77–79, 106, 247–48n37; patriarchy in, 21, 68, 69, 70, 73, 74; Puerto Rican identity and, 69, 79–81, 231n15; race in, 68, 70, 72, 73, 74–75; *Rashomon* (film) and, 70, 77, 106; truth as unreachable in, 67–71, 74–78, 80–81; United States in, 76, 79,

81; and *Wide Sargasso Sea* (Rhys), 21, 67, 81, 88–89, 101, 103, 231n16
Mallarmé, Stéphane, 81
Manktelow, Emily J., 220n2
Mann, Thomas: *Doktor Faustus,* 246n28
Mansilla, Lucio V., 236n5
Marcos, Ferdinand, 221n7
Mardorossian, Carine M., 82, 231n17
marginalia, 14, 195, 245n26
Markov, Georgy, 129–30
Mars, Kettly, 195–96, 205–6, 210, 248n41; *L'heure hybride,* 248n42. *See also Saisons sauvages*
Martin, Nicholas, 7–8, 13, 218n18
Martínez Alvarez, Rafael. *See* Alva, Martin
Martínez, Orlando, 165–66, 186
Martínez de Medina, Zoila, 242n8
Martínez San Miguel, Yolanda, 224n22
Martinique, 82, 83, 84, 85, 219n20
Martyr d'Anghiera, Peter: *De Orbe Novo,* 219n20
masculinity, 43–44, 66, 73, 224n22; and the *hombre nuevo,* 118; and hypermasculinity, 17, 182; and virility, 225n27, 226n30. *See also machismo*
Massillon, Yves, 155
Mawby, Spencer, 138
May, Todd, 227n35
McAlister, Elizabeth A., 223n17
McKeever, Stuart A., 247n35
McKenzie, Kirsten, 220n2
Mehta, Kamal, 243n14
memoirs, 19, 168, 242n8; Balaguer's, 22, 160–67, 173, 186, 190, 240n8; Duvalier's, 158; Greene's, 155, 157; of the Trujillo era, 167–68, 242n6. *See also* autobiography; *Memorias de un cortesano de la "era de Trujillo"* (Balaguer)
Memorias de un cortesano de la "era de Trujillo" (Balaguer), 160–67, 242n8; blank page in, 165–67, 186, 200; *Foro Público* and, 163–64, 190; gossip in, 160–67, 172, 173, 241n4, 242n7; Haitian massacre (1937) in, 162; history and, 161, 164–67, 172, 173, 179, 242n7; inside knowledge and, 161–62, 165, 242n8; and *Los que falsificaron la firma de Dios* (Sención), 168–69, 172; "Mujeres en mi Vida" (poem), 166; paranoia in, 163; reception of, 161, 173

memory, 1, 63, 90, 113, 166, 140, 198, 248n40; and exile, 129; invention of, 178, 245n21; preservation of, 91–92, 122, 132, 143, 193, 196, 205, 206; suppression of, 76, 79–80, 191, 200–201, 205, 245n25. *See also* forgetting; nostalgia
Méndez, José Luis, 35
men's talk: gossip as, 1, 17–18, 34, 49, 53, 56, 73, 91, 182, 218–19n18, 226n30, 237n8. *See also* women's talk
Merry, Sally Engle, 221n6
Mexico, 133, 134, 157, 209, 218n15, 230n14, 240n30
Miller, D. A., 188–89
Miller, T. S., 245n26, 246n28
Milne-Smith, Amy, 219n18
Minta, Stephen, 222n11
Molloy, Sylvia, 216n6, 236n5
Monsiváis, Carlos, 105, 106
Montaigne, Michel de, 2
Morales, Amparo: *Tesoro lexicográfico del español de Puerto Rico* (with Vaquero), 11
morality: cannibalism and, 233–34n29; and community, 6, 33, 38–39, 41–42, 42, 57, 93, 94, 97, 224n23; gossip and, 1, 5, 6, 16, 39, 48, 58, 137, 160, 181, 187–89, 195, 215n4, 217n12; moral judgment, 1, 33, 38–39, 41–42, 42, 60, 69, 94, 181, 186, 229n5; and politics, 33–34, 136–37, 157, 165, 166–67, 176, 203, 246n29; sexual, 58, 71, 73, 135, 229n6
Moreno, Marisel, 68, 73
Morrison, Toni, 229n9
Mouffe, Chantal, 112–13, 136–37
Mullen, Patrick B., 247n36
Munro, Hope, 216n7
Munro, Martin, 19, 143, 145, 205
music and song, 1, 19, 178, 207, 243n14; calypso, 18, 224–25n25, 243n14; gossip and, 174, 217n13, 223n17, 243n14, 245n24; Haitian, 18, 223n17, 243n14; "Maldito amor" (*danza*), 76, 230n10; mentos, 243n14, 245n24; merengue, 160, 173–74, 176–78, 243n14–244n16, 245n23; "El Venao" (merengue), 42–43, 224n22

Naipaul, V. S., 1, 232n20; *Miguel Street*, 243n14; *The Mystic Masseur*, 232n23

Nair, Rukmini Bhaya, 8
Nancy, Jean-Luc, 59, 224n23, 227nn34–35
Napoleon, 158, 166, 181, 241n2
narrative: ambiguity of, 107, 176, 226n30; anticolonial, 137–38, 139; and authoritarianism, 20, 22, 121, 130, 137, 142, 168, 180, 191, 245n21, 248n38, 248n42; authority, 21, 55, 70, 89, 97, 166; in *The Brief Wondrous Life of Oscar Wao* (Díaz), 179–80, 184–89, 191–92, 194, 247n34, 247–48n37; Caribbean, 24, 66–67, 206, 207–14, 235n34; and community, 7, 29, 37, 49, 96–97, 99, 101, 189; conflict, 18–19, 68, 71–72, 76–79, 88, 101, 112, 145, 160, 178, 180, 189, 191, 207, 211–13, 228n2; control, 17, 22, 23, 77, 130, 182, 186, 189, 192, 228n2; disruption, 23, 24, 55, 200; in *La fascinación de la víctima* (Torres), 100–101, 103–7; gossip as form of, 4, 5, 17, 73, 174, 180, 187, 193, 195, 206, 208, 210, 214, 244n20; gossip as narrative strategy, 4, 145, 179, 185, 187–88, 209, 246n28; in *El hombre del acordeón* (Maggiolo), 160, 174–79, 180; incompleteness of, 24, 40–42, 66, 69–70, 78, 103, 175, 186, 205; instability of, 24, 178, 193; in *Maldito amor* (Ferré), 21, 68–81, 101, 106, 200, 228n2, 247–48n37; master, 21, 68, 76, 81, 89, 99, 107, 247–48n37; monstrous, 98; and nationhood, 79–80, 186, 194; official, 65–67, 74, 106, 179–80, 189, 210; patriarchal, 21, 68–69, 74; plurality or fragmentation of, 24, 35, 68, 77, 82, 88, 97, 103, 106, 137, 194, 212, 247n33, 247–48n37; postmodern, 98; public, 5, 92, 94, 121, 189, 211; recomposition, 103, 106, 176, 235n35; resistance, 237n9; revision and correction of, 16, 68, 74, 79, 80–81, 180, 192, 210–11, 220n1, 228n2
Natarajan, Nalini, 8, 139
nation and nationhood: in Antigua, 139; in the Caribbean, 5, 18, 19, 23, 205–6; in Cuba, 135; in the Dominican Republic, 174, 176, 179, 184–86, 191, 194; forgetting and, 79–81, 245n25; in Haiti, 142–43, 156, 196; in Puerto Rico, 69, 216n5, 230n11, 231n15; public sphere

and, 111–13; in Trinidad, 138. See also *Maldito amor* (Ferré); *specific countries*
Nayar, Pramod K., 244n17
Negrón, Luis, 29; "Muchos o de cómo a veces la lengua es bruja" (short story), 56–57, 60
Negrón-Muntaner, Frances, 231n15
neocolonialism, 79, 138–39, 153, 235n34. See also colonialism; postcolonialism
news media, 23, 25, 50, 216n8, 243n15; gossip columns, 14, 18, 25, 149, 151–52, 159, 163–64, 190, 237n8; newspapers, 1, 28, 49, 91, 124, 142, 147, 149, 151, 157, 232n23, 243n15; radio, 90–91, 241n5, 243n15. See also *Foro Público* (Dominican newspaper column); internet; public sphere; rumor
Nicaragua, 237n9
Nichols, Elizabeth Gackstetter, 243n15
nihilism, 2, 31, 35, 213
Noelle-Neumann, Elisabeth: *The Spiral of Silence*, 246n30
nostalgia, 23, 117, 166, 220n5
Nunez, Elizabeth: *Bruised Hibiscus*, 91, 232n23

Oates, Joyce Carol, 3
Obeah, 82–83, 231n17
Ocasio, Rafael, 117, 124
Ollivier, Émile: *La discorde aux cent voix*, 225n27, 234n30
Onetti, Juan Carlos, 4, 216n6
oppression, 5, 27, 63, 111, 125, 189, 223n16; gossip as means of 1, 6, 28, 44–45, 179, 191, 218n17, 230n11. See also authoritarianism; totalitarianism
orality, 25–29, 182, 207–8, 219–20n1, 218n5, 223n16; and *Antes que anochezca*, 238n14; in the Caribbean, 66, 110, 207–8; and community, 52, 226n27; gossip and, 14, 25–26, 28, 110, 139, 208; in *Maldito amor* (Ferré), 73; oral grapevine, 12, 22, 90, 174; in *Wide Sargasso Sea* (Rhys), 82; oral traditions, 99, 207–8, 221n8
Ortega, Julio, 77
otherness: in the Caribbean, 5, 29, 87, 228n1, 235–36n37; in *Célanire cou-coupé* (Condé), 233–34n29; gossip and, 10, 18, 23, 29, 57, 93, 208, 209; in "¡Jum!" (Sánchez), 52; Latin American, 30

outsider(s): in Cabrera Infante's essays, 134; and Caribbean identity, 23, 84; in *La fascinación de la víctima* (Torres), 102, 106, 235n35; gossip and, 16, 27, 29, 93; Graham Greene, seen as, 134, 153, 157; in "Le Loupgarou" (Walcott), 232–33n27; in Mais's fiction, 46–47; in Rhys's fiction, 48–50, 84–86; in Sánchez's fiction, 52–53, 56
Owen, Walter C., 221n7

Padilla affair, 121, 126, 127, 129
Padura, Leonardo, 235n34
Paine, Robert, 215n4, 220–21n6
panopticon, 4, 29, 33, 38, 61, 63, 198, 227n38
paranoia, 4, 6, 20, 33, 50, 62–64, 163, 212, 227n37, 238n12
Paravisini-Gebert, Lizabeth, 231n16
Parry, Benita, 82
pasquinades, 20, 30–35, 38, 44, 115, 177, 221–22nn10–15, 223nn17–19, 241n2, 241–42n5. See also *mala hora, La* (García Márquez)
Pasquino (Vatican worker), 221–22n10
Pavel, Thomas: "Literary Criticism and Methodology," 6
Penuel, Arnold, 39, 42
Pereira, Manuel, 114
Pérez, Mario Emilio, 11
Pérez Jiménez, Marcos, 241n2
Perez Sarduy, Pedro, 129
Perice, Glen, 23, 248n40
Perkowska-Alvarez, Magdalena, 237n9
Peru, 90, 91, 96, 227n37
Phelps, Anthony, 239n23; "Mon pays que voici" (poem), 143
Philby, Kim, 135, 155, 156
Phillips, Susan E., 3, 218n18, 239n20; *Transforming Talk: The Problem with Gossip in Late Medieval England*, 7
philosophy, 136, 180; and community, 59–60, 224n23, 227n35; and gossip, 27–28, 107–8, 215n4, 227n34, 247n37; and the public sphere, 111–13
Piglia, Ricardo, 23, 234n34
Pinochet, Augusto, 124, 241n2
Pino-Ojeda, Walescka, 70
Piñera, Virgilio, 114, 122, 126, 130, 237n6
Plato, 27–28

plausibility: gossip and, 22, 24, 92–93, 147, 169, 193–95, 212, 229n3, 233n28; history and, 168, 173, 186, 188, 195; narrative and, 67, 74–75, 175, 188, 194
Plutarch, 2, 126–27, 240n28
PM (film), 127
Ponce de León, Juan, 79
Ponte, Antonio José: *La fiesta vigilada*, 4, 20, 29, 61–64; surveillance society in, 61–63, 132, 198, 227n38, 228n40
pool hall. *See* billiard hall
postauthoritarianism. *See under* authoritarianism
postcolonialism: Antiguan, 141; in the Caribbean, 3, 5, 25–26, 89, 210, 223n16, 232n21, 236n3; epistemology and, 81, 89, 210; gossip and, 8, 110; Haitian, 142; Puerto Rican, 81; society and, 59, 60. *See also* colonialism
Postman, Leo, 247n36
postmodernism, 98, 99; gossip as postmodern, 194, 248n39
potin, 10–11
power: and authoritarianism, 158, 241n2, 242n11; in *The Brief Wondrous Life of Oscar Wao* (Díaz), 179–82, 188–90, 193, 194–95; in the Caribbean, 18–19, 24, 44, 65, 87, 112, 211, 235–36n37, 236n3; of Castro, 122, 123, 130; and colonialism, 8, 27, 81, 84, 87, 138, 207; of Duvalier, 3, 196, 239n22, 240n29; of gossip, 11, 21, 23, 24, 60, 72, 98, 101, 103–4, 151–52, 166, 170–72, 194, 198, 210–13, 217nn11–13, 218nn16–17; gossip and, 2, 3, 8, 15–16, 22, 24, 29, 88, 171–72, 195, 210–13, 215n4, 218nn16–17, 223n16, 236n1; knowledge and, 150–51, 152, 228n2; in *Maldito amor* (Ferré), 68, 72–73, 78, 229n5; of merengue, 178; and morality, 60, 181, 189, 229n5; of pasquinades, 32, 33, 34, 222n14; and reputation, 16, 72, 190, 217n13; in *Saisons sauvages* (Mars), 197–98, 200, 202; surveillance and, 61–62, 171–72; of Trujillo, 22, 179, 189–90, 192; truth and, 104, 107, 233n28. *See also* authoritarianism; totalitarianism
Prats, Delfín, 236–37n6
Preble-Niemi, Oralia, 75
Presagio (film), 224n21

Prestol Castillo, Freddy, 247n33
privacy: and the body, 108, 117; boundaries of public and private, 32, 34, 107–8, 110, 211, 248n41; and community, 47, 48, 220–221n6, 226n28; gossip as private act, 92, 110, 211, 223n17; gossip as violation of, 101, 107, 108, 110, 172, 173, 211, 229n5; private information, 13–14, 182; private lives, 16, 61, 73, 161, 162, 181, 196, 197, 198, 228n2; private sphere, 32–33, 34, 110–11, 190, 211; private stories, 101, 131, 185, 188–89, 191, 194; private truths, 68, 78; and shame, 72, 121; and surveillance, 63–64, 171–73. *See also* public sphere
Proust, Marcel, 7, 77–78, 103, 214, 218n18
Providencia (Colombia), 17
psychoanalysis: connections to gossip, 103–7, 234n33; and detective work, 21, 67, 100, 103–6, 235n35. *See also fascinación de la víctima, La* (Torres)
psychology, 116, 159, 165, 215n4, 247n36, 248n41
public sphere: in *Antes que anochezca* (Arenas), 113, 116, 122, 123–25, 126, 137–38; Cabrera Infante and, 126, 130, 132–36, 137–38; Caribbean, 236n3; Creole and, 145; in *Crónica de una muerte anunciada* (García Márquez), 42; Dalleo on, 18, 110–11, 236n3; François Duvalier and, 152–54, 155, 157–58, 198; global public sphere, 111–13, 116, 130, 132, 133–34, 138, 152–55, 236n3; gossip and, 3, 5, 18–19, 20, 21, 23, 110–58, 182, 211; Habermas on, 32–33, 112–13; in *La mala hora* (García Márquez), 32–33, 34; Williams and, 137–38. *See also* counterpublic
Puerto Rico: *gran familia* and, 69, 79, 230n13; nationhood of, 69, 79–81; patriarchy in, 68, 73, 74; slang terms for "gossip" in, 11; social tensions in, 57, 67, 68, 79, 230n11, 231n15; "El Venao" (merengue) in, 42, 43. *See also gran familia*; *Maldito amor* (Ferré)
Puig, Manuel, 4, 127–28
punishment: gossip as, 20, 50, 55, 56, 60, 191; for gossiping, 131, 142, 218n16, 221n7, 227n37. *See also* laws against gossip

race and racism, 8, 28, 58, 66, 83–84, 87, 91, 97, 138–39, 153, 155, 233–34n29; gossip and, 48, 49; in *Maldito amor* (Ferré), 68, 72, 73, 74–75
Radio Bemba, 91, 99
Radio Caribe, 241n5
Rafael, Vicente, 242n7
ragot, 11
Rama, Angel, 40–41, 124
Ramchand, Kenneth, 47
Ramírez, Sergio: *Margarita, está linda la mar*, 237n9
Rashomon (film), 70, 77, 106
Read Vittini, Mario, 167
regulation of gossip. See laws against gossip
Renan, Ernest, 79–80, 245n25
reputation, 17, 202, 211, 217n13; in *Antes que anochezca* (Arenas), 115, 117; Castro's reputational attacks, 130, 131; community and, 53, 56, 58, 59, 184, 224n22; Duvalier's reputational attacks, 21, 113, 142, 154–58; in García Márquez's work, 31, 33, 34, 38; and gender, 56, 226n30; gossip and destruction of, 2, 6, 16, 33, 49, 71–72, 177, 184–85, 190, 204, 211, 221n7, 228n2, 233n28, 236n2, 246n30; gossip as means of bolstering, 56, 57, 190
resistance, 4, 58, 145, 174, 198, 200, 220n1, 222n12, 249n42; gossip and, 5–6, 24, 110, 170, 180, 210, 236n1, 237n9
respectability, 17, 56, 58, 94, 177, 190, 225n26, 228n2
revenge, 29, 44, 55, 70, 149, 176, 243n16, 248n40; gossip as means of, 56, 116–17, 126, 233n28, 246n28, 245n22
Rhys, Jean, 3, 21, 29, 211; "Fishy Waters" (short story), 51; on gossip and community, 20, 60; "Heat" (short story), 50; and *Jane Eyre* (Brontë), 3; "Pioneers, Oh, Pioneers" (short story), 48–50, 51, 53; *Sleep It Off, Lady*, 48; "Sleep It Off, Lady" (short story), 50, 226n29. See also *Wide Sargasso Sea*
Riley, Nerea, 117
riverside, 52–53; as site of gossiping, 45, 225n25, 225n27
Roa Bastos, Augusto, 4, 241n2
Robbins, Timothy R., 243n15

Rodríguez, Armando, 120
Rodriguez, Néstor, 242n9
Rodríguez Feo, José, 114, 116
Rodríguez Monegal, Emir, 127–28, 133
Rogoff, Irit, 194
Rohlehr, Gordon, 243n14
Rohter, Larry, 242–43n12
Rojas, Rafael, 136, 246n29
romans à clef, 7, 146, 168, 196
Romay Chacón, Tomás, 1
Rowe, William, 222n11
Rulfo, Juan: *Pedro Páramo*, 230n14
rumor, 30, 31, 43, 166, 226n28, 226n30, 229n7, 233n28, 242n7, 244n17, 244n20; definition of, 217–18n14; and gossip, 9, 14–15, 71, 88, 90–91, 147, 151, 154, 225–26n27, 232n24, 233–34n29, 234n30, 234n33, 236n2; and history, 22, 127, 138, 168, 185–87, 205, 247nn34–35; and legend, 247n36; as news, 92, 144, 146–47, 148, 149–51, 170, 196–8, 204, 241n2; and the public sphere, 22–23, 110, 139, 216n8, 248n40; and race, 97, 205; terms for, 11–12. See also hearsay
Rushdie, Salman, 4, 8
Russia, 128, 228n2. See also Soviet Union

Sada, Daniel, 241n2
Saer, Juan José, 234n34
St. Vincent, 217n13
Saisons sauvages (Mars), 22, 160, 195–206, 249n44; community in, 198–99, 249n43; Duvalier regime in, 195, 196, 199, 201, 204–5, 249n43; history in, 198, 201, 248n41; and *Los que falsificaron la firma de Dios* (Sención), 197; and *Maldito amor* (Ferré), 200; and *Memorias de un cortesano de la "era de Trujillo"* (Balaguer), 200; memory in, 200, 205–6; as *roman de dictature*, 195–96; silence in, 200–201, 205; surveillance in, 197; zombification in, 200
Salovey, Peter, 12
Sánchez, Luis Rafael, 1, 20, 29, 60, 211; "Etc." (short story), 55–56; *La importancia de llamarse Daniel Santos*, 17, 225n27, 226n30; "¡Jum!" (short story), 4, 51–53, 57, 226n31; orality and, 219n1, 226n30

Sánchez-Eppler, Benigno, 125
Santamaría, Haydée, 128, 132
Santí, Enrico Mario, 230n14
Santos, Lidia, 68
Sarduy, Severo, 124, 237n6
Savory, Elaine, 48
scandal, 48, 70, 105, 114, 181, 220n2, 233n28, 240n30, 243n14; avoidance or fear of, 47, 88, 117, 120, 200, 204, 222n11; as feature of gossip, 7, 11, 12, 14, 25, 91, 217n12; pasquinades and, 32, 222n11, 223n17; provoked by governments, 121, 154, 156; scandalization of history, 112, 117, 139–40, 153, 158, 167, 173, 245n26. *See also* accusations; denunciation
Schantz, Ned, 3, 7
Schelling, Vivian, 222n11
scold's bridle, 221n7. *See also* punishment
Scott, James C., 24, 222n11, 236n2
Scott, Lindsey, 248–49n42
Sell, Roger, 194
Sellers, Julie A., 174, 245n23
Sención, Viriato, 22, 168–69, 179, 242nn9–10, 242–43n12; "La Marimanta" (short story), 173. See also *Los que falsificaron la firma de Dios*
Senior, Olive, 17, 29, 51, 57, 60, 93, 216n7; "Ballad," 57–58; *Dancing Lessons,* 58–59; "Lily, Lily," 58; "The Lizardy Man and His Lady," 58; "Real Old Time T'ing," 58
Shakespeare, William, 166; *Hamlet,* 81; *Macbeth,* 137
Shelton, Marie-Denise, 232n21
Shining Path guerrillas, 227n37. *See also* Peru
Silva, María Guadalupe, 61
Simek, Nicole, 94, 97
Sims, Robert L., 222n12
skepticism, 50, 79, 98–99, 194, 212, 232n21. *See also* doubt
slander, 2; accusations of, 156, 157, 190; in *Antes que anochezca* (Arenas), 116; *The Comedians* (Greene) as, 156, 157; gossip and, 9, 45, 93, 154, 217n12, 225n26, 226n30, 233n28, 243n14, 246n30; in memoirs, 168; in news media, 18, 49; perpetrated by authority figures, 18, 130–31, 149, 154–58, 191, 241–42n5, 246n30. *See also* libel

slavery, 25, 207, 220n1; and the body, 236n37; in the Caribbean, 4, 23, 111, 138, 140, 210, 219n20; emancipation, 65, 140, 219n20; in Greece, 28; slave owners, 27, 74, 84, 140; slaves' gossip, 27
Sloan, Cynthia, 68
Smith, Barbara Herrnstein, 12
social media. *See* internet
sociology, 2, 8; of gossip, 215n4, 216n9, 220–21n6, 232n26, 244n20; of rumor, 244n20; of witchcraft, 232n26. *See also* anthropology
Solomon, Nathalie: *Potins, cancans et littérature* (with Chamayou), 7, 217nn11–12
song. *See* music and song
soplones, 10, 227n37
Souza, Raymond D., 127
Soviet Union, 4, 114, 135, 168. *See also* Russia
Spacks, Patricia Meyer: on definition of gossip, 12–13, 15, 217n11; Gluckman and, 6; on "good" gossip, 3, 6, 8, 59, 207, 216n7, 216n9; *Gossip,* 6; on gossip and community, 2–3, 7, 18, 59, 64, 226n33; on gossip and gender, 16; on gossip as a resource for the marginalized, 229n9; on harmlessness of gossip, 16, 218n16; on interpretive gossip, 104, 226n33, 230n12; on intimacy of gossip, 2, 4, 18, 64, 218n17, 226n33; on orality and gossip, 14; Pavel and, 6; Senior and, 60; Spacksian scholarship, 4, 7–8, 15, 215n4, 217n12, 230n14; sociology and, 216n9
Spain, 133, 147, 158. *See also* Europe
Spear, Thomas, 239n22
speculation: becoming accepted fact, 53, 94, 95, 107; blank page and, 165–66; and community, 6, 53, 93, 101, 223n17; gossip as, 38, 92–93, 147–49, 156, 187, 197; interpretive, 6, 97; and narrative, 88, 89, 96, 98, 99, 107
Spenser, Edmund, 216n10
Spivak, Gayatri, 82
spying. *See* surveillance
Stewart, Pamela J., 232n26
Stovel, Bruce, 14
Strathern, Andrew, 232n26
Suetonius, 154, 240n28
Sunstein, Cass R., 216n8

supernatural, 54, 83, 173, 187, 189–90, 224n21, 232–33n27, 241n4, 243n13
superstition, 82, 95, 97, 155, 169–70, 232n22, 232–33n27. See also witchcraft
surveillance, 33, 45, 50, 227n37, 227–28n38, 228n39; in Cuba, 20, 29, 61–64, 123, 132, 144, 198, 227n36, 228n40; in the Dominican Republic, 170–71; in Haiti, 197–98, 240n29. See also panopticon
suspicion, 109, 142–43, 144, 162–63, 205, 211; and community, 31, 35, 59, 92–93; and gossip, 2, 45, 57, 61–63, 86–89, 92–94, 168, 213, 242n11; of official narratives or institutions, 24, 66, 105–6, 232n21, 247n33
Sylvain, Patrick, 29, 51, 211; "Odette" (short story), 53–55

tabloid gossip, 28. See also news media
talk, 1, 51, 58, 66, 91, 127, 156, 170, 226n27, 227n33, 231n19; bad-talk, 17; children's, 49, 50; and community, 15, 29, 30, 42, 46, 47–48, 52, 54, 55, 84; in García Márquez's texts, 31, 34, 36, 37, 42, 55, 221n8, 222n15; gossip as, 2, 7, 8, 9, 10, 14, 17, 182, 218n18, 225n25, 227n34; ole talk, 1, 12; and rumor, 217n13, 244n17; servants', 88, 151; as substitute for action, 37, 42, 141; talkativeness of gossips, 2, 11; as term for gossip, 12. See also idle talk; men's talk; orality; whispering; women's talk
Talmud, 2
Taussig, Michael, 180
télédiol, 12, 17, 22–23, 90–91, 248n42
telenovela, 70, 209
telephone, 43, 62, 129, 147, 170–72, 233n28; *téléphone arabe* (Arab telephone), 12, 127
testimonio, 125, 238n15
testimony, 2, 50, 74, 93, 151, 175, 215n4, 237n6, 244n17; gossip as pathology of, 92, 99, 238n15
Thelwell, Michael: *The Harder They Come*, 56
Tokunaga, Robert, 228n39
Tönnies, Ferdinand, 59, 228n40
Tontons Macoutes, 145–48, 149, 151–52, 198, 199, 203, 205, 243n13
Torrents, Nissa, 132, 133

Torres, Ana Teresa: *Doña Inés contra el olvido*, 234n31; *Los últimos espectadores del acorazado Potemkin*, 234n31. See also *fascinación de la víctima, La*
Torres-Saillant, Silvio, 3, 4, 5, 242n9
totalitarianism, 29, 211, 227n35; in *La fiesta vigilada* (Ponte), 29, 61–64; of gossip, 20, 29, 44, 52, 60–61, 180, 214, 227n38; masculinity and, 44; and narrative control, 111, 130, 180, 193–95, 246n29, 248n38. See also authoritarianism
tourism, 111, 113, 131, 138–39, 141
trauma, 111, 188, 195, 205, 246n28
Trinidad, 6, 91, 137–38, 216n7, 224n25, 232n23, 243n14
Trujillo Ricart, Aida: *A la sombra de mi abuelo*, 167
Trujillo, María de los Ángeles (Angelita): *Trujillo, mi padre en mis memorias*, 167
Trujillo, Rafael Leónidas, 3, 22, 142, 159–60, 162, 168, 169, 172, 227n37, 241n4; era of, 11, 18, 159–60, 161, 163, 164, 167, 179–194, 242n7, 246n30; *Foro Público* and, 163, 190, 241–42n5; merengue and, 173–74, 177–78, 243–44n16. See also *Brief Wondrous Life of Oscar Wao, The* (Díaz); *hombre del acordeón, El* (Veloz Maggiolo); *Los que falsificaron la firma de Dios* (Sención); *Memorias de un cortesano de la "era de Trujillo"* (Balaguer)
Trujillo, Ramfis, 164, 167, 181
truth, 80, 107–8, 135–36, 165, 167, 229n3; arrived at through gossip, 100, 104, 107, 168, 180, 228n12; in the Caribbean, 23, 65–67, 87–89, 111, 138, 211–13; and community, 59, 111; in García Márquez's works, 35, 41, 223n19; and gossip, 28, 92–93, 99, 104, 193, 201–3, 209, 211, 212, 213; in Haiti, 147, 233n28; and *Maldito amor* (Ferré), 69, 71, 75–78; and narrative, 77–78, 92, 104, 175; and postmodernism, 98, 99, 194, 248n39; truthfulness of gossip, 6, 15, 21, 35, 67, 69, 71, 93, 116, 149–50, 186, 191, 202–3, 237n6, 244n17, 248n38; and *Wide Sargasso Sea* (Rhys), 82, 85–89. See also *Brief Wondrous Life of Oscar Wao, The* (Díaz); *hombre del acordeón, El* (Veloz Maggiolo)

292 *Index*

Turner, Patricia A., 205, 233–34n29, 244n20

United Kingdom, 4, 27, 28, 129, 138, 139–40, 141, 153, 155, 239n18, 245n24; expatriates of, 48–50, 51, 84–87, 220n2; gossip in, 7, 88, 207, 219n18, 221n7, 237n8, 239n20; literature of, 3, 7, 16, 25, 62, 113, 134, 208, 216n10, 218n16; society of, 51. *See also* Anglophone Caribbean; British West Indies; colonialism; diaspora; Europe; Greene, Graham

United States: and Cuba, 124, 131, 133, 238n13; and the Dominican Republic, 164, 179, 181; and Haiti, 23, 149, 151, 153; gossip of, 207, 216n8; literature of, 3, 7, 8, 16, 66, 207, 208, 209, 213, 217n10; and Puerto Rico, 79, 81; and Rama, 124. *See also* African American culture; colonialism; diaspora

Vaquero, María: *Tesoro lexicográfico del español de Puerto Rico* (with Morales), 11

Vargas Llosa, Mario, 125, 221n9, 223n18; *La fiesta del chivo*, 247n33

Vega, Ana Lydia, 99–100, 216n7

Veloz Maggiolo, Marcio, 22, 210, 245n21; *La memoria fermentada*, 245n21; *La mosca soldado*, 243n13; "Nido de Volanderas" (short story), 197, 244n19. See also *hombre del acordeón, El*

"Venao, El" (merengue), 42–43, 224n22

Venegas, José Luis, 130

Venezuela, 43, 102, 105–6, 241n2. See also *fascinación de la víctima, La* (Torres)

Verity, Jeremy, 245n24

Victor, Gary, 206

Vieux, Antonio, 239n22

violence, 221n18, 246n40; in Caribbean history, 19, 20, 83, 191, 212; in Caribbean society, 106; and community, 29, 33, 35–36, 44, 50, 52–53; domestic, 139; epistemic, 76, 82, 108, 211; of gossip, 2, 6, 17, 30, 45, 53, 109, 177, 198, 207, 210–11, 212, 218n16; in Haiti, 151, 154, 248n40, 249n42; homophobic, 51–53, 57; mob, 49, 52, 53, 54–55; racial, 84, 160; sexual, 55, 90, 121, 148, 185, 201–3, 249n42; state-sponsored, 146, 154, 162, 164, 178, 188, 193, 205, 222n14. *See also* adversarialism

violencia, la (Colombia), 35–36, 223n18, 223n20. See also *mala hora, La* (García Márquez)

virility. *See* masculinity

Vodou, 145, 146, 152–53, 155, 187, 232n25, 240n29, 244n18. *See also* zombification

voyeurism, 108–9, 171–72, 211

Voznesensky, Andrei: "Ode to Gossips" (poem), 4

Walcott, Derek, 1, 26, 28, 208; "Le Loup-garou" (poem), 232–33n27

Walford, Lynn, 31

Walls, Jeannette, 216n8

Walonen, Michael K., 220n2

Walsh, John P., 195, 198, 248n41

Weir-Soley, Donna, 225n25

Welsh, Sarah Lawson, 224n24

Wert, Sarah, 12

whispering, 32, 52, 53, 88, 124, 131, 138, 156, 166, 170, 183, 190, 191, 233n28, 241n2, 247n35; as feature of gossip, 9, 12, 14, 25, 206; and informants, 132, 144; and rumor, 147, 196; of secrets, 25, 90, 91, 129

Wickerson, Erica, 246n28

Wide Sargasso Sea (Rhys), 3, 67, 81–89; epistemology and, 82, 86–89, 103; *La fascinación de la víctima* (Torres) and, 101; *Jane Eyre* (Brontë) and, 3, 82, 89; *Maldito amor* (Ferré) and, 21, 67, 81, 88–89, 103, 231n16; Obeah practices in, 82–83, 231n17

Wiegmink, Pia, 112, 133

Wiese Delgado, Hans Paul, 167

Wilkes, Roger, 216n8

Wilkinson, Stephen, 235n34

Williams, Eric, 137–38, 139, 140; "Massa Day Done" (address), 138

Wilson, Peter, 17, 56

witchcraft, 54, 95–96, 197, 232n22, 232n26, 233n27, 244n19

women's talk: gossip as, 7, 10, 16, 17, 30, 49, 57–58, 82, 182, 217n11, 218–19n18, 226n30, 227n33; aggressive aspects of, 45, 55; in Ferré's work, 73–74, 228n2; in

Saisons sauvages (Mars), 199; stigmatization of, 34, 45, 224–25n25
Wood, Michael, 30, 221n8
Woolf, Virginia, 229n9
Wynter, Sylvia, 224n24

yard, as site of gossiping, 46, 58, 225n27, 228n38

Yerkovich, Sally, 215n4
Yoruba vocabulary, 12

Zard, Philippe, 227–28n38
Zephaniah, Benjamin: "The SUN" (poem), 28
zin, or *zen*, 12, 154, 233n28
zombification, 145, 200, 229n3, 240n24

Recent Books in the New World Studies Series

Supriya M. Nair, *Pathologies of Paradise: Caribbean Detours*

Colleen C. O'Brien, *Race, Romance, and Rebellion: Literatures of the Americas in the Nineteenth Century*

Kelly Baker Josephs, *Disturbers of the Peace: Representations of Madness in Anglophone Caribbean Literature*

Christina Kullberg, *The Poetics of Ethnography in Martinican Narratives: Exploring the Self and the Environment*

Maria Cristina Fumagalli, Bénédicte Ledent, and Roberto del Valle Alcalá, editors, *The Cross-Dressed Caribbean: Writing, Politics, Sexualities*

Philip Kaisary, *The Haitian Revolution in the Literary Imagination: Radical Horizons, Conservative Constraints*

Jason Frydman, *Sounding the Break: African American and Caribbean Routes of World Literature*

Tanya L. Shields, *Bodies and Bones: Feminist Rehearsal and Imagining Caribbean Belonging*

Stanka Radović, *Locating the Destitute: Space and Identity in Caribbean Fiction*

Nicole N. Aljoe and Ian Finseth, editors, *Journeys of the Slave Narrative in the Early Americas*

Stephen M. Park, *The Pan American Imagination: Contested Visions of the Hemisphere in Twentieth-Century Literature*

Maurice St. Pierre, *Eric Williams and the Anticolonial Tradition: The Making of a Diasporan Intellectual*

Elena Machado Sáez, *Market Aesthetics: The Purchase of the Past in Caribbean Diasporic Fiction*

Martin Munro, *Tropical Apocalypse: Haiti and the Caribbean End Times*

Jeannine Murray-Román, *Performance and Personhood in Caribbean Literature: From Alexis to the Digital Age*

Anke Birkenmaier, *The Spectre of Races: Latin American Anthropology and Literature between the Wars*

John Patrick Leary, *A Cultural History of Underdevelopment: Latin America in the U.S. Imagination*

Raphael Dalleo, *American Imperialism's Undead: The Occupation of Haiti and the Rise of Caribbean Anticolonialism*

Emily Sahakian, *Staging Creolization: Women's Theater and Performance from the French Caribbean*

Candace Ward, *Crossing the Line: Early Creole Novels and Anglophone Caribbean Culture in the Age of Emancipation*

Ana Rodríguez Navas, *Idle Talk, Deadly Talk: The Uses of Gossip in Caribbean Literature*

www.ingramcontent.com/pod-product-compliance
Lightning Source LLC
Chambersburg PA
CBHW031538170125
20545CB00003B/166